THE INVISIBLE HAND OF PEACE

Capitalism, The War Machine, and International Relations Theory

The Invisible Hand of Peace shows that the domestic institutions associated with capitalism, namely private property and competitive market structures, have promoted peace between states over the past two centuries. It employs a wide range of historical and statistical evidence to illustrate both the broad applicability of these claims and their capacity to generate new explanations of critical historical events, such as the emergence of the Anglo-American friendship at the end of the nineteenth century, the outbreak of World War I, and the evolution of the recent conflict across the Taiwan Strait. By showing that this capitalist peace has historically been stronger than the peace among democratic states, these findings also suggest that contemporary American foreign policy should be geared toward promoting economic liberalization rather than democracy in the post-9/11 world.

Patrick J. McDonald is an Assistant Professor in the Department of Government at the University of Texas at Austin. He received a Ph.D. in political science from the Ohio State University in 2002. He then served as a postdoctoral Fellow at the Christopher H. Browne Center for International Politics at the University of Pennsylvania until 2004. Professor McDonald's research has been published in the *American Journal of Political Science, International Studies Quarterly, Journal of Conflict Resolution, The Washington Quarterly*, and *World Politics.*

The Invisible Hand of Peace

Capitalism, The War Machine, and International Relations Theory

PATRICK J. McDONALD
The University of Texas at Austin

CAMBRIDGE UNIVERSITY PRESS
Cambridge, New York, Melbourne, Madrid, Cape Town,
Singapore, São Paulo, Delhi, Tokyo, Mexico City

Cambridge University Press
32 Avenue of the Americas, New York, NY 10013-2473, USA

www.cambridge.org
Information on this title: www.cambridge.org/9780521744126

First published 2009
Reprinted 2011

A catalog record for this publication is available from the British Library.

Library of Congress Cataloging in Publication Data

McDonald, Patrick J., 1973–
The invisible hand of peace: capitalism, the war machine, and international relations theory / Patrick J. McDonald.
p. cm.
Includes bibliographical references.
ISBN 978-0-521-74412-6 (pbk) – ISBN 978-0-521-76136-9 (hardback)
1. War–Economic aspects. 2. Peace–Economic aspects. 3. Capitalism. 4. International relations. I. Title.
HB195.M34 2009
330.12′2–dc22 2008044607

ISBN 978-0-521-76136-9 Hardback
ISBN 978-0-521-74412-6 Paperback

For Deanna

Contents

Tables

Acknowledgments

Although my inability to complete this project in a timely fashion has been a source of constant frustration to me (and I am sure to those close to me as well), I hope that the delay and the opportunities it has created to broaden the scope of this book have been worth it. Special thanks go to my three mentors: Dave Rowe, Ed Mansfield, and Harrison Wagner. Dave managed to keep me in graduate school when I was ready to take my terminal master's degree and go find some job that would not be nearly as rewarding as I have found this one to be. His seminars continually provoked me to rethink my own ideas, and his work on World War I spawned the initial idea that became this book. Ed has continually offered steady encouragement and sound advice, even though he was aware early on that I did not know what I was getting myself into. I have learned most about careful research by trying to follow his example. A postdoc at the Christopher H. Browne Center for International Politics at the University of Pennsylvania gave me the time and freedom to transform this project so that it looks very different from the dissertation it once was. I am most grateful though that my time in Philadelphia enabled us to become good friends. My job interview at the University of Texas at Austin in 2004 quickly convinced me that an opportunity to be Harrison Wagner's colleague was one I simply could not pass up. I have learned much more from him than I expected. Harrison has tirelessly and repeatedly read this manuscript and spent more hours than I can count discussing with me the ideas contained here. His patience, insight, and willingness to help have been a gift.

I have been extremely fortunate to receive important feedback on the ideas contained here from many people at three great institutions – the Ohio State University, the University of Pennsylvania, and the University of Texas at Austin. Looking back now, I can see numerous portions in the book that would have been either omitted or glossed over in a careless fashion had this process not taken me to each of these places. Thank you to all those mentioned here for reading portions of this project at various stages or giving me your time to bounce ideas back and forth. Even though only one of them remains at Ohio State University, I was extremely fortunate that my time there allowed me to put together a dissertation committee of Ed Mansfield, John Mueller, Dave Rowe, and Tim Frye. I still remember my defense as one of the most productive two-hour discussion sessions this project has seen. Thanks to my graduate school colleagues – David Bearce, Paul Fritz, Yoav Gortzak, Andrea Grove, Yoram Haftel, Ted Lehmann, Jon Pevehouse, and Chris Scholl – for enduring repeated questions and arguments over the beginnings of the ideas contained here. A special thanks to Kevin Sweeney: Even though we took the same classes and progressed through graduate school at the same rate, we possessed very different ways of thinking about the world. These differences undoubtedly made this a better book. I am grateful for his continuing friendship.

Thank you to the Christopher H. Browne Center for International Politics and the Department of Political Science at the University of Pennsylvania for financing a postdoctoral fellowship that enabled me to expand the research here in two critical ways. I began work on the nineteenth-century era of globalization while I was there. Avery Goldstein pushed me to think about how my arguments applied to East Asian politics, specifically China. Chapter 8 of this book would not have appeared without Avery's prompting and support. I appreciate his encouragement of my fieldwork, particularly because it broadened my own thinking. Thanks also to David Rousseau and Rudy Sil for serving as continual sounding boards about both my project and academia while I was at Penn.

The University of Texas has provided a great environment to bring this project to its conclusion. Many colleagues have taken an active interest in this book, helping me to wade through numerous struggles either by reading portions of the manuscript or by offering advice on how to attack a problem. Thanks to Zoltan Barany, Gary Freeman, Eugene Gholz, Jim Granato, Ron Krebs, Rob Moser, Bat Sparrow, Devin Stauffer, and Peter Trubowitz. While some have since left Austin, I would also like to thank the junior faculty group – including Jason Brownlee, Jason Casellas, Ken Greene, Andy Karch, Eric McDaniel, Tasha Philpot, John Sides, Ismail White, and Corrine McConnaughy – for allowing me to present portions of this project to our working group, offering good advice on the manuscript, and keeping me sane with numerous diversions out of the office. Special thanks go to both George Gavrilis and Terry Chapman for being incredibly generous with their time. I know both have read and reread multiple portions of the manuscript. I would also like to thank Tse-min Lin for his mentorship and encouragement of my interest in Taiwan. Thank you to Mary Love, Chih-shian Liou, Eugene Kuan, and Mark LaBrayere for their excellent research assistance.

A number of individuals helped facilitate my research outside of the United States. Thanks to the Houston branch of the Taiwanese Cultural and Economic Representative Office for inviting me to participate in a scholarly delegation to Taiwan in the summer of 2005. Thanks to Cathy Chen and Angel Liu for coordinating this visit and continuing to answer all of my questions about Taiwan. My colleague at the University of Texas, Liu Xuecheng, helped me organize a visit to China in 2005. I worked out of the Institute for International Studies at Tsinghua University in Beijing. Thank you to Shi Zhiqin, Yan Xuetong, and Yuan Yuhong for being wonderful hosts there. Two of my graduate students at the University of Texas, Eugene Kuan and Chih-shian Liou, deserve special thanks for all of their help preparing for and assisting me on a research trip to Taiwan in 2006. They know very well that I would have struggled mightily without them. Thank you also to the Marquess of Salisbury for granting me permission to use quotations from his family's archives in Chapter 6.

I was fortunate to have obtained financial support for this research at a number of stages. A grant from the American Philosophical Society enabled me to conduct archival research in the United Kingdom in the summer of 2005. A grant from the Office of Vice President for Research at the University of Texas funded trips to China and Taiwan. A Dean's Fellowship from the College of Liberal Arts at the University of Texas granted me a semester break from teaching that allowed me writing time to complete the manuscript.

Multiple portions of this book have appeared in papers previously published. Portions of Chapters 3 and 4 appeared in the 2004 paper "Peace Through Trade or Free Trade?" that was published in the *Journal of Conflict Resolution*. Portions of Chapters 3 and 9 appeared in a 2007 paper "The Purse Strings of Peace," which was published in the *American Journal of Political Science*. Portions of Chapters 3 and 5 appeared in a 2007 paper "The Achilles' Heel of Liberal IR Theory? Globalization and Conflict in the Pre–World War I Era," which was published in *World Politics*. And portions of Chapter 10 appeared in a 2007 paper "Revitalizing Grand Strategy: America's Untapped Market Power," which was published in *The Washington Quarterly*. Thank you, respectively, to Sage Publications, Blackwell Publishing, The Johns Hopkins University Press, and MIT Press for allowing me to reprint portions of those papers in this book.

Finally, my family deserves the most gratitude for enduring the challenges associated with being a graduate student and an assistant professor while writing a first book. My mother Doreen and my sister Heidi have been constant sources of encouragement and support. They know only too well the challenges we faced long ago that could have derailed this project before it even had a chance to get off the ground. My wife Deanna has been amazing in her willingness to forgive all my repeated failures to meet deadlines and in her determination to reassure me that I remain on the right path. I am proud to be able to dedicate this book to her with all my love.

ONE

American Grand Strategy and the Liberal Peace

The United States has a long history of responding to strategic challenges and opportunities by promoting the spread of its own political and economic institutions abroad. Rooted firmly in a political culture defined by its attachment to individual freedom, this penchant often manifests itself in foreign policies supporting democratic transitions and economic liberalization around the world. Democracy and trade are trumpeted for two key reasons: states that possess liberal political and economic institutions do not go to war with each other, and they also tend to share common national interests. As democracy and commerce proliferate around the world, the United States should face fewer enemies while cultivating more political allies.

Many American political leaders over the past two centuries have reaffirmed these principles. Outlining the benefits of annexing Texas in his inaugural address, President Polk (1845) noted, "Foreign Powers do not seem to appreciate the true character of our Government... To enlarge its limits is to extend the dominions of peace over additional territories and increasing millions... While the Chief Magistrate and the popular branch of Congress are elected for short terms by the suffrages of those millions who must in their own persons bear all the burdens and miseries of war, our Government can not be otherwise than pacific." At the Paris Peace Conference of 1919, Woodrow Wilson launched a bold and revolutionary plan to end balance-of-power politics that seemed to lead to war by creating a democratic global political order. Secretary of State Cordell Hull championed free trade in the 1930s as a device to remove the economic causes of conflict that he saw emerging as states shifted toward protectionism in Europe. The Truman administration implemented the Marshall Plan to foster economic recovery and strengthen democracy while preventing the spread of communism in Western Europe in the larger emerging struggle with the former Soviet Union.

This proclivity to foster the expansion of America's own political and economic institutions has only been strengthened following the implosion of the Soviet Union, which left the United States as the sole superpower in the world. Just as the American triumph over Germany and Japan created an opportunity for presidents Roosevelt and Truman to promote American interests by transforming these political systems into liberal democracies, the collapse of the Soviet Union in 1991 created another opportunity to foster the development of liberal institutions around the world. Referring to American encouragement of democratization, President Clinton's National Security Advisor Anthony Lake (1993) announced that American strategy would shift from "containment to democratic enlargement" in the wake of the Soviet collapse. Clinton defended this policy in his 1994 State of the Union address by evoking the absence of war among democracies. He stated, "Ultimately, the best strategy to ensure our security and to build a durable peace is to support the advance of democracy elsewhere. Democracies don't attack each other."

The peaceful Soviet collapse stands out as more than a chapter in the centuries-old conflict among great powers for global influence that offered another strategic opportunity for the United States to promote liberal institutions. It also marked a watershed in the struggle between governments and decentralized markets to shape the daily choices of individuals and social behavior. The collapse of the Soviet Union emphatically symbolized the defeat of socialism and political authority as a device to control economic activity. This triumph constitutes part of what Francis Fukuyama (1992) has labeled the "End of History" in which no viable alternative economic order exists besides that of free market capitalism. Similarly, Thomas Friedman (2005) describes the fall of the Berlin Wall on November 9, 1989, as the revolution of 11/9 that flattened the world by redistributing power so that economic decision making is driven by the wants of billions of individuals around the world rather than small numbers of political officials in central planning bureaucracies. Propelled by the economic revolutions of Ronald Reagan, Margaret Thatcher, and Deng Xiaoping, governments around the world have increasingly adopted neoliberal economic policies privatizing domestic industry, cutting trade barriers that insulate domestic firms from international competition, eliminating domestic price controls, and substantially reducing the size of Keynesian fiscal outlays.

This book seeks to understand what implications these historic developments in the organization of economic activity have for stability in the international system. When the ability of governments to manipulate the forces of globalization is limited and markets play a large role in the coordination of social behavior, is the international system marked by more or less military conflict among states? Do the domestic institutions often associated with free market capitalism, namely private property and competitive market structures, cause peace?

These questions carry enormous implications for American grand strategy. The attacks on September 11, 2001 (9/11), motivated President George W. Bush to strengthen the American commitment to the liberal vision of transformation, particularly in the nascent struggle with Islamic fundamentalism. His administration made political reform a centerpiece of his strategy to remake the Middle East. In his 2004 State of the Union address, Bush declared, "As long as the Middle East remains a place of tyranny and despair and anger, it will continue to produce men and movements that threaten the safety of America and our friends. So America is pursuing a forward strategy of freedom in the Middle East . . . We have no desire to dominate, no ambitions of empire. Our aim is a democratic peace."

Economic reform has more quietly been made the junior partner supporting the cause of liberty in the Middle East. Bush has argued that trade indirectly promotes peace by encouraging individual liberty. In a statement outlining a proposal for a free trade zone with the Middle East, President Bush (2003) observed, "Over time, the expansion of liberty throughout the world is the best guarantee of security throughout the world. Freedom is the way to peace . . . Across the globe, free markets and trade have helped defeat poverty, and taught men and women the habits of liberty. So I propose the establishment of a U.S.–Middle East free trade area within a decade, to bring the Middle East into an expanding circle of opportunity, to provide hope for the people who live in that region." Similarly, U.S. Trade Representative Robert Zoellick chided domestic proponents of protectionism for ignoring the capacity of globalization to strengthen the forces of reform and tolerance in the Middle East. He wrote in 2004, "Economic isolationists are too short sighted to see the full mosaic of America's interests. Their fight to defeat such trade agreements would rob the United States of one of its most powerful tools, just when we should be integrating trade and economic reforms with the struggle for democracy and tolerance that is vital to our security."

Such references to the social virtues of markets often elicit rejoinders from those who see capitalism not for its capacity to promote economic opportunity and peace but instead for its tendency to concentrate wealth and expand, often rapaciously, from the economic centers of the developed world.[1] If unfettered markets raised living standards in Western societies and stimulated the fall of the Berlin Wall, they have also left many developing societies trapped in poverty and subject to the demands of a global class of capitalists and their political representatives, like the United States and the International Monetary Fund. Rather than diffusing peacefully throughout the world, the beneficiaries of capitalism have often relied on the sword to secure raw materials and outlets for surplus goods in Latin America, Africa, and the Middle East. If international trade promoted reconciliation between France and Germany during the Cold War, then it also stimulated American intervention in places like Iran, Chile, and Guatemala. Along these lines, current American attempts to transform the Middle East are not viewed for their self-proclaimed goals of promoting freedom and liberty but are instead seen as a device to secure stable access to oil. Contemporary skepticism over the benevolent effects of commerce is reinforced by the legacy of the first era of globalization, which ended in 1914. Even without accepting Leninist arguments tracing the origins of World War I to competition among European powers over the rapidly dwindling supply of colonial outlets for surplus capital, the decisions for war in July 1914 suggest that globalization failed in its most crucial test to prevent war.

REVISING THE FOUNDATIONS OF THE LIBERAL PEACE

This book challenges the intellectual foundations of a series of academic findings, known collectively as the liberal peace, which are intimately tied to this broader national debate over American foreign policy.[2] Perhaps the most prominent in international relations theory over the past two decades, this contemporary research program has utilized insights from such classical scholars as Adam Smith, Baron de Montesquieu, Immanuel Kant, Joseph Schumpeter, and Richard Cobden to refine and affirm two

[1] For a recent examination of this tension associated with market development see James (2006).

[2] For example, John M. Owen (2005, p. 122) writes of their intimate connection with the policies of George W. Bush: "... [F]ew other presidents – certainly none since Woodrow Wilson, a former president of the American Political Science Association ... – have tied their foreign policies more explicitly to the work of social science. The defining act of Bush's presidency was grounded in a theory that the political scientist Jack Levy once declared was 'as close as anything we have to an empirical law in international relations,' namely that democracies do not fight each other."

critical propositions.[3] First, democratic states have created a zone of peace among themselves. Second, high levels of international commerce between states create similar effects, raising the costs of military conflict to unacceptable levels for modern economies.[4]

The relationships among democracy, international trade, and peace are more tenuous than previously thought. The capacity of democracy to promote peace is much weaker than this literature has yet to acknowledge. In addition, the capacity of commerce to constrain war is much stronger than this literature has yet to acknowledge. However, these pacific effects generated by trade depend critically on the presence of liberal economic institutions. I utilize the question of whether market-promoting institutions limit war to advance two central claims. First, liberal economic institutions – namely, the predominance of private property and competitive market structures within domestic economies – promote peace. Second, this liberal economic peace has historically been much stronger than the liberal democratic peace frequently cited by both scholars and policymakers. Together these claims carry important implications for contemporary debates over American grand strategy. They challenge the conventional wisdom about the national security benefits provided from democracy promotion and suggest instead that economic liberalization offers a more robust path to peace.

Democracy and Peace?

The democratic peace debate has extensively studied how regular and competitive elections can empower society to constrain abuses of political authority and generate peace among states. These claims linking democracy to peace generally take one of two forms.[5] The first, which has garnered more

[3] A third finding linking membership in international organizations to peace has received increasing attention. The arguments made here possess fewer implications for this research. For important contributions to this debate, see Oneal, Russett, and Davis (1998), Mansfield, Pevehouse, and Bearce (1999/2000), Mansfield and Pevehouse (2000), Russett and Oneal (2001), Bearce (2003), Boehmer, Gartzke, and Nordstrom (2004), Pevehouse and Russett (2006), and Haftel (2007).

[4] A wide array of contemporary evidence has been accumulated supporting these respective claims. See, for example, Polachek (1980), Rummel (1983), D. Lake (1992), Bremer (1993), Maoz and Russett (1993), Mansfield (1994), Oneal and Russett (1997, 1999), Oneal, Russett, and Berbaum (2003), Owen (1997a), Russett and Oneal (2001), Schultz (2001), Huth and Allee (2002), and Rousseau (2005).

[5] There also is a third version of the democratic peace hypothesis that examines how the number of democracies in the international system shapes the aggregate conflict outcomes in the system. For examples of this research see Gleditsch and Hegre (1997), Mitchell et al. (1999), and Gleditsch (2002).

empirical support, is known as the *dyadic democratic peace proposition.*[6] It restricts the capacity of democracy to promote peace to pairs of democratic states. Democratic governments are only pacific when interacting with fellow democracies. A second hypothesis, known as the *monadic version of the democratic peace hypothesis*, drops this pairing restriction. It holds that the constraints on war imposed by democracy should operate in interactions with all types of regimes in the international system, democracies and autocracies alike.

Numerous theories have been offered to explain the empirical regularities linking democracy to peace. The literature has developed around three primary variants. Two rely on the institutional qualities of democracy; the third on the normative characteristics that tend to emerge from such regimes. The first institutional explanation points to such features as regular elections; the separation of powers among an executive, legislature, and judiciary; and the rule of law within democracies as sources of peace. The process of holding regular and competitive elections increases the political costs to a leader for going to war. When the segments of society that pay the real costs of war in terms of higher taxation and death in battle are granted the means to punish the government officials by removing them from office, states use force much more cautiously. Democratic states tend to win the wars they fight, suggesting that they only fight when they expect to win (Lake 1992; Bueno de Mesquita et al. 1999, 2003; Reiter and Stam 2002). A second institutional explanation highlights how democracy increases transparency and adjusts informational asymmetries in the bargaining process between states. These traits enhance the credibility of promises to avoid the use of military force made between democracies, reduce the dangers of cheating endemic to anarchy, and increase the probability of reaching a cooperative settlement to a dispute (Fearon 1994; Smith 1998; Schultz 2001; Lipson 2003).

A third set of explanations focuses on the normative aspects of democracy (e.g., Maoz and Russett 1993; Dixon 1994; Owen 1994, 1997a; Risse-Kappen 1996; Rousseau 2005). It argues that the political culture that evolves within democracies helps to promote peace. As the norms of

6 The empirical support for the dyadic version of this argument is remarkably robust (e.g. Rummel 1983; Bremer 1992; Maoz and Russett 1993; Dixon 1994; Rousseau et al. 1996; Russett and Oneal 2001; Bueno de Mesquita et al. 2003; Oneal, Russett, and Berbaum 2003; Rousseau 2005). For arguments supporting the monadic version see Benoit (1996), Ray (1998), Macmillan (2003), Rousseau (2005), and Souva and Prins (2006). For critiques of the democratic peace literature see Layne (1994), Spiro (1994), Oren (1995), Gates et al. (1996), Gowa (1999), Green, Kim, and Yoon (2001), and Rosato (2003).

conciliation, compromise, and reciprocity shape the resolution of conflicts within democracies, democratic leaders tend to adopt such procedures when negotiating with other democratic states. These norms help to facilitate peaceful dispute resolution.

Despite substantial empirical and theoretical progress, at least three important questions remain for the democratic peace research program. First, numerous scholars have pointed out that democracy, and the threat of electoral punishment in particular, often insufficiently constrains decisions for war (e.g., Gowa 1999; Mansfield and Snyder 1995, 2002a, b, 2005; Rosato 2003). For example, if a ruling political circle wishes to embrace aggressive foreign policies that heighten the risks of war, the choice to oppose such policies can be politically costly for both opposition politicians and members of society. Opposition leaders must weigh the likely consequences, both domestic and international, before going to war. If victory in war generates a policy success, opposition leaders run the risk of being cast as supporting foreign policy weakness by opposing war (Schultz 2001; Levy and Mabe 2004). Similarly, nonmyopic democratic leaders may be able to circumvent electoral constraints and attempt to check their authority by legislators. Given the costs of organizing opposition, active political opposition from society may fail to materialize as individuals choose to free-ride on the protests and threats of electoral punishment by fellow citizens (Gowa 1999). Mansfield and Snyder (2005) show that elected leaders can exploit appeals to nationalism when state institutions regulating political participation are weak, like in the early stages of a democratic transition, to pursue aggressive foreign policies. The failure of recently democratizing states to grant constitutional freedoms and civil liberties that help regulate political participation and constrain the policy outcomes produced by majoritarian institutions like elections casts doubt on their ability to join the "zone of peace" (Zakaria 1997, 2003). In part, these possibilities reflect the legacy of the French Revolution and the subsequent debate within liberal thought throughout the nineteenth century over the role played by nationalism in promoting or constraining individual liberty (Howard 1978). Even democratic leaders can exploit domestic institutional instability and public fears of insecurity to construct broad swaths of public support for war.

Second, an abundance of candidate explanations for the tendency of two democracies to avoid war with each other has failed to yield a consensus on which among these is best. New contributions in this research program have historically been motivated by this theoretical uncertainty. For example, Bueno de Mesquita et al. (1999, p. 791) write, "Although these observations about democracy and war are part of an important pattern, they lack a coherent explanation. Several possibilities have been put forward, but none has gained broad acceptance." Similarly, Lipson (2003, pp. 1–2) writes, "That is exactly the question about peace among democratic states. It works well in practice, but there is considerable confusion about how it works in theory. The lack of an answer is no joke, however. Despite extensive research, all we have is a remarkable correlation. We still lack a convincing explanation about why democracies do not fight each other."

This lack of theoretical consensus is perhaps most damaging to the research program's central claim when confronting a critical empirical limitation that challenges most existing theoretical explanations of the democratic peace. As will be discussed in Chapter 9, the peace among democratic states does not emerge until after World War I.[7] In both monadic and dyadic research designs, autocrats rather than democrats were more pacific before World War I. This shift in the foreign policy behavior of democracies between the nineteenth and twentieth centuries creates at least two significant problems for most claims linking democracy to peace. The first is simply a new theoretical question that needs to be answered: Why were democratic regimes aggressive in the nineteenth century? The second related problem carries important theoretical implications for most of the existing explanations of a democratic peace because they do not specify that the constraints on war created by democracy are likely to vary over time.[8] Consequently,

[7] Although some segments of the democratic peace literature have acknowledged this extreme shift in the relationship between regime type and war, it remains relatively understudied. While arguing that the peace among democratic states does not emerge until the post–World War II era, Gowa (1999) presents some evidence that dyads possessing two democratic states were more likely to engage in low-level military disputes than all other dyads in the period prior to World War I. Cederman (2001) attributes this "initial democratic belligerence" in the nineteenth century to colonial competition among the United States, Britain, and France. Similarly, Blank (2000) argues that the decline of imperialism allowed the democratic peace to emerge after 1945. Although finding that democracy reduced the likelihood of military disputes from 1886 to 1939, Oneal and Russett (1999) and Russett and Oneal (2001) observe that these pacific effects are weaker in the period before World War I. In a sample of politically relevant dyads, they point to the emergence of a democratic peace around 1896 and suggest that a widespread expansion of suffrage occurring around the turn of the twentieth century may account for this shift. This date shifts to 1900 when all dyad are included in the sample.

[8] Even time-variant explanations of the democratic peace (e.g., Mitchell et al. 1999, Cederman 2001) insufficiently address this empirical anomaly because they generally begin with the expectation of the null hypothesis positing no relationship between regime type and war. In other words, this hypothesis suggests that democrats were just as likely to go to war as autocrats were in the period before the democratic peace emerged. However, the results presented in Chapter 9 contradict this null finding. Instead, democratic regimes were more likely than autocratic ones to go to war before World War I.

if existing explanations are correct, democratic constraints on war should operate irrespective of the time period under investigation. This dramatic switching relationship between democracy and conflict after World War I thus contradicts most theories claiming that democracy promotes peace and stands out as a critical empirical anomaly yet to be explained.

Third, much of this research program has proceeded by making one of two assumptions.[9] First, democratic institutions are assumed to be exogenous. Often reflected in assertions that political institutions are somehow more fundamental than other social institutions that regulate individual behaviour, this assumption necessarily points to the presence or absence of democracy as the best theoretical vehicle to understand the domestic causes of war and peace. Second, if democratic institutions are instead endogenous, or caused by some larger socioeconomic structure or development, it is assumed that any systematic source of variation in regime type does not simultaneously affect the conflict propensities of governments.[10] The costs of such assumptions loom large in light of multiple claims within classical liberal thought and contemporary research suggesting that political freedom is nested within economic freedom. The emergence of democracy has long been traced to institutions and outcomes normally associated with liberal economic institutions, like respect for private property, the emergence of an educated middle class, and economic development (e.g., Smith 1937; Cobden 1868, 1870; Hayek 1994; Moore 1966; North and Weingast 1989; Pipes 1999; Przeworski et al. 2000; Lipset 1994; Boix 2003). For example, in one of the twentieth century's classic works of liberal thought, *The Road to Serfdom*, F. A. Hayek writes, "If 'capitalism' means here a competitive system based on free disposal over private property, it is far more important to realize that only within this system is democracy possible" (1994 [1944], pp. 77–8). This possibility suggests that the peace observed among democratic states may be caused by their tendency to possess relatively liberal market institutions rather than their embrace of open political competition in elections.

Even if liberal economic institutions are not responsible for causing the observed peace among democratic states, do they play a larger role in limiting war among states? One of the most prominent contributions to the academic literature argues that a virtuous relationship exists among democracy, commerce, membership in international organizations, and peace, in which each of these traits reinforces the others (Russett and Oneal 2001).

9 Weede (1995), Gartzke (1998), and Mousseau (2000), are exceptions to this.

10 For a similar critique see Thompson (1996).

Democracy not only promotes peace, it also increases commerce among states, which in turn promotes peace. More recent research critiquing the democratic peace suggests instead that the commercial peace created by capitalism or economic development is stronger than that of democracy (Mousseau 2000; Mousseau, Hegre, and O'Neal 2003; Gartzke, Li, and Boehmer 2001; Gartzke 2007).

The possibility that the democratic peace is weaker than the commercial peace carries important implications for both the central role played by democracy promotion in American grand strategy and for the repeated tendency in policy and academic debates to conflate political and economic freedom. Throughout the Cold War, the United States was cast as engaged in a Manichaean struggle with the totalitarian Soviet Union that controlled all aspects of the political and economic lives of its citizenry. The end of this bifurcation of the world into two vastly different and opposing camps has made it easier to recognize that states often make very different institutional choices with respect to their economic and political institutions. China, for example, stands out as a critical case in which its regime has chosen to sequence political and economic reforms, opting to embrace economic integration before political openness.

The Bush Doctrine suggests that democratic and economic reforms should complement each other, at least as devices to defend American interests around the world. However, a series of recent studies by Mansfield and Snyder (1995, 2002a, b, 2005) caution against overlooking the risks associated with utilizing democracy promotion as an instrument of foreign policy in places like Iraq. They present a wide range of evidence showing that the likelihood of military conflict increases during periods of democratic transition. Similar concerns have arisen in studies of civil war and ethnic conflict (Snyder 2000; Chua 2002). Whereas stable and mature democracies are unlikely to fight each other, the process of transforming an autocratic regime into a democratic regime may be a dangerous one marked by more and not less military strife. If democratization results in a short-term increase in military conflict, American grand strategy should perhaps focus on promoting liberty through markets instead. For example, this possibility suggests that the absence of democratic reform in China may not hinder the building of cooperative ties with the United States that are capable of smoothing any global power transition between the two. Exploring this possibility first necessitates examining whether and how liberal economic institutions have historically influenced decisions for war or peace among governments.

Commercial Liberalism

The commercial peace research program displays perhaps even more variation in explaining the long-hypothesized and more recently confirmed tendency for international commerce to promote peace between states. One segment of this literature focusing on international trade presents up to five potential mechanisms by which commerce promotes peace. The first has been labeled the *opportunity cost* or *deterrence model.* Because conflict or even the threat of it tends to disrupt normal trading patterns, potentially large economic costs will deter dependent states from using military force to solve their political conflicts (e.g., Polachek 1980; Russett and Oneal 2001). A second mechanism compares the relative costs of acquiring productive resources. As commerce grows, the incentives for plunder or conquest decrease simply because it is a more costly means of generating economic growth (Rosecrance 1986). Third, a sociological hypothesis concentrates on how trade helps to increase contact and communication across societies. By building a broader cosmopolitan identity across societies, trade enables common interests to emerge while displacing national loyalties and competitive relations among governments that generate military conflict (e.g., Deutsch et al. 1957). Fourth, drawing on bargaining models, some scholars argue that international commerce provides an important signaling mechanism that can help states achieve a negotiated compromise short of war during a crisis (e.g., Morrow 1999; Gartzke, Li, and Boehmer 2001; Reed 2003). A fifth segment focuses on how regional trading arrangements among states promote heightened trade levels and peace (Mansfield, Pevehouse, and Bearce 1999/2000; Mansfield and Pevehouse 2000; Bearce 2003; Haftel 2007).

A second strand of this research focuses instead on domestic economic attributes to explain the absence of military conflict. Mousseau (2000, 2005) and Mousseau, Hegre, and O'Neal (2003) point to the emergence of contractual norms within societies based on exchange as the link between markets and peace. Hegre (2000) claims instead that economic development conditions the relative value of commerce and conquest. Development raises the costs of conquest and increases the returns from international trade.[11] Souva (2004) shows that the similarity of domestic economic institutions promotes peace. Defined by the absence of capital controls, common

[11] Boehmer and Sobek (2005) find a curvilinear relationship between development and conflict. Extremely poor and wealthy states are both less warlike.

political interests, and economic development, Gartzke (2007) argues that capitalism reduces military conflict by reducing the incentives for conquest and by facilitating communication about resolve in diplomatic crises.

The commercial peace research program faces challenges like those that raise doubts about the capacity of democracy to limit war. Three stand out. They concern the historical capacity of trade to promote peace, the process by which trade causes states to adopt peaceful foreign policies, and the endogeneity question – namely whether the causes of trade also influence decisions for war and peace.

First, the commercial peace literature faces a different version of the historical inconsistency critique. Rather than being bypassed as in the democratic peace literature, it has served as a foundational argument for criticism of any claim that international commerce promotes peace. Even though substantial trading ties helped build cooperative political relationships in Europe following World War II,[12] the abrupt end of a sustained era of globalization caused by the outbreak of World War I stands out as a glaring anomaly for any claim linking international commerce to peace. If substantial trading links failed then to prevent one of the defining military conflicts in human history, why should globalization be able to prevent war in the contemporary period? This empirical weakness looms larger than the single but important case of World War I. European and American competition for colonial markets in Africa, South America, and Asia at the end of the nineteenth century seems to confirm Marxist–Leninist claims associating capitalist development with imperialist expansion and war. These assertions linking international trade and capitalism with conflict in the nineteenth century survive in part because of the absence of systematic research examining the links between trade and conflict during this first era of globalization. The limited data on bilateral trade flows before 1950 have led much of the commercial peace literature to focus on empirical evidence after World War II to validate its claims.[13] When scholars expand their analysis to include cases from the nineteenth century, data across the two periods are aggregated and potential differences between these eras of globalization are obscured.[14]

[12] On the relationship between trade and peace in post–World War II Europe, see Verdier and Eilstrup-Sangiovanni (2005).

[13] Edward Mansfield and Brian M. Pollins (2003, p. 8) write, "Instead, large-N studies have focused almost exclusively on the past half century and have largely ignored whether and how the effect of interdependence have changed over time."

[14] Barbieri (1996), Oneal and Russett (1999), and Russett and Oneal (2001) examine samples between 1870 and 1939. However, all three studies aggregate data before and after World War I into a single sample.

Second, the mechanisms by which the economic interests of private individuals exposed to international markets get translated into public policies that support either war or peace remain understudied.[15] For example, one classical hypothesis points to the natural division of resources among societies as generating a mutual need to establish cooperative trading relationships and peace.[16] This claim associates international trade with the emergence of common interests among governments. Ricardo's principle of comparative advantage reinforces such a link by demonstrating that international trade tends to increase the aggregate income of all countries engaging in it. Accordingly, the economic gains from trade create a joint interest in peace by offering countries a strong material incentive to avoid the severed trading links that accompany war.[17]

Standard trade theory that has moved beyond Ricardo's key insight illustrates the risks associated with focusing on macro-level propositions to understand how globalization promotes peace. The processes associated with integrating national markets into a single world economy generate intense conflicts within societies by altering the domestic distribution of income. For example, the Heckscher–Ohlin framework shows that trade increases the real income of owners of relatively abundant factors of production in an economy (Flam and Flanders 1991). At the same time, owners of scarce factors of production see their real incomes decline from globalization. This insight carries an important implication. Because international trade redistributes income within society, it simultaneously creates conflicting pressures for and against more open commercial policies. This domestic conflict implies that gains from trade accruing to an economy as a whole will not necessarily translate into uniform lobbying pressures from society for the promotion of trade and peace. Unless the domestic beneficiaries of trade

[15] For examples of such critiques see Mansfield and Pollins (2001), Barbieri and Schneider (1999) and Schneider and Schulze (2003).

[16] For a discussion of this variant and its classical roots, see Chapter 1 of Howard (1978).

[17] Moreover, this straightforward proposition linking high levels of trade with peace is readily testable with the use of modern statistical techniques. Much of the contemporary commercial peace literature has adopted this very approach using broad claims rooted in classical liberal international relations theory to test whether aggregate economic outcomes, like heightened bilateral trade flows, reduce military conflict. More limited attention has been devoted to using alternative empirical techniques, like intense case studies, capable of discriminating among multiple commercial peace hypotheses and moving beyond broad propositions that neglect the process by which economic interests are translated through the domestic institutions to shape decisions for war or peace. For a similar critique see Ripsman and Blanchard (2003) and Rowe (2005).

also possess sufficient political clout to ensure that domestic markets stay open and military conflict is avoided, these uneven effects of globalization cast doubt on the classical insight that international trade always generates a common interest for peace among states. At the very least, these possibilities suggest that the domestic process by which the economic interests derived from international trade get translated into pacific foreign policies is crucial to understanding how globalization limits war. At the same time, the theoretical opportunity created by revising Ricardo's basic insight necessitates additional empirical research – quantitative and qualitative alike – that moves beyond relying on such aggregate economic indicators like bilateral trade flows to confirm whether and how globalization limits military conflict between states.

Third, economists and political scientists have long recognized that trade flows expand between states for a variety of reasons, including technological innovations that drive down transportation costs, differences in relative factor endowments, and variation in domestic political institutions that influence the scope of regulatory barriers like tariffs. The source of expanding trade flows carries important consequences for the possibility of peaceful relations among states. For example, during the Cold War economic flows within the Soviet bloc were driven by very different mechanisms than those within the Western bloc. In the case of the former, hierarchical political relationships between the Soviet Union and its client states directed trade.[18] In the case of the latter, international trade flows responded instead to the signals created by competitive markets. Today, surging worldwide demand for oil has made economic growth in many Middle Eastern countries completely dependent on a single global integrated market. However, like the conditions in Soviet bloc countries, production decisions and levels of trade in these economies are shaped by government agencies responsible for administering these public assets. Similarly, economic historians agree that the dramatic growth of international commercial flows during the first era of globalization was driven by technological innovations such as the railroad and steamship. Many states even responded to these declining transportation costs by increasing political barriers to trade. Expanding trade flows coexisted with higher tariffs. These brief examples illustrate that the presence of aggregate trade flows, on their own, often tells us little about the causes of this exchange and the political and economic institutions that

[18] For a discussion of the role of hierarchical relationships in international relations, see D. Lake (1996, 2007).

underpin it. Consequently, all trade may not be alike in its capacity to promote peace.[19]

The empirical and theoretical questions surrounding these two research programs carry important implications for the study here of the relationship between liberal economic institutions and peace. Most important, they underscore the need to expand the range of institutions that regulate state–society interactions within a domestic political system and shape a country's international relationships. As suggested by the arguments of Doyle (1983, 1986, 1997, 2005) and Zakaria (2003), the democratic peace may really be a liberal peace in which the peace is jointly created by multiple domestic institutions that protect civil liberties, ensure competitive markets, and widen political participation. This possibility suggests another theoretical implication. The peace among democratic states may really be caused by liberal economic institutions. Just as respect for private property and relatively laissez faire economic policies promote democracy, they could simultaneously promote peace. At the very least, these possibilities underscore the need to examine the relative capacity of liberal political and economic institutions to promote peace.

THE INVISIBLE HAND OF PEACE

One key thesis runs throughout this book: the domestic institutional foundations of liberal economic systems promote peace between states. This broader claim is rooted in two conceptual shifts from the broader liberal peace literature and decomposed into two constituent parts – one that focuses on the predominance of private ownership in a domestic economy, and another that concentrates on government efforts to limit the capacity of globalization to make domestic markets more competitive. I draw on classical liberal theory, standard trade theory, selectorate theory, the new institutionalism in economics, and the bargaining model of war to explain how these two institutions empower societal actors to prevent war. Just as Adam Smith suggested that an invisible hand facilitated the emergence of collective societal benefits from self-interested actions by individuals interacting within markets, the pursuit of wealth by *private individuals interacting in competitive markets* reduces the risks of war among states.

19 For a similar argument see Dorussen (2006) along with the literature cited earlier that examines how preferential trading arrangements promote peace. For example, Mansfield and Pevehouse (2000) show that trade only promotes peace between states that are also members to a common regional economic institution.

The first conceptual shift from the existing literature challenges the central role that the presence or absence of democracy has been accorded as a source of social order within domestic political systems and consequently as a cause of peace. Liberal international relations theory holds that the institutional relationship between a government and its citizenry plays a critical role in shaping the character of a state's foreign policy (Moravcsik 1997). Just as elections have been extolled for their capacity to protect individual liberty, the degree to which markets shape the allocation of scarce resources in an economy reflects government capacity to regulate, shape, and control individual and collective choices within society. In one of the foundational statements of the liberal peace, Michael Doyle (1983, pp. 207–8) points to four sets of domestic institutions that classical liberal theory identifies as advancing or protecting individual freedom: democratic elections, juridical equality among citizens, private property, and the allocation of scarce resources through decentralized markets rather than by bureaucratic authorities. Liberal peace research and policy proclamations associated with its claims have largely focused on the first two of these institutions while neglecting the role of private property and competitive markets.

The second conceptual shift redirects attention away from such concepts as interdependence and aggregate trade flows that have traditionally been the focus of commercial liberalism and toward such liberal economic institutions, such as private property and competitive market structures, which shape both domestic and international commercial activity. This shift enables an exploration of the limitations and conditions under which international trade promotes peace among states. Although classical liberalism suggests that the material incentives generated by trade facilitate the emergence of common political interests and peace among states, standard trade theory shows how trade can be politically divisive between and within societies. Just as trade increases aggregate consumption possibilities for an economy, it simultaneously shifts the distribution of income within it. These distributional implications suggest that not all commercial flows are alike in their capacity to promote peace. As trade theorists note (e.g., Leamer 1993), commerce can be driven by multiple factors, including consumer tastes, transaction costs, transportation costs, relative factor endowments between countries, and political barriers to trade. Only one of these attributes – political barriers to trade – directly reflects the structure of domestic institutions that enables governments to influence prices within a domestic economy and thus shape individual choices within that political system.

These conceptual shifts facilitate the construction of the two critical component claims of this book – one focusing on how the relative predominance of private property in an economy promotes peace; the second on how competitive domestic market structures promote peace. Given the centrality of these two institutions in capitalist economies, this twin institutional foci implies a much broader claim: capitalism promotes peace.[20]

Large quantities of public property enable government officials to shape the allocation of scarce resources in an economy and simultaneously diminish the role played by decentralized markets in coordinating economic activity. State-owned enterprises act as political firms in which management decisions often reflect political expediency and bureaucratic pressures before profit. Large quantities of public property generate fiscal autonomy for governments and strengthen their hold on the domestic reigns of power. This fiscal autonomy increases the likelihood that governments will engage in military conflict for two reasons. First, it decouples domestic survival from foreign policy performance and decreases the domestic political risk governments face when pursuing aggressive foreign policies. Second, this financial autonomy enables governments to sustain arms races that both reduce the relative military power of adversaries and tempt those adversaries to launch preventive military attacks. *Governments possessing access to large quantities of public property are more likely to engage in military conflict than governments overseeing more privatized economies.*

Commercial policies shape the extent to which competitive market prices determine the allocation of resources within a domestic economy and the conditions under which globalization promotes peace. By restricting the entry of foreign goods, import tariffs decrease the size of domestic markets and increase the ability of domestic firms to influence prices (Varian 1996, pp. 418–19). The elimination of barriers to trade provides an important mechanism by which more competition can be "imported" into the domestic economy (e.g., Irwin 2002).

The ability of globalization to promote peace depends on the outcome of this crucial domestic political struggle over commercial policy. When free trading interests dominate the domestic political game, governments adopt fewer barriers to international trade and pursue more restrained national interests that create opportunities for cooperation with other states. When protectionist interests enjoy more domestic influence, governments adopt more aggressive foreign policies, including greater control over foreign territories, which raise the risks of military conflict with other states. The capacity

[20] The definition of capitalism employed in this book relies on the key domestic institutions, namely private property and the allocation of scarce resources through competitive price signals, which modern economists generally use to define it. For examples of this definition, see Friedman (1962) and Kornai (1992, 2000).

to intervene in the domestic economy and shape this domestic struggle creates opportunities for governments to build coalitions supporting its entire range of policies, including those that heighten the risk of war with other states. These arguments point to the state's capacity to regulate flows of goods, services, people, and capital across national boundaries as critically shaping the relationship between globalization and peace. *Governments that adopt more restrictive policies toward international trade and investment flows are more likely to engage in military conflict.*

The empirical sections of the book first test these two primary hypotheses linking private property and liberal commercial policies to peace; and then compare these findings with the existing body of work in the liberal peace literature that focuses on how democracy and economic interdependence promote peace between states. They draw on statistical analysis, archival research, and contemporary fieldwork to generate the following key findings:

1. Governments overseeing economies with high quantities of private property are less likely to engage in military conflict than governments overseeing economies with lower quantities of private property.
2. Governments embracing free-trade policies engage in fewer military conflicts than governments managing more closed economies.
   - 2a. This link between free-trade policies and peace spans both modern eras of globalization – one from the middle of the nineteenth century until 1914 and another during the post–World War II period.
3. The capacity of liberal economic institutions to promote peace has historically been stronger than that of democracy.
   - 3a. The democratic peace, or the claim that any two democracies are less likely to engage in military conflict than any other pair of regimes, does not emerge until after World War I.
   - 3b. Before World War I, democratic states were more likely than autocratic states to engage in all levels of military conflict, including war.
   - 3c. Moreover, in the twentieth century, the democratic peace holds only among states that also possess substantial quantities of private property.
   - 3d. Such a restriction does not apply to the peace created by liberal economic institutions. Liberal economic institutions promote peace irrespective of regime type.

3e. Whereas the democratic peace holds only in a dyadic setting (between two democracies), the peace created by liberal economic institutions holds in both dyadic and monadic research designs.

These arguments also create opportunities to rethink important historical cases that have been used both to confirm and challenge the arguments associated with the liberal peace. For example, the evolution of the relationship between the United States and Great Britain over the nineteenth century from one of rivalry and competition to one of cooperation and friendship has been repeatedly examined in the democratic peace debate (Owen 1994, 1997a, b; Layne 1994; Rock 1997; Way 1998; Blank 2000). Rather than reaffirm the capacity of democracy to promote peace, I show how normal democratic processes facilitated the emergence of expansionist foreign policy interests in the United States that heightened political conflict with Great Britain. The conflicts over Oregon and Venezuela in the nineteenth century illustrate that the predominant emphasis on democracy in the literature has obscured a much larger role within these respective countries for economic interests in both starting and stopping these disputes. Although protectionist interests in both countries helped to stimulate and prolong these conflicts, economic interests that were competitive in international markets and their political representatives played a critical role in halting these disputes and thus preventing war.

The conflict over Venezuela in 1895, in particular, carries important implications for larger historical debates over the role played by capitalist development in American foreign policy. Multiple historians have long pointed to economic factors as crucial in America's transition from a continental to a global power in the 1890s (Williams 1959; LaFeber 1998). Because American territorial expansion during this period relied largely on projecting and using military force, these arguments suggest that commerce promotes conflict rather than peace. My reexamination demonstrates instead that the domestic economic interests most supportive of territorial expansion and conflict in this case were mercantilist and anticapitalist in nature.

Critics of liberal international relations theory have long pointed to the nineteenth-century era of globalization and the outbreak of World War I as powerful evidence contradicting the claim that commerce promotes peace. My arguments focusing on the domestic institutions underpinning economic exchange show why this skeptical conventional wisdom is wrong. Instead of asking why globalization failed to stop war, I examine how political intervention in markets shaped the decision for war in July 1914. French capital controls and substantial quantities of public property in Russia helped shift the European balance of military power between 1905 and 1914. These market constraints contributed to a disproportionate Russian capacity to finance an arms race on land that precipitated the German decision to launch a preventive war in July 1914. Apart from reaffirming the explanatory strength of liberal international relations theory, these claims challenge the predominant focus in the historiography of World War I on German decision making. The key cause of World War I lies within the domestic institutions of Russia rather than Germany.

Finally, the evolution of the political conflict between China and Taiwan stands out as a critical case to test claims associated with the liberal peace in the contemporary era of globalization. As Taiwan has embraced democratization and liberalized trade with the mainland, the relationship has deteriorated with both periodic military exercises and bold political statements that raise the threat of war. These trends suggest that political and economic liberalization have stimulated, rather than dampened, conflict across the Taiwan Straits. I show that liberal economic institutions, but not liberal political institutions, have helped to stabilize the recent conflict between China and Taiwan. Although democratization has created incentives for some Taiwanese politicians to pursue pro-independence policies that heighten the risk of war, economic reforms are both restraining the mainland's stance toward Taiwan and shifting Taiwan's internal balance of power toward groups opposed to independence and the potential war it could bring.

THE STRUCTURE OF THE BOOK

The book is organized into three key sections. The first section, in Chapters 1 through 3, examines how a concentration on the pacific effects generated by liberal economic institutions interacts with existing research on the liberal peace and debates about American grand strategy. Chapter 2 examines the liberal peace debate in the context of contemporary international relations theory and Western philosophy. It shows how a focus on institutions regulating the domestic economy can generate new insights into unanswered questions in these debates. Chapter 3 develops the theoretical explanations linking private property and competitive market structures to peace.

The second section of the book, in Chapters 4 through 8, tests these arguments linking private property and competitive markets to peace by examining their historical capacity to limit military conflict. For the most part, the liberal peace literature has predominantly drawn on multivariate statistical analysis to check the empirical veracity of various propositions linking either democracy or commerce to peace and then refine them. To ensure comparability of the findings here with this broader literature and to establish that my domestic variant of commercial liberalism has promoted peace across time and in multiple countries, Chapters 4 and 5 adopt a similar research strategy. Chapter 4 tests the capacity of these institutions to promote peace in the twentieth century. Chapter 5 then extends this statistical analysis by looking at the nineteenth-century era of globalization that ended in 1914. Together, the findings of these two chapters illustrate the historical depth of this domestic variant of commercial liberalism, showing that it existed across both modern eras of globalization.

Chapters 6 through 8 deepen this empirical analysis by presenting a series of detailed case studies chosen for their capacity to confront the most critical tests of liberal international relations theory over the past two centuries and to reveal the mechanisms by which an invisible hand pushes governments to adopt more pacific foreign policies. Given the implications of the arguments here for debates over American foreign policy, Chapter 6 examines how struggles over trade, tariff policy, and imperialism in the United States shaped the relationship with its chief rival in the international system during the nineteenth century. Chapter 7 reexamines the Achilles' heel of liberal international relations theory – the outbreak of World War I following more than a fifty-year period of globalization. Chapter 8 investigates the recent evolution of the conflict between China and Taiwan.

The final section, in Chapters 9 and 10, explores the relative capacity of democracy and liberal economic institutions to promote peace and then revisits the policy implications of these conclusions. Chapter 9 draws on a wide range of statistical tests to show that market-based exchange, not democracy, has historically acted as a more significant constraint on war. Chapter 10 presents a summary of the book's key arguments and then returns to where it began. What are the implications of this capitalist peace for American foreign policy in the twenty-first century, when it faces multiple challenges like the rise of China, Islamic fascism, terrorism, and a backlash against globalization in much of the developing world? It argues that the relative emphasis between promoting markets and democracy should be switched in American grand strategy. The United States possesses the largest and most vibrant market in the global economy. American grand strategy can integrate this unique political asset more effectively. A comparison among British economic statecraft in the 1840s, American attempts to rebuild the European economy following World War II, and contemporary efforts by China to utilize economic incentives to transform its political relationship with Taiwan suggests how similar broad-based economic liberalization strategies by the United States could release the invisible hand to promote development, democracy, and peace in the contemporary world.

TWO

Liberal International Relations Theory on War

The expansion of individual liberty promotes peace between states by limiting governmental abuses of political authority, particularly manipulations of external threat for domestic political gain.[1] This classical insight has served as the foundation for liberal international relations theory, including the contemporary democratic peace research program. According to this line of reasoning, governments often wage war for particularistic or selfish reasons that undermine the broader welfare of society while simultaneously fortifying the domestic political status of the governing elite. To prevent war, society needs mechanisms such as elections to constrain and punish political leaders who would pursue these selfish goals. For example, the limited fear of domestic punishment allows autocratic regimes to enter into more wars because they can do so while holding onto power at home. The presence of democratic elections limits war by empowering citizens, who bear its real costs, to replace political leaders that pursue aggressive foreign policies.

This chapter builds on this central insight in two ways. First, it examines why an expanded range of domestic institutions capable of promoting liberty should be integrated in the liberal peace research program. Political scientists have traditionally focused on "political" institutions as critical sources of individual liberty.[2] Although competitive elections expand

[1] See for example Waltz (1959), Howard (1978), and Doyle (1997).

[2] Political institutions aggregate individual preferences and create social outcomes through authority relationships in which some small subset of actors has the capacity to direct or command the behavior of others. Alternatively, the economic institutions that will be the focus of this chapter – private property and competitive market structures – coordinate social behavior via voluntary exchange relationships. For a discussion of this distinction see Lindblom (1977).

political participation and force governments to be more responsive to the demands of its citizens, state and society interact in multiple institutional settings outside of elections. The domestic institutions shaping the allocation of resources within an economy also shape the capacity of governments to control individual choice. Society can be empowered through the market to limit abuses of government authority. This possibility combines with the basic liberal claim linking liberty to peace to suggest that such market-based interactions should also influence choices for war and peace.

Second, this chapter blends contemporary bargaining theory and this classical explanation of why wars occur to construct a theoretical framework capable of generating hypotheses linking liberal economic institutions to peace. Classical liberalism is perhaps more accurately described as possessing a theory of peace rather than war. It focuses on the incentives governments face when deciding to enter a military conflict. Peace emerges when war becomes too costly, primarily with the expansion of democratic political freedom or international trade.

Bargaining theory shows that a singular focus on incentives is incomplete (e.g., Fearon 1995; Morrow 1999; Powell 1999, 2006; Gartzke et al. 2001; Schultz 2001; Wagner 2007). The outbreak of war is not necessarily limited simply by making it more costly. Predatory rulers may draw liberal states into military conflict by exploiting the strategic restraint created by democracy or substantial trade ties. If this is the case, there may be no relationship between liberal institutions and war if the former restrains a government from initiating a military conflict while simultaneously making it an enticing target for aggression by other states in the international system.

Rather than cast these theoretical frameworks as competing, I show how they fundamentally complement each other. The central focus of each – one focusing on incentives, the other focusing on the strategic nature of interactions between governments – is necessary to understand why wars occur.

This chapter thus combines these two arguments – one showing how individual liberty can emerge through the market, and a second blending classical insights and contemporary bargaining theory – to construct a general liberal framework on war. It builds this theoretical framework with four parts. The first section explores how the contemporary liberal peace research can be revised in light of classical arguments discussing how private property and competitive market structures have historically constrained state authority. The second section summarizes classical liberal views on war and peace. A third section reexamines classical arguments about why wars occur in light of contemporary research using models of strategic interaction. A final concluding section combines these discussions to lay out the theoretical foundation that guides the hypotheses constructed in Chapter 3.

MARKET CONSTRAINTS ON PUBLIC AUTHORITY

A wide variety of literature in both economics and political science has explored how the desire of rational politicians to remain in office can lead to economic policies that reduce economic welfare either for an entire society or components of it.[3] As such, the regulation of an economy becomes an arena of competition and struggle in a domestic polity. Barry Weingast (1995, p. 1) summarizes this tension:

> The fundamental political dilemma of an economic system is this: A government strong enough to protect property rights and enforce contracts is also strong enough to confiscate the wealth of its citizens. Thriving markets require not only the system of property rights and a law of contracts, but a secure political foundation that limits the ability of the state to confiscate wealth. Far from obvious, however, are the circumstances that produce a political system that plays one role instead of the other.[4]

Private actors need governments, and the coercive power they possess, to transact regularly through competitive markets. At the same time, the possession of these powers creates opportunities for governments to manipulate economic activity for their own benefit and expand their authority over society. Just as more commonly identified political institutions like elections, federalism, and the separation of power between an executive and a legislature prevent the concentration of political power in the hands of a few individuals, institutions regulating market transactions also influence and reflect the balance of authority between a government and its citizenry. By limiting a government's ability to bypass the market and direct the allocation of scarce resources in an economy, society can constrain government authority and shape public policy.

Private Property

Often first attributed to John Locke's *Two Treatises of Government*, the link between private property and individual liberty has long been a key

[3] For a good review of work by economists on this topic, see Keech (1995). One of the classics in political science on how the desire to remain in office can lead politicians to distort economic outcomes is Bates (1981).

[4] Echoing this theme, Douglass North (1981, p. 20) notes, "The existence of the state is essential for economic growth; the state, however, is the source of manmade economic decline."

foundation of modern liberal theory.[5] Its publication, themes, and underlying motivations were a product of the pressures leading up to the Glorious Revolution, a critical transition era of English history. The tract emerged from collaboration with the Earl of Shaftesbury, who was quite active in the broader Whig political movement to assert parliamentary control over the crown. Locke's intellectual foil was Robert Filmer, whose *Patriarcha* provided the ideological and intellectual rationale for the divine right of absolutism (Filmer and Sommerville 1991 [1680]). Filmer argued that existing political institutions that endowed the monarchy with political authority reflected the initial granting of earthly authority from God to Adam. All men were not created equal before God; instead, both individuals and their material possessions on earth were part of a monarch's dominion.

Locke sought to construct the requirements of a social contract that challenged Filmer's assertion that all men were not equal before God and thus undeserving of an active participatory role in the political order. Locke argued that men had to be free and equal in order to fulfill their duties to God (Dunn 1969, p. 121). Humans left the state of nature and formed a political society to protect their property, broadly defined to include life, liberty, and material possessions.[6] Private property, justified through natural law granting individuals the right to own property in themselves, helped create the independence necessary for liberty (Gray 1995, p. 14). Locke equates the absence of individual property with the presence of despotic power in which one has absolute and arbitrary power over others (Laslett 1988, p. 103).[7]

Locke's arguments about property challenged the right of royal authority to seize property via taxation, a recurring source of conflict between the monarchy and the emergent class of British wealth in seventeenth-century England.[8] Given that the right to hold property emerged, not from positive

[5] This discussion of Locke relies primarily on Dunn (1969), Laslett (1988), and Tully (1980).

[6] For example, Locke writes at the beginning of Chapter 11 in the Second Treatise, "The great end of Men entering into Society, being the enjoyment of their Properties in Peace and Safety, and the great instrument and means of that being the Laws established in that Society . . ." II, §134.

[7] Laslett cites Locke, II, §174.

[8] Both Dunn (1969) and Tully (1980) point to this critical historical frame of reference, namely the recurring conflict between the crown and the emerging bourgeoisie, as motivating Locke's arguments rather than the conflict between capital and labor that is the focus of the more Marxist interpretation of Locke by MacPherson (1962). Dunn (1969, p. 216) writes, "Nor is there any reason to suppose that he believed the life of unlimited capitalist appropriation to exemplify a greater level of moral rationality than the life of the devout peasant. It is essential to recollect the challenge which the property rights which he wished to defend were *in fact* undergoing. The spectre which haunted the English

or manmade law, but from natural law and that man entered the basic social contract to protect his property, a government did not have the right to seize or expropriate these possessions without first acquiring the consent of its citizens through parliamentary approval. Repeated seizures of property violated this contract, threatened other property holdings, and justified rebellion by society. Most important, repeated seizures of property constituted a vehicle by which the government could extend its power over its citizens.[9]

Contemporary research examining the broader conflict between monarch and parliament in seventeenth-century England confirms many of Locke's central insights about the role that private property can play in constraining the concentration of political authority (e.g., Kiser 1986/87; North and Weingast 1989; Pipes 1999). Successive monarchs in the sixteenth and seventeenth centuries escaped popular attempts to limit their authority by possessing independent sources of revenue, such as substantial landholdings, that could finance public policy. Absent the need to acquire more revenue, the crown did not need to call the British Parliament into session to request financial assistance. This financial independence deprived parliament, and the interests that dominated it, of a lever by which to constrain the crown's authority. For example, the massive confiscation of all church lands by Henry VIII (1509–47) limited his need to rely on parliament for finance and thus increased his political autonomy.[10] Successive monarchs eventually sold these assets and had to seek alternative revenue sources like taxation. Their repeated attempts to compensate for these dwindling financial resources through forced loans and the institution of new taxes without parliamentary approval threatened private property and played a central role in the political crises of the seventeenth century. The merchant and aristocratic interests that dominated both houses of parliament did not grant access to their growing private holdings without winning important political concessions that limited the crown's political authority.

Pipes (1999) draws a direct comparison between England and Russia to illustrate the central role that private property plays in the emergence of

property-owner in 1680 or between 1685 and 1688 was the threat of non-parliamentary taxation and the confiscation of freeholds in order to consolidate executive authority. It was not a determined policy of redistributive social justice" (italics in original).

9 Locke notes that the expropriation of property can help expand a government's power in II, § 138. He discusses violations of property as justifying rebellion in II, § 222.

10 Although carrying more implications for the next chapter, it is important to note that Kiser (1986/87, 282) and Kiser, Drass, and Brustein (1995) link this confiscation of property by Henry VIII to his strategy of empire building that led him to fight more wars than any other English monarch.

democracy. He argues that the confiscation of nearly all landed property in Novgorod by Ivan III and Ivan IV in the sixteenth century prevented the emergence of an aristocracy capable of limiting the concentration of political authority in the tsarist state. This absence of private property and the simultaneous concentration of political power and wealth in the patrimonial Russian state insulated the government from societal pressures for democratic reform. Pipes (1999, p. 180) writes, "As can be seen, the evolution in Russia of property in land ran in the diametrically opposite direction from the rest of Europe... No single factor in Russia's history explains better the divergence of her political and economic evolution from the rest of Europe, because it meant that in the age of absolutism in Russia, unlike most of Western Europe, property presented no barrier to royal power."

These links among the absence of private property, substantial quantities of public property, and the absence of societal constraints on government authority also find contemporary support in the resource curse literature (e.g., Ross 2001; Boix 2003; Weinthal and Jones Luong 2006). The ease by which governments can extract wealth from large natural resource endowments shapes the structure of domestic institutions. States possessing large natural resource endowments, such as oil and minerals, often derive substantial revenues upon nationalizing these assets and avoid demands for accountability associated with alternative systems of public finance that rely instead on the imposition of taxes. In short, because it is easily susceptible to expropriation by governments, oil and mineral wealth is often associated with authoritarian regimes.

These ideas linking the concentration of political authority and economic wealth can also be found in Friedrich Hayek's *The Road to Serfdom*, one of the classic critiques of communism in the twentieth century. He explores the implications for individual freedom of economic planning by comparing systems of private property with those in which all assets are owned or controlled by a single person or collective. In the latter arrangement, one individual or collective possesses the authority to direct the lives of other members of society by controlling the means of subsistence. Hayek (1994 [1944], p. 115) writes:

> What our generation has forgotten is that the system of private property is the most important guaranty of freedom, not only for those who own property, but scarcely less for those who do not. It is only because the control of the means of production is divided among many people acting independently that nobody has complete power over us, that we as individuals can decide what to do with ourselves. If all the means of production were vested in a single hand, whether it be nominally that of society as a whole or that of a dictator, whoever exercises this control has complete power over us.

As property diffuses to multiple owners, social behavior is increasingly coordinated by voluntary interactions in decentralized markets rather than the authoritative decisions of any single body. This weakening of a central authority necessarily enhances the liberty of individuals in society.[11]

Competitive Market Structures

The relationship between private property and liberty parallels the connections between decentralized exchange through markets and liberty. Once again, Hayek (1994) describes how political interference with free and competitive markets can abridge individual liberties and enhance the power of the state.[12] Hayek argued the origins of the Nazi totalitarianism lay in the socialist-leaning policies first inaugurated by Bismarck.[13] Defined by the absence of private property and allocation of productive resources via bureaucracy, socialism must rely on coercion to function effectively. The implementation of a central economic plan requires both the identification of a central goal, which productive decisions seek to fulfill, and a strategy to achieve these ends. Some means of deciding among competing plans was a fundamental prerequisite to the centralization of economic life. Seeing unanimous consent within society on these issues as impossible, Hayek argued that some coercion was necessary to make such collective decisions.

The use of coercion via government-administered central plans contrasts significantly with relying instead on competitive market structures to determine production and consumption decisions in an economy. The availability of multiple alternatives prevents all parties in a competitive market transaction from coercing each other. If a buyer does not like the seller's

[11] Recent studies about the role played by state-owned enterprises in the internal politics of a country support Hayek's claims. In a study of Egypt, India, Turkey, and Mexico, Waterbury (1992) argues that such public resources strengthen regime stability by building broad-based coalitions of support, including labor, which depend on such benefits as lifetime employment and guaranteed supply contracts. Moreover, when publicly held firms constitute a large portion of national product, even private firms come to depend on business transactions conducted with them. State-owned enterprises thus enable governments to build large networks of political patronage, tie large portions of society to their survival in office, and minimize the potential for resistance to costly public policies.

[12] I qualify this a bit by noting that Hayek recognized the important role of the state in supplying such public goods as a legal infrastructure, or the rule of the law, and national defense. Thus, it would be incorrect to characterize his arguments as not recognizing any role for authority in social behavior.

[13] Hayek (1994, p. 6) writes, "Few are ready to recognize that the rise of fascism and nazism was not a reaction against the socialist trends of the preceding period but a necessary outcome of those tendencies."

price, he or she can simply find another seller or choose instead to withdraw from the exchange.[14] Accordingly, command over societal resources in competitive markets is generally governed by mutually beneficial and voluntary exchange relationships.[15]

State and society often interact within markets on the basis of an exchange relationship in which the price mechanism constrains both sets of actors. When the state makes a commitment to respect private property or agrees to compete with private-sector firms for the right to acquire scarce societal resources, it necessarily surrenders some of its authority to direct or control the behavior of private individuals. Competitive markets render both the state and members of society weak in the sense that neither can control prices or the terms of their exchange relationship. For example, governments that rely on voluntary enlistment to build and sustain their armed forces must compete with the same wage pressures faced by firms in the private sector trying to expand their number of employees. Conscription offers the state a means to bypass these labor market pressures and unilaterally set wages for soldiers.[16] If conscripted, a citizen must either accept the payment offered by the state or face legal sanctions. Similarly, states that finance spending deficits by selling bonds in international credit markets must pay interest rates that the market offers.

Even if a government is not acting as a participant in market transactions with private individuals in society, it can still utilize its capacity to make markets to augment its political authority. For example, governments often construct supportive domestic coalitions by instituting regulations, like tariffs, that restrict competition in local markets. Once governments forego these opportunities to create revenue-generating regulations, they simultaneously surrender their capacity to capture the political benefits they can create. Most importantly, whether acting as a market participant or market maker, these possibilities suggest that competitive market structures can limit a government's capacity to direct and control the allocation of resources and, as a consequence, the political and economic activities of its citizenry.

Adam Smith's discussion of the links between commerce and liberty focuses on how the expansion of markets first led sovereigns to grant

[14] Hirschman (1970) describes this as the exit option.

[15] Friedman (1962) focuses on these links between the availability of multiple alternatives in competitive markets and the absence of coercion in these social interactions to argue that capitalism promotes freedom.

[16] For a study of how such labor market pressures constrain a government's ability to raise an army see Rowe, Bearce, and McDonald (2002).

increasing freedom to cities – effectively creating independent republics – to generate a tax base and foster an alliance that could be used to offset the power and influence of feudal landlords.[17] The spread of commerce within the cities then created opportunities for large landowners to dispose of surplus production and led them to adopt innovations, like allowing peasants to retain larger portions of their surplus by granting them longer leases, to expand production.[18] These innovations decreased the dependence of the peasants on the landlord for subsistence and would eventually serve to curtail the authority of the latter. Smith writes (1937, p. 385), "[c]ommerce and manufactures gradually introduced order and good government, and with them, the liberty and security of individuals, among the inhabitants of the country, who had before lived almost in a continual state of war with their neighbors, and of servile dependency on their superiors." In effect, the greed of the government and landlords had led them to allow cities and peasants to hold or lay claim to greater quantities of property that then altered the fundamental relationship between the two parties from one based on authority to one governed by decentralized exchange.

Contemporary studies of the links between economic regulation and political power confirm many of these insights. The capacity to restrict competition in markets, namely by preventing the entry of competitors or by simply setting price ceilings and floors, allows governments to create valuable economic assets that can be sold in exchange for revenue or political support. These restrictions have long taken the form of monopoly rights granting recipients the right to sell goods at an above-market price to consumers that then lack access to alternative producers. For example, Ekelund

[17] This discussion of the links between commerce and liberty is largely based on Book 3, "Of the Different Progress of Opulence in Different Nations," of *Wealth of Nations*. However, Smith also notes that commerce can also expand liberty by establishing judicial independence from the executive (Book 5). For a discussion of Smith's ideas on the reciprocal interaction between commerce and liberty see Chapter 4 of Winch (1978) and Hirschman (1997 [1977], pp. 100–13).

[18] Smith (1937 [1776], p. 390) writes, "[t]he merchants and manufacturers soon furnished him with a method of spending upon his own person on the same manner as he had done to the rest. The same cause continuing to operate, he was desirous to raise his rents above what his lands . . . could afford. His tenants could agree to this on one condition only, that they should be secured in their possession, for such a term of years as might give them time to recover with profit whatever they should lay out in the further improvement of the land. The expensive vanity of the landlord made him willing to accept of this condition; hence the origin of long leases . . . But if he (referring to the peasant) has a lease for a long term of years, he is altogether independent . . . The tenants having in this manner become independent, and the retainers being dismissed, the great proprietors were no longer capable of interrupting the regular execution of justice, or of disturbing the peace of the country."

and Tollison (1981, 1997) trace the emergence of mercantilist policies in sixteenth- and seventeenth-century Europe to a government's capacity to meet its revenue demands through the sale of monopoly rights. Facing repeated financial crises, English monarchs resorted to this tactic regularly until institutional changes following the Glorious Revolution helped the crown reassure bondholders that loans would be repaid on time (Kiser 1986/87; North and Weingast 1989; Macdonald 2006). The English government could then turn to capital markets more regularly to meet its fiscal challenges. In a study of postcolonial Africa, Bates (1981) explores how newly democratic leaders exploited colonial institutions that granted the state monopsony purchasing rights of agricultural production for their own political gain. Governments pushed down agricultural prices, which eventually decreased rural production, to keep food prices low in the cities and prevent mass political opposition. These programs of wealth redistribution from the countryside to the cities shrunk aggregate economic activity by undermining a sector with relatively high levels of productivity. Finally, studies of trade policy (e.g., Grossman and Helpman 1994; Gawande and Hoekman 2006) also illustrate these dynamics. Politicians "sell" protective regulations, like tariffs, that insulate domestic producers from foreign competition in exchange for campaign contributions that help them to remain in office. In sum, the capacity to restrict market competition can often be a device by which government officials extend their political authority.

One of Hayek's overarching themes provides an appropriate means to conclude this section. It highlights how the relative relationship between capitalism and democracy in promoting individual liberty may influence a government's foreign policy and the capacity of democracy to promote peace. Hayek argued that the reliance of economic planning on coercion to function inevitably rendered democratic socialism impossible. This claim was rooted in an examination of the difficulties of administering a central plan to govern an economy. Because democracies cannot debate every aspect of a central plan down to the daily productive decisions of each firm, they must necessarily delegate such decision making over the plan to either a separate governing body or a set of individuals.[19] This act of delegation necessarily removes important components of the implementation of the plan from democratic oversight. These arguments, in turn, led Hayek to claim that capitalism was necessary for democracy to function

[19] Hayek (1994, p. 78) writes, "Our point, however, is not that dictatorship must inevitably extirpate freedom but rather that planning leads to dictatorship because dictatorship is the most effective instrument of coercion and the enforcement of ideals and, as such, essential if central planning on a large scale is to be possible."

(Hayek 1994, pp. 77–8). This theoretical possibility carries important implications for liberal peace research. By arguing that the presence of democracy depends on capitalism, Hayek's claims suggest that the peace among democratic states may really be caused by such institutions like private property or competitive market structures.

CLASSICAL LIBERALISM ON WAR

By first promoting individual liberty, classical liberal theory implies that private property and competitive market structures may promote peace. This possibility is nested in a conception of war that generally casts it in instrumental terms, focusing on the interests that encourage governments to go to war.[20] Peace is viewed as the opposite side of the same coin. Its presence requires altering this set of national incentives so that either the costs of war or the benefits of peace are increased. Classical liberal theory emphasizes two broad sets of interests that heighten the risk of war. Drawing heavily on critiques of monarchical and despotic political systems, the first mechanism focuses on the domestic political benefits that some subset of society or the government derives from war. Peace is promoted through institutions like democratic elections, which simultaneously protect individual liberty and punish the pursuit of such domestic political gains through war. The second class of explanations, built from the theories of Smith and Ricardo showing the mutual gains generated by trade, highlights instead the economic benefits of peace. The elimination of trade barriers facilitates the emergence of common political interests among societies stemming from mutual economic dependence. These two incentive structures motivate the contemporary research programs on the democratic and commercial peace.

Constraining the Despots: Democracy and Peace

The first classical liberal explanation of war focuses on institutions and relationships that exist within states. This distinguishes it from realism, and its neorealist structural variant in particular, which generally traces the origins of war to conditions that exist among states – like the balance of power, alliance dynamics, or the relative efficacy of military conquest (e.g., Waltz 1959, 1979; Jervis 1978; Van Evera 1984; Mearsheimer 2001). While

[20] There are exceptions of course to this statement. Both Kant and Smith understood that constraints imposed by anarchy and the security dilemma could lead states possessing strong interests for peace to wage war against each other. For a discussion of this element in their writing see Walter (1996), Doyle (1997), and Jahn (2006).

incorporating the truism that war is an inherently destructive activity, the liberal framework focuses on how the unequal distribution of the costs and benefits of military conflict within society can create incentives for ruling political elites to use war to extend or consolidate their domestic political power.[21]

Classical liberals identified a number of political benefits that might accrue to a ruling government once war broke out. James Mill claimed that war benefited the state and a minority of society by enlarging the former's financial base.[22] The public head of the Manchester School, Richard Cobden, argued that war and war scares allowed governments to postpone domestic reforms that would necessarily expand individual liberty and limit the role of government in domestic life (e.g., Cobden 1868, pp. 44–5; 1870, p. 429). England's central role in maintaining the European balance of power increased the need for British intervention in the affairs of other countries and justified the maintenance of unnecessarily high and costly levels of armaments in peacetime.[23] Thomas Paine criticized hereditary monarchy as an unjust and corrupt system of government that heightened the risks of war.[24] Monarchs went to war because it provided an opportunity to strengthen their domestic power by increasing public taxation. Paine writes:

> War is the common harvest of all those who participate in the division and expenditure of public money, in all countries. It is the art of conquering at home; the object of it is an increase of revenue; and as revenue cannot be increased without taxes, a pretence must be made for such expenditures. In reviewing the history of the English government, its wars and its taxes, a by-stander, not blinded by prejudice, nor warped by interest, would declare, that taxes were not raised to carry on war, but that wars were raised to carry taxes (1995[1791], p. 128).

[21] Michael Howard characterizes this liberal conception of war: "By the end of the eighteenth century a complete liberal theory of international relations, of war and peace, had thus already developed . . . According to this doctrine, mankind would naturally live in a state of perfect harmony if it were not for the vested interests of governments . . . The whole 'war system' was contrived to preserve the power and the employment of princes, statesmen, soldiers, diplomats, and armaments manufacturers, and to bind their tyranny ever more firmly upon the necks of the people" (1978, p. 31).

[22] See the discussion of James Mill's views on the origins of war in Silberner (1946, pp. 37–50).

[23] See Chapter 3 in the pamphlet entitled *Russia* (Cobden, 1868, pp. 255–6). He writes, "Our history may during the last century may be called the tragedy of 'British intervention in the politics of Europe;' in which princes, diplomatists, peers, and generals, have been the authors and actors – the people the victims; and the moral will be exhibited to the latest posterity in 800 million pounds of debt."

[24] Michael Howard (1978) credits Thomas Paine with the most complete expression of these liberal principles on the origins of war. See also Walker (2000) for a discussion of Paine's contributions to international relations theory.

Schumpeter (1951[1919]) adopts a similar logic when attributing imperialism and war to the political dominance of a premodern warrior class within societies. These "atavistic" elements were tightly aligned with the state and needed military conflict to justify their political status.

This focus on the domestic political incentives behind war resembles a broader principle–agent problem between a state and its citizenry (Downs and Rocke 1994, 1995; Goemans 2000). The state is hired by society to provide security from external threats. Due to the costs of monitoring and control, the state can shirk its responsibilities or use conflict with other states as a means to cement its domestic political power. Because rulers are able to pass on most of the costs of war to their societies, they remain unaffected by its consequences and are relatively unconstrained in the decision-making process leading up to war. Governments wage war for particularistic or selfish reasons that fortify their domestic political status while simultaneously undermining the broader welfare of society.[25] To prevent war, society needs mechanisms to constrain a government's authority and punish, when necessary, the pursuit of selfish goals on the part of its political leaders.

While pointing out the dangers to international peace posed by governments constituted solely by the aristocracy, despots, or monarchs, most classical liberal writers looked to some form of popular representation as the solution to this dilemma. When broad swaths of society that directly bore the costs of war possessed the means to remove officials through elections, the pursuit of aggressive foreign policies would prove to be a domestic political hindrance rather than an opportunity. For example, the first definitive article in Kant's (1971) essay *Perpetual Peace* highlighted how requiring leaders to gain the consent of the citizenry bearing war's costs would induce caution in foreign policy. Similarly, Paine looked favorably toward a future in which the French Revolution catalyzed the collapse of monarchical rule and the construction of peace among the subsequent democratic regimes. He (1995[1791], pp. 194–5) wrote, "Monarchical sovereignty, the enemy of mankind, and the source of misery, is abolished; and sovereignty is restored its natural and original place, the Nation. Were this the case throughout Europe, the cause of wars would be taken away." Schumpeter argued that democracy helps prevent particularistic economic interests from capturing the state in the pursuit of imperialist expansion and war.

[25] Reviewing the domestic causes of war, Waltz (1959, p. 100) writes, "Why do governments make war? Because war gives them an excuse for raising taxes, for expanding the bureaucracy, for increasing their control over their citizens. These are the constantly iterated accusations of liberals." For contemporary examples of this liberal explanation of war see Moravcsik (1997, pp. 530–33) and Snyder (1991).

Unleashing Common Interests: Commerce and Peace

The writings of Cobden and Schumpeter provide the perfect transition from the domestic reform to commercial interest variants of classical liberal international relations theory because they incorporated the insights of both.[26] Their respective plans for domestic reform were not limited to expanding political participation via democracy. They both also embraced economic reform, and in particular the pursuit of free trade, as a means to erode the domestic political power of groups, like the landed aristocracy and export monopolists who derived economic gains from territorial expansion and war. Moreover, Cobden in particular recognized how the elimination of trade barriers would simultaneously curtail material incentives for war by tying countries together in a condition of mutual economic dependence.

Free-trade policies struck at the foundation of privilege crucial to maintaining the power of aristocratic and autocratic interests that had long captured the premodern state. Cobden was a prominent leader in the anti–Corn Law campaign in Great Britain, which sought to reduce the political influence of the landed aristocracy that still dominated parliament by cutting tariffs. While propping up prices for land and food that directly raised the incomes of the aristocracy, the costs of these tariffs were borne by growing industrial and working classes centered in Manchester. The Corn Laws helped to close off foreign markets by encouraging protectionist responses in potential trading partners. These tariffs also drove up food prices, which constituted a significant portion of spending by working classes, and subsequently increased their demands on factory owners for higher wages. Here are two samples of Cobden's arguments:

> The single and undisguised object of the League is to put down commercial monopoly; but that cannot be done by saddling upon our backs a fixed duty on corn, which means a differential duty on sugar, on coffee, and monopoly in every other article. The Corn-law is the great tree of Monopoly, under whose baneful shadow every other restriction exists. Cut it down by the roots, and it will destroy the others in its fall. The sole object of the League is to put an end to and extinguish, at once and forever, the principle of maintaining taxes for the benefit of a particular class (1870, p. 78).

And similarly:

> The laws for the encouragement of trade are direct and important; and their tendency is to destroy the privileges of the nobles, by raising up a middle class . . . (1868, p. 186).

26 Doyle (1997) and Cain (1979) offer valuable reviews of the contributions made respectively by Schumpeter and Cobden to liberal international relations theory.

By eliminating a principle source of aristocratic political strength – import protection for landed interests – free trade would promote political change within Britain by empowering the emerging industrial and working classes.

Over a half century later, Schumpeter also pointed to redistributive economic regulations, like tariffs, as a source of domestic political inequity and ultimately war. While challenging Lenin's teleological claims that capitalism necessarily fostered industrial concentration, export monopolism, and imperialism, Schumpeter argued that the origins of tariffs lay in the protection of traditional sources of power within the state. This fundamentally political process then enabled the construction of domestic trusts and cartels responsible for imperialism. Autocrats restricted commercial activities, including international trade, to generate a tax base, which simultaneously created a social class whose political standing and economic livelihood depended on the continuance of such regulations.[27] In the early stages of precapitalist economic development, merchants recognized that they needed the state to provide public goods such as safe trading routes. They also understood that their monarchs could not provide such public goods without stable sources of revenue. Autocratic leaders thus utilized tariff protection to co-opt the emerging bourgeois class in the early stages of the Industrial Revolution.[28]

In a fashion similar to Cobden, Schumpeter held that the political power of the bourgeoisie was further constrained by a tight premodern alliance forged between the state and the nobility. Because the competitive pressures associated with capitalism were less capable of penetrating agricultural production, the political foundations of feudalism, which protected the political influence of the aristocracy by creating an alliance with autocratic leaders, remained strong (Schumpeter 1951[1919], p. 121).

Limited political power for the beneficiaries of capitalism, whether the bourgeoisie or working classes, helped prevent the emergence of peace. Both Cobden and Schumpeter drew on the common liberal heritage that traces the origins of war to the particularistic interests of the ruling classes within

[27] For a similar characterization of mercantilism that uses price theory to illustrate such claims see Ekelund and Tollison (1981, 1997).

[28] Schumpeter (1951 [1919], p. 121) writes, "Trade and industry of the early precapitalist period thus remained strongly pervaded with precapitalist methods, bore the stamp of autocracy, and served its interests, either willingly or by force . . . Existing economic interests, artificially shaped by the autocratic state, remained dependent on the "protection" of the state. The industrial organism, such as it was, would not have been able to withstand free competition."

a political system.[29] For Schumpeter, war provided few economic benefits. Instead, the primary purpose of war was political. It created a demand for the services of a warrior class – which tended to be tightly aligned with the state – that needed conflict to justify its existence. Similarly, Cobden saw war as a device to curtail individual liberty and expand the role of government in domestic life. He wrote (1868, pp. 1, 42–3), "The middle and industrious classes of England can have no interest apart from the preservation of peace. The honours, the fame, the emoluments of war belong not to them; the battle-plain is the harvest-field of the aristocracy, watered with the blood of the people."

The emerging economic transformation sparked by the Industrial Revolution could thus promote peace by undermining the domestic political power of the landed aristocracy, the state, the warrior class, and export monopolists – groups that were most responsible for the outbreak of conflict.[30] Free trade would render the emerging bourgeois class less dependent on the state for protection and less willing to support foreign policies, like war, that were contrary to its economic interests. Enrichment of the working and industrial classes also strengthened their political influence within democratically elected parliaments. Similarly, free trade eliminated the economic incentives behind the forcible annexation of new territories. These incentives included guaranteed markets for surplus production, access to cheap raw materials, and the prevention of foreign capital holders from developing the infrastructures of these emerging economies.

Cobden also recognized a second virtue of free trade that received relatively more attention from liberal writers in the nineteenth century. This tradition proceeded from a supposition that an underlying harmony of interests existed among individuals living in different societies around the world. The natural dispersion of economic resources had bound people together in relations of mutual dependence. Cobden characterized this natural commercial order in the following manner: "Free Trade is a Divine Law: if it were not, the world would have been differently created. One country

[29] Cobden argued that trade promoted peace in two key ways. The first involves the transformation of domestic power discussed in this section. Cobden also argued that trade promoted peace by rendering states dependent on trade with other countries. Writing of England's substantial commercial ties with the New World, "England . . . has by the magic of her machinery, united for ever two remote hemispheres in the bonds of peace, by placing European and American in absolute and inextricable dependence on each other (1868, pp. 1, 193).

[30] Nicholls (1991) compares Cobden's condemnation of the alliance between the aristocracy and the military to Eisenhower's warnings of the military–industrial complex in the United States.

has cotton, another wine, another coal, which is proof that, according to the Divine Order of things, men should fraternize and trade their goods and thus further Peace and Goodwill on Earth."[31]

These views were shared by the likes of Charles Montesquieu, Thomas Paine, Jeremy Bentham, John Stuart Mill, and Frederic Bastiat.[32] The economic incentives for conquest would be eliminated by enabling countries to acquire what they did not possess through peaceful exchange that simultaneously increased the wealth of all its participants. Mercantilist policies, based instead on a zero-sum view of the quantity of wealth in the world, restricted trade and increased the chances for war by reducing "the incentives for countries to remain at peace with each other" (Silberner 1946, p. 49). In the *Spirit of the Laws*, Montesquieu (1966[1748]) wrote, "The natural effect of commerce is to lead to peace. Two nations that trade with each other become reciprocally dependent; if one has an interest in buying, the other has an interest in selling, and all the unions are founded on mutual needs."[33] In the second part of *Rights of Man*, Paine (1995[1791], pp. 265–6) echoed these themes while emphasizing the capacity of commerce to "improve the condition of man by means of his interest." He went on:

> Commerce is no other than the traffic of two individuals, multiplied on a scale of numbers; and by the same rule that nature intended the intercourse of two, intended that of all. For this purpose she has distributed the materials of manufactures and commerce, in various and distant parts of a nation and of the world; and as they cannot be procured by war so cheaply or so commodiously as by commerce, she has rendered the latter the means of extirpating the former.

John Stuart Mill agreed that international trade facilitated the emergence of an underlying harmony of interests among countries around the world by increasing communication across societies and encouraging individuals to reject nationalism (Miller 1961).

This second classical liberal view on the origins of war thus focused on the capacity of trade to promote common interests among states. Once governments became more aware of their fundamental economic dependence on each other, they possessed little interest in jeopardizing these material gains through war. Any political barrier to this exchange necessarily prevented people from realizing these common interests and reaping the benefits of an international division of labor. The construction of peace necessitated maximizing commercial intercourse between countries.

31 As quoted in Cain (1979, p. 240).

32 For reviews of these writings see Flournoy (1946), Hirschman (1997[1977]), Howard (1978), and Silberner (1946).

33 Book 2, Chapter 20.

CAUSES OF WAR: INTERESTS AND STRUCTURES

Given this broader classical liberal framework focusing on the capacity of democracy and trade to remake perverted incentive structures and discourage war, a first wave of liberal peace research set about testing the validity of such claims with increasing statistical sophistication. The widespread integration of bargaining models in security studies challenged the theoretical foundations of these research programs and spawned a second wave of theoretical revision. This section reexamines classical liberal insights about the origins of war in light of more recent developments in bargaining theory. It builds the broader argument that both frameworks – one focusing on interests, the other on strategic interaction – are necessary to understand how private property and competitive markets promote individual liberty and peace.

Fearon's (1995) now classic application of bargaining theory helped reorient research on war by shifting the motivating question.[34] Beginning from the assumption that war is costly, he shows that a set of settlements exists that both states in a dispute should prefer rather than going to war. Consequently, solving the puzzle of why wars occur requires an understanding of why states fail to reach a peaceful compromise that avoids these costs.

He models this negotiation process as an interaction between two states, say Home and Foreign, locked in a disagreement over how to distribute some pool of resources. The governments of Home and Foreign want to maximize the portion of resources they control. If they cannot agree on some distribution, they settle the dispute by going to war. The balance of military capabilities then shapes the war's outcome. States possessing more military capabilities are more likely to win. The victor captures the entire pool of resources. The use of military force, though, is inefficient as it destroys some portion of this pool of resources. Consequently, peace provides a bonus by offering a larger pool of resources to be divided between Home and Foreign. Fearon shows that this bonus is large enough to compensate both governments so that they are at least as well off as if they had gone to war.

Why then should governments squander the rewards of peace? Fearon attributes the collapse of bargaining, and thus the cause of war, to three sources: private information, commitment problems, and issue indivisibilities. Private information is an endemic problem that hinders all negotiations.

[34] For reviews of bargaining applications to the study of war and Fearon's significant contribution see Powell (2002), Reiter (2003), and Wagner (2007).

It refers to each government possessing more accurate assessments of its own resolve, military capabilities, or the domestic political costs that emerge once war has broken out. The presence of private information combined with the incentives to misrepresent this information during the bargaining process limits the willingness of both parties to restrain their demands for the sake of reaching an agreement.

For example, believing that some recent, but secret, military innovation is likely to enable its victory on the battlefield, Home demands nearly the entire pool of resources under dispute and threatens war if Foreign offers anything less. If this innovation was likely to alter the balance of military power between the two states and Foreign was aware that it faced near certain defeat on the battlefield, Foreign would prefer to accede to Home's demand, salvage some small portion of the pool of resources, and simultaneously avoid military defeat and the attendant costs of war. However, Foreign also knows that Home has an incentive to bluff about the extent of its military capabilities. Home would rather let Foreign capitulate before war so that it avoids having to pay the military costs of imposing the settlement on the battlefield. Given Home's incentives to misrepresent its bargaining power, Foreign's military situation may not be as hopeless as Home claims. Foreign must consider the possibility that Home is lying when deciding how to respond to Home's demand. Foreign might capture a larger portion of the resources by rejecting Home's offer. If Home was bluffing, Home stands down and accepts less of the resources than it initially demanded. Alternatively, if Home was not bluffing, Foreign's rejection of Home's offer leads to war. Foreign thus faces a dilemma. Although it wishes to avoid war, it simultaneously hopes to maximize the proportion of resources it controls. Given Home's private information and its inability to reveal this to Foreign, Foreign will sometimes mistakenly believe that Home is bluffing and go to war when it should have conceded and accepted Home's initial offer. The uncertainty of the situation and the difficulty for both states in revealing any private information they possess prevent peaceful compromise.

This framework suggests that states are more likely to settle their disputes and avoid war when they possess mechanisms that facilitate the revelation of this private information. Applications of this framework to liberal peace research have examined how democracy and international commerce help governments to escape some of these information dilemmas (e.g., Fearon 1994, 1997; Morrow 1999; Gartzke, Li, and Boehmer 2001; Schultz 1999, 2001; Reed 2003). For example, democratic leaders can utilize their domestic publics and the possibility of being removed for policy failures to convince an adversary about the sincerity of their bargaining position. Imagine that

Home is a democracy. Once democratic leaders publicly commit to successfully securing some issue, or in the previous example, some proportion of the resources under dispute, they expose themselves to electoral punishment if they fail to fulfill that commitment. This public commitment by Home provides an effective signal that conveys to Foreign that Home is unlikely to back down in the dispute. Foreign's desire to avoid the costs of war and its belief that Home is unlikely to back down leads Foreign to accede to Home's demand, which then helps both parties avoid war.

Now imagine if Home instead were an autocratic government. Home could try and signal its resolve in the dispute by telling Foreign that its domestic opposition is likely to stage a violent coup if it does not secure some diplomatic victory in the form of significant concessions. However, this claim reveals less information about Home's real situation because Home's public is likely to face relatively higher costs to remove it from power than if competitive elections were regularly held. The credibility of Home's threat thus remains uncertain. As a consequence, the signals sent by autocratic governments convey less information and increase the likelihood that the dispute will escalate to open military conflict.

Substantial trade ties can similarly signal resolve in a dispute. Because war between interdependent economies threatens to impose additional costs in the form of embargoes and interrupted trading routes, only states resolved to securing large concessions from an adversary would risk such assets in a dispute. This willingness to risk extensive trading links signals that a government is unlikely to be bluffing and encourages an adversary to make concessions necessary to sustain peace.

Despite disproportionate attention to these information problems as a cause of war, Powell (2006) argues that important cases, like the outbreak of World War II, are best explained by commitment problems.[35] Commitment problems occur when one party doubts the willingness of the other party to fulfill the obligations of any accord or to refrain in the future from exploiting any new bargaining advantage that might accrue from an agreement made in the present. For example, he suggests that a hypothetical absence of private information about British, American, and German military capabilities and resolve in the late 1930s would not have prevented World War II. Both Britain and the United States possessed relatively good information about

[35] Powell also argues that Fearon's third cause of war – issue indivisibilities – should instead be cast as a commitment problem. Lipson (2003) and Verdier and Eilstrup-Sangiovanni (2005) apply the commitment problem framework to the democratic and commercial variants of the liberal peace.

Hitler's intentions. However, they still went to war because further concessions would simply have strengthened Hitler's power and encouraged him to demand even more. Any promise by Hitler not to exploit the growing military power of the German war machine was simply not credible. In this case, as in others plagued by such commitment problems, states go to war to avoid having to make even more concessions in the future as their bargaining power further deteriorates. Fearon (1995, p. 406) writes of this situation: "[t]he declining state attacks not because it fears being attacked in the future but because it fears the peace it will have to accept after the rival has grown stronger." The commitment problem stems from the inability of one state to promise not to exploit either its growing power or the improvement in its bargaining position after receiving concessions. A preventive war, in which a declining power attacks a rival that is growing more powerful, is one such example of how commitment problems cause war. The rising state cannot credibly commit to forego exploiting its power to extract concessions from its adversaries in the future. Consequently, the declining power goes to war to prevent the rising state from consolidating its capabilities.[36]

Bargaining models exposed an important limitation in explanations of war that rely strictly on national interests as classical liberalism does. In particular, they demonstrated how classical propositions about how democracy and trade promote peace were not nested in a broader theoretical framework capable of understanding how the structure of the strategic interaction between states shapes their decisions for war. For example, Paine's conception of how democracy promotes peace is essentially a constraint-based model of war that focuses on the actions of one government. The threat of electoral punishment makes a government less likely to go to war.

War, however, needs at least two participants. One state can always choose to walk away from the fight by making significant concessions. In light of this strategic nature of a dispute, states often exploit each other's relative weakness. If the threat of electoral punishment prevents one government from going to war, such domestic constraints simultaneously create a strategic opportunity for its rivals in the international system. Those adversaries could demand greater concessions in the midst of that diplomatic crisis,

[36] Along with preventive war, Powell (2006) discusses two more commitment problems – a preemptive attack created by an offensive advantage and bargaining over issues (what I referred to earlier as the pool of resources) that affect future bargaining power. He argues that all three problems are caused by rapid shifts in the distribution of power.

fully aware that its democratic adversary faces an unhappy public likely to penalize any decision for war. The net effect on the likelihood of conflict is unclear. While democracy prevents one government from acting boldly in a conflict, it simultaneously encourages its adversary to do the opposite.

Moreover, the threat of electoral punishment may not always push a government to avoid war. Sometimes this domestic constraint can paradoxically encourage a government to go to war. This possibility emerges when expanding the time horizon of the democratic government in power. If these domestic constraints are dynamic, namely if they will increase over time, a government may rationally choose to fight sooner rather than at some point in the future when the domestic costs of going to war will be even higher. Powell (2006) characterizes this situation as another example of a commitment problem that can lead to war. In this case, however, the shifting balance of power occurs within the domestic political system. Governing parties often share some portion of their domestic resources with the opposition to maintain domestic stability and prevent repeated challenges to a regime. As a government's hold on power becomes more tenuous, they share more resources with the opposition. War may sometimes offset this trend by increasing a government's capacity to remain in power. A dramatic shift in the domestic balance of power between the governing and opposition parties in favor of the latter can encourage a government to go to war. The inability of the opposition to promise not to demand greater portions of the domestic pool of resources in the future leads the current governing regime to opt for war in the present period. This logic resembles that of the diversionary theory of war. In this case, governments deflect internal difficulties by sparking an international crisis that rallies support for the nation and hopefully its government (e.g., Levy 1989; Downs and Rocke 1994; Smith 1996; Goemans 2000).

Despite the importance of incorporating the strategic situation in theoretical approaches to understanding war, the broader liberal focus on the domestic process by which national interests are defined should not be jettisoned or relegated to secondary theoretical status. There are at least two reasons to view these two approaches as both complementary and necessary to understanding how domestic institutions, including democracy and those associated with regulating economic activity, shape decisions about war and peace.

First, most applications of bargaining theory adopt the unitary actor assumption that abstracts out much of the domestic political process that is the central focus of liberal international relations theory. Fearon (1995) characterizes his presentation of the bargaining model of the war as a formalization of neorealist insights that focuses on how structural conditions outside of domestic politics shape interactions among states.[37] This modeling decision, often made to limit technical complexity by restricting the number of actors in a hypothetical interaction to two, comes at the cost of not incorporating the focus of classical liberalism on how domestic political incentives can shape decisions for war. Reiter (2003) discusses the limitations of this neglect of domestic politics. The costs and benefits of war are not only shaped by a state's position within the international distribution of power or the possibility of seizing some disputed issue or pool of resources from an adversary in the international system.

The decision for war also influences the structure of domestic politics and the capacity of a government to hold on to or consolidate its power at home. Classical liberalism suggests that war can provide an opportunity to alter the domestic distribution of power and wealth. Paine (1995 [1791]) described war as the art of conquering at home. Schumpeter (1951 [1919]) pointed to war as a device to increase demand for the services of a warrior class that valued war more for the act itself than any benefits that might be garnered after victory. Such ideas echoed President Eisenhower's warnings of the growing military–industrial complex in the United States, which needed tension with the Soviet Union to justify its necessity to the American public. If governments can redistribute the costs of war onto their publics, as Kant (1971), Paine (1995 [1791]), and Cobden (1868) suggested they could and did, war is no longer costly for the principal groups responsible for making the decision of whether or not to participate. Under these circumstances, many of the insights of the bargaining framework no longer apply.

Second, the bargaining approach begins by assuming some conflict of interest between states. Both states wish to possess the same piece of territory or pool of resources. The avoidance of war requires finding some division of these resources that leaves both parties as well off or better than had they instead chosen to settle the dispute with military force. Classical liberal theory, particularly the commercial variant, suggests states may not always possess such conflicts of interest. Just as the exchange of food for manufactured products promotes domestic peace and leaves little reason for urban dwellers to conquer farmers, the international division of labor holds out similar opportunities to bind economies together in a web of

[37] Fearon (1995, p. 379, fn 1) writes, "[w]ar may be rational for civilian or military leaders if they will enjoy various benefits of war without suffering costs imposed on the population. While I believe that 'second-image' mechanisms of this sort are very important empirically, I do not explore them here. A more accurate label for the subject of the article might be 'rational unitary-actor explanations,' but this is cumbersome."

mutual dependence. Under these circumstances, states simply possess few political disputes. Peace emerges not from the successful resolution of disputes but from the absence of disputes that heighten the possibility of war. This possibility suggests that national interests or preferences, and the degree to which they conflict, also play an important role in determining the conditions under which governments go to war with each other.

This final point emphasizes that explanations of war need to take into consideration at least two things: the national interests held by respective governments that give rise to political disputes with the potential to escalate into war, and once engaged in dispute, the structure of the bargaining employed to resolve the dispute.[38] The conjunction of these conditions underscores the essential complementarity of classical liberal insights about war that focus on incentives with contemporary bargaining approaches that concentrate instead on the context of strategic interaction. The final section of this chapter integrates these conceptions of why wars occur to construct the broader framework from which to generate the hypotheses linking capitalism to peace.

NEOCLASSICAL LIBERALISM ON WAR

Together, classical liberalism and bargaining theory suggest that three general factors play a critical role in shaping the outbreak of war among states: national preferences and the degree to which they conflict; the domestic structure of power between government and society that can both encourage and discourage the former to use military force as an instrument of foreign policy; and the structure of the strategic interaction between states that shape their capacity to reach a peaceful compromise that avoids the costs of war. This final section integrates these elements into a single framework that is then utilized in the next chapter to examine how the neglected domestic institutions of liberal international relations theory – private property and competitive market structures – influence the likelihood of war in the international system.

The recent restatement of liberal international relations theory by Moravcsik (1997) reflects the classical focus on incentives, or national interests, to explain the outbreak of war among states. He argues that liberal

[38] Moravcsik (1997, p. 544) echoes this essential complementarity between incentive-based and bargaining models of war discussed in this section. He writes, "States first define preferences – a stage explained by liberal theories of state–society relations. Then they debate, bargain, or fight to particular agreements – a second stage explained by realist and institutionalist (as well as liberal) theories of strategic interaction."

international relations theory explains variation in the character and quality of relations among states by focusing on how the state–society relationship, or that between a government and its citizenry, shapes national foreign policy goals. This central insight is built from three critical assumptions. First, societal actors, rather than the state, are the primary actors in international system. This bottom-up view of international relations holds that the demands or interests of some subset of societal actors shape the content of the foreign policies of states. For example, governments would not sign free-trade pacts unless many individuals and groups within their society stood to gain from such a policy. Similarly, governments would not go to war unless some portion of society supported such a decision and stood to gain from it, whether in the form of acquiring access to new markets or eliminating a threat to security.

Second, in addition to the content of preferences, the structure of domestic institutions shapes which groups, and thus which set of societal interests, win out in the domestic political game and thus have their demands constitute the "national interest." This structure also influences the degree of autonomy governments possess relative to society. This autonomy allows a government to either restrict the subset of society to which it responds or actively intervene in the domestic struggle so that the national interest reflects its political goals. By highlighting the importance of domestic institutions, Moravcsik (1997, p. 518) differentiates this liberal framework from a strictly pluralist conception of domestic politics that simply treats the state as a vehicle to aggregate conflicting demands from within society. The state does not necessarily act neutral in this domestic struggle and can instead shape it to further its own more narrow particularistic goals, such as consolidating its power over society.

Third, variation in the degree to which the national goals of one state conflict or complement the national goals of another state critically influences their actions relative to one another and thus the character of the international system. This focus on the structure of national interests among states differentiates Moravcsik's liberalism from realism, which focuses on the international structure of power, and neoliberal institutionalism, which focuses on the international structure of information. Relations among states are characterized by three broad configurations of interests. Interests may be compatible, fundamentally at odds with each other, or contain elements of both accord and disagreement. For example, classical ideas about how commerce promotes peace suggest that the elimination of all trade barriers would make the national interests of states complementary, thus removing all material incentives for war. In short, the process by which national interests move into a stage of relative harmony creates the peaceful condition among states.

This formulation of liberal international relations theory provides the first set of mechanisms linking private property and competitive market structures to peace in the international system. Variations in these institutional structures transform the economic interests of different components of society into foreign policy interests, particularly those with respect to territory. For example, domestic economic sectors capable of surviving open competition from foreign producers generally support restrained national interests and cooperative foreign policies. These groups advocate peaceful solutions to political disputes with other countries and help block both their government and rival imperialist groups from within society from pursuing policies designed to conquer new territory. When these groups possess disproportionate influence within domestic political systems, governments deploy military force less often against other governments.

Second, market-promoting institutions also shape decisions for war by limiting the capacity of governments to use restrictions on market exchange to generate tangible political assets that further their own political goals. Governments often intervene in markets by nationalizing private assets or erecting trade barriers to construct domestic coalitions that support their own policy goals. Just as restraints on market exchange generate economic rents and redistribute wealth within a society, they also create opportunities for governments to alter the domestic distribution of political power. These coalition-building dynamics extend to the domain of foreign policy. Governments have historically used trade barriers and public property to limit the power of opposition groups, create foreign policy autonomy, and strengthen their hold on domestic power. The transformation of these resources generated by economic regulation into political assets enables a government to pursue riskier foreign policies like war with limited fear of domestic punishment. These dynamics reflect the concerns of classical liberal writers who link the outbreak of war to efforts by governments to alter the domestic distribution of power and wealth.

Although most of the explanatory focus will be on these first two mechanisms, I will also examine two instances where market conditions shaped the bargaining dilemma faced by governments with conflicting national interests. Most applications of bargaining theory to the liberal peace focus on how democracy and commerce help mitigate the problem of private information.[39] I will instead look at how market constraints shape decisions for

39 Lipson (2003) is an exception.

war by altering the ability of governments to commit to upholding peaceful agreements in the future. In the case of World War I, large quantities of public property in Russia generated a commitment problem by facilitating a rapid shift in the balance of military power on the continent. In the contemporary period, extensive commercial links have helped solve a commitment problem between China and Taiwan by reassuring the mainland that future governments in Taiwan are unlikely to pursue political independence.

CONCLUSION

This chapter has engaged in a dialogue between classical liberalism and contemporary research to develop two arguments. First, drawing on one of classical liberalism's central insights linking individual liberty to peace, an expansion of the institutional arenas by which state and society interact provides the opportunity to answer some of the questions facing the contemporary liberal peace research program. Although studies of the domestic sources of interstate relations have often looked to the presence or absence of democratic institutions to characterize societal capacity to influence foreign policy, domestic institutions that regulate the market also shape a government's authority and the domestic distribution of power. Consequently, they too may possess important foreign policy consequences. Second, on their own, classical liberal theory and contemporary bargaining theory provide insufficient explanations for why war occurs. The next chapter builds on the neoclassical liberal framework presented here to construct a series of hypotheses linking private property and competitive market structures to the presence of peace in the international system.

THREE

Releasing the Invisible Hand

Multiple socialist writers – including Lenin, Hilferding, and Hobson – have linked the ills of capitalism, particularly the concentration of wealth, within countries to relationships of rivalry and military conflict among states in the international system. The same pressures within capitalism that encouraged ruthless competition and the acquisitiveness of wealth by private individuals simultaneously encouraged territorial expansion by governments. By pressing down wages at home, capitalists undermined the purchasing power of the local labor class and contributed to falling profits. These economic losses at home could be offset by securing cheap sources of raw materials and new outlets for manufactured products in the developed world. Once the supply of these new market outlets dried up in the periphery, the developed countries turned against each other in a zero-sum competition to protect existing markets and deprive competing powers of the same imperialist relief. Thus European great powers and the United States first carved up Africa, Asia, the near East, and South America into colonial outlets. The ensuing conflict in these rivalries eventually gave way to both World War I and World War II. Contemporary descendants of such claims (e.g., Williams 1959; LaFeber 1998 [1963]; McCormick 1995 [1989]; Layne 2006) suggest that the outbreak of peace in Europe after 1945 failed to bring a reprieve from these expansionist tendencies. The United States and Soviet Union continued to vie for political and economic influence in these regions of the world. The recent wars in the Persian Gulf, seemingly fueled by the need of industrial countries to secure stable access to oil, appear to confirm this link among capitalism, territorial expansion, and military conflict.

This chapter presents a theoretical framework that challenges the intellectual foundations of these popular claims associating capitalism with war. Although recognizing that economic interests per se can motivate some domestic groups to advocate territorial expansion with the aid of military force, I examine how such sectors tend to rely on barriers that limit the capacity of competitive markets to coordinate economic activity. These advocates for conflict tend to be proponents not of capitalism but of alternative economic systems like mercantilism, which simultaneously insulate their economic interests from the pressures associated with competitive markets. Alternatively, I show why the beneficiaries of liberal economic orders tend to support peaceful foreign policies. Just as Adam Smith suggested that an invisible hand facilitated the emergence of collective societal benefits from self-interested actions by individuals interacting within markets, the pursuit of wealth by *private individuals interacting in competitive markets* reduces the risks of war among states. The predominance of private ownership and competitive market structures within domestic economic systems promote peace by limiting the economic benefits of military expansion, preventing the concentration of domestic political power, and helping governments to secure political compromise when faced with the threat of war.

This chapter breaks down the broader claim connecting market-promoting institutions and peace into two component parts: one linking the predominance of private property in a domestic economy to peace and the other linking the competitiveness of domestic markets to peace. The capacity of these institutions to promote peace is examined by tracing how they respectively influence the three general mechanisms associated with the outbreak of war described at the end of Chapter 2. The first section examines how large quantities of public property generate fiscal autonomy for governments, which strengthens their hold on the domestic reigns of power and creates opportunities to pursue more aggressive foreign policies. The second section examines how government barriers to international commerce hinder competition in domestic markets and shape the conditions under which globalization promotes peace. Foreign policy restraint, particularly with respect to territorial demands, and peace emerge when the beneficiaries of open, global markets possess disproportionate domestic political influence.

THE PURSE STRINGS OF PEACE

There cannot be a greater security for the continuance of peace, than the imposing on ministers the necessity of applying to the people for taxes to support a war.

– David Ricardo in *Funding System* (1951[1820])

The contemporary liberal peace literature grounds many of its claims in Kant's famous essay *Perpetual Peace*. This research can be extended through one of the lesser known writings of David Ricardo. More generally recognized for his discussion of comparative advantage and its implications for how international trade could increase national wealth, Ricardo's concern over the size of the British public debt in the aftermath of the Napoleonic Wars led him to explore how the process of securing finance for war shaped the potential for peace.[1] He argued that the immediate imposition of an income tax upon the onset of conflict, rather than the flotation of a series of public loans to pay the costs of war, would provide benefits to both the economy and the polity. Economically, it would force citizens to anticipate the possibility of war and save for its economic costs. Consumed in wartime, these savings would minimize the postconflict costs of repaying debt and allow the economy to reach normal consumption levels as soon as military hostilities ceased. Politically, it would prevent the citizenry from passing the costs of war onto future generations while depriving the state of a discretionary reserve that could be tapped for aggressive conquest.

Ricardo's arguments illustrate one of the foundational propositions of liberal international relations theory. As citizens acquire the means to limit government power, their ability to resist war effectively and the possibilities for peace grow. A government's need and ability to secure private-sector resources to finance the construction of a war machine capable of defending its territory, projecting its national interests, and even conquering other states critically shape its decision for war. By forcing the state to rely on the private sector for revenue and simultaneously restricting its ability to tax or seize these assets, individuals in society can be empowered to establish a more pacific foreign policy.

Public Finance and the State–Society Relationship

The predominance of privately held property pushes a government toward peace by influencing the distribution of political power between a government and its citizenry within a domestic political order. As discussed in Chapter 2, a wide variety of scholarship in comparative political economy argues that public revenue needs shape the structure of domestic institutions and the character of state–society relations. Because governments do not own all of the productive resources contained within a state's geographic boundaries, their ability to implement public policy depends on their capacity to draw on the total pool of economic resources contained within its territory. Neoclassical theories of the state claim that governments can

[1] For a review of Ricardo's writings on the problem of war, see Chapter 2 of Silberner (1946).

extend their authority at home and abroad when their ability to mobilize the wealth of society grows (e.g., North 1981; Levi 1988; Eggertsson 1990).[2]

Governments face a series of difficult political choices when deciding how to mobilize wealth from their economy. They can choose to rely on the coercive power of the state and simply seize private assets. However, this strategy is not without its costs. A long literature in economics recognizes why it is rational for leaders to privatize resources and then commit not to seize these assets in the future (e.g., Smith 1937[1776], Book 3; North 1981). Repeated seizure of assets and violation of commitments to respect private property ultimately impede long-term economic growth and weaken a ruler's foundation for national power. Perhaps more significantly, the expropriation of private assets restricts consumption and often provokes societal opposition to the government's rule. Through promising to regularize and limit their seizure by taxing only a portion of the returns that accrue to such resources, leaders can stimulate investment and increase total national production. Moreover, because positive assessments of government performance often hinge on the ability of business and the interests of capital to supply goods such as employment and growth, governments often choose to protect the interests of these groups by upholding a commitment to protect private property (e.g., Lindblom 1977; Block 1977; Przeworski and Wallerstein 1988; Barnett 1990). Policies that might threaten business profits, such as expropriating private assets, often do not even find their way to the public agenda.

Large quantities of public property serve as an independent source of revenue that strengthens the state and insulates it from societal oversight in the selection and implementation of public policy. These resources free a regime from making political concessions that circumvent or limit its power over society, often made necessary to mobilize a portion of the economy's wealth to fund the administration of the state. If a state owned all of the assets within an economy, it would not need to surrender authority or subject itself to greater societal oversight to generate revenue. Privatization necessarily reduces the amount of resources owned by the state and forces it to extract more wealth through taxation to hold expenditures constant. As the evolution of parliamentary constraints in England suggests, regular taxation requires some societal consent that often simultaneously places limits

2 Margaret Levi (1988, p. 2) writes, "One major limitation on rule is revenue, the income of the government. The greater the revenue of the state, the more possible it is to extend rule. Revenue enhances the ability of rulers to elaborate the institutions of the state, to bring more people within the domain of those institutions, and to increase the number and variety of collective goods provided through the state."

on the conditions under which such resources can be extracted and the ends to which they can be directed. For example, Barnett (1990, p. 538) writes:

> Because the state is institutionally separated from organized production, it does not produce its own source of revenue. Therefore, all state managers must be attentive to and are constrained by the flow of resources upon which the deployment of the state's means depends. The state's ability either to develop alternative sources of financial means or to loosen its dependence on the capitalist class substantially increases its autonomy.

Levi (1988, p. 19) echoes the logic of these arguments by noting that the relative bargaining power of a ruler attempting to raise revenue is enhanced as its dependence on the economic resources of its constituents is reduced. In sum, the ability of the state to rely on sources of wealth that its citizenry does not own increases its autonomy and limits societal influence over public policy.[3]

Financial Autonomy and Military Conflict

Neoclassical liberalism holds that a government's ability to avoid the domestic costs associated with war shapes the character of its foreign policy. Kant and Paine argued that citizens could use regular elections to prevent war by threatening to remove political officials who pursued policies that heightened its likelihood. Just as the absence of competitive elections enhances the authority and autonomy of authoritarian regimes, small quantities of private property can influence decisions for war by depriving society of an important mechanism capable of limiting a government's ability to evade punishment for failed public policies.

Governments gain a relatively free hand in foreign policy to pursue territorial expansion and war when they possess large quantities of public property. These financial resources expand the political options governments possess to counteract domestic political opposition to such policies as increased defense spending or the decision for war. Governments can choose to divert large financial rewards to small but critical constituencies

[3] Similar predictions can be generated by examining alternative sources of nontax revenue like foreign aid or easy access to foreign credit. Like public property, these resources relieve a government from having to seize a portion of a citizenry's wealth – and free it from the accompanying political concessions – to fund its bureaucratic apparatus and the policies it wishes to implement. Chapter 7 will examine how the French government leveraged capital controls to direct huge sums of domestic savings into emergency loans for the Russian government in 1905 and 1906. These loans were critical in helping Russia avert bankruptcy and weather the storm of domestic revolution in 1905 following the Russo–Japanese War.

like the military, the internal security apparatus, and business leaders to prevent the emergence of leaders capable of organizing opposition parties or movements. Alternatively, governments can use nationalized economic sectors to widely distribute economic rewards like jobs and social welfare benefits to society to prevent grassroots opposition to the regime. By increasing the opportunity costs of organizing political opposition, this relaxation of the domestic fiscal and political constraints on war enables patrimonial leaders to utilize military force in their foreign policies.

The consolidation of economic wealth and political power within a regime can also accentuate commitment problems that create incentives for adversaries to target the illiberal economy in a preventive war. The absence of domestic constraints heightens the anxiety of other governments aware of the risks posed to international order by leaders unlikely to face any domestic backlash to failed military adventures. Moreover, the ability to evade the political constraints generated by mobilizing financial resources through taxation can enable a government to sustain an arms race that destabilizes regional and global distributions of power. In sum, governments possessing large quantities of public property are likely to both initiate and be the targets of military challenges.

Conflict Initiation

This basic logic whereby large quantities of public property encourage a government to embark on military expansion can be illustrated with selectorate theory (Bueno de Mesquita et al. 1999, 2003, 2004).[4] It traces variations in conflict participation between democratic and authoritarian regimes to institutional differences that influence their respective capacities to hold onto power at home. Governments are more likely to go to war when they possess stable coalitions of domestic support that will continue to sustain their regime irrespective of the outcome of the conflict. An incumbent government builds such support by disbursing a larger combination of benefits to members of its winning coalition than can be credibly promised by a political challenger. It offers two types of benefits: public goods, such as security from external threats, which are consumed by all members of the polity; and private benefits, such as subsidies, direct payments, or privileged

[4] This theory possesses an important similarity with classical liberal insights about why wars occur. It focuses on how the capacity of government officials to redistribute valuable resources within a political system toward political supporters helps strengthen their hold on domestic power. The disbursement of these resources heightens the risks of war by increasing the capacity of governments to remain relatively insulated from its domestic political costs.

access to government contracts, *which flow only to those members of the government's winning coalition.*

Individuals in the polity make the decision of whether or not to retain an incumbent based on the mix of public and private goods received. Winning coalition size shapes the cost that leaders must pay for private goods (Bueno de Mesquita et al. 2003, p. 91). As the polity grows more democratic, the size of potential equal disbursements of private benefits to each member of the winning coalition shrinks. Shrinking private benefit receipts make the success of public policy and the public goods generated by such policies more important in the decision by society of whether or not to retain a government.

Alternatively, as the polity grows less democratic, the size of private benefit payouts looms larger in the decision of each member of the selectorate over whether to continue to support the incumbent. Because selectorate members risk losing these private benefits by supporting an unsuccessful takeover bid by a political challenger, they tend to be loyal supporters of the incumbent. Consequently, these high opportunity costs of switching political allegiance contribute to regime stability and reduce the need for the incumbent to rely on public policy successes to remain in office.

Bueno de Mesquita et al. focus primarily on the relationship between the size of the winning coalition and public goods provision to explain decisions to use military force. Victory on the battlefield creates opportunities to provide public benefits, such as eliminating an important threat to national security, that are consumed by all members of the polity. However, ensuring victory often requires the diversion of discretionary resources away from private benefit spending, which subsequently jeopardizes an incumbent's ability to remain in office.[5] Autocratic leaders with small winning coalitions generally forego investments in military victory and instead opt to reward their supporters when facing this dilemma. By doling out large quantities of private benefits, their capacity to remain in office depends not on the war's outcome but on continuity in the delivery of these benefits. This domestic strength encourages leaders with small winning coalitions to enter more wars because they face fewer risks of being deposed after the war.[6]

[5] For additional evidence linking war participation to the survival of regimes and political leaders, see Bueno de Mesquita, Siverson, and Woller (1992) and Bueno de Mesquita and Siverson (1995).

[6] These domestic incentives simultaneously encourage them to divert fewer resources away from private benefits spending necessary to achieve victory. This lower war effort influences the strategic game with international adversaries. Hesitation to expend extra resources in war makes leaders with small winning coalitions attractive targets to predators in the international system.

Winning coalition size is just one component in the size of private benefits payouts flowing to members of the winning coalition. The total pool of economic resources controlled by a government also shapes private benefit payouts and, along with them, variations in public policy. Bueno de Mesquita et al. assume that revenues are generated by taxing the economic activity of polity members. Consequently, they assume that all politicians face the same dilemma associated with generating government revenues through taxation. If the marginal tax rate is too high, citizens devote more time to leisure activities, reduce their individual contribution to aggregate economic activity, and simultaneously shrink the total pool of resources that governments rely on to fund public expenditures. However, the discussion here distinguishing between generating public revenues through taxation or public property illustrates that all governments do not face this dilemma in the same fashion. Many governments possess large quantities of publicly owned assets that relieve them of having to tax the incomes of private individuals directly. As previous sections have discussed, these differences in public finance can shape such domestic political characteristics as autonomy and regime type, and subsequently influence decisions for war and peace.

Public assets are unique in that they are already owned and controlled by the government. Unlike decisions on taxation, government officials do not withhold a portion of private-sector wealth to gain access to the pool of societal resources. As public resources grow, governments can increase private benefit payouts without increasing taxation rates on private economic activity. Alternatively, they can choose to maintain constant private benefits payoffs and expand the size of the winning coalition. In short, large quantities of public property create political flexibility for governments wishing to consolidate their regime by enabling them to either raise the opportunity costs to their coalition members for supporting an opposition candidate or by co-opting potential opposition forces. This financial autonomy enables governments to redistribute publicly owned wealth within the economy toward political supporters (members of the winning coalition), tie significant portions of society to their survival in office, and prevent the emergence of active opposition to its policies.

One recent example of these dynamics can be seen in Venezuela. Rather than forcing Hugo Chavez to resign, a general strike in December 2002 led by management at PDVSA, Venezuela's state-owned oil firm, instead allowed him to reorganize the firm, purge management that had opposed his regime, and establish his control over it. Chavez has successfully funneled oil profits into massive social spending programs that expanded his base of support among groups struck by poverty and previously left out of Venezuelan politics. These programs helped Chavez achieve victory in a recall referendum of August 2004 (Gott 2005). Moreover, control over these revenues has enabled Chavez to cultivate regional and global influence by subsidizing oil sales to neighboring states in the Caribbean and South America, modernizing the military with significant arms purchases, and building a new reservist army that could eventually number two million members.[7]

How does such financial autonomy influence decisions for military conflict? Because the survival of autocrats in office depends largely on their ability to provide private benefits and not on their performance in war, selectorate theory holds that such regimes require lower probabilities of victory before entering a war. Large private benefits payments to members of the support coalition reduce the risk of being ejected from office after a foreign policy failure (Bueno de Mesquita et al. 2003, pp. 269–72). Similarly, large quantities of public property increase the pool of resources that governments can draw upon to generate private benefits for members of the winning coalition. These political assets help governments maintain their capacity to hold office even after defeat in war and reduce the expected threshold of victory they need to reach before entering a conflict.[8] Political challengers that do not possess access to such financial resources find it difficult to build a viable opposition movement by encouraging members of the winning coalition to abandon the incumbent. Consequently, governments with large quantities of public resources can confidently initiate military conflicts because they are often highly insulated from the domestic political costs of military failure.

Egyptian foreign policy under Nasser illustrates how public property can simultaneously strengthen a regime and enable it to pursue aggressive foreign policies. Upon removing King Faruk from power in 1952, Nasser's Revolutionary Command Council pursued a sustained policy of nationalization until 1966 that led to massive redistribution of landholdings, limited the political influence of the old landowning elite, placed major industrial firms and most of the banking sector under state control, and substantially reduced foreign holdings, including the Suez Canal, in the Egyptian

[7] Michael Shifter (2006) writes, "Chavez regards Venezuela's state-owned enterprise PDVSA as the foundation of his grandiose political project . . . He has skillfully managed to establish himself as a global and regional leader, using oil money and brash anti-Americanism to attempt to construct a counterweight to U.S. power."

[8] A more detailed explication of this logic and its derivation from the propositions associated with selectorate theory can be found in McDonald (2007a).

economy. Secure at home and flush with substantial economic resources, Nasser then embarked on a steady program to expand Egyptian influence in the region. Waterbury (1983, p. 78) writes, "Dismantling the upper reaches of the private sector therefore contributed directly and commensurately to regime strength by placing the levers of economic control in its hands. With this control he (Nasser) could better defend Egypt's stature among Arabs through a regional policy founded on aggressive Arabism and socialism." Similarly, Barnett (1992, p. 95) argues that these nationalizations consolidated Nasser's political control and became an important lever of political power, allowing him to distribute economic rewards to counter opposition. This consolidation of political power was a necessary precursor to his broader goals of eliminating imperialist interference and promoting Egypt's position abroad (p. 84). During his reign from 1952 until 1970, Nasser's attempts to extend his influence in the Middle East would contribute to Egyptian participation in three wars: the war over the Suez in 1956, the Yemeni civil war of 1962 to 1967, and the Six-Day War of 1967. During this same period, Egypt participated in thirty-nine new militarized disputes, ten of which involved at least one battle death. The near-constant militarization of Egyptian foreign policy illustrates what selectorate theory would identify as a low threshold for entering conflict. Finally, the links between risk acceptance toward war and Nasser's efforts to build a strong base of domestic support that enabled his political survival are perhaps best demonstrated by his capacity to remain in office following the disastrous defeat of 1967.

Targeted in Preventive Strikes

Governments with large quantities of public property are also more likely to be targeted in a military attack. This financial bonanza can create a commitment problem that tempts an adversary to launch a preventive war by strengthening a regime's domestic position or by enabling it to divert massive quantities of domestic resources to the military. Both mechanisms highlight how the inability of domestic society to place limits on a government's authority at home frees that government to violate present and future promises to uphold the international status quo.[9]

[9] The logic of the selectorate model suggests a third mechanism that will not be examined here. Bueno de Mesquita et al. argue that coalition size determines how hard politicians try to achieve victory in war. Small-coalition leaders are hesitant to divert resources from private goods spending to the war effort because their ability to remain in office depends less on victory than on the continued ability to provide these benefits. In comparing the limiting cases of whether to spend all of their discretionary resources on the war

The first focuses on the possibility that a government's domestic political insulation enables it to pursue future renegotiation of any peaceful settlement with another state in the international system. Because public property reduces the risks of being removed from office after war, governments can adopt an intransigent bargaining position by demanding more concessions. In effect, by reducing the domestic political costs associated with executing threats – like the use of military force – once engaged in a political dispute, these public resources enable a government to bargain with more resolve. If an adversary decides to construct a peaceful negotiated settlement with a government secure at home, it cannot be sure that the same government will not use this domestic political security to demand more concessions in the future. Aware that they are likely to hold onto power at home even after military defeat, governments holding substantial quantities of public property cannot credibly commit to forego exploiting the opportunities for political expansion generated by their domestic political security.

One of the political motivations behind British intervention in Egypt in 1956 illustrates this commitment problem created by the nationalization of critical national resources. Apart from threatening Europe's access to Middle Eastern oil, British advisors feared that control of the Suez Canal and its revenues would enable Nasser to consolidate his internal position and then extend his influence in the region, which could include toppling moderate Arab regimes (Yergin 1991, pp. 485–8; Pearson 2003, p. 44). This logic suggests that the British would have been less willing to try and topple Nasser if they believed him to be capable of committing to preserving

or spend it all instead on private benefits, they show that politicians choose an all-out effort when winning coalition size is greater than total revenues (W > R) (2003, p. 234). As winning coalition size grows (W), politicians devote more discretionary resources to outlays that increase the probability of military victory. This increased effort level simultaneously makes large coalition states less attractive targets. Given this relationship between winning coalition size and the total pool of resources controlled by government officials, the converse proposition also holds. As total revenues (R) increase, politicians are simultaneously less willing to engage in an all-out effort in war. Large quantities of state-owned assets increase the total pool of economic resources controlled by politicians and enhance their ability to provide private benefits to members of their winning coalition. These domestic dynamics decouple the regime's capacity to remain in office from its performance in war and lead it to spend less on the war effort. Reduced effort levels render these states more attractive targets for military conflict. Although the statistical results presented in Chapter 9 confirm that governments with large quantities of public property are more likely to be targeted in military disputes than those with small quantities, the examples discussed in this chapter and Chapter 7 suggest instead that the commitment problems posed by these resources provide a stronger explanation of this relationship. For an extended discussion of the logic behind this mechanism and how it is generated from the claims associated with selectorate theory see McDonald (2007a).

the territorial status quo in the region. However, his broad program of nationalization facilitated his consolidation of power at home by limiting the capacity of private wealth holders to participate or mobilize political opposition. Thus, Britain prepared to launch a war to retake the Canal and prevent Nasser from embarking on a broader program of regional expansion in support of socialist regimes abroad by either dislodging him from power or by depriving him of the financial resources that could facilitate such political goals.

Second, such governments can be targeted because their financial autonomy enables them to accelerate military spending without making domestic political concessions that often accompany increases in taxation. Extended arms races often push governments to locate new financial resources to sustain higher levels of military spending. Unless governments are free to borrow money on international credit markets, this often necessitates some type of renegotiation with the holders of private wealth within a society. Property owners often demand political concessions – either in the form of greater political representation, new constraints on a government's ability to raise more taxes in the future, or a larger influence in the making of public policy – before agreeing to any revision in the basic tax contract between state and society. In short, once engaged in an arms race, governments often face a dilemma. They can concede defeat in the arms race and watch their subsequent bargaining power relative to other states erode. Or they can choose to try and sustain the arms race at the cost of accepting new constraints on their political authority at home that could ultimately limit their capacity to remain in power.

Large quantities of public property provide one institutional escape out of this dilemma for governments. Such governments do not need to renegotiate the basic tax contract with society because they already possess significant financial resources that can be diverted to military spending. This domestic political insulation enables a government to start an arms race confident that it will be able to sustain it longer than an adversary, who will eventually face the choice of whether or not to make new domestic concessions to remain in the competition.

By creating differential capacities to sustain arms races, this financial disparity carries the potential both to alter the future balance of military power between rivals and to heighten the risks of war. The government with substantial public property holdings can continually enhance its bargaining leverage with augmented military spending. Adversaries that would be forced to renegotiate the basic tax contract with their own domestic population to generate new revenues for military spending may opt instead to launch a preventive war that relieves them of the political and economic burdens of the arms race.[10] Fearing a future in which a growing military disparity forces them continually to make diplomatic concessions whenever engaged in an international political dispute, a government with limited public property fights both because it cannot sustain the costs of the arms race and its competitor with public property cannot commit to refrain from exploiting these resources to enhance its bargaining leverage.[11]

The reexamination of the origins of World War I in Chapter 7 illustrates how large quantities of public property can generate this commitment problem stemming from differential domestic organizational capacities to sustain an arms race. The domestic political insulation created by substantial quantities of public property was critical to the arms race on land that eventually gave way to the German decision to launch a preventive war against Russia in 1914. Although German and French politicians were forced to make important political concessions to the political left in the immediate years before 1914 to keep pace in armaments competition, large amounts of public property, particularly in railroads and vodka distillation, insulated the Russian government from these domestic pressures and enabled them to accelerate the race without provoking domestic opposition. Aware of Russia's financial strength and the pending completion of its Great Program of military expansion in 1917, Germany launched a preventive war in 1914 while it still possessed a reasonable hope of achieving victory on the battlefield. The relative ease by which the tsar could procure financial resources for the military rendered it difficult for him to commit not to exploit this advantage. The growing financial incapacity of Germany to keep pace with Russia in the arms race contributed to its decision to launch a preventive war against Russia in the midst of the July crisis (Ferguson 1994).

In sum, governments possessing large quantities of public property are more likely to engage in military conflict than those overseeing more privatized economies. This section described two key theoretical mechanisms linking the financial autonomy created by public property to conflict. First, these resources help strengthen regime stability, insulating governments from the domestic political costs of military conflict and allowing them to initiate military disputes in support of aggressive foreign policies. Second,

[10] This link among arms races, commitment problems, and war is discussed in Powell (2006).

[11] On its own, this logic implies that two governments, each in possession of large quantities of public property, may be able to reach peaceful settlements once engaged in political disputes. The likelihood of this possibility is reduced by the mechanism discussed in the previous section. Both governments would still be tempted to initiate military conflict because they remain relatively insulated from its domestic political costs.

these resources tempt adversaries to attack such governments. Adversaries target such governments to prevent them from adopting a hostile foreign policy after consolidating their position at home; and to prevent them from running an arms race that upsets regional or global distributions of military power.

Substantial public assets reduce the role of markets in domestic economic activity by empowering bureaucrats to allocate resources for political rather than economic gain. Similarly, attempts by governments to insulate domestic firms from international markets reduce competition within the domestic economy. These barriers to commerce, both in the form of tariffs and capital controls, limit the capacity of globalization to promote peace. The next section focuses on these barriers to construct the second set of theoretical mechanisms linking neoliberal domestic institutions to peace.

GLOBALIZATION, CREATIVE DESTRUCTION, AND PEACE

> Commerce, which ought naturally to be, among nations, as among individuals, a bond of union and friendship, has become the most fertile source of discord and animosity. The capricious ambition of kings and ministers has not, during the present and preceding century been more fatal to the repose of Europe, than the impertinent jealousy of merchants and manufacturers. The violence and injustice of the rulers is an ancient evil, for which, I am afraid, the nature of human affairs can scarce admit of a remedy. But the mean rapacity, the monopolizing spirit of merchants and manufacturers, who neither are, nor ought to be, the rulers of mankind, though it cannot perhaps be corrected, may very easily be prevented from disturbing the tranquility of any body but themselves.
>
> – Adam Smith, *The Wealth of Nations* (1937[1776], p. 460)

Adam Smith held that one of the primary virtues of international trade lay in its capacity to discipline the "monopolizing spirit of merchants and manufacturers" by exposing them to more competition from abroad. Once domestic markets open to foreign competition, domestic producer arrangements restricting output and propping up prices are no longer sustainable. Left out of such arrangements and eager to penetrate vulnerable markets, foreigners sell their products at lower prices and force domestic industry to face the uncomfortable choice of either innovation and survival or stagnation and bankruptcy. Governments surrender their capacity to support high prices necessary to sustain inefficient domestic firms by eliminating entry barriers on foreign producers. This process of importing competition into the domestic economy facilitates the creative destruction that Schumpeter (1942) described as fundamental to capitalism. The threat of external competition simultaneously forces economic organizations to reform while rendering the survival of those incapable of adaptation both costly and unsustainable. In much the same way, this section argues that forces of competition imported via globalization destroy much of the economic demand for war and a government's capacity to wage it without broad public support while simultaneously creating a material foundation for peaceful cooperation between states.

While classical scholars of trade, like Adam Smith and David Ricardo, understood that international trade could increase the aggregate income of a society, contemporary research shows that these material benefits do not come without cost. The process of importing competition into the domestic economy necessarily redistributes income as jobs are lost and inefficient firms halt production. Just as globalization creates political coalitions that embrace its opportunities, it also generates a political backlash that seeks to halt the intensification of competition within the home economy. This dynamic of creative destruction suggests that the outcome of a continual domestic struggle over commercial policy shapes the degree to which governments embrace globalization, which then carries important implications for the capacity of international trade to restrict military conflict between states.

Here I explore two related mechanisms by which this struggle over commercial policy influences the capacity of globalization to heighten competition in the local economy and promote peace. The first focuses on the conflict within society over the distribution of the economic costs and benefits generated by international trade. This domestic political conflict shapes national interests, particularly those which governments are willing to defend with military force. When domestic groups that benefit from international trade – like consumers and internationally competitive firms – win this domestic struggle, governments respond by pursuing more restrained national interests and by embracing political cooperation with other states so as to not risk these material benefits. Alternatively, groups benefiting from protection are more willing to support aggressive foreign policies that create opportunities to slow imports, restrict competition in the home economy, or secure preferential access to new or existing markets via military force. The tendency of governments to use military force to promote national interests increases as the domestic influence of protectionist groups grows.

The second mechanism alters the role of the state from simply mediating this societal struggle to actively shaping its outcome for political benefit. War and political conflicts between states are not always driven by economic incentives such as securing access to new markets. To protect national security, governments are often forced to balance aggressive powers or rescue allies in danger of being conquered. The capacity of governments to defend these national political interests depends critically on their ability to remain in office while implementing costly foreign policies that may include the deployment of military force. Just as public property helps governments to consolidate power at home, regulations like subsidies or tariffs that strengthen the position of local producers in domestic markets create similar opportunities to cultivate political support from the beneficiaries of such policies. In short, economic regulation can be utilized by governments to minimize the domestic political costs of deploying military force in defense of national interests.

Significant restrictions on international trade limit the capacity of globalization to heighten competition in the domestic economy and suggest that the beneficiaries of trade have enjoyed little success in the domestic struggle over commercial policy. They also empower governments to shape the allocation of scarce resources and redistribute income toward political supporters. These consequences point to the same testable hypothesis derived from the larger argument linking market-promoting institutions and peace. *Large political barriers to international trade raise the likelihood that governments deploy military force to settle their political disputes.*

These arguments differ from traditional studies of commercial liberalism in two key ways. First, they shift the conceptual focus of the economic causes of peace from global trade flows to the domestic institutions that underpin them. Some studies of trade policy and commercial liberalism often assert that liberal institutions regulating the domestic economy can be inferred from such aggregate outcomes as higher levels of international trade. However, trade flows between countries are shaped by multiple causes, including differences in relative factor endowments, economies of scale, transportation costs, and political barriers to trade. Only one of these causes – political barriers to trade – directly reflects the institutions regulating the domestic economy.

Second, the conceptual focus on the struggle over commercial policy necessarily places the state–society relationship, the foundation of liberal international relations theory, at the center of hypotheses linking international trade to peace. The capacity of globalization to promote peace depends critically on whether it alters the domestic balance of political power in favor of groups that gain from international trade.

Commercial Liberalism, National Interests, and Peace

This section merges the classical foundations of commercial liberalism found in the writings of Cobden and Schumpeter with standard trade theory to present two processes by which this domestic conflict over globalization shapes the definition of national interests and a government's propensity to utilize military force in support of those interests. In the first, the outcome of a domestic struggle within society between free traders and protectionists shapes the willingness of governments to defend national interests with military force. In the second, the state actively influences this internal struggle over commercial policy as part of a larger political strategy whereby it builds domestic support for the implementation of its preferred foreign policy. This focus on the domestic filtering process requires two shifts from traditional explanations of how commerce promotes peace. The first alters the underlying trade model from one that focuses on the aggregate benefits of international commerce to a family of models that turn attention to how international trade alters the distribution of income within an economy. The second redirects conceptual attention toward commercial policy, namely the level of free trade in an economy, and away from aggregate trade flows.

The basic mechanics linking trade to peace are often rooted in the simple, but powerful insight of David Ricardo (1951[1820]). He used the concept of comparative costs to illustrate how two economies could both increase their aggregate consumption possibilities through trade by specializing in the production of goods where they possessed respective efficiency advantages. This conclusion implies that any policy or event that constricts international commerce will necessarily decrease national income and impose economic costs on a society. Because military hostilities tend to reduce economic exchange between countries, these aggregate economic costs promote peace by making a state less willing to enter a war or by facilitating compromise in diplomatic crises by helping political officials to communicate their resolve over the issue in dispute. This theoretical dependence on Ricardo carries important implications for any conclusion linking commerce to peace.

By focusing on the aggregate economic benefits derived from international trade, the commercial peace has neglected key insights from standard trade theory illustrating that these gains are not distributed evenly within economies. For example, the Heckscher–Ohlin framework shows that trade increases the real income of owners of relatively abundant factors of production in an economy (Flam and Flanders 1991). Owners of relatively scarce factors simultaneously see their relative incomes decrease. If it is costly for factors to move between sectors, owners of factors specific to the exporting industry receive increasing incomes from international trade (Jones 1971). At the same time, owners of factors specific to import-competing industries face declining incomes.

These models yield a simple but important insight. Because international trade redistributes income within society, it simultaneously creates conflicting pressures for and against more open commercial policies. This domestic conflict implies that aggregate gains from trade will not necessarily translate into uniform lobbying pressures from society for the promotion of trade and peace. For example, politically powerful constituencies owning scarce factors of production may be able to resist this process and reap economic gains from the closure of international markets. Trade models highlighting these uneven effects within societies can shed light not only on which sectors seek open international markets but can also provide a deductive foundation linking domestic economic interests to the foreign policies of states.

Insights into these domestic pressures can be generated by moving beyond Ricardo and shifting the underlying model of international trade used in commercial peace hypothesis. By redistributing income within economies, greater exposure to international trade simultaneously generates domestic conflict over whether commercial policy should be more or less restrictive. Commercial policy disputes help shape broader domestic cleavages over the role of military force in foreign policy, territorial expansion, and war. The following analysis builds on the complementarity between liberal international relations theory and bargaining models of war. It focuses on the first step in this war-generating process to identify how domestic struggles over globalization can lead states to define their national interests, particularly with respect to territory, more broadly or narrowly.

Consumers and Internationally Competitive Firms: Advocates for National Restraint and Peace

Consistent with Ricardo's central insight, the economic gains from trade arise from multiple factors.[12] Two particularly stand out: the decline in prices of consumer goods and the growth in nominal income received by

[12] For a brief overview of the many gains from trade including economics of scale, expanded consumer choice, more competitive prices in domestic markets, and real income growth, see Irwin (2002, pp. 29–39).

firms that are competitive in international markets without state assistance. First, by introducing consumer goods produced at lower costs from around the world into the domestic market, integration tends to drive down the price of traded goods in an economy. Economists have characterized this as the process of importing competition into domestic markets (Levinsohn 1993). Imports produced by relatively more efficient foreign firms reduce monopoly rents in previously noncompetitive markets and lower the prices of final goods in the domestic economy. As the cost of consumer goods falls, the purchasing power or real income of society increases. Given these gains, consumers should strongly support policies, including the elimination of trade barriers and the avoidance of military conflict, likely to promote trade.

Similarly, some groups within the domestic economy receive additional income gains from trade if they are employed in an exporting industry or own factors that are relatively abundant in the domestic economy with respect to the world.[13] For example, as a reduction in import barriers spurs trading partners to reduce tariffs, exporters will lobby their home government for lower tariffs. As lower foreign tariffs allow home exporting industries to seek out new markets or higher prices for their final goods, they also increase the income of factors employed by them.[14]

These trade policy preferences carry implications for the broader foreign policy preferences of these groups.[15] Firms or industries that are competitive in international markets without state assistance (such as tariffs, quotas, or export subsidies) are more likely to advocate restrained national interests

[13] Different predictions about the distributional effects of globalization between the Heckscher–Ohlin and specific factors model of trade derive largely from the different assumptions about the costs of moving a factor from one sector to another. The Heckscher–Ohlin model assumes zero costs and has been used to predict that societal cleavages created by globalization depend on class (Rogowski 1989). Owners of abundant factors favor globalization, whereas owners of scarce factors oppose it. However, the specific factors model becomes more appropriate as these costs become positive. Under these circumstances, societal cleavages are more likely to be based on industry differences (Hiscox 2002). I will not explore these distinctions any further here. Rather I wish to exploit the simple insight that globalization produces societal conflict and not all domestic groups will necessarily support the further integration of national markets into the global economy.

[14] Again this depends on the assumptions made about the costs of moving across industries. As costs approach zero, then owners of abundant factors employed in the exporting industry will see incomes rise. As the costs of redeployment increase, factors specific to the exporting industry will see their incomes rise.

[15] This analysis is similar to that found in Solingen (1998), Trubowitz (1998), and Fordham (1998). All three examine how economic interests stemming from globalization shape domestic struggles over a state's broader foreign policy interests.

that limit potential military conflicts with other states.[16] These foreign policy goals are driven by material interests seeking to avoid the well-known economic costs of military conflict, including higher taxes, export controls, embargoed export markets, higher transportation costs, and higher costs for imported inputs for production. Moreover, such internationally competitive groups lack further economic incentive to support military expansion. The goods produced by these firms penetrate new markets and generate larger revenues because of their cost advantages. This competitiveness is best measured via existing restrictions on imports in the home market. If foreign firms are free to compete there and the home firm can survive, then that same home firm should be competitive vis-à-vis those same competitors in foreign economies. Such firms or industries are generally unwilling to pay the costs, such as higher taxes or the temporary disruption of trade, associated with forcibly opening new markets because they can achieve this same economic outcome without military force. Governments seeking to build domestic support for open trading policies and peaceful foreign policies should be able to draw heavily on consumers and these internationally competitive economic interests. Governments seeking to adopt a more aggressive foreign policy need to marginalize the influence of these constituencies and find alternative bases of societal support.

Import-Competing Interests and Military Conflict

Standard trade theory illustrates, however, that the income gains from trade are not captured by all segments of the domestic economy. For example, the Stolper–Samuelson (1941) theorem demonstrates that protection increases the real income of scarce factors of production. Owners of scarce factors should benefit from any policy or event that constricts international exchange. Extending this insight to commercial liberalism implies that the beneficiaries of protection, or firms that are not competitive in global markets, may support aggressive foreign policies or war for the economic benefits it provides to them. By slowing imports, military conflict raises the domestic price of traded goods and enables import-competing firms to expand their domestic market share. Even if they do not actively

[16] I distinguish here between export-oriented firms and firms that are competitive in international markets without state assistance for the following reason. Firms or industries may orient their sales to international markets but rely on state assistance to be competitive there. For reasons that I shall discuss shortly, namely that they have been captured by the state, such firms are less likely to support restrained national interests and peace. Prussian landowners prior to World War I were an example of this dynamic. Export subsidies allowed them to sell grain in Western Russia. These groups also supported an aggressive stance against Russia during the press war in the six months prior to July 1914.

lobby for military expansion, such groups are unlikely to spend resources lobbying for greater openness and peace if the economic costs of these policies disproportionately fall on them. A government trying to build a pacific or conciliatory foreign policy is unlikely to find much support from this segment of society.

The economic incentives for conflict do not stem solely from the latter's ability to restrict trade and drive up domestic prices. Classic writings about imperialism (e.g., Lenin 1993[1916]; Schumpeter 1951[1919]) suggest another mechanism that focuses on the use of military force to defend existing external markets or secure new outlets for domestic production. Because protected sectors rely on the state to enact barriers to make their products more competitive in domestic markets, their opportunities for capturing new global markets are relatively restricted. If they already rely on tariffs to survive in the domestic economy, they will be unable to survive in more competitive international markets without this assistance. To capture larger profits, they may be willing to pay some of the costs of larger defense burdens, including higher taxes, necessary to open new markets with military force. The conquest of another economy offers economic rewards by enlarging the size of the protected domestic market.[17] Alternatively, military force can be deployed to prevent foreign firms from penetrating third-party markets. These potential economic gains accruing to protected firms from the use of military force can be contrasted with more competitive firms that do not need regulatory assistance to remain profitable. The goods of the latter group penetrate new markets because they are produced more efficiently and at lower costs. Consequently, firms that do not rely on protection to remain profitable lack any economic incentive to pay the costs associated with war.

Such economic pressures behind expansion existed in the United States in the nineteenth century. Some of President Cleveland's most vocal support for his aggressive stance over Venezuela with Great Britain in 1895 came from manufacturing, industry, big business, and Republicans – precisely the groups that had always opposed him for supporting free-trade policies (Blake 1942). These interests saw the Venezuelan issue as an opportunity to solidify the Monroe Doctrine while defending new markets in Latin America made even more important given chronic problems of overproduction exposed by the depression in the latter part of the nineteenth century and British competition in these markets (LaFeber 1998[1963]).

[17] Unlike Lenin, however, these arguments do not imply that capitalist development necessarily allows these mercantilist interests to win out over more internationally competitive firms in the domestic struggle to capture the state and shape its foreign policy.

In sum, the relative balance of societal influence between the beneficiaries and losers from unrestricted trade shapes the willingness of governments to deploy military force in the support of national interests. When the beneficiaries of trade have defeated import-competing interests and enjoy more domestic political influence, governments are less likely to deploy military force abroad to defend economic interests.

The State and Protection: Constructing Coalitions for War

By itself, this discussion focusing on the relationship domestic economic actors have with the broader global economy[18] implies that the state acts in a politically neutral fashion by simply implementing the foreign policy goals of the dominant group within society. Furthermore, it suggests that territorial expansion and war are driven solely by these economic interests emanating from society. Although these incentives sometimes may be sufficient to generate political conflicts with states that culminate in military conflict, governments also face a set of external political constraints governed by anarchy and the global distribution of power that shape their willingness to use military force in defense of national interests. Under these circumstances, economic regulation can facilitate the construction of domestic coalitions of support necessary to sustain costly militarized foreign policies.

Governments actively shape the outcomes of domestic battles over globalization. Given its regulatory role over the domestic economy, the state can restrict access to the domestic economy and generate tangible assets that societal actors are willing to acquire for either revenue or political support (e.g., Stigler 1971; Grossman and Helpman 1994). For example, tariffs create competitive advantages for firms by insulating them from international competition. Because these regulations cannot be transferred to another economy, they can be regarded as a specific asset (Williamson 1985). If firms oppose a government's policy and wish to move their operations to another country, they risk losing the regulatory benefits they rely on to remain profitable. Or at the very least, they will need to invest more productive resources lobbying a new government for tariff protection. Consequently, the threat to withhold these regulatory benefits absent active political support from its recipients can provide an important resource by which governments build coalitions behind their entire range of policies. As governments intervene more in the domestic economy, they create more "pork" that can be used to

[18] Trubowitz (1998) has a similar theoretical focus.

co-opt opposition groups. For example, if a government wishes to conquer another state to shift the balance of power in its favor, its ability to implement this policy goal will depend partly on its capacity to carve out a domestic support coalition capable of keeping it in office during and after this war. As a government embraces more competitive international markets and constrains itself from intervening in the domestic economy, it simultaneously relinquishes a policy tool that may prove crucial to implementing a costly foreign policy.

This logic resembles that discussed in the previous section on public property. Governments pursue risky policies like war when the likelihood of being removed from office following policy failures is low. Governments can generate this domestic security, and the policy autonomy it creates, by tying the economic welfare of societal groups to its continuation in power through the provision of such material benefits as direct subsidies or tariffs. Because these societal groups risk losing these benefits by withdrawing their political support, governments can utilize such power to regulate the domestic economy to construct and then maintain a base of societal support capable of keeping it in office following costly foreign policy failures like defeat in war. This domestic insulation then makes governments more willing to take on the political risks associated with deploying military force.

The domestic political dynamics underlying the construction of a German navy to implement Weltpolitik and challenge British hegemony illustrate how governments can use tariff policy to manufacture support for policies that provoke political conflicts with other states and raise the dangers of war.[19] The naval component created an opportunity for the government to reestablish the alliance between conservatives and industrial interests that had been undermined by the Caprivi tariff reforms. Industrial interests favored the construction of a navy because it offered strategic protection to international commerce if the global economy were to break apart into trading blocs, as Joseph Chamberlain's campaign for imperial preference in Great Britain suggested. Steady government demand for new battleships also insulated this sector from downturns in the business cycle. Agrarian interests instead preferred that the resources devoted to the navy had gone to the army.[20] However, the decision to pay for the navy by reestablishing a broad set of agricultural tariffs that reduced grain imports from its

[19] The following section draws on the arguments of Fischer (1975), Berghahn (1993[1973]), and Snyder (1991).

[20] For a good discussion of the relative breakdown of economic and political interests within Germany and England during this period see Chapter 17 in Kennedy (1980).

American, Argentine, and Russian competitors helped solidify agricultural support behind Weltpolitik. The imposition of the tariffs thus allowed the government to generate side payments for conservative support of its navy and divert the massive armament costs to the left wing of the German electorate. Germany's global policy to expand its colonial holdings directly challenged fundamental British interests and provided a focal point for the emerging Anglo-German rivalry (e.g., Kennedy 1980; Steiner 1977). The agricultural tariffs also alienated powerful groups within Russia and played a large role in the steady deterioration of Russo-German relations in the decade prior to 1914 (Spring 1988b).

Using Protection to Assess Domestic Outcomes and Foreign Policy Interests

These domestic political dynamics linking the distributional consequences of globalization to national foreign policy interests suggest multiple observable implications. The beneficiaries of international commerce, such as consumers and exporters, should lobby the state to pursue conciliatory foreign policies that diminish the risks of armed conflict. When deciding to pursue an aggressive foreign policy, the state should utilize economic regulation like tariffs to mobilize societal support. More importantly, these pressures also imply that a state's likelihood of entering military conflict decreases under one of two conditions: when the domestic influence of the beneficiaries of international commerce increases or when the state's regulation of the domestic economy declines.

How then might we assess the domestic balance of power among the state, protected economic sectors, and the beneficiaries of trade? Just as battlefield outcomes reflect the balance of military power between states (e.g., Fearon 1995; Wagner 2000), trade policy outcomes provide a good measurement of the relative influence possessed by these groups. Larger barriers to trade indicate larger societal coalitions that depend on the state for regulatory protection. The regime has tied the interests of these groups to its survival and should be able to rely on them to support its policies. Larger barriers to trade also indicate that protectionist interests have been relatively more successful in lobbying the state for favorable regulations and possess greater domestic political influence. However, relatively small barriers imply that free-trading interests, such as consumers, have been able to realize their economic goals and possess relatively more influence in the domestic system. Larger barriers to trade also indicate that substantial components of the domestic economy are unlikely to be competitive in international markets. Import barriers eliminate competition from foreign firms in domestic markets. Unable to thrive without this insulation in the domestic economy, such firms are less likely to be successful against heightened international competition in more open global markets.

Political barriers to trade also reflect government efforts to restrict the role of competitive prices in allocating scarce resources. Larger barriers to trade restrict the entry of foreign goods, decrease the size of domestic markets, and increase the ability of domestic firms to control prices (Varian 1996, pp. 418–19). If a domestic monopoly exists prior to free trade, the elimination of trade barriers enables foreign competitors to erode the market position of the domestic monopolist (Bhagwati 1991, pp. 110–15). Finally, firms within competitive domestic markets lack any incentive to expend costly resources lobbying the government for protection from foreign producers. Any benefit received from import protection will be eroded by competition among domestic producers. For these reasons, domestic monopolies cannot exist without barriers to international competition. Consequently, the absence of trade barriers suggests the presence of competitive domestic markets. Conversely, as trade barriers increase, the probability that domestic prices will be influenced by political collusion between the government and producers increases as well.

This subtle shift in the primary independent variable under investigation, from aggregate trade flows to the degree to which states regulate international commerce, creates important theoretical leverage for the commercial peace research program. Such a shift enables the integration of important insights from standard trade theory that push beyond Ricardo's claim that trade enhances national income. Because trade based on comparative advantage redistributes income within a society, it generates political conflict between groups within society. Groups benefiting from international trade that successfully lobby for free trade policies are also likely to favor conciliatory foreign policies that avoid the economic losses associated with conflict. As the relative influence of these groups grows, we should expect states to possess fewer political conflicts with other states that precipitate military disputes. Conversely, as an economy becomes more insulated from the international economy, the constraints provided by competitive international markets on expansionary national interests and military conflict diminish. Trade policy outcomes provide one means to assess this domestic struggle. As protection levels increase, the likelihood of military conflict should grow as well.

CONCLUSION

The predominance of private property and the absence of government barriers to international trade enable competitive markets to coordinate domestic economic activity. This chapter has generated a series of theoretical mechanisms linking these institutions to the adoption of restrained national interests with respect to territory, a limited capacity for governments to escape the domestic political costs of war, and the attenuation of commitment problems that render peaceful compromises in the midst of diplomatic crises difficult. Figure 3.1 summarizes these various mechanisms. The vertical axis is differentiated by the two critical institutions of capitalism. The horizontal axis separates the hypothesized mechanisms linking these institutions to conflict according to three general sources of war presented at the end of Chapter 2.

The following six chapters test these claims with a wide range of evidence. The next chapter examines the capacity of these market-promoting institutions to generate peace within the most familiar confines of liberal peace research. Drawing on statistical methods, it examines whether the predominance of private property and free trade policies have limited military conflict between states in the post–World War II period.

General Mechanisms of War

Key Institutions of Capitalism	*National Interests*	*Domestic Regime Strength*	*Strategic Interaction*
Property rights regimes		Large quantities of public property strengthen regime by enabling it to co-opt opposition. This political security insulates governments from domestic punishment following war. *Examples*: Nasser's Egypt; Russia 1905–1914	Large quantities of public property make commitments to abide by international status quo and restrain arms spending less credible. *Examples*: Russo-German arms race 1912–1914
Openness of domestic markets to international competition	Free trading sectors favor limited territorial demands, cooperative foreign policies. *Examples*: Merchants, financial sector, and cotton sector in 19th century U.S.; British industrialists in 19th century; Taiwanese business interests with investment on mainland after 1987 Protectionists favor territorial expansion. *Examples*: Northeast industrial interests and western populists in 19th century U.S.; Russian agriculture 1914	State coopts society via economic regulation in support of aggressive foreign policy. *Examples*: Iron and Rye coalition in Germany; French financial sector 1905–1914; Taiwan's DPP	

Figure 3.1. Theoretical overview

FOUR

Liberal Economic Institutions and Peace in the Twentieth Century

This chapter begins the empirical evaluation of this book's two key hypotheses linking the predominance of private property and competitive market structures to peace. It draws on well-established practices in the large-liberal peace literature to ensure comparability with the findings presented here. For the most part, this research program has drawn on multivariate statistical analysis to evaluate whether democracy and international trade promoted peace during the post–World War II period. This research technique identifies broad relationships among variables that measure such concepts as commercial integration, regime type, military power, and military conflict across multiple countries and over multiple time periods. The statistical analysis presented here thus tests for the presence of any historical association between liberal economic institutions and the outbreak of military conflict between states.[1]

This analysis is comprised of two parts. Each part focuses on whether one of the two domestic institutions alters the likelihood that governments utilize military force to settle their political disputes with each other. If these hypotheses are correct, the following relationships should be observed. First, governments possessing high quantities of public property should utilize military force to settle political disputes with other governments at a higher rate than governments with more privatized economies. Second,

[1] Subsequent empirical chapters will identify the presence of critical theoretical mechanisms in a series of key historical cases. For example, I will examine whether firms that are competitive in international markets lobby their governments to adopt peaceful foreign policies. I will also examine whether noncompetitive firms and sectors instead support military aggression and potentially war. These chapters will utilize specific examples to illustrate how these institutions promote peace by pushing governments to adopt complementary national interests; by increasing the political difficulty to governments of redistributing the costs of war away from them and their supporters; and by facilitating the location of peaceful compromises once engaged in political disputes.

governments adopting free-trade policies should enter military disputes at a lower rate than those adopting more mercantilist or autarkic commercial policies. Apart from examining broad trends across thousands of cases over time and in different regions of the world, this statistical analysis controls for – and thus eliminates – the role of confounding factors like democracy or the military balance of power when estimating the extent to which these liberal economic institutions alter participation rates in military conflict.

The rest of this chapter proceeds as follows. The two primary sections examine how large quantities of public property and the adoption of free-trade policies alter the likelihood of military conflict between states. The first part of each section presents the basic research design. It discusses how the central concepts (namely, public property, free-trade policies, and military conflict) and confounding factors (like geographic contiguity, the military balance of power, and regime type) are measured. The second part of each section then describes estimation techniques and presents the statistical results. This analysis strongly supports the two principle hypotheses of this book: both private property and free trade promote peace.

PUBLIC PROPERTY AND MILITARY CONFLICT: AN EMPIRICAL TEST

This section examines whether the prevalence of private property in the domestic economy is associated with peace. It does so by testing the converse proposition – that high levels of public property raise the likelihood of military conflict. The previous chapter discussed how large quantities of public property create financial autonomy for a government. This financial autonomy reduces the domestic political risks associated with adopting aggressive foreign policies. Such resources enable governments to build robust domestic coalitions of support that remain resilient even after significant policy failures, such as defeat in war. Moreover, this domestic political strength invites military challenges by adversaries in the international system. Consequently, large quantities of public property embolden foreign policies and raise the risks that governments possessing these assets will engage in war.

Measuring the Central Concepts: Property Regimes and Military Conflict

The quantity of public property in an economy shapes military conflict between states by influencing the political process by which governments mobilize wealth from their economies and then use these assets to implement policies and strengthen their rule. To construct a valid measurement that captures this link between public ownership and public finance, I use data that distinguish among different sources of government revenue for a wide range of countries across time. The International Monetary Fund's (IMF) *Government Finance Statistics* and the World Bank's *World Development Indicators* (IMF 2001; World Bank various years) both carry information on the distribution of public revenue. Their breakdown of revenue sources includes categories for income taxes, sales or consumption taxes, tariffs, foreign aid, and public property. One class of revenue is labeled nontax revenue. It measures the proportion of annual receipts derived from the following sources: a government sale of its property, goods and services produced by state-owned enterprises, interest from financial assets owned by the government, dividends from public ownership in corporations, rents from leasing natural resources, and administrative fees.[2] I utilize this statistic to measure the size of public property within a domestic economy. Higher values of nontax revenue are taken to indicate a greater availability of public assets in the domestic economy that can be tapped to fund public policies. Although this variable is not a direct indicator of the distribution of assets in a domestic economy between the public and private sectors, it directly measures the state's dependence on its own property to implement its public spending priorities. Given the use of selectorate theory and the subsequent focus on public revenues as shaping incentives for military conflict, this measurement provides a crucial indicator of variation in public finance regimes. Higher values of nontax revenue indicate relatively lower private contributions to the state's treasury and thus more autonomy for the government in the policymaking process.

I construct the variable named PUBLIC from these data on nontax revenues. By measuring the proportion of public revenues generated from publicly owned assets, it can take on a value anywhere between zero and one. These two sources possess data on nontax revenue beginning in 1970. The sample used for the subsequent quantitative tests of the relationship between public property and military conflict spans from 1970 to 2001, the year the data on military conflict end.

Over this period, the number of states in the international system for any given year ranges from 139 to 191. Because some states have ceased to exist (e.g., Czechoslovakia, East Germany, South Vietnam) over this sample period, there are potentially 197 states that could have entered this sample at least once. Within the sample, 144 countries have at least 1 annual

[2] Chapter 5 in IMF (2001) describes the different classes of government revenue.

observation. There are a total of 2,782 annual observations for PUBLIC during this period. Among the countries that are completely absent from the sample, these missing data are most pronounced for two regions: the Caribbean and Oceania. Of the fifty-three countries in the sample that do not have any data for PUBLIC, nine come from the Caribbean (out of a potential thirteen countries in the region) and ten come from Oceania (out of a potential fifteen in the region). Thus, although data problems make it difficult to test for anyrelationship in the Caribbean and Oceania, other regions in the world have relatively strong data coverage.[3] The average value for PUBLIC is 0.16 and the median value is 0.12 during this period.

I measure military conflict by following standard conventions in the international relations literature. Generally, this concept is measured with some derivation of the militarized interstate dispute (MID) data set created under the auspices of the Correlates of War research program (Jones, Bremer, and Singer 1996). The data set explicitly focuses on instances in which a government threatens or uses military force against another government.[4] It also classifies these actions according to a 5-point scale of hostility level in which 1 represents no militarized action, 2 is a threat to use force, 3 is a display of force, 4 is the use of force, and 5 is war. All of the statistical tests examining the use of military force in this book will use version 3.0 of this data set (Ghosn and Palmer 2003) that was recently updated to identify all military disputes between states from 1816 until 2001.

Table 4.1 presents a preliminary look at the relationship between PUBLIC and participation in military disputes. It classifies all the annual observations of PUBLIC for states that are not great powers for the period from 1970 to 2001 into five groups.[5] These groups are created according to the proportion

[3] Here is a brief list of the most prominent missing countries from the sample by region. Within Europe, eight countries do not have any data. These are Monaco, Liechtenstein, Andorra, East Germany, San Marino, Malta, Macedonia, and Bosnia-Herzegovina. For Africa, eight countries out of a potential fifty-four do not have any data – Cape Verde, Sao Tome Principe, Equatorial Guinea, Eritrea, Angola, Mozambique, Seychelles, and Libya. In the Middle East, data are completely missing over the duration of the sample for Iraq, Lebanon, Saudi Arabia, South Yemen, and Qatar. And in Asia, ten countries are missing from the sample – Afghanistan, Turkmenistan, Uzbekistan, Taiwan, North Korea, Maldive Islands, Cambodia, Laos, South Vietnam, and Brunei.

[4] The following actions are classified as threats of force: explicit threats to use force, as well as threats to blockade, occupy territory, or declare war. The following actions are classified as a use of force: shows of force, nuclear alerts, border violations, blockades, occupations of territory, attacks, declarations of war, or the use of chemical or biological weapons.

[5] I drop great powers, primarily the United States, the Great Britain, France, Russia/Soviet Union, and China, from the data in this table for two reasons. First, as noted in the bottom of the table, these states enter five times as many annual disputes during this time period than states that are not great powers. Second, because the data for

of a government's revenues that are derived from publicly owned assets. For example, the first category of states generates less than 10 percent of total government revenues from publicly owned assets. Below each of the five categories are multiple examples of states in each of these categories.

The number under MILITARY DISPUTES indicates the average number of new military disputes entered by a state in a given year for all the observations in that category of PUBLIC.[6] In the first category of annual observations where states possessed relatively fewer public assets, governments engage in 0.32 new military disputes per year. Or alternatively, this group of states enters on average approximately one new military dispute every three years. This propensity for military conflict is lower than the average of 0.41 new military disputes per year for all countries in the sample. A downward scan of the numbers under MILITARY DISPUTES illustrates that the annual recourse to military force in foreign policy grows as governments derive larger portions of their total revenues from public assets. Countries like India, Pakistan, and Venezuela, which generally derive between 20 percent and 30 percent of their total revenues from state-owned assets, participate in 0.45 new military disputes each year. Governments

PUBLIC is only available for IMF members, the observations for Russia and China are few and concentrated in the 1990s. A second, less precise measurement of state-owned assets can be created with an indicator found in the first two versions of the POLITY data set that coded the extent to which governments tried to regulate and organize the economic and social life of the citizens of the state (Gurr 1997 [1989]). SCOPE is subjectively defined along a continuum ranging from one (totalitarian) to nine (minimal), with higher values indicating less state control of social and economic life. Data for this variable are available until 1986. Lower values for SCOPE indicate more government direction in the domestic economy and higher quantities of public property. I briefly examine the aggregate relationship between SCOPE and military conflict here for two reasons. First, while a number of socialist states are excluded from empirical studies of conflict because of irregular reporting of their aggregate economic indicators, the polity project explicitly coded these states as high (generally 1 or 2) on the grading scale evaluating government direction in the economy. Second, SCOPE expands the temporal domain back to 1950 rather than 1970. For the period from 1950 to 1986, all states participated in an average of 0.54 military disputes per year (n = 4030). States with relatively higher quantities of private property (scores of 3 to 9 on SCOPE) entered 0.48 military disputes per year (n = 3463). States with SCOPE scores of either 1 or 2 entered 0.85 military disputes per year. Some examples of these states with SCOPE scores of either 1 or 2 include Cuba, East Germany, Poland, Soviet Union, Egypt, China, Sudan, Iraq, North Korea, Cambodia, and Myanmar.

[6] Disputes that last more than one year do not show up in the coding of annual military disputes in the second or any other subsequent year of the dispute. For example, imagine that France engaged in a two-year military dispute that begins with Germany in 1971 and ended in 1972. Imagine that France also engaged in a dispute with Belgium lasting less than a year and both beginning and ending in 1972. France's military dispute score would be one in 1971 and one in 1972.

Table 4.1. *Average number of new military disputes entered by a country in a year according to PUBLIC score*

PUBLIC	MILITARY DISPUTES	N
Less than 10% of government revenues *Example countries*: Argentina, Australia, Belgium, Burundi, Colombia, Finland, Greece, Indonesia, Italy, Japan, the Netherlands, Nicaragua, Portugal, Senegal, Spain, South Africa, Switzerland, Thailand, Uganda, West Germany, Zambia	0.32	1,031
Greater than 10%, but less than 20% of government revenues *Example countries*: Canada, Costa Rica, Cyprus, Denmark, Ghana, Hungary, Ireland, Israel, Kenya, Luxembourg, Mexico, Paraguay, Peru, Philippines, South Korea, Sweden, Turkey	0.40	1,030
Greater than 20%, but less than 30% of government revenues *Example countries*: Bolivia, Brazil, Bulgaria, Chile, Ethiopia, India, Jordan, Nigeria, Pakistan, Panama, Tunisia, Venezuela	0.45	311
Greater than 30%, but less than 40% of government revenues *Example countries*: Bangladesh, Egypt, Myanmar, Singapore	0.60	131
Greater than 40% of government revenues *Example countries*: Bahrain, Botswana, Congo, Iran, Kuwait, Oman, Romania, Syria	0.87	164
SAMPLE AVERAGE	0.41	2,669

Note: Countries identified as great powers (China, France, Germany 1991–2001, Japan 1991–2001, Russia/Soviet Union, United States, Great Britain) excluded from the sample. The average number of annual military disputes entered by these great powers in the sample is 2.04 (n = 113).

with the most public property also possess the most violent foreign policies, entering on average 0.87 new military disputes every year.

Although these numbers are suggestive of a strong relationship between public property and military conflict, caution is in order before reaching such a conclusion. A large literature on the origins of war has demonstrated that military conflict between states can be caused by multiple factors acting independently or simultaneously. As the note at the bottom of Table 4.1 illustrates, great power status also appears to raise the likelihood that a government engages in military force. Great powers participate on average in five times as many annual military disputes as states that are not great powers. Similarly, the democratic peace literature suggests that democratic states are less likely to engage in military conflict than autocratic regimes. It could be that any relationship between public property and conflict is spurious. For example, the states listed at the top of Table 4.1 with low quantities of public property could also be more democratic on average. This possibility suggests that democracy causes governments both to limit their ownership of productive assets in an economy and participate in fewer military conflicts. In short, confidence in any assertion that public property heightens the risk of military conflict requires the use of more sophisticated statistical techniques that control for the possibility that some third variable is responsible for this relationship. The remainder of this section turns to this task.

Multivariate Tests of Public Property and Conflict

Most of the international relations literature utilizing quantitative methods to identify factors that correlate with the outbreak of military conflict between states relies on the dyad year as its primary unit of analysis. For example, the democratic peace hypothesis is explicitly dyadic in that it refers to the relationship between pairs of states. Democratic states only adopt more pacific foreign policies when they interact with fellow democratic states. Therefore, a dyad composed of the United States and the Great Britain should engage in fewer military disputes (with each other) than a dyad composed of two autocratic states, like Iran and Iraq, or a dyad composed of one democratic state and one autocratic state, like the United States and Iraq.

The initial set of statistical tests examining the size and direction of any relationship between liberal economic institutions and military conflict relies on this dyadic research design for two reasons. First, it ensures comparability of any conclusions reached here with the democratic peace literature and the broader quantitative literature on the origins of conflict. Second, because the theoretical discussion from Chapter 3 generates multiple expectations about how domestic economic institutions in one state shape both that government's incentives to initiate a military dispute and an adversary's decision to target it in a military attack, a dyadic research design is particularly appropriate. It incorporates both of these initiating and targeting possibilities while controlling for other dyadic characteristics, like the balance of military power between states.

In this framework, the unit of analysis is the dyad year. For example, a dyad composed of the United States and France in 1980 would compose one observation. That dyad composed of the United States and France in 1981 would compose another observation. A dyad composed of the United States and Belgium in 1981 would compose a third observation.

The sample of observations used to perform this analysis includes all potential dyads created by matching every state in the international system with every other state. The temporal domain of this analysis is a function of data availability for the indicator of public property regimes, PUBLIC. The sample will thus be composed of all possible dyads in the international system for the period from 1970 to 2001.[7] The subsequent statistical tests investigate how a series of dyadic traits correlate with the outbreak of a military dispute within that same dyad during any given year.

Key Variables: $PUBLIC_H$ and CONFLICT

The primary independent variable in these tests measures variation in property rights regimes. Like democracy, this trait characterizes the economic structure of a state, not of a dyad. The construction of a dyadic indicator of property rights regimes draws on the common strategy employed in the democratic peace literature to build dyadic concepts from state attributes. Employing the weak-link assumption, I assume that the least restrained state in the dyad drives the conflict potential of a dyad (e.g., Dixon 1994). In the democratic peace literature, this means the least democratic state drives the conflict dynamics of a dyad. Its democracy score is used to represent the level of democracy within the dyad. Thus, as the most autocratic state in the dyad introduces liberal political reforms and becomes more democratic, the dyad should engage in fewer military disputes.

The application of this assumption to property rights regimes means that the state possessing the highest PUBLIC score of the two states within the dyad drives the conflict potential of that same dyad. Governments possessing more public property possess fewer constraints from private economic actors on their decisions for conflict. For example, in 1978 the PUBLIC scores for the United States, Egypt, and Israel were 0.07, 0.21, and 0.12, respectively. The utilization of the weak-link assumption means that the dyadic score for the U.S.–Egypt dyad in 1978 is 0.21. The corresponding dyadic score for the Egypt–Israel dyad is also 0.21. The dyadic score for the U.S.–Israel dyad is 0.12.

The theoretical discussion from the previous chapter suggests the following relationships among these three countries: Egypt's higher quantity of public property raises the likelihood that it will initiate a military dispute against either the United States or Israel. Similarly, Egypt's higher quantity of public property raises the likelihood that it will be targeted by either the United States or Israel in a military dispute. If the hypothesis is correct, dyads like either the Egypt–Israel one or the Egypt–U.S. one should have a

[7] The sample of cases was created with version 3.03 of Eugene (Bennett and Stam 2000a).

higher expected probability of conflict than those like the U.S.–Israel dyad based solely on PUBLIC scores.[8]

The following statistical tests utilize the variable $PUBLIC_H$ to assess the role that public property plays in the outbreak of military conflict within the dyad. Because governments might nationalize private assets once engaged in war, I measure $PUBLIC_H$ in the year prior to which military conflict is observed.[9]

The dependent variable, CONFLICT, draws on the militarized interstate dispute data set. It takes on a value of one if a new militarized dispute breaks out between the dyadic partners in a given year. For all other years, it is coded as zero. For example, if the United States and Iran engage in a military dispute in 1979 that lasts until 1981, CONFLICT would only take on a value of one in the first year of the dispute, 1979.

Control Variables

Any relationship between public property and military conflict could be obscured by the presence of some third variable, like autocracy, that causes high values of both public property and conflict. This possibility can be controlled through multivariate regression analysis that incorporates these alternative variables and simultaneously makes it possible to isolate the effects of public property on conflict.

The democratic peace stands out as perhaps the most important argument to control for in any examination of the role that liberal economic institutions play in conflict. Because extensive support has been offered for the proposition that democratic states are less likely to go to war with each other (e.g., Russett and Oneal 2001), I include a variable measuring the level of democracy in the dyad. It draws on the Polity IV data set that creates a democracy and autocracy score for each regime in their sample (Jaggers and Gurr 1995). As is common in the literature, a democracy value for each state is constructed by subtracting the autocracy score from the democracy score of regimes. These scores range from −10 to 10, with higher values indicating a more democratic regime. To move from state to dyadic attributes, I again draw on the weak-link hypothesis asserting that the least domestically

[8] This prediction also includes the caveat that all other predictors of military conflict are held constant for this hypothetical example.

[9] I also conducted statistical tests utilizing nontax revenue divided by GDP (rather than total government revenue) to operationalize PUBLIC. Although this alternative indicator shrinks the sample size a bit because some of the observations for GDP on developing countries are missing, it does not generate any changes in the statistical conclusions.

constrained government drives the conflict potential of the dyad. The variable, $DEMOCRACY_L$, is simply the Polity IV score for the least democratic member of the dyad.[10] Finally, like the variable for public property, I measure this variable for democracy within the dyad in the year prior to the year in which conflict is observed. This measurement decision creates some protection from the possibility that governments restrict political freedoms and limit democratic participation upon entry into a war.

In addition to democracy, liberal peace research has explored whether and how international commerce promotes peace between states. Chapter 1 critiqued this commercial peace literature for its neglect of how the domestic institutions underlying this exchange may condition this peace. To ensure that the capacity of property rights regimes to promote peace is independent of the broader pressures created by international trade, I include the standard variable in the liberal peace literature used to measure the latter concept. $DEPEND_L$ again draws on the weak-link hypothesis. It is the lowest ratio of the following two variables: the bilateral trade (measured as annual imports plus exports) between the two members of the dyad divided by the first state's gross domestic product (GDP); or the bilateral level of trade between the two members divided by the second state's gross domestic product. $DEPEND_L$ is also measured in the year prior to which military conflict is measured.[11] As bilateral trade constitutes a larger portion of the more weakly constrained member's GDP, the likelihood of conflict within that dyad should decrease.

Some variants of commercial liberalism have focused on the constraints created by development levels, rather than trade, on military conflict (Mousseau 2000, 2005; Hegre 2000; Mousseau, Hegre, and O'Neal 2003; Boehmer and Sobek 2005; Gartzke 2007). Such studies focus on how economic development either enhances democratic constraints on war or shapes state interests in military conquest. To ensure that the findings linking the distribution of property rights to conflict are not explained by development levels, I add two variables, $DEVELOP_L$ and $DEVELOP_L^2$, to the baseline regression. The first variable measures the lower development level of the two economies in the dyad. The second variable squares this term. This specification allows the direction of the relationship between

[10] I utilize version 2 of the Polity IV, which converts regime scores previously classified as "interregnum" or "transition" to the 21-point scale. For a discussion of these coding rules see http://www.cidcm.umd.edu/inscr/polity/convert.htm.

[11] The data sources for this variable are Oneal and Russett (1999), version 6.1 of Heston, Summers, and Aten (2002), and the *Direction of Trade Statistics* from the International Monetary Fund (various years).

development and military conflict to change as development levels change. The inclusion of both of these terms makes it possible to examine whether a curvilinear relationship exists between development and military conflict. Boehmer and Sobek (2005) expect that governments possessing both low and extremely high development levels to be the most pacific. At low levels of development, states lack the resource base and capability to project their interests abroad and consequently engage in relatively few military conflicts. As states climb the development ladder, their foreign policies become more militarized before becoming more pacific at high income levels. Imagine that states were categorized into three groups according to income levels: poor, middle income, and wealthy. This model specification tests whether dyads are likely to have more military conflict as the poorest state in the dyad moves from the poor to the middle-income category; and then whether the dyad will be marked by less military conflict as its poorest member moves from the middle to the wealthy category. I utilize per capita gross domestic product to measure development levels for each member of the dyad.[12]

Numerous realist arguments suggest power is a key determinant of national willingness to use force in international politics. I include two variables to control for the multiple mechanisms by which power shapes the outbreak of conflict among states. First, the most powerful states in the international system generally possess the most broadly defined interests and are the most capable of defending those interests. As shown in Table 4.1, great powers on average engage in five times as many annual military disputes as states that are not defined as great powers. I control for this increased propensity toward using military force by incorporating GREAT-POWER – a dummy variable that takes on a value of one when either member of a dyad is defined as great power. This group of great powers includes the United States, Great Britain, France, China, and the Soviet Union/Russia for the entire sample and Germany and Japan from 1991 to 2001.

Second, some variants of realism suggest that substantial power disparities between states reduce the likelihood of military conflict. Weaker states have no incentive to use military force because it is unlikely to be successful. This weakness simultaneously allows powerful states to demand and receive political concessions without using force. I include the variable POWER PREPONDERANCE to control for this possibility. This variable is built from the Correlates of War (COW) Project's Composite Index of National Capability (Singer, Bremer, and Stuckey 1972). The COW project creates

[12] Data for GDP is taken from version 6.1 of the Penn World Tables.

an annual observation measuring the military capability for each country in the international system. This capability score is based on six characteristics: military expenditure, military personnel, energy consumption, iron and steel production, total population, and urban population. An indexed score uses these six components to measure the proportion of military capabilities a state possesses relative to the entire pool of military capabilities for all states in the international system. POWER PREPONDERANCE is the natural log of the ratio of the state possessing the largest capability score divided by the capability score of the weaker state within the dyad. As this score increases, the gap in military capabilities between the two states grows. Under this circumstance, they should be less likely to enter a new military dispute.

Realist and liberal theories alike expect that states possessing common political interests are unlikely to engage in military conflict with each other. I include two variables to control for this possibility. First, common alliance memberships suggest that states possess similar political goals. Consequently, I include the variable, ALLIES, which takes on a value of one if both states are member to the same alliance and zero for all other cases.[13] Second, I include the variable, INTERESTS, which is the weighted global s-score measuring the similarity of two states alliance portfolios (Signorino and Ritter 1999).

I also include control variables for geographic conditions that might contribute to the outbreak of disputes. As states become closer to each other, they are more likely to have territorial disagreements and have more opportunities for interactions that can become conflictual. CONTIGUOUS is a dummy variable indicating whether or not the two states border each other on land or are separated by less than 150 miles by sea. The source of this definition and data is Stinnett et al. (2002). DISTANCE is the natural log of the distance in miles between the capitals of the two states. States that are further apart are likely to have fewer interactions and thus likely to have fewer opportunities to come into conflict.

Estimating the Relationship between Public Property and Conflict

Due to the dichotomous nature of the dependent variable, the baseline regression model employs a standard estimator in the literature–logistic regression. I also incorporate a series of independent variables (SPLINES) that account for the previous history of conflict between the two states in the

[13] For a discussion of some of the problems of using alliance scores as an indicator of political interests see Bearce, Flanagan, and Floros (2006).

dyad (Beck, Katz, and Tucker 1998).[14] The baseline regression thus models the outbreak of military conflict between two states in a dyad as a function of eleven concepts: property rights regimes (PUBLIC_H), democracy ($\text{DEMOCRACY}_\text{L}$), bilateral trade ($\text{DEPEND}_\text{L}$), development ($\text{DEVELOP}_\text{L}$ and $\text{DEVELOP}^2_\text{L}$), great power status (GREAT-POWER), the distribution of power between the two states (POWER PREPONDERANCE), whether or not the two states are allied (ALLIES), the degree of similarity in their political interests (INTERESTS), whether or not they border each other (CONTIGUOUS), the geographic distance between the two states (DISTANCE), and the previous history of conflict in the dyad (SPLINES).[15]

The results for the baseline model are displayed in the first column of Table 4.2. The estimated coefficient for each variable in each model is listed at the top of a cell. The estimated standard error associated with each coefficient is listed below it in parentheses. Two things are important to remember in a preliminary examination of the information in this table. First, the number of asterisks marked next to the coefficient associated with each independent variable indicates the level of confidence associated with that estimation. When two asterisks are present, we can be 95 percent confident (i.e., we will be mistaken only 5 percent of the time) that the value of the coefficient is distinguishable from zero. This confidence allows the rejection of the null hypothesis that the variable under investigation is unrelated to the outbreak of military conflict. This statistical significance means that the variable under investigation has some effect on the likelihood of observing military conflict within the dyad in a given year. If the variable does not have any asterisks associated with it, the estimation does not possess sufficient confidence to reject the null hypothesis. In this situation, we cannot be sure that the variable has any effect on military conflict. Second, the direction of the coefficient indicates how the probability of conflict changes as the independent variable increases in value. If the coefficient on the variable is positive, then the likelihood of military conflict increases as level of that variable increases. If the coefficient is negative, then the likelihood of conflict declines as that independent variable increases in value.

Displayed in the first row of values in Table 4.2, the positive and statistically significant coefficient on PUBLIC_H illustrates that larger quantities

[14] I do not include these coefficient estimates in the tables for reasons of space. This technique includes a counter and cubic splines in each of the models (Beck, Katz, and Tucker 1998). To counter within-panel heteroskedasticity I employ Huber–White standard errors, which are reported in parentheses below the parameter estimates.

[15] Descriptive statistics for the variables in this baseline model can be found in the data appendix at the end of the chapter.

Table 4.2. *Dyadic tests, 1970–2001*

	CONFLICT	CONFLICT (VIOLENT)
$PUBLIC_H$	0.016***	0.020***
	(0.004)	(0.004)
$DEMOCRACY_L$	−0.035***	−0.037**
	(0.013)	(0.016)
$DEPEND_L$	−5.506	−3.818
	(5.382)	(4.600)
POWER-PREPONDERANCE	−0.102*	−0.030
	(0.056)	(0.065)
GREAT-POWER	1.358***	1.057***
	(0.206)	(0.272)
INTERESTS	−1.072***	−0.471
	(0.327)	(0.369)
ALLIES	0.681***	0.601***
	(0.208)	(0.232)
DISTANCE	−0.266***	−0.253***
	(0.088)	(0.093)
CONTIGOUS	2.364***	2.582***
	(0.273)	(0.315)
$DEVELOP_L$	$1.5*10^{-4}$**	$1.1*10^{-4}$
	$(6.8*10^{-5})$	$(7.1*10^{-5})$
$DEVELOP_L^2$	$-1.1*10^{-8}$**	$-7.2*10^{-9}$*
	$(4.7*10^{-9})$	$(4.3*10^{-9})$
CONSTANT	−1.642*	−2.804***
	(0.853)	(0.922)
N	102,052	102,052
Log-Likelihood	−1490.03	−1157.23

Note: Top number in each cell is estimated coefficient. Robust standard errors clustered on dyad listed below in parentheses. Two-tailed estimates are conducted for all estimates. $^{***}p \leq 0.01$; $^{**}p \leq 0.05$; $^{*}p \leq 0.10$. Splines (not shown) added to all models.

of public assets in the least constrained member of the dyad raise the likelihood of military conflict between the two states in any year. Alternatively, as the size of the private sector in the least constrained state increases (and $PUBLIC_H$ declines), the two governments become less likely to engage in military conflict. This test offers important empirical support for the broader claim linking private property to peace. Even while holding a series of well-known causes of military conflict constant, higher public property levels in an economy still independently heighten the risks of military conflict between states.[16]

The other variables in the model generally perform according to standard expectations in the literature.[17] More common political interests (INTERESTS), larger power asymmetries (POWER PREPONDERANCE), and greater geographical distances between two states (DISTANCE) all reduce the likelihood of military conflict within a dyad. The presence of at least one great power (GREAT-POWER) in the dyad and geographic contiguity (CONTIGUOUS) between the two members of a dyad both heighten the likelihood of military conflict within the dyad.

Apart from the variable for international trade, the coefficients on the remaining liberal peace variables are statistically significant and in their hypothesized directions. The negative and statistically significant coefficient on DEMOCRACY_L confirms the presence of democratic peace between states by showing that higher levels of democracy reduce the likelihood of military conflict. The results for the two other potential mechanisms of the commercial peace are mixed. Although negative, the coefficient associated with aggregate levels of international trade (DEPEND_L) is not statistically significant. However, the coefficients on the two terms for economic development are both statistically significant. These results confirm the findings of Boehmer and Sobek (2005) suggesting that middle-income countries are the most violent in the international system.

These regressions that include variables for development levels are particularly important in controlling for an alternative hypothesis often associated with variants of Marxist–Leninist theory. Just as Marx argued that class and the broader position individuals hold relative to the means of production determine the distribution of political power within a society, extensions of this logic characterize the global distribution of power as being driven

[16] I also conducted a series of regressions that utilized slightly adjusted data for PUBLIC. Many of the observations for socialist states and members of OPEC are missing for the period under investigation. Both sets of states tend to have relatively higher quantities of public property than other states in the international system. Consequently, I utilized existing data on PUBLIC to create sample average values for socialist states as identified by Kornai (1992) and members of OPEC. These average values were, respectively, 0.241 for socialist states and 0.361 for members of OPEC. I then included these average values whenever data for PUBLIC were missing and ran the baseline regression again. The number of observations in the sample increased from 102,052 to 114,988. The inclusion of these additional observations generated the same substantive results. The coefficient on PUBLIC_H remains positive and statistically significant.

[17] Contrary to standard expectations in the literature, the coefficient on joint alliance membership (ALLY) is positive and significant. For a discussion of this relationship see Bearce, Flanagan, and Floros (2006).

by the distribution of national wealth between societies. Accordingly, the wealthiest states deploy military force against developing countries to secure access to raw materials and stable markets for their surplus production.[18] While the curvilinear relationship between development and conflict suggests that this hypothesis might characterize the foreign policy of states in their early stages of development, the coefficient on PUBLIC_{H} illustrates that these possibilities do not alter any of the conclusions linking public property to conflict. Even while incorporating variables measuring economic development, large quantities of public property still independently raise the likelihood of military conflict.[19]

The remaining model (displayed in column 2 of Table 4.2) checks the robustness of this result to an alternative coding of the dependent variable – military conflict. In this model, the dependent variable only takes on a value of one (i.e., shows up as conflict being present within the dyad in a given year) when the hostility level in a militarized dispute is greater than or equal to four. Thus, it codes instances in which states use military force or go to war. This regression ensures that the positive relationship between public property levels and military conflict does not depend on the inclusion of a large number of minor military disputes between states. Although the coefficient estimates for dyadic balance of power (POWER PREPONDERANCE) and common political interests (INTERESTS) are no longer statistically significant, the size of the positive relationship between public property levels and military conflict has grown slightly larger. More importantly, these results confirm that high public property levels raise the probability that states will engage in military disputes with high levels of severity.

Having demonstrated that the positive relationship between public property and military conflict is statistically significant across multiple specifications, the final section of this chapter examines the relative magnitude of this relationship. How does the probability of military conflict change as the states within a dyad possess more or less public property? Estimates of these predictions about the likelihood of military conflict are displayed in Table 4.3. The baseline-predicted probability listed at the bottom of the

[18] Similarly, if private ownership of property is associated with economic growth and higher levels of national wealth, then governments overseeing capitalist economies could simply possess more military resources to implement an aggressive foreign policy because they enjoy access to a larger pool of societal resources.

[19] I also ran a regression that used GDP rather than development as a control variable. It yielded results similar to those with the control for development with one exception. While PUBLIC remained positive and significant, the coefficient on GREAT-POWER was insignificant and the coefficient on GDP was positive and significant. A strong correlation (between GDP and GREAT-POWER [0.68]) accounts for this difference.

Table 4.3. *Predicted probabilities of conflict for Model 1, Table 4.2*

	Value of independent variable	Predicted probability of conflict	Change in predicted probability of conflict
$PUBLIC_H$ (+)			
10th percentile	0.088	0.00059	56.1
90th percentile	0.366	0.00093	
$DEMOCRACY_L$ (−)			
10th percentile	−9.0	0.00093	−89.0
90th percentile	9.0	0.00049	
$DEVELOP_L$ (−, +, −)			
10th percentile	787.89	0.00062	48.7
90th percentile	8203.21	0.00093	
POWER PREPONDERANCE (−)			
10th percentile	0.327	0.00085	−31.6
90th percentile	4.070	0.00058	
INTERESTS			
10th percentile	0.357	0.00072	−30.0
90th percentile	0.996	0.00050	
BASELINE		0.00072	

Note: Baseline predicted probability of conflict calculated from baseline model (column 1 of Table 4.2). All continuous variables ($PUBLIC_L$, $DEMOCRACY_L$, $DEPEND_L$, POWER PREPONDERANCE, INTERESTS, DISTANCE, $DEVELOP_L$, $DEVELOP_L^2$, SPLINES) are held constant at respective sample means. All dichotomous variables (GREAT-POWER, ALLIES, CONTIGUOUS) are held constant at respective modes.

table indicates that a dyad has a 0.00072 probability of having a military dispute in a given year when all continuous variables in the baseline regression model possess a value of their sample means and all dichotomous variables possess a value of their sample mode. The first obvious thing to note about this value is its relatively small size. When the unit of analysis is a dyad year, the likelihood of military conflict is much smaller. This provides a stark contrast to statistics presented in Table 4.1 showing that states, on average, enter a new military conflict about once every 2.5 years.[20] Table 4.1 counted

[20] Another reason for this substantial discrepancy between the likelihood of military conflict apart from a shift in the unit of analysis is the manner in which disputes are counted in Tables 4.1 and 4.3. In the state year analysis found in Table 4.1, I count all new military disputes, including multiple disputes in a year. The outbreak of multiple disputes in a year is not captured in the dyadic analysis. Rather the dependent variable only identifies when a new military dispute has occurred in a given year. Thus, dyads in which five new disputes break out are not distinguished from dyads in which only one new dispute has occurred.

a state's participation in military conflict in a given year relative to all states in the international system. This dyadic statistic in Table 4.3 counts a state's participation in military conflict relative to only one other state in the international system in a given year. Despite the infrequency of conflict when examining pairs of states in a given year, it is still possible to estimate how a shift in value for the primary variables in the model alters the likelihood of military conflict.

Table 4.3 examines how the likelihood of conflict changes by moving between low and high values for a given variable.[21] These high and low values are set by the distribution of values within the sample for a given variable. The first group of values examines how the likelihood of conflict changes as the score for PUBLIC moves from 0.088 (10 percent of the cases in the sample are lower than this value) to 0.366 (10 percent of the cases in the sample are higher than this score). These values can be classified as relatively liberal (0.087) and illiberal (0.366) property rights regimes. When the least restrained member of the dyad has a relatively liberal property rights regime (i.e., 8.7 percent of government revenues are derived from public assets), that dyad has a 0.00059 percent chance of engaging in military conflict in a given year. However, when the least restrained member of the dyad has a relatively illiberal property rights regime (i.e., more than 36 percent of the government's revenue is derived from state-owned assets), that dyad has a 0.00093 percent chance of engaging in military conflict in a given year. Given that these likelihoods are so small, we can get a better sense of the relative magnitude of this shift by exploring the percentage change in the likelihood of military conflict. This statistic is displayed in the final column of Table 4.3. Here we see that likelihood of military conflict in a given year increases by over 50 percent when a dyad moves from being composed of two states with relatively liberal property rights regimes (low PUBLIC_H value) to possessing just one state with an illiberal property rights regime (high PUBLIC_H value).

Some additional context for these numbers can be created by associating representative countries with these values. In 1992, the United States, Austria, and Myanmar had PUBLIC scores of 0.079, 0.089, and 0.353, respectively. Holding all other variables constant at their means or modes, these predicted probabilities estimate that the United States and Myanmar (or any other state with a similar PUBLIC score) are approximately 50 percent

[21] Descriptive statistics for the variables in this baseline model and subsequent models in this chapter are displayed in the data appendix at the end of the chapter.

more likely to engage in at least one new military dispute with each other that year than the United States and Austria.

These shifts in the likelihood of military conflict caused by variations in the scope of public property compare relatively favorably with the remaining liberal peace variables in the baseline regression model. The second row of values in Table 4.3 corresponds to shifts in the level of democracy in the dyad. As the least constrained member of the dyad moves from an autocratic regime with a Polity score of −9 to democratic regime with a score of 9, the likelihood of military conflict declines by nearly 90 percent. A movement from extremely low to high development levels heightens the likelihood of a new military dispute by nearly 50 percent. A comparable shift in the balance of political power or the similarity of political interests within the dyad reduces the likelihood of military conflict by approximately 30 percent. In short, the influence of property rights regimes on the outbreak of military conflict within a dyad is both statistically and substantively important.

Economists generally assess the level of capitalism within an economy by the nature of the institutions that underpin its exchange relationships. The predominance of privately held property in an economy stands out as one of the hallmarks of capitalism. Previous chapters have outlined classical arguments linking private ownership to the protection of individual liberty and peace. This section has tested a converse proposition, linking high levels of public property to the increased presence of military conflict between states. Drawing on one of the standard research designs in the liberal peace literature, a series of statistical tests confirmed this hypothesis.

FREE TRADE AND PEACE: AN EMPIRICAL TEST

This section tests whether a second key liberal economic institution, namely the scope of competition within domestic markets, shapes the likelihood of military conflict between states. The scope of government barriers to international commerce is used here to measure the extent to which competitive prices allocate scarce resources in a domestic economy. Larger barriers to trade restrict the entry of foreign goods, decrease the size of domestic markets, and increase the ability of domestic firms to control prices (Varian 1996, pp. 418–19). If a domestic monopoly exists prior to free trade, the elimination of trade barriers enables foreign competitors to erode the market position of the domestic monopolist (Bhagwati 1991, pp. 110–15). In short, as government barriers to trade fall, the extent to which competitive markets allocate resources in the domestic economy should increase. More importantly, the arguments linking market competition to peace suggest that lower barriers to international trade should be correlated with lower likelihoods of military conflict.[22]

This focus on government barriers to international commerce possesses a second virtue relative to most variants of commercial liberalism that focus instead on whether international trade promotes peace. Chapter 3 discussed how trade policy outcomes, namely whether a government adopts free trade or protectionist policies, could be used to measure the relative balance of political power between domestic groups that benefit from access to open global markets and those groups that rely instead on government protection from such competitive pressures to remain profitable.

The theoretical distinction between trade and free trade possesses important empirical implications for the commercial peace literature. By often offering multiple causal mechanisms as the foundation for empirical investigations, studies of trade and peace have often neglected the possibility that its multiple variants each demand separate tests for their validation. This problem is most apparent when comparing classical liberal references to free trade with the sociological or opportunity cost variants. The sociological hypothesis that focuses on the quantity of transnational contacts suggests that all commerce promotes peace. Accordingly, the proper specification of this variable is simply the total trade of a state with either its trading partner or the rest of the world. Variants like the opportunity cost hypothesis that focus on an economy's dependence on trade suggest instead that a measure of trade's role relative to total national income serves as the best indicator for the pacifying effects of commerce. The focus here on free trade and the size of the protected sector in the domestic economy directs attention to the state's ability to shape this commerce through such regulations as tariffs or import quotas. This section draws on the basic dyadic framework introduced in the previous section to test whether protection influences the onset of military conflict between states.

Measuring the Central Concept: Protection

The quality of trade policy indicators has long been a source of controversy in the economic growth literature (e.g., Edwards 1993, 1998; Leamer 1988; Rodrik 1995; Hiscox and Kastner 2002). A number of measures have been suggested, including the ratio of total trade to national product, the ratio of duties to total imports, black market premiums for foreign exchange, subjective evaluations of trade policy orientation, and residuals from models

22 These tests draw on McDonald (2004).

predicting aggregate trade flows. Because states possess a wide variety of instruments – including tariffs, quotas, subsidies, and quality controls – to shape trade flows, measurements that rely on any one of these tools may poorly reflect the aggregate level of regulation.[23] Moreover, protection is often industry specific, complicating efforts to create a measure of protection for an entire economy. Given these problems and the number of trade policy indicators, one recent study notes that "attempts to construct a single indicator of trade orientation may be futile" and suggests that empirical studies of the effects of openness on growth must shift to assessing the robustness of findings across multiple indicators of openness (Edwards 1998, p. 384).

This debate has particular relevance for empirical studies of trade and conflict because of the their reliance on trade intensity ratios, such as imports and exports divided by GDP, to assess commercial integration. While warning of the dangers of relying on any single indicator to assess openness, it also suggests that trade intensity ratios (like trade divided by GDP) may poorly measure political barriers to trade. Leamer (1988, pp. 147–9) notes trade is a function of resource supplies, international prices, technology, tastes, natural barriers to trade, and artificial barriers to trade in traditional small country models. Without controlling for all these sources, high dependence ratios (total trade divided by GDP) may simply reflect dramatically different factor endowments instead of political barriers to trade.

To test whether protection heightens the risk of military conflict, I rely on two indicators of regulatory barriers to trade. The first is the ratio of a country's customs duties to its total imports.[24] This indicator offers a number of conceptual benefits over total trade to GDP ratios. First, the depth of tariff protection provides an indicator of the quantity of free trade in an economy. As tariffs increase, the quantity of free trade should decrease. Fewer goods are likely to enter an economy duty-free as customs revenue comprises a larger share of total imports. Instead of assuming that a strong negative correlation between tariff levels and trade exists, this indicator

[23] Bhagwati (1988) refers to dangers associated with these dynamics as the "law of constant protection." As states reduce tariffs, they may simultaneously substitute alternative restrictions such as nontariff barriers. Therefore, a measure of openness that focused solely on tariffs may be in danger of incorrectly characterizing a reduction in these barriers as a period of increasing openness.

[24] Data from the World Bank Development Indicators (2003) is available from 1970 to 2001. The World Bank defines import duties in the following manner: Import duties comprise all levies collected on goods at the point of entry into the country. They include levies for revenue purposes or import protection, whether on a specific or ad valorem basis, as long as they are restricted to imported products. Data are shown for central government only.

recognizes that there are a number of costs captured in the price of a traded good, including input costs, transportation costs, insurance, foreign exchange contracts, and tariffs, among others.[25] All these costs can affect the price of a traded good and consequently the size of aggregate trade flows. A measure of tariffs provides one means to isolate the component of the total price of a good that reflects government intervention.

Second, as already discussed, protection levels can measure the relative domestic strength of groups within society that benefit or are hurt by free trade. Higher barriers to trade suggest that import-competing sectors have successfully lobbied the state and purchased regulations from the government that redistribute income toward them. However, lower barriers indicate that free-trade lobbies and consumers have been more successful in defeating protectionist interests.

Third, the inclusion of these measures also provides an opportunity to test different hypotheses within commercial liberalism. Bilateral total trade to GDP ratios (labeled DEPEND in the following tables) are normally used to operationalize such concepts as the extent of transnational ties across societies and the relative dependence of an economy on trade. Consequently, these aggregate trade ratios test the opportunity cost and sociological variants of commercial liberalism. The inclusion of measurements for protection levels along with DEPEND in statistical tests allows me to compare the domestic version of commercial liberalism with these alternative explanations commonly presented in the literature.

Despite these advantages, the use of tariffs to measure protection possesses some shortcomings that suggest the need for additional indicators to ensure the robustness of any empirical conclusions. The quantity of import tariffs cannot capture the extent to which states use nontariff barriers to shield noncompetitive domestic producers. Moreover, the imposition of prohibitive tariffs may not be reflected in measures of protection that rely on customs revenue. If large enough, tariffs can eliminate the trading of foreign goods in a domestic economy. A government would then not collect any customs revenue and a measure of protection relying on import duties may then remain unchanged.

[25] Economic historians examining the prewar period of globalization argue that the negative correlation between tariffs and trade did not emerge until the Bretton Woods area. The expansion of trade in the latter part of the nineteenth century was largely the result of technological developments that dramatically reduced transportation costs whereas the current period of globalization has been stimulated by liberal trade policies (O'Rourke and Williamson 1999, p. 29). The implications of this difference across the two eras of globalization will be examined in Chapter 5.

To respond to these potential shortcomings, the following statistical tests also employ a second measure of protection. Leamer (1988) suggests that the residuals from econometric models of trade provide one means to measure protection. By modeling well-accepted covariates of trade such as factor endowments, distance, GDP, and development, unexplained variance can be attributed to political barriers to trade. Hiscox and Kastner (2002) offer a slightly different approach. They utilize a gravity model of trade predicting the size of bilateral trade flows between a pair of states (or dyad), given the GDP of each trading partner and the distance between the economies. They then add to this baseline model a series of dummy variables for each country-year in the sample.[26] Because the gravity model has been used to estimate normal or natural patterns of trade among nations, the coefficients on the country-year variables provide a means to measure country-specific deviations from a baseline free-trade state in a year. This deviation can then estimate the size of all political barriers to trade that a government erects in a year.

They argue that such an approach to measuring protection offers a number of advantages over previous attempts. First, it extends coverage of protection levels both spatially and temporally from existing data sets. Second, by tracing a series of changes in trade policy across a number of countries, they illustrate how their measure responds to the implementation or elimination of tariff and nontariff barriers.[27] Finally, they also demonstrate that their indicator correlates reasonably well with alternative measures of protection, including customs collected as a portion of imports.[28]

The need for employing new measures is underscored by their relatively small correlation with the predominant measurement in the commercial peace literature, total trade over GDP ratios. Hiscox and Kastner report a bivariate correlation between their measure of protection and the trade intensity ratio of −0.21 in a sample of 82 states from 1960 to 1992

[26] Their data set also possesses an alternative specification of the gravity model that includes relative capital and labor ratios between the two countries. The correlation between these two figures is 0.99. I subsequently ran models with each of these specifications. The results did not change so I only reported those with their base specification that included just the income of the exporting country and distance on the right-hand side of the gravity model.

[27] Hiscox and Kastner (2002, pp. 3–4) write, "[o]ur measure differs markedly from the most commonly used indexes of trade restrictions in a variety of important ways and cases. In particular, it does not understate policy openness in economies less predisposed to trade for natural reasons having to do with geography and resource endowments, but it also does not overstate policy openness in countries that favor nontariff forms of protection over tariffs."

[28] They report the bivariate correlation between import duties and the gravity estimation of protection as 0.45 in their sample.

(Hiscox and Kastner 2002, p. 36). In the samples here, the correlations between dyadic measurements of duties and aggregate trade levels divided by GDP (labeled DEPEND_{L}) are relatively small. In the sample using import duties as a measure of protection, the bivariate correlation with total trade to GDP ratios is −0.19. In the sample using the Hiscox/Kastner indicator, the bivariate correlation is −0.14. These low correlations suggest that these different operationalizations are measuring different concepts and again underscore the need to control for protection in tests of the commercial peace.[29]

Multivariate Tests of Protection and Conflict

To test the hypothesis that greater levels of protection increase the probability of interstate conflict, the same statistical approach used in the previous section to examine whether public property heightened the likelihood of military conflict is used here. A variable for protection levels is initially substituted for the public property variable. Subsequent estimations include variables for property rights regime and market competition. The dependent variable remains the same. CONFLICT takes on a value of one when a new militarized interstate dispute occurs in a year between the two states of a dyad. For all other situations, it takes on a value of zero. The dyad year again serves as the unit of analysis. All interstate dyads in the international system provide the spatial domain of cases whereas the temporal domain is a function of how protection is measured. When using data on import duties, the cases span from 1970 to 2001. Data utilizing the Hiscox and Kastner indicator are available from 1960 to 1992.

Protection or openness is operationalized in two ways. Both rely on the weak-link hypothesis, which asserts that the least constrained member of a dyad drives the conflict potential of the dyad. With respect to protection, the government with the highest barriers to trade faces the fewest domestic constraints on its decision to utilize military force to promote national interests. Societal opponents to the income losses stemming from trade interruptions are relatively weaker in this economy than if there were lower barriers. Moreover, larger protected sectors suggest greater societal pressures for broader interests with respect to territory and a larger pool

[29] These indicators for protection also have relatively low correlations with democracy, the other primary liberal peace variable. The bivariate correlation between the World Bank indicator and democracy is −0.34; and the bivariate correlation between the Hiscox and Kastner indicator and democracy is −0.12.

of societal support from which the government can draw if it chooses to pursue aggressive foreign policies.

The first indicator of protection measures the proportion of customs revenue divided by total imports in the state possessing the greater such ratio in the dyad. A similar logic follows for data from Hiscox and Kastner (2002). They present protection scores as deviations from the sample maximum, or free trade, state in their data set – the Netherlands in 1964. Larger values for a state in a year indicate greater deviations in imports from a gravity model prediction and subsequently of more regulatory barriers to imports. For both indicators of protection, $PROTECT_H$ measures the score of the state in the dyad possessing higher barriers to trade. This value is measured in the year prior to which military conflict is measured to account for potential endogeneity effects between conflict and protection. I expect $PROTECT_H$ to be positively related to military conflict between states.

The remaining control variables in the baseline model are the same from the previous section. The baseline regression thus models the outbreak of military conflict between two states in a dyad as a function of eleven concepts: protection levels ($PROTECT_H$) democracy ($DEMOCRACY_L$), bilateral trade ($DEPEND_L$), development ($DEVELOP_L$ and $DEVELOP_L^2$), great power status (GREAT-POWER), the balance of power between the two states (POWERBALANCE), whether or not the two states are allied (ALLIES), the degree of similarity in their political interests (INTERESTS), whether or not they border each other (CONTIGUOUS), the geographic distance between the two states (DISTANCE), and the previous history of conflict in the dyad (SPLINES).[30]

Empirical Results

The statistical results can be seen in Table 4.4. It includes four regressions. The results for the baseline model that utilize import tariffs to measure the extent to which governments subject domestic firms to international competition can be seen in the first column. This coefficient associated with the variable $PROTECT_H$ directly tests the hypothesis linking higher levels of protection to a heightened risk of military conflict between states. The positive and statistically significant coefficient indicates that the likelihood of military conflict between two states in a dyad grows as the protection level of the most regulated economy within the dyad grows. Alternatively, as both governments adopt free-trade policies and expose their domestic

[30] Descriptive statistics for the variables in this baseline model can be found in the data appendix at the end of the chapter.

Table 4.4. *Dyadic tests, 1970–2001*

	CONFLICT	CONFLICT	CONFLICT	CONFLICT
$PROTECT_H$ (tariffs)	0.024***		0.020***	
	(0.007)		(0.007)	
$PROTECT_H$ (gravity)		0.047***		0.041***
		(0.009)		(0.012)
$PUBLIC_H$			0.014***	0.025***
			(0.004)	(0.005)
$DEMOCRACY_L$	−0.046***	−0.027*	−0.036**	−0.028*
	(0.013)	(0.014)	(0.013)	(0.015)
$DEPEND_L$	−2.691	−16.368	−3.415	−21.600
	(5.442)	(18.479)	(5.158)	(20.655)
POWER- PREPONDERANCE	−0.116*	−0.138***	−0.112*	−0.022
	(0.061)	(0.053)	(0.060)	(0.066)
GREAT-POWER	1.408***	1.253***	1.445***	1.073**
	(0.210)	(0.224)	(0.203)	(0.233)
INTERESTS	−1.074**	−1.731***	−0.998**	−1.474**
	(0.359)	(0.363)	(0.352)	(0.486)
ALLIES	0.657**	0.697*	0.684**	0.742***
	(0.205)	(0.248)	(0.207)	(0.263)
DISTANCE	−0.298***	−0.549***	−0.279***	−0.375***
	(0.091)	(0.087)	(0.094)	(0.109)
CONTIGOUS	2.187***	1.685***	2.211***	1.588***
	(0.282)	(0.280)	(0.286)	(0.302)
$DEVELOP_L$	$1.9*10^{-4}$***	$3.1*10^{-4}$***	$1.7*10^{-4}$***	$2.4*10^{-4}$***
	$(7.1*10^{-5})$	$(8.0*10^{-5})$	$(7.0*10^{-5})$	$(7.8*10^{-5})$
$DEVELOP_L^2$	$1.2*10^{-8}$**	$1.6*10^{-8}$***	$1.2*10^{-8}$**	$1.1*10^{-8}$**
	$(5.1*10^{-9})$	$(5.6*10^{-9})$	$(4.9*10^{-9})$	$(4.7*10^{-9})$
CONSTANT	−1.398	0.709	−1.825*	−2.243**
	(0.901)	(0.844)	(0.952)	(1.062)
N	87,708	92,354	85,416	42,547
Log-Likelihood	−1359.06	−1506.79	−1334.85	−758.27

Note: Top number in each cell is estimated coefficient. Robust standard errors clustered on dyad listed below in parentheses. Two-tailed estimates are conducted for all estimates. $^{***}p \leq 0.01$; $^{**}p \leq 0.05$; $^{*}p \leq 0.10$. Splines (not shown) added to all models.

economies to more competition from foreign firms, they become less likely to settle their political disputes with military force. Given the hypothesized role played by protection levels in understanding how societal interests and institutions mediate between the pressures of globalization and foreign policy, these results directly support the domestic version of commercial liberalism presented here. Free trade promotes peace.

These results carry larger implications for the primary argument of this book, linking liberal economic institutions to peace between states. Economists have long argued that the elimination of political barriers to trade, like tariffs on imports, quotas, and subsidies, increases the level of competition within the domestic economy. This greater competition reduces the capacity of both private firms and governments to control the prices at which goods and services are exchanged between individuals and firms. In addition to the predominance of private ownership in an economy, the allocation of scarce resources through the signals of competitive prices stands out as one of the hallmark institutions of capitalist economies. Together with the evidence presented in the previous section, these statistical results confirm that the two key domestic institutions often used to define capitalist economies promote peace between states.

The second model, displayed in the second column of Table 4.4, provides additional support for the claim that free trade promotes peace by utilizing an alternative measurement of political barriers to international trade. As noted in the previous section, tariffs are only one regulatory device by which governments can insulate domestic firms from the pressures of international competition. Since the end of World War II, governments have increasingly relied on nontariff barriers, such as subsidies, quotas, and voluntary export restraints, to protect domestic industry. This regression utilizes this measure of protection derived from Hiscox and Kastner (2002).[31] It generates the same conclusion drawn from the previous regression displayed in column 1 of the table. The positive and statistically significant coefficient on protection levels again indicates that political barriers to trade are correlated with a greater propensity to engage in military conflict. Alternatively, the elimination of trade barriers reduces the likelihood of military conflict. By utilizing this alternative indicator of trade barriers, these results offer an important robustness check confirming the broader claim linking free trade to peace.

[31] The sample generated by using the Hiscox and Kastner indicator differs from the one using tariff barriers in two important respects. First, the gravity sample (column 2) spans from 1960 to 1992 while the tariff sample (column 1) spans from 1970 to 2001. Second, the gravity sample includes more countries that are both more autocratic and poorer. The differences in the variation across the range of key independent variables in the respective samples can be seen in the data appendix at the end of the chapter. The mean democracy score is −1.5 for model 1 and −3.4 for model 2. The mean development score for model 1 is $3,796 and the mean development score for model 2 is $3,178. The fact that protection levels remain positive and statistically significant in both samples demonstrates the robustness of this empirical relationship.

The remaining coefficients in the models perform similarly to the results from the previous section. With the exception of the positive and significant coefficient on ALLIES, the results on the control variables conform to standard expectations. As the democracy score for the more weakly constrained member of the dyad increases, the probability that a new dispute breaks out between the two states decreases. The positive and significant coefficient on contiguity indicates that governments engage in more disputes against states with which they share common borders. This link between geography and conflict is further supported by the negative coefficient on distance. As distance increases, new military disputes are less likely to break out between dyadic partners. The negative sign on POWER PREPONERANCE indicates that larger power disparities between states decrease conflict. Dyads possessing at least one great power engage in more military disputes.

If we turn to the coefficient on DEPEND_{L}, we can compare how the domestic version of commercial liberalism presented here fares relative to more standard explanations in the literature. Because bilateral trade ratios have been used to indicate both mutual trade dependence and the scope of transnational ties across societies, the negative coefficient on DEPEND_{L} offers tentative support for these hypotheses. However, this coefficient does not achieve statistical significance, suggesting that the capacity of trade to promote peace depends instead on the extent to which governments regulate this trade.

Another way to examine the relative role of protection and trade flows in shaping military conflict between states is through the addition of an interaction variable to the baseline equation that multiplies DEPEND_{L} and $\text{PROTECT}_{\text{H}}$. This variable checks the possibility that the respective effect of these variables on the outbreak of military conflict depends on the value of the other variable (Friedrich 1982; Braumoeller 2004). If this is the case, the coefficients and standard errors on DEPEND_{L} are conditioned by the value of $\text{PROTECT}_{\text{H}}$. For example, as suggested by the arguments of Cobden (1868) and Schumpeter (1951 [1919]), larger bilateral trade flows may only limit military conflict between states if they both have relatively low levels of import barriers.

This possibility is explored in Table 4.5. Here I replicate the models from Table 4.4 with one exception.[32] Each model possesses one additional variable, $\text{DEPEND}^{*}_{\text{L}}$ $\text{PROTECT}_{\text{H}}$, which tests for these interaction effects between trade flows and political barriers to trade. In these regressions, the coefficient on DEPEND_{L} illustrates its effect on the probability of a

[32] I also deleted the control variables from Table 4.5 to conserve space.

Table 4.5. *Dyadic tests with trade and tariff interaction term, 1970–2001*

	Conflict	CONFLICT	CONFLICT	CONFLICT
$PROTECT_H$ (tariffs)	0.019**		0.015*	
	(0.008)		(0.008)	
$PROTECT_H$ (gravity)		0.044***		0.039***
		(0.010)		(0.013)
$PUBLIC_H$			0.014***	0.025***
			(0.004)	(0.005)
$DEPEND_L$	−24.483*	−85.369	−24.410*	−49.997
	(14.210)	(63.151)	(13.353)	(56.328)
$DEPEND_L^*$ $PROTECT_H$	3.737**	2.313	3.615*	0.949
	(1.898)	(1.933)	(1.850)	(1.791)
N	87,708	92,354	85,416	42,547
Log-Likelihood	−1356.23	−1505.76	−1332.17	−758.17

Note: Control variables deleted to conserve space. Top number in each cell is estimated coefficient. Robust standard errors clustered on dyad listed below in parentheses. Two-tailed estimates are conducted for all estimates. $^{***}p \leq 0.01$; $^{**}p \leq 0.05$; $^{*}p \leq 0.10$. Splines (not shown) added to all models.

dispute when $PROTECT_H$ equals zero.[33] As shown in the first model, when import tariffs are used to operationalize protection levels, the coefficient on $DEPEND_L$ is negative and statistically significant. Thus, for dyads in which neither government erects any import barriers to trade, larger trade flows reduce the probability of military conflict between two states. However, the positive and significant coefficient on $DEPEND_L^*$ $PROTECT_H$ shows that these negative results will not be maintained for all values of $PROTECT_H$. As the latter reaches higher levels, the tendency of import duties to enhance the likelihood of conflict overcomes the inhibiting role of $DEPEND_L$. In model 1, $DEPEND_L$ only remains negative and significant ($p < 0.10$) until $PROTECT_H$ reaches a value of approximately 1.0. For the current sample, slightly less than 2 percent of the total cases (1,547) meet this condition.

[33] In a standard regression, say $Y = B_0 + B_1X_1 + B_2X_2$, the effects of X_1 and X_2 are estimated, respectively, by the size and the direction of the coefficients, B_1 and B_2. Moreover, the effect of X_1 on Y is independent of the level or value of X_2. This is not the case if a conditional relationship exists between the two variables. This possibility can be examined by adding another variable, X_1X_2, to the regression yielding: $Y = B_0 + B_1X_1 + B_2X_2 + B_3X_1X_2$. Now, the effect of X_2 on Y changes as the level of X_1 changes. We can see this by rearranging terms: $Y = B_0 + B_1X_1 + (B_2 + B_3X_1)X_2$. Now, the effect of X_2 on Y is estimated by the "new" coefficient $B_2 + B_3X_1$. When X_1 equals zero, this effect of X_2 is reduced to the coefficient B_2.

In short, the ability of greater bilateral trade flows to reduce military conflict is largely restricted to dyads in which both governments have essentially eliminated all tariffs.

Moreover, aggregate trade flows do not condition the relationship between protective barriers and military conflict to the same extent. In model 1 of Table 4.5, the coefficient on PROTECT_H is positive and significant. Even when bilateral trade is absent between the two members of a dyad, higher levels of regulatory barriers still increase the likelihood of military conflict. The positive and significant value on $\text{DEPEND}_\text{L}^{*}$ PROTECT_H shows that these effects of protection on conflict only increase as bilateral trade grows. Although the size of the effect of PROTECT_H on conflict changes across values of DEPEND_L, it remains statistically significant for all observed values of DEPEND_L.

The second model of Table 4.5 tests for these interaction effects while using the Hiscox and Kastner indicator for regulatory barriers to trade. As previously illustrated in the baseline regression, the links between aggregate trade flows and peace are again relatively weak. The coefficient on DEPEND_L is negative but never achieves standard levels of statistical significance for any observed values of PROTECT_H. PROTECT_H is positive and statistically significant across all observed values for DEPEND_L.

Table 4.6 examines the substantive implications of the baseline regression results from model 1 of Table 4.4. It displays the predicted probabilities that a new military dispute breaks out between two states in a year given a set of assumptions about the values taken on by all the variables in the model. For the baseline predicted probability of conflict, 0.00078, displayed in the bottom row, all continuous variables are held constant at their respective means and all dichotomous variables are held constant at their respective modes.[34]

Table 4.6 then illustrates how this predicted probability of conflict changes by shifting the value of one variable between low and high scores across the range of possible values it can take in this sample (the 10th and 90th percentiles). These values can be thought of as representing a free-trade and an autarkic economy relative to the rest of the world. The top row of values in Table 4.6 shows how the predicted probability of military conflict changes as both states within the dyad possess relatively few barriers to international trade. It initially sets the level of PROTECT_H to 0.049 – a case in which a government collects taxes on imports totaling 4.9 percent of an economy's

[34] The descriptive statistics for the variables in this baseline regression are displayed in the data appendix.

Table 4.6. *Predicted probabilities of conflict for Model 1, Table 4.4*

	Value of independent variable	Predicted probability of conflict	Change in predicted probability of conflict
$PROTECT_H$ (+)			
10th percentile	0.049	0.00060	67.9
90th percentile	0.269	0.00101	
$DEMOCRACY_L$ (−)			
10th percentile	−9.0	0.00109	−56.3
90th percentile	9.0	0.00048	
$DEVELOP_L$ (−, +, −)			
10th percentile	630.88	0.00060	92.3
90th percentile	8203.21	0.00116	
POWER-PREPONDERANCE (−)			
10th percentile	0.333	0.00094	−35.2
90th percentile	4.081	0.00061	
INTERESTS			
10th percentile	0.358	0.00078	−29.7
90th percentile	0.996	0.00055	
BASELINE		0.00078	

Note: Baseline predicted probability of conflict calculated from baseline model (column 1 of Table 4.2). All continuous variables ($PROTECT_H$, $DEMOCRACY_L$, $DEPEND_L$, POWER PREPONDERANCE, INTERESTS, DISTANCE, $DEVELOP_L$, $DEVELOP^2_L$, SPLINES) are held constant at respective sample means. All dichotomous variables (GREAT-POWER, ALLIES, CONTIGUOUS) are held constant at respective modes.

annual imports. While holding all other variables constant at either their respective means or modes, this protection level predicts that the annual likelihood of military conflict within the dyad will be 0.00060. A shift in this protection value to 0.269 (90th percentile score for the sample) increases the likelihood of military conflict by nearly 70 percent to 0.00101.

The magnitude of these shifting likelihoods of conflict generated by changes in protection levels compares favorably with the remaining liberal peace variables in the model – democracy and aggregate trade levels. A similar shift in $DEMOCRACY_L$ from its 10th percentile (−9) to its 90th percentile (9) decreases the likelihood of conflict by more than 50 percent from 0.00109 to 0.00048. An increase in development levels from extremely low to high levels again increases the likelihood of military conflict.

The tendency of protective trade policies to increase military conflict is both statistically and substantively significant. The change in likelihood of military conflict generated by altering the makeup of a dyad to include a government eschewing the political virtues of economic competition rather than one embracing them is as large as or larger than similar changes in a set of key variables – like geographic distance, democracy, and the balance of power – that have been long linked to the outbreak of war between states.

The final group of statistical results, displayed in the third and fourth columns of Table 4.4, checks whether the conclusions linking free trade to peace depend on excluding a variable for private property. Even if private property and competitive prices are conceptually distinct, do they each independently constrain a government's decision to enter a military conflict? The regressions displayed in the first two columns of Table 4.4 show that trade policy outcomes influence the likelihood of military conflict in a dyad. The final two regressions in Table 4.4 demonstrate that both competitive markets and private property independently reduce military conflict between states. The models in columns 3 and 4 each add the variable for the quantity of public property in an economy utilized in the previous section.

Before turning to these results, it is first important to note that measurements for protection and public property levels are distinct. The bivariate correlation between import tariffs and public property is positive but relatively low (0.12). Although the correlation between these two concepts grows when using the gravity model estimate for protection, it remains relatively low (0.26). In short, we can be confident that these numerical indicators are measuring distinct concepts.

These statistical results are displayed in the third and fourth columns of Table 4.4. The variables for protection levels and public property are both positive and statistically significant in both of these model estimations. Even while controlling for quantities of public property in an economy, more protection from the pressures associated with international market competition raises the likelihood of military conflict. At the same time, higher levels of public property also raise the risk of conflict while controlling for the quantity of free trade in a domestic economy. Private property and free trade both promote peace between states.

CONCLUSION

This chapter has presented the first empirical tests of the broader argument linking liberal economic institutions to peace. The liberal peace literature has predominantly utilized multivariate statistical analysis to identify the correlates of military conflict between pairs of states (dyads) in the post–World War II period. I utilized this basic framework to examine whether variations in property rights regimes and trade policy outcomes influenced the likelihood of military conflict between states. Utilizing thousands of observations across more than thirty years of time and over one hundred countries, this analysis strongly supported the central component hypotheses of this book. First, higher levels of public property heighten the likelihood of military conflict. Alternatively, higher quantities of private ownership in a domestic economy promote opportunities for peaceful interactions between states. Second, lower regulatory barriers to trade reduced the likelihood that states engage in military conflict. Conversely, as governments insulate domestic firms from global markets, they become more likely to deploy military force to promote their national interests.

The next chapter continues this examination of how domestic struggles over commercial policy shape the definition of national interests and the capacity of globalization to promote peace. It extends the present research by examining a period long held out as challenging claims associated with a liberal peace among states, namely the first era of globalization from the middle of the nineteenth century until 1914.

APPENDIX: DATA

Distribution of values for independent variables for baseline dyadic models Model 1, Table 4.2

Variable	Mean	10th	25th	50th	75th	90th
$PUBLIC_H$	0.207	0.086	0.115	0.159	0.250	0.366
$DEMOCRACY_L$	−1.505	−9.0	−7.0	−5.0	6.0	9.0
$DEPEND_L$	7.4×10^{-4}	0.0	0.0	1.2×10^{-5}	2.6×10^{-4}	2.8×10^{-3}
POWER-BALANCE	1.997	0.328	0.816	1.712	2.869	4.076
GREAT-POWER	0.088	0.0	0.0	0.0	0.0	0.0
INTERESTS	0.663	0.357	0.504	0.596	0.955	0.996
ALLIES	0.089	0.0	0.0	0.0	0.0	0.0
DISTANCE	8.283	7.138	7.935	8.501	8.839	9.096
CONTIGUOUS	0.031	0.0	0.0	0.0	0.0	0.0
$DEVELOP_L$	3796.3	787.9	1163.2	2647.1	4645.0	8203.2
$DEVELOP_L^2$	3.0×10^{7}	6.2×10^{5}	1.4×10^{6}	7.0×10^{6}	2.2×10^{7}	6.7×10^{7}

Model 1, Table 4.4

Variable	Mean	10th	25th	50th	75th	90th
$PROTECT_H$ (tariffs)	0.157	0.049	0.091	0.152	0.208	0.269
$DEMOCRACY_L$	−1.505	−9.0	−7.0	−5.0	6.0	9.0
$DEPEND_L$	7.4×10^{-4}	0.0	0.0	9.6×10^{-6}	2.4×10^{-4}	1.2×10^{-3}
POWER-BALANCE	2.006	0.333	0.821	1.730	2.886	4.081
GREAT-POWER	0.088	0.0	0.0	0.0	0.0	0.0
INTERESTS	0.663	0.357	0.509	0.599	0.960	0.996
ALLIES	0.089	0.0	0.0	0.0	0.0	0.0
DISTANCE	8.289	7.165	7.943	8.503	8.847	9.103
CONTIGUOUS	0.031	0.0	0.0	0.0	0.0	0.0
$DEVELOP_L$	3772.1	787.6	1163.2	2578.3	4583.3	8169.7
$DEVELOP^2_L$	3.0×10^{7}	6.2×10^{5}	1.4×10^{6}	7.0×10^{6}	2.1×10^{7}	6.7×10^{7}

Model 2, Table 4.4

Variable	Mean	10th	25th	50th	75th	90th
$PROTECT_H$ (gravity)	36.169	25.800	29.877	35.348	41.802	48.372
$DEMOCRACY_L$	−3.364	−9.0	−8.0	−7.0	1.0	8.0
$DEPEND_L$	6.4×10^{-4}	0.0	0.0	6.8×10^{-6}	2.6×10^{-4}	1.2×10^{-3}
POWER-BALANCE	2.017	0.320	0.793	1.732	2.926	4.069
GREAT-POWER	0.106	0.0	0.0	0.0	0.0	1.0
INTERESTS	0.643	0.326	0.475	0.588	0.914	0.996
ALLIES	0.120	0.0	0.0	0.0	0.0	1.0
DISTANCE	8.265	7.163	7.901	8.491	8.801	9.055
CONTIGUOUS	0.038	0.0	0.0	0.0	0.0	0.0
$DEVELOP_L$	3178.3	845.4	1086.8	2010.8	3762.7	7295.6
$DEVELOP^2_L$	2.2×10^{7}	7.1×10^{5}	1.2×10^{6}	4.0×10^{6}	1.4×10^{7}	5.3×10^{7}

FIVE

Free Trade and Peace in the First Era of Globalization

Dating back to Lenin's intellectually and politically transformative pamphlet *Imperialism*, the fateful summer of 1914 has been used to challenge any connection between capitalism and peace. This challenge has generally centered on the failure of a sustained period of globalization, beginning with the elimination of the Corn Laws in 1846, to prevent the outbreak of World War I. The dramatic war-induced end to this long era of globalization has also been referenced to question the broader foundations of liberal international relations theory, cast doubt on any claim linking trade and peace in the period following World War II, and assert that the contemporary era of globalization possesses an underlying fragility overlooked by those forgetting the lessons of history (Rowe 2005; Ferguson 2005). Those skeptical about the pacific consequences of commerce, such as Realist and Marxist–Leninist scholars, have long relied on this first era of globalization to claim that commerce either heightens military tensions between states or simply has no effect at all on conflict (Lenin 1993[1916]; Waltz 1979; Buzan 1984; Copeland 1996; Ripsman and Blanchard 1996/97; Rowe 1999, 2005; Mearsheimer 2001; Jervis 2002).

Apart from the example of World War I, these criticisms have remained strong for multiple reasons. Few studies systematically examine the links between trade and conflict during this first era of globalization (Mansfield and Pollins 2003, p. 8). The limited data on bilateral trade flows before 1950 have led much of the commercial peace literature to focus on empirical evidence after World War II to validate its claims. When scholars expand their analysis to include cases from the nineteenth century, data across the two periods are aggregated and potential differences between these eras of globalization are obscured.[1] Perhaps more importantly, when faced with

[1] Barbieri (1996), Oneal and Russett (1999), and Russett and Oneal (2001) examine samples between 1870 and 1939. However, all three studies aggregate data before and after World War I into a single sample.

this apparent anomaly between markets and conflict, liberal peace scholars often invoke some alternative set of causes, like the absence of democracy, to explain the outbreak of war rather than revisiting the theoretical foundations of their claims.

This chapter begins a three-pronged response to the conventional wisdom that this earlier era of globalization contradicts claims linking market-based exchange to peace. It utilizes recent research by economic historians to examine how protection levels influenced the likelihood of military conflict across this first era of globalization. Drawing again on multivariate statistical analysis, it shows that the foreign policy effects of free trade were the same in both the nineteenth and twentieth centuries. Free trade promoted peace during both eras of globalization. Chapters 6 and 7 then move beyond examining broad aggregate trends among many states to conduct in-depth analyses of two critical sets of historical relationships in the nineteenth and early twentieth centuries. The evolution of Anglo-American relations in the nineteenth century illustrates how liberal market institutions give rise to powerful domestic pressures for peace. Alternatively, the increasingly inflexible struggle between the Triple Alliance and Triple Entente in the decade before 1914 illustrates how government constraints on capitalism can give rise to war.

The consequences of economic integration on military conflict during this period have remained largely misunderstood because scholars have generally defined globalization according to a rise in trade flows and neglected other factors, like domestic institutions, which shape the quantity and character of this exchange. This oversight has key implications for the first era of globalization. Unlike the trade expansion following World War II that resulted largely from the adoption of more liberal commercial policies, a sustained drop in transportation costs instead drove economic integration in the earlier era (O'Rourke and Williamson 1999). Moreover, in response to this shock of exploding imports, most governments reversed earlier trends of regulatory liberalization by reinstituting wide-ranging tariffs in the decades leading up to the war. Trade – but not necessarily free trade – was on the rise. Declining transportation costs had created a situation in which rising trade flows and rising tariffs could coexist.

A shift in the central theoretical concept, from economic interdependence that has long been the focus of international relations theory to the underlying institutions that regulate the domestic economy, creates the opportunity to cast new light on one of the enduring theoretical puzzles of international relations. This first era of globalization was not the archetypal liberal economic order as has often been suggested by those who characterize globalization according to growing aggregate commercial flows between states. Apart from a rise in tariffs across continental Europe fueled by the grain invasion from the Americas and the interior of Russia, some of the largest economies possessed important capital controls that enabled their governments to control sovereign lending and divert capital toward political allies and away from political enemies. Substantial quantities of public property helped Russia to escape the critical financial crisis, precipitated by arms races on land and at sea in the decade before World War I, faced by all other European governments. Russia's financial strength loomed large in German calculations for war in July of 1914.

Despite these institutional differences between these two eras of globalization, the same pressures linking liberal economic institutions to peace in the twentieth century shaped interstate relations during this first era of globalization. Groups benefiting from free trade lobbied their governments for restrained national interests and cooperative foreign policies that avoided the economic costs of war. Noncompetitive industries pushed their governments to embrace expansionist foreign policies of imperialism that would grant them protected access to raw materials and outlets for their surplus production. Governments drew on their regulatory capacity to carve out secure coalitions of domestic support that then facilitated ambitious strategies of expansion, like Weltpolitik.

This chapter examines the validity of these arguments in two ways. It first challenges the traditional characterization of this first era of globalization as a liberal order. Despite exploding international trade flows, governments still possessed important mechanisms by which they limited the capacity of decentralized markets to allocate resources and influence the behavior of private individuals. Second, it examines the long trends between free trade and peace during this earlier era of globalization. It utilizes a newly constructed data set on tariff levels to test statistically the claim that protection heightened the risk of military conflict before 1914. Consistent with the results presented in Chapter 4, the expansion of free trade, or a reduction in barriers to commerce, decreased the willingness of governments to initiate military conflict during this first era of globalization.

Together these findings lead to two important conclusions. First, this earlier era of globalization does not undermine the foundations of liberal international relations theory as often suggested. Like the current period, free trade promoted peace between states during the nineteenth century. Second, the statistical tests reveal a result that has long been relegated to the footnotes of research on the democratic peace. Higher levels of democracy correlate with greater levels of military conflict before World

War I. These results linking free trade to peace and democracy to conflict during the nineteenth century begin to lay the foundations for another critical argument of this book: liberal economic institutions have historically played a larger role in promoting peace between states than liberal political institutions.

This chapter has two main sections. The first describes many national regulations on commercial activities during this first era of globalization to challenge depictions of it as a liberal economic order. The second presents series of statistical tests showing that the basic predictions of commercial liberalism hold during this first era of globalization – free trade promotes peace.

A LIBERAL ECONOMIC ORDER?

Even though the aggregate quantity of trade flows between states was growing rapidly during the latter half of the nineteenth century, the major combatants in World War I still possessed a variety of means to interrupt flows of goods and capital. As will be discussed in Chapter 7, tariffs and capital controls loomed large in the decade before July 1914 by shaping the fiscal ability of states to fund rearmament and build political coalitions in support of more aggressive foreign policies. The presence of growing international trade flows did not imply free trade and open domestic markets in this era.

Trade

A simple glance at the expansion of nineteenth-century trade flows provides a strong *prima facie* case for the critics of commercial liberalism. Table 5.1 illustrates this growth in terms of export volumes for some of the world's historically largest economies. It utilizes 1913 as a base year for exports. British exports grew by more than a factor of thirty-five between 1820 and 1913. The volume of French exports in 1820 was only a little more than 4 percent of its level in 1913. These dramatic increases remained strong even in the final years before the World War I in July 1914. For example, French, German, and American exports all grew by more than 30 percent in the three-year period before the outbreak of war in July 1914.

More importantly for the commercial peace hypothesis, economic historians now argue that the rapid globalization and integration of national economies that occurred in the nineteenth century were entirely the product of a sharp reduction in transportation costs and were not attributable to a more liberal trading order. O'Rourke and Williamson write, "*all* of the

Table 5.1. *Export volume index for main economies, 1820–1989 (1913 = 100)*

	France	Germany	Italy	U.K.	U.S.
1820	4.31		7.33	2.86	1.31
1830	4.24			4.47	2.13
1840	6.51	4.30		7.38	4.08
1850	10.56	5.90		13.07	4.07
1860	19.55	9.80		22.68	9.61
1870	31.10	17.70	38.70	31.10	13.00
1880	43.50	22.40	51.70	41.20	35.00
1890	53.00	29.80	43.20	55.10	40.40
1900	61.60	44.70	64.40	58.60	72.80
1910	75.10	77.40	91.70	88.00	73.10
1913	100.00	100.00	100.00	100.00	100.00
1920	86.00	36.70	105.50	70.70	141.80
1930	132.00	87.00	104.70	66.70	130.30
1940	40.00	38.50	63.30	41.30	153.60
1950	149.20	34.80	126.50	100.00	224.60
1960	298.40	154.70	366.90	120.00	387.90
1970	678.20	386.60	1265.00	192.00	680.60
1980	1371.20	683.30	2303.00	313.40	1337.60
1989	1900.70	1060.80	3363.50	446.10	1894.10

Source: Maddison (1991).

commodity market integration in the Atlantic economy after the 1860s was due to the fall in transport costs between markets, and *none* was due to more liberal trade policy. In contrast, most of the commodity market integration after the 1950s was (we suspect) due to more liberal trade policy" (1999, p. 29). Two key technological developments in this era were largely responsible for this change. Dramatic railway construction after 1850 integrated national markets and reduced the costs of bringing goods from the interior of a country to coastal regions. The advent of the steam engine also reduced the costs and time of transportation along waterways. The effects of these technological innovations can be seen through changes in the proportion that transportation costs made up in the total price of traded goods. Bairoch (1989, p. 56) estimates that transportation costs of wheat and bar iron comprised 76–82 percent and 89–94 percent, respectively, of the price of these goods in 1830. By 1910, these percentages had been reduced to 25–30 and 27–31 percent, respectively.

These radical changes in the cost of transporting goods led to an explosion in international trade, the erosion of the relative income of scarce factors of production within economies, and the creation of political pressures demanding protection from these shocks (Williamson 1998). One of the largest dislocations occurred in European agriculture as cheap grain from land-abundant economies like Russia and the United States eroded returns accruing to land. These pressures were particularly intense in Germany. Seeing his nation become a net importer of grain, Bismarck reversed earlier trends toward liberalization in 1879 and introduced new tariffs protecting both agriculture and industry. This action then touched off a series of protectionist responses by most other governments in Europe (among large countries, Britain was the exception) and effectively ended the one brief period of trade liberalization in Europe begun with the signing of the Cobden–Chevalier Treaty in 1860. This shift toward protectionism would continue until the outbreak of World War II (Bairoch 1989). Contrary to the conventional wisdom often used to characterize this first era of globalization, free trade was not on the rise during this period. Tariffs actually increased across Europe in the final two decades of the nineteenth century as demands for protection in response to the transportation revolution grew too loud for politicians to ignore. Paul Bairoch (1989, p. 57) notes of this phenomenon, "It can be concluded that the tariff barriers set up during the period of 1880 to 1914 merely replaced the previous natural barriers provided by high transport costs." In short, the ability of states to control international commerce increased as tariffs replaced transportation costs in the price of traded goods.

Apart from sheltering noncompetitive domestic producers, tariffs also constituted a large component of public revenues for some states during this period. Table 5.2 shows the significance of customs revenue to multiple economies during this era and compares these ratios to the current period of globalization. Germany stands out as a prime case of a state dependent on customs revenue. The federal system within the Reich allowed the separate German states to defend their capacity to impose incomes taxes while forcing the federal government to rely on tariffs for funding the largest expenditure of its budget – defense (Ferguson 1994). Moreover, indirect means of taxation, of which customs duties were often the largest component, served as the primary means of generating revenue in the other Great Power continental combatants of World War I: France, Austria–Hungary, and Russia (Ferguson 1998).

Even though governments depended more on tariffs for public revenue in the nineteenth century than today, the decades prior to and after World War I illustrate how the same domestic conflict sparked by globalization fueled similar struggles over the distribution of the burdens of public finance.

Table 5.2. *Customs revenues as a percentage of total central (or federal) government revenue*

	1850–1852	1862–1864	1876–1878	1892–1894	1911–1913	1992[c]
Belgium	10.6	9.6	7.1	7.3	9.3[a]	0.0
France	10.0	7.9	7.3	12.6	15.2	0.0
Germany			42.2	35.8	43.9[a]	0.0
Italy		11.3	12.2	13.0	10.8	0.02
Russia	14.6	9.8	12.4	15.2	10.6	
Spain	12.9	9.7	9.3	18.4	16.7	0.54
The Netherlands	8.8	7.4	5.8	5.1	9.8	0.0
Great Britain	38.8	34.0	25.4	20.3	17.5	0.08
United States	91.5	94.2[b]	49.1	49.0	44.6	1.55
Canada	–	–	71.7	70.1	82.9	2.84

[a] 1910–12.
[b] 1859–61.
[c] Measured as taxes on international trade – includes import duties, export duties, profits of export or import monopolies, exchange profits, and exchange taxes.
Sources: Bairoch (1989, p. 59); World Bank (various years).

This political choice to rely on tariffs for revenue disproportionately placed the burdens of public finance on those portions of society (namely the left) that spent large components of their income on consumption (i.e., food). Thus, the same constituents lobbying for free trade as consumers saw the reduction of tariffs as a device for making the burdens of public finance more democratic. Not only would the elimination of tariffs reduce the costs of consumer goods (and thus increase the political left's real income), it would also force the state to replace this lost revenue via property and income taxes, whose burdens would fall on wealthier segments of the electorate.[2]

Global Financial Markets and Capital Controls

The period prior to World War I also witnessed a dramatic expansion in the flow of capital across national boundaries. As markets opened in the Americas, Australia, Asia, and Africa, European capital from the financial centers of London, Paris, and Berlin quickly sought out these outlets. In terms of foreign investment as a percentage of domestic savings, no Organisation for

[2] The relationship between these distributional struggles over public finance and European relations, particularly among France, Germany, and Britain, are examined in Kent (1989), Stevenson (1996), and Herrmann (1996).

Economic Co-operation and Development (OECD) economy today exports as much capital as did Britain during this period (O'Rourke and Williamson 1999, p. 209). Bordo, Eichengreen, and Irwin (1999) offer similar conclusions when measuring globalization in terms of capital exports as a percentage of gross domestic product (GDP). Strands of liberal theory suggest that capital market integration during this period should also have reduced conflict among states.[3] These arguments claim that private capital holders can penalize governments and force policy changes by moving their assets out of an economy. The widespread exit of capital then threatens growth and broader investor confidence. However, like with trade, aggregate expansion in capital flows tells us little about the state's ability to channel this investment and use it for its own political purposes.

To understand the extent of government's ability to control capital flows during this period, it is first important to note that the financial centers of London, Paris, and Berlin dominated capital markets in this first era of globalization. Staley (1935, p. 9) estimates that more than 80 percent of total global capital exports came from these three sources in 1913. He puts this figure at more than 95 percent in 1900. Perhaps more importantly though, Germany and France, unlike Great Britain, actively intervened and controlled the flow of surplus capital to foreign destinations. They did this largely by regulating the listing of foreign government securities at the Berlin and Paris exchanges. The chancellor in Germany gained his right of interference through two formal means (Laves 1977). The first was exercised through the chancellor's position on the directorate for the Reichsbank. If the chancellor wished to prevent a foreign government from obtaining loans in Germany, he could direct the Reichsbank to stop accepting its bonds as collateral for loans. Dramatically decreasing the value of these securities, financial intermediaries would be discouraged from attempting to place any more of that government's debt in the future with its investors. Bismarck had effectively used this instrument to close German capital markets to Russia in 1887.[4] Second, as the Prime Minister of Prussia, the chancellor could prevent any foreign securities from being listed in that state. Under a stock exchange law introduced in 1896, each state was required to comply with the restrictions imposed on foreign securities in all other states. The

[3] Stein (1993) calls this financial liberalism.

[4] Many have argued that this action played a large role in the origins of the Franco-Russian alliance as the latter was desperate for a foreign loan at the time. Moreover, because British investors were hesitant to invest in Russian securities without an alliance between the governments, this left the Russian government with little choice but France. For examples of these arguments see Viner (1951, pp. 49–85) and Geyer (1987).

chancellor's right of control within Prussia was thereby extended to all other exchanges in Germany.

Through decrees in 1823 and 1873 both the minister of finance and the minister of foreign affairs in France obtained the right to veto any public listing of a foreign government. Although in practice these restrictions could be circumvented by buying securities listed in foreign exchanges such as in Brussels, they generally were not.[5] In a report to the British foreign secretary on the health of the German financial system, F. Oppenheimer agrees, writing, "French finance is always to a certain extent dependent upon the Government of the day because the French Bourse is at the latter's mercy: no issue could there be effected against the wishes of the cabinet" (Gooch and Temperley 1932, Vol. 7, p. 799). Consequently, whenever a foreign government wished to tap the supply of capital in either France or Germany, the official position of the government with respect to the loan had to be included in negotiations.

This veto power was even more significant because government loans made up a large portion of the total capital market activity during this period. For example, Feis (1930, p. 57) estimates that more than half of French foreign investment was made up of loans to foreign governments. Bordo, Eichengreen, and Irwin (1999) note that contractual problems, information asymmetries, and the failure to adopt standard accounting practices led most investors throughout Western Europe to be skeptical of private ventures. As a consequence, holdings of government bonds and railway securities dominated capital exports. The former was often chosen on the basis of political alliances and the latter because of the ease of shareholders in monitoring how their funds were being spent. Investors could more easily evaluate the risk of these investments by verifying the extent of new track construction and the volume of traffic on these lines.

These capital controls enabled the governments to co-opt support from the wealthiest members of their societies in the implementation of foreign policies that tightened alliance blocs, influenced the capacity of other governments to arm for war, and shaped the resolution of key diplomatic crises in the decade before World War I. Bismarck prevented the Russian government from obtaining loans from the pool of German savings, thereby contributing to the Russian political tilt toward France. France seized on Russia's need for capital during the revolution and severe fiscal crisis sparked

[5] Feis (1930, pp. 121–2) writes, "Despite these means of evasion, the powers possessed by the French government were sufficient to make its will effective. Listing on the official Bourse or some direct manifestation of government favor was essential to the success of a large foreign security emission."

by defeat in the Russo-Japanese War. It opened the Paris Bourse by granting formal approval to Russian financing requests in exchange for political support at the Algeciras conference in 1906 (Long 1968). During this same period of Russian weakness, the kaiser also offered access to the German capital market in hopes of reaching a political agreement with Nicholas that would split the Franco-Russian alliance. When the Russians sided with France at Algeciras, the German government forbade its firms to participate in the giant bailout loan of the Russian government in 1906. The German market remained closed to Russian government securities throughout the period leading up to World War I (Viner 1951, p. 56). Austro-Hungarian attempts to gain access to the Paris Bourse were denied three times by the French government in 1909, 1910, and 1911, sometimes at Russia's request (Viner 1951, pp. 64–6). Russia persuaded the French government to open the Paris Bourse to Serbia and help fund its military build-up following the Bosnian annexation crisis in 1908 (Feis 1930, pp. 262–6). Worried about the ability of Russia to launch an effective offensive against Germany, the French government made the construction of strategic railways in Poland a condition for a series of government-backed railroad loans beginning in 1913 (Krumeich 1984; Spring 1988a; Stevenson 1996, pp. 323–6).

These examples cast doubt on the ability of business interests and financiers to direct foreign policies toward compromise and peace.[6] Instead they illustrate how governments relied on capital controls to capture these sectors and steer them into financially supporting policies that would eventually culminate in war. The capacity of globalization to promote peace depends critically on the presence of institutions that lead private actors to respond to market incentives. French and German control over sovereign lending forced capital holders to respond instead to political incentives that simply reinforced the long-standing political conflict on the continent.

This discussion also illustrates the risk of assuming that globalization is necessarily caused by the adoption of free-trade policies. Because growing trade flows can be caused by multiple factors, including relative factor endowments, falling transportation costs, or the elimination of political barriers, observations of such large commercial flows do not necessarily imply that economies are regulated by relatively liberal institutions. Governments still possessed important instruments of economic control despite substantial trade growth prior to World War I. The first era of globalization was not

[6] For a discussion of the argument that financiers tried to prevent a general European war in 1914, and then failed to do so, see Ferguson (1998, pp. 186–97).

as institutionally liberal as is often inferred by those drawing comparisons with the contemporary period. The next section tests the implications of these arguments by examining how protection levels correlated with military conflict during this era of illiberal globalization.

FREE TRADE AND PEACE IN THE NINETEENTH CENTURY?

This section presents a statistical analysis of interstate conflict during the first era of globalization from 1865 to 1914.[7] This starting point is a function of the data used for the key independent variable – tariffs. The primary source, the Williamson tariff data set, provides substantial cross-national coverage for most countries in the international system beginning in 1865 (e.g., Blattman, Clemens, and Williamson 2002). The analysis includes observations up to 1914, given the widespread consensus identifying the outbreak of World War I as the end of this historical period of globalization.

It presents another test of one of the primary hypotheses outlined in Chapter 3: higher levels of protection from international trade increase the likelihood that governments utilize military force to settle their political disputes. The primary research design utilized to test this hypothesis differs slightly from the results presented in Chapter 4. It is a monadic approach that draws on the state year as the unit of analysis. Each observation in the statistical tests represents a state's characteristics for a given year in the sample. Thus the United States in 1890 constitutes one observation. The United States in 1891 makes up another observation. Russia in 1890 constitutes a third observation.

The unit of analysis is altered from the dyad year in previous tests for multiple reasons. First, I initially utilized the dyad year in studies of the relationship between protection and public property on military conflict to facilitate comparison of these findings with the broader body of work on the liberal peace. Most of this research relies on the dyad year as its primary unit of analysis. To ensure that any conclusions did not depend solely on the unit of analysis deployed to test them, I wanted to draw initially on established practices in this literature. Second, data limitations, particularly on bilateral trade flows, in this first era of globalization suggest that a monadic research design poses fewer risks associated with deleting observations when data are not present for all the independent variables contained in the statistical model.

[7] This work draws on collaboration with Kevin Sweeney (McDonald and Sweeney 2007). I thank him for allowing me to include some of this research here.

Although fairly good data for total exports and imports are available for many countries in this first era of globalization, bilateral import and export data are more limited to the largest economies and their respective trading partners. A dyadic research design requires bilateral trade data between both countries in a given year for an observation to be complete and enter the sample. Thus it carries with it the risk of systematically deleting smaller economies from the sample. However, the monadic research design only requires aggregate data on the economic attributes of one state to exist for that country to enter the sample in a given year. Third, this choice to use the state year as the unit of analysis follows directly from my theoretical approach that focuses on how a series of internal struggles over globalization and commercial policy correlate with a government's decision to engage in military conflict in a given year. Although these internal debates can sometimes be shaped by the particular economic characteristics of a single trading partner, they are more often shaped by the larger issue of how deeply the home economy is integrated into the broader global economy. Fourth, I present monadic results here and in future chapters to underscore the breadth of the peace created by liberal economic institutions. Whereas a large part of the research community agrees that the democratic peace is dyadic, namely it is restricted only to interactions among pairs of democratic states, this monadic research design helps illustrate that the liberal economic peace does not possess a similar restriction. Liberal economic institutions generally pacify the foreign policies of governments, irrespective of the internal attributes of the states with which they are interacting.

Measuring Key Variables: Military Conflict and Protection

The primary dependent variable again utilizes data from the most recent version (3.0) of the Militarized Interstate Dispute (MID) project (Ghosn and Palmer 2003). A theoretical focus on how the domestic distributional struggle over globalization shapes the definition of national interests suggests a need to isolate a specific class of military disputes. The theoretical framework presented here focuses on the first stage in a war-generating process in which states first possess some conflict over an issue in dispute and then bargain over the distribution of this issue while trying to avoid the costs associated with war. An operationalization of the dependent variable must then be able to identify situations when states possess national interests that they are willing to promote with military force. This indicator must capture both national interests and the state's participation in military conflict. Bennett and Stam (2000b, p. 658) write, "The indicator that comes closest to a measure of intent in existing data is the COW MID data set's variable that marks 'revisionist' states, defined as those who want to change the status quo." This leads me to focus on military disputes that states engage in while possessing revisionist interests. I define the dependent variable as REVMIDON. It takes on a value of one for each year in which a state enters a new military dispute and is classified as possessing revisionist interests in that dispute.[8] It takes on a value of zero for all other remaining years. As a robustness check, I also conduct separate tests that utilize a government's initiation of a new military dispute as the dependent variable. This variable is labeled MIDINITIATION. It takes on a value of one when a state is identified by the MID project as initiating a new military dispute in a given year.

I measure the annual amount of protection in a given economy with PROTECT.[9] It indicates a state's annual revenue from import tariffs as a percentage of its total imports. Data for this indicator draw on two sources. Utilized in a series of papers on the historical causes and consequences of globalization (e.g., Blattman, Clemens, and Williamson 2002), the Williamson tariff data set includes a sample of thirty-five countries across the nineteenth and twentieth centuries. I draw on tariff data for only twenty-seven of these thirty-five countries to construct the basic measurement of PROTECT. The remaining eight countries are colonies that the Correlates of War project does not define as independent states.[10] When data are missing from Williamson, I augment it by including data from B. R. Mitchell's *International Historical Statistics*.[11] Based on these two data sources, data

[8] In a description of MID data set, Jones, Bremer, and Singer write (1996, p. 178), "We . . . based our indicator of what constitutes a revisionist state on the prevailing status quo ante prior to the onset of any militarized action and recorded as revisionist the state or states that sought to overturn the status quo ante." This explicit coding criterion raises confidence that the definition of national interests occurs prior to the onset of the dispute. Consequently, this variable is particularly appropriate to the theoretical framework here, which focuses on the first stage of a war-generating process in which a domestic struggle over the costs and benefits of globalization shapes the definition of national interests over which states are willing to employ military force to defend.

[9] The measurement for PROTECT is taken in the year t-1, or the year prior to which the presence or absence of military conflict is observed.

[10] The eight deleted colonies from the Williamson data set are: Australia, Burma, Canada, Ceylon, India, Indonesia, New Zealand, and the Philippines.

[11] Mitchell's data allow me to add Belgium, the Netherlands, Switzerland, Romania, and Bulgaria to the sample. These cases account for 168 cases in the baseline model sample of 1,293. Additionally, data from both Williamson and Mitchell (various years) are available for 519 of these 1,293 cases. The bivariate correlation between these two data sources is 0.9851.

for PROTECT were available for thirty-two states in the international system from 1865 to 1914.[12]

Control Variables

The central role of the democratic peace in the liberal peace literature necessitates a control variable in the baseline regression for regime type. DEMOCRACY uses the Polity IV data set to measure the degree of political freedom in a political system (Marshall and Jaggers 2003).[13] DEMOCRACY reflects a state's autocracy score subtracted from its democracy score. This yields the familiar −10 to 10 scale, where a 10 represents pure democracy. I lag this variable, measuring the level of democracy in the time period prior to when the presence of a dispute is coded. Given the nature of this research design, this variable does not control for the typical result in the democratic peace literature, namely that the peace is restricted to pairs of democratic states. Instead, it controls for the monadic claim that democratic states should be less likely to engage in military conflict (e.g., Rummel 1983; Ray 1995; Benoit 1996; MacMillan 2003; Souva and Prins 2006).

The baseline model also includes control variables for the role of power, interests, and geography in the outbreak of conflict. CAPABILITY measures the quantity of material power held by a state in a year. It is the score generated by the Correlates of War project's Composite Index of National Capability (COW CINC). Stronger states are expected to be more likely to engage in militarized disputes as they possess more wide-ranging interests that could lead to conflict with other states in the system. I add a second control variable for this possibility, MAJORPOWER. It is a dummy variable taking on a value of one if the state is a major power according to the COW project. To control for the possibility that hegemony, and in particular close political ties with hegemonic leaders, shapes a state's interests and its willingness to engage in military conflict, AFFINITY is added to the baseline model. It is the weighted global S score for alliance portfolios of a state with the system leader. CONTIGUOUS COUNT counts the number of countries

[12] While annual counts ranged between thirty-three and forty-four during this period, there were on average thirty-nine states in the international system during this period. The following thirty-two states are included in the sample: United States, Cuba, Mexico, Colombia, Peru, Chile, Argentina, Uruguay, Austria–Hungary, Serbia, Greece, Russia, Turkey, Egypt, China, Netherlands, Belgium, Switzerland, Bulgaria, Romania, Brazil, Great Britain, France, Spain, Portugal, Germany, Italy, Sweden, Norway, Denmark, Japan, and Thailand.

[13] I utilize Version 2 of the Polity IV, which converts regime scores previously classified as "interregnum" or "transition" to the 21-point scale. For a discussion of these coding rules see http://www.cidcm.umd.edu/inscr/polity/convert.htm.

Table 5.3. *Monadic statistical tests, 1865–1914*

	REVMIDON	MIDINITIATION
PROTECT	0.025***	0.027***
	(0.009)	(0.009)
DEMOCRACY	0.037**	0.044***
	(0.015)	(0.016)
AFFINITY	−0.269	−0.383
	(0.311)	(0.288)
CAPABILITY	3.501***	3.775***
	(0.904)	(0.821)
MAJORPOWER	0.749**	1.028***
	(0.316)	(0.372)
CONTIGUOUS COUNT	0.006	0.017
	(0.047)	(0.046)
CONSTANT	−1.399***	−1.685***
	(0.337)	(0.280)
N	1,293	1,293
Log-Likelihood	−471.68	−502.03

Note: Top number in each cell is estimated coefficient. Robust standard errors clustered on state listed below in parentheses. Two-tailed estimates are conducted for all estimates. $^{***}p \leq 0.01$; $^{**}p \leq 0.05$; $^{*}p \leq 0.10$. Splines (not shown) added to all models.

a state borders on land. It controls for the possibility that more border partners raise the likelihood for revisionist interests and territorial disputes. CAPABILITY, MAJORPOWER, and AFFINITY were all generated with EUGene Version 3.02 (Bennett and Stam 2000a). CONTIGUITY was coded with the updated COW contiguity data set (Stinnett et al. 2002).

Statistical Results

These monadic results are presented in Table 5.3.[14] The coefficient on PROTECT offers encouraging results for the hypothesis linking protection to military conflict. It is both positive and statistically significant. As the

[14] Due to the dichotomous nature of the dependent variable, I employ a standard statistical technique in the literature – logistic regression with the Beck, Katz, and Tucker (1998) correction for within-panel correlation – to examine how protection levels correlate with a government's decision to engage in military conflict. Although I do not include these coefficient estimates in the tables for reasons of space, this technique includes a counter and cubic splines in each of the models (Beck, Katz, and Tucker 1998). To counter within-panel heteroskedasticity, I employ Huber–White standard errors, which are reported in parentheses below the parameter estimates.

theoretical framework suggested, protection levels raise the likelihood that a state possesses revisionist interests that lead it to engage in a militarized interstate dispute.[15] Conversely, these results also indicate that as governments erect fewer barriers to international commerce, or as the quantity of free trade grows, they are less likely to engage in military disputes. This serves as direct evidence that the first era of globalization reaffirms rather than contradicts the commercial peace hypothesis. By turning to protection levels instead of aggregate trade flows to understand the links between globalization and foreign policy, we see that the adoption of free-trade policies limited revisionist interests that led to the use of military force in the fifty-year period prior to the outbreak of World War I.[16]

The second column offers further confirmation of the broader hypothesis that protection increases a government's proclivity to engage in military force. Here the dependent variable is coded in a slightly different manner. It takes on a value of one when a government initiates a new military dispute. Once again, the coefficient on PROTECT is positive and statistically significant. This coefficient indicates that governments enacting large tariffs to insulate their economies from the forces of international competition in the nineteenth century were more likely to initiate military disputes against other states in the international system than governments that adopted

[15] Endogeneity concerns suggest that the positive relationship between tariffs and conflict in this regression stems from the tendency of governments to increase tariffs once at war. A two-stage estimating framework can be utilized to check for such a possibility. It simultaneously tests for the capacity of protection to increase conflict and conflict to increase protection. I have employed such a test in McDonald and Sweeney (2007). These tests show that military conflict did not increase tariff levels during this first era of globalization. However, higher levels of protection did heighten a state's participation in military conflict.

[16] Largely for reasons of space, I have not presented a series of regression results that include a monadic control for aggregate trade flows. Normally, this concept is measured with an indicator for openness, or an economy's total imports and exports divided by national income. Because data for national income are less readily available during this period, the inclusion of this variable shrunk the number of cases that could be included in the regression from 1,293 to 939. As expected by the arguments of economic historians linking globalization in the nineteenth century to declining transportation costs, the correlation between protection levels and openness was fairly low (-0.155). While this reduced sample imposed costs on the estimates of the remaining coefficients (in terms of smaller coefficients and larger standard errors), these regressions illustrated that these costs of its inclusion outweighed the benefits. While the coefficient on openness was negative, it did not come close to achieving standard levels of statistical significance ($p = 0.688$). Moreover, a log-likelihood test illustrated that the constraint of assuming that the coefficient on openness equaled zero was justified. Consequently, I present here results that did not include this variable in the baseline model. A full discussion of these statistical models can be found in McDonald and Sweeney (2007).

free-trade policies. In short, just as in the twentieth century, free trade promoted peace during this first era of globalization.

The coefficient estimates on the control variables in this first model largely conform to initial expectations with one important exception. Although not achieving standard levels of statistical significance, the negative coefficient on AFFINITY suggests that possessing political interests in line with the hegemon reduces incentives to engage in military conflict. Powerful states in the international system, as indicated by MAJORPOWER or CAPABILITY, are more likely than weaker states to engage in a military dispute in a given year. The coefficient on CONTIGUOUS COUNT is positive but fails to achieve statistical significance. Perhaps most surprising, the coefficient on DEMOCRACY is positive and statistically significant. As the level of political freedom increased in nineteenth-century polities, governments became more likely to possess revisionist interests that led them to engage in military disputes.

This finding that democracy promotes military conflict does not directly contradict the most standard empirical conclusion in the literature, namely that the democratic peace is restricted to pairs of democratic states (or democratic dyads). It carries more implications for the monadic version, which claims that democratic states adopt more peaceful foreign policies toward both democratic and autocratic regimes. At the same time, these results are consistent with some studies that have highlighted the limitations of a democratic peace in the nineteenth century. While arguing that peace among democratic states does not emerge until the post–World War II era, Gowa (1999, p. 65) presents some evidence that dyads possessing two democratic states were more likely to engage in low-level military disputes than all other dyads in the period prior to World War I. Cederman (2001, pp. 22–3) finds evidence for this "initial democratic belligerence" in the nineteenth century and attributes it to colonial competition among the United States, Britain, and France. Moreover, while finding that democracy reduces the likelihood of military disputes from 1886 to 1939, Oneal and Russett (1999) and Russett and Oneal (2001) observe that these pacific effects are weaker in the period before World War I. In a sample of politically relevant dyads, they point to the emergence of a democratic peace around 1896 (2001, p. 114). This date shifts to 1900 when all dyads are included in the sample (1999, p. 24).[17] Russett and Oneal (2001, p. 114) suggest that a widespread expansion of suffrage occurring around the turn

[17] In a series of regressions where the sample was restricted to the observations in a given year, my tests show a positive coefficient on democracy until 1905. In the remaining years before 1914, it is negative in 1906, 1907, 1912, and 1914.

Table 5.4. *Predicted probabilities of conflict, 1865–1914*

Variable (predicted relationship to conflict)	Value of independent variable	Predicted probability of conflict	Percentage change in predicted probability of conflict
PROTECT (+)			
10th percentile	0.030	0.078	91.2
90th percentile	0.325	0.149	
DEMOCRACY (−)			
10th percentile	−9.0	0.077	76.1
90th percentile	8.0	0.135	
CAPABILITY (+)			
10th percentile	0.0014	0.090	49.1
90th percentile	0.1297	0.134	
BASELINE		0.101	

Note: Baseline predicted probability of conflict calculated from baseline model (column 1 of Table 5.3). All continuous variables (PROTECT, DEMOCRACY, CAPABILITY, AFFINITY, CONTIGUOUS COUNT, SPLINES) are held constant at respective sample means. All dichotomous variables (MAJORPOWER) are held constant at respective modes.

of the twentieth century may account for this shift. Democratic regimes of the nineteenth century did not possess as many societal constraints on the use of force given more restricted franchises.[18] In short, while the positive coefficient on democracy directly challenges claims of a possible monadic democratic peace, multiple studies have already acknowledged this discrepancy in the foreign-policy behavior of democracies across the nineteenth and twentieth centuries. I probe the strength of these results along with their broader theoretical implications in Chapter 9.

To get a better sense of the substantive implications of these statistical models, Table 5.4 shows how changes in the value of key independent variables alter the likelihood that a government utilizes military force in a given year. The baseline predicted probability is much larger here than in the dyadic tests presented in the previous conflict. When all continuous variables in the model are held constant at their respective means and the state is not a great power, there is a 10 percent chance of that average government entering a new military dispute in a year. Military conflict is a more common event when using the state year as the unit of analysis.

[18] These suggestions about the foreign-policy implications of limited political participation in nineteenth-century democracies are consistent with the arguments of the selectorate model that focuses on the proportion of society responsible for selecting political leaders (Bueno de Mesquita et al. 1999, 2004).

Turning to the top row of Table 5.4, we can see that tariff levels have a substantial effect on the likelihood that governments entered military conflicts during this first era of globalization. Holding all other variables constant, free-trading states (those whose import tariffs constituted approximately 3 percent of total imports) entered at least one military dispute in slightly less than 8 percent of the country-years under analysis. This predicted probability nearly doubled to 15 percent when assuming that the hypothetical government was relatively more protectionist (import tariffs constituted approximately 33 percent of total imports).

The magnitude of these pacifying effects compare favorably to a key rival liberal peace hypothesis focusing on democracy and a key realist hypothesis focusing on military capabilities. As noted earlier, democratic regimes were actually more likely than autocratic regimes to engage in military conflict before 1914. Governments possessing Polity scores of 8 were more than 75 percent more likely to engage in military disputes than more autocratic regimes possessing Polity scores of −9. Similarly, some of the weakest states in the international system entered in a new dispute in approximately 9 percent of the years under analysis. This predicted probability rose to 13.4 percent for some of the strongest states in the international system.

CONCLUSION

Critics of commercial liberalism have long coupled the nineteenth-century era of globalization with the outbreak of World War I to cast doubt on claims linking commerce and peace. This critique has remained strong partly for its singular focus on the outbreak of this one war and its apparent correlation with a sustained period of international trade. This chapter challenges this conventional wisdom by examining broad trends during the half century prior to 1914 rather than concentrating on the events of that single year in which this period of globalization ended. It draws on earlier arguments to illustrate the costs associated with drawing on misspecified theoretical mechanisms to examine the relationship between globalization and peace. A focus on the domestic distributional implications of international trade rather than its aggregate costs and benefits uncovers important similarities between the two eras of globalization in the nineteenth and twentieth centuries. Free trade, but not aggregate trade flows, promoted peace during both periods. These statistical results strongly support the claim that this first era of globalization does not undermine some of the central tenets of liberal international relations theory as the conventional wisdom often asserts. They also demonstrate the historical breadth of commercial liberalism by extending the link between free trade and peace to include the first era of globalization. Moreover, these statistical results strongly support the second key claim of this book: liberal economic institutions have historically played a larger role in promoting peace than liberal political institutions. During the nineteenth-century era of globalization, free trade promoted peace whereas democracy promoted conflict.

The next two chapters continue challenging conventional wisdoms associated with the liberal peace. They move beyond correlations across thousands of cases to trace the presence and influence of property rights regimes and domestic struggles over commercial policy in critical cases of both peace and war in the nineteenth and early twentieth centuries. Chapter 7 directly confronts the challenge of 1914. Instead of asking why trade failed to stop war, I examine how government restraints on capitalism contributed to its outbreak.

SIX

From Rivalry to Friendship

The nineteenth century witnessed a profound transformation in the political relationship between the existing and aspiring global superpowers of the era, Britain and the United States. It began with American efforts to remain aloof from European balance-of-power politics so that internal democratic reform could be safely consolidated. The Napoleonic Wars challenged this strategy of withdrawal as Britain and France both pressed for American support in their ongoing continental struggle for political supremacy. The United States quickly found itself at war again with its former imperial power.

The end of the War of 1812 failed to create the foundations for a lasting peace between the erstwhile imperial center and its political scion. Outstanding territorial disputes over the Oregon territory, the northeastern boundary that is present-day Maine, and in the Great Lakes region kept the possibility of war lurking throughout the first half of the century. The outbreak of the Civil War tempted Britain to intervene as the Northern embargo of the Southern cotton economy simultaneously endangered the industrial prowess of Britain. A final cathartic dispute over Venezuela in the 1890s, fueled partly by an American willingness to assume the responsibilities associated with the hemispheric supremacy implied by the Monroe Doctrine, ended with a stark and shared realization that war would be ruinous across both sides of the Atlantic. How were these political hazards continually navigated throughout this dynamic century so that the special relationship marked by conciliation, cooperation, and peace that endures today could emerge from one of rivalry, war, and economic competition?

This chapter uses the claims made here linking liberal economic institutions and peace to revisit this critical historical question. It replaces the quantitative approach of the previous chapters with evidence from archives and the secondary historical record to trace the mechanisms by which domestic struggles over commercial policy shaped the resolution of two critical disputes that nearly descended into war. Internal cleavages over globalization shaped political struggles in both Great Britain and the United States to define national interests with respect to disputed territory in Oregon and Venezuela. The resolution of these domestic conflicts in favor of free-trading interests facilitated peaceful compromise between the United States and Great Britain.

These arguments challenge predominant claims in two sets of debates important to both political scientists and historians. Political scientists (Rock 1989, 1997; Owen 1994, 1997a, b; Layne 1994; Way 1998; Blank 2000; Kirshner 2007) have examined nineteenth-century Anglo-American relations within the broader theoretical debate over the veracity and causes of a liberal peace among states. Skeptics and proponents alike find ammunition for their relative positions. Layne and Rock point to the extreme power imbalances and broader geostrategic interests as shaping the outcomes of these conflicts. Owen and Way attribute peaceful compromise to liberal causes, namely democracy and trade. Instead, I show how normal democratic process and protectionist demands for territorial expansion in the United States helped stoke conflict with Britain. These pressures for war were quelled by the triumph of interests trumpeting free trade and open financial markets. Pushed by his free-trading treasury secretary, Robert Walker, President Polk abandoned significant components of his own Democratic Party demanding all of the Oregon territory when the escalation of the dispute in 1846 threatened to derail his larger goal of tariff reform. Similarly, President Cleveland in 1895 buckled to Republican and Populist pressures demanding a more assertive line against Britain only until the Venezuelan crisis threatened his preeminent economic goal – keeping the United States on the gold standard.

The internal struggles between protectionists and free traders in the United States, particularly in the dispute over Venezuela, carry important implications for historical arguments linking capitalist development to American expansion at the end of the nineteenth century (Williams 1959; LaFeber 1998[1963]). While agreeing with one component of this debate, namely the importance of economic interests in shaping the evolution of the larger political conflict between Great Britain and the United States, I show how the relative need for state support to remain economically competitive shaped interests inside the United States for either compromise or conflict. Mercantilist, not capitalist, interests demanding tariffs or its monetary substitute, currency devaluation (Frieden 1997), advocated territorial expansion and willingly countenanced military conflict with Great Britain in support of these economic goals.

These arguments are explored in four sections. An introductory section briefly outlines the empirical expectations drawn from the theoretical framework constructed in Chapter 3 and discusses the rationale behind the use of these cases to study some of the mechanisms by which liberal economic institutions promote peace. The second and third sections analyze how internal political struggles over commercial policy in both countries played a critical role in the resolution of the conflicts over Oregon and Venezuela. A final section examines the implications of these findings for the liberal peace debate.

ANGLO-AMERICAN RELATIONS, METHODS, AND THE LIBERAL PEACE

Although extremely valuable for their capacity to identify broad patterns across time and across thousands of cases, the statistical tests found in Chapters 4 and 5 confirmed only two implications of the multiple arguments linking liberal economic institutions to peace. Highly restrictive commercial policies are correlated with the outbreak of military conflict; and large quantities of public property heighten the risks of military conflict. The hypothesis linking free trade to peace, however, was built from multiple secondary claims that generate additional observable implications that are often difficult to identify with statistical analysis. This chapter begins the task of evaluating these subsidiary claims by confirming whether the hypothesized causal mechanisms actually operated to prevent military conflict in specific historical instances.

These mechanisms focus on three sets of actors – the beneficiaries of globalization, the losers from globalization, and the state. Groups that benefit from open global markets, like consumers and internationally competitive firms, should lobby their public officials for open commercial policies, restrained territorial claims, and peace. When a political dispute between governments threatens to provoke open military conflict, the economic interests of these domestic actors should lead them to oppose publicly policies and government maneuvers that heighten the risk of war. In the midst of these crises over Oregon and Venezuela, such groups – such as cotton growers from the South – should lobby political officials to avert war or publicly voice their support for peaceful compromise. Congressional officials who represent such interests should oppose presidential maneuvers or legislative initiatives that hinder political compromise with Britain. Alternatively, groups that rely on government intervention in markets, like northeastern industrial interests dependent on tariff protection, should lobby instead for territorial annexation and aggressive foreign policies that heighten the risk of war. Finally, it must be recognized that governments do not always play a neutral role in this struggle within society over globalization. Economic regulation can be used to construct stable domestic coalitions of support necessary to implement aggressive foreign policies that include territorial expansion. Alternatively, politicians who have built stable bases of domestic support by embracing free trade should be more likely to embrace restrained national interests. In summary, the outcome of this domestic struggle among these three groups plays a critical role in the eventual decision over whether to escalate or peacefully settle international political disputes.

The Oregon and Venezuela cases provide unique opportunities to examine the veracity of these claims within the confines of existing debates over the liberal peace and American grand strategy. First, as noted earlier, liberal peace research by multiple scholars has already drawn heavily on the American and British cases in the nineteenth century to examine whether democracy and commerce promote peace. A reexamination of the disputes over Oregon and Venezuela in light of the arguments presented here facilitates theoretical comparison with existing explanations for a liberal peace between states. A concentration on the presence or absence of democracy has led political scientists to minimize the importance of key economic factors over the course of both conflicts.

These cases also facilitate a comparison of the relative role played by political and economic institutions in the outbreak of war and peace among states. Although some liberal peace scholars (e.g., Russett and Oneal 2001) hold that these constraints reinforce each other in a virtuous circle, others (e.g., Weede 1995; Mousseau 2000; Gartzke, Li, and Boehmer 2001; Gartzke 2007) suggest instead that market-based constraints are more effective institutions for preserving peace than democracy. A study of diplomatic relations between two nineteenth-century democracies possessing substantial commercial ties offers an important opportunity to compare directly whether these sources of a liberal peace are competing or complementary.

Second, these cases allow me to check whether the invisible hand of peace has operated across both modern eras of globalization. Skeptics of commercial liberalism often use the case of World War I to cast doubt on the capacity of trade to promote peace across the entire nineteenth century or to suggest that the current era of globalization could suffer a similar fate (Ferguson 2005). Although the connections between globalization and the origins of World War I will be explored more in Chapter 7, a study of

Anglo-American relations here facilitates the evaluation of such criticisms outside the single case often used to substantiate them.

Third, as noted in this chapter's introduction, the Anglo-American march toward peace presents an important theoretical puzzle for realist propositions arguing that transitions of global influence between great powers often end in war (Gilpin 1981). How were these two countries able to avoid the hot and cold wars associated with French, German, and Soviet bids for military hegemony across the past two centuries? An answer to this question also carries important contemporary policy implications as scholars and commentators alike look to historical shifts in the distribution of power among great powers for clues as to whether Chinese and American relations will progress peacefully over the coming decades (Goldstein 2005; Shirk 2007). Although a realist perspective focusing on potential military threats may warn of a growing resemblance between contemporary Sino-American relations and the Anglo-German rivalry in the decades before World War I, the arguments here suggest that this contemporary relationship rooted strongly in complementary economic interests may instead resemble the Anglo-American rivalry throughout the nineteenth century.

Fourth, the Venezuelan case has been used by historians to suggest that capitalism played a central role in the transition of the United States from a continental to a global power. Along these lines, capitalism has fueled American territorial aggrandizement and war rather than peace. This reexamination in light of the arguments presented here addresses directly the broader debate about how capitalism influences the foreign policy of states.

Fifth, these cases are important and worthy of intensive study because debates over the liberal peace in American universities are intimately connected to discussions about the character of American foreign policy. Scholarly claims that democracies tend not to go to war with each other have been used by presidents to justify American promotion of elections abroad. Have these constraints historically operated in the state whose recent grand strategy seems centered on reaffirming a central role for liberal institutions in the peaceful conduct of international affairs? What lessons does the domestic conflict over American grand strategy in the nineteenth century carry for today?

THE OREGON DISPUTE

Following the War of 1812, the United States still possessed multiple outstanding disputes with Great Britain in North America.[1] Along the Great

[1] This summary section draws heavily on Merk (1967), Pletcher (1973), and Dykstra (1999).

Lakes region, the threat of Americans fomenting rebellion in Canada reduced the willingness of British politicians to compromise on the northeastern boundary dispute in Maine. They worried that concessions could embolden resistance to imperial rule in Canada. A brief Aroostook War was fought in 1838 as a militia organized in Maine ejected lumberjacks from Canada operating in this disputed territory. In the northwest, both countries possessed rival claims to the Oregon territory.

Great Britain and the United States attempted multiple times between 1818 and 1846 to negotiate a final division of the Oregon territory.[2] In 1818, the two countries agreed to establish a ten-year period of a joint occupation of the disputed territory. Attempts to construct a final division of the territory failed in negotiations from 1825 to 1827 and the two sides agreed to an indefinite period of joint occupation in which either party needed to give a year's notice if they intended to withdraw from this agreement.

Anxious to improve relations with the United States, Robert Peel, the prime minister of the British government, and his foreign secretary, Lord Aberdeen, appointed Lord Ashburton to conduct negotiations with Daniel Webster in 1842 to settle their outstanding disputes in North America with the United States. While these negotiations settled the northeastern boundary dispute over Maine, they failed to reach a compromise over Oregon. The United States was willing to partition the territory, including Vancouver Island, at the 49th parallel. The British were only willing to accept this boundary from the Rocky Mountains to the Columbia River. Anxious to preserve a water outlet for the Hudson Bay Company's operations south of the 49th parallel, they insisted on using the Columbia River as the southern border for their territorial claims. This disputed territory made up much of present-day Washington State.

The dispute rose in intensity with the ascendancy of James K. Polk to the presidency in the United States. The political wrangling associated with Polk's surprise nomination at the Democratic National Convention held in May of 1844 in Baltimore committed him to expansive claims over Oregon.[3]

[2] Both countries dated their claims back to explorations conducted in the eighteenth century. John Jacob Astor had established an American settlement for fur trading at the mouth of the Columbia River in 1811. The Hudson Bay Company also managed a substantial fur trading business in this territory, although their operations increasingly occurred north of the Columbia River in the 1840s.

[3] This section draws heavily on Paul (1951) for a discussion of the events leading up to the convention and the political maneuvers there that led to Polk's nomination. Before this meeting, state nominating conventions around the country pledged a majority of votes to the presumptive nominee and Andrew Jackson's choice, Martin Van Buren. However, the debate over the annexation of Texas changed these expectations by inserting questions of

Party leaders constructed a platform supporting the annexation of Texas and Oregon to unify the southern and western factions of the party and ease some of the rancor that had gripped the convention. When Polk arrived in office, his role as party leader committed him to adopting this expansionist policy on Oregon. Polk affirmed these commitments in two key public addresses – his inaugural address and his annual message to Congress in December of 1845.

A growing rhetoric for expansion and war in the United States, particularly from western senators demanding all of the disputed territory, placed Peel and Aberdeen in an awkward position. While they desired stronger relations with the United States, public perceptions of weakness created by being too conciliatory to the inflammatory posturing of the United States could undermine the effectiveness of their own government. Lord Palmerston, the foreign secretary in the previous Melbourne government and the likely replacement for Aberdeen if a Whig government returned to power, had sharply criticized the extent of British concessions in the Webster–Ashburton negotiations. As a way out of this impasse, Aberdeen and Peel preferred to resolve the dispute through arbitration. This could allow them to abdicate responsibility for substantial concessions if an arbitrator insisted upon them. In the final offers of arbitration in December of 1845, the British representative in Washington, Richard Pakenham, had even signaled that his government would not oppose an award of the entire disputed territory if an arbitrator chose to do so.

Polk, however, continually refused arbitration on two grounds. First, given that arbitrators were often European monarchs, he felt that any arbitrator's ties to the British throne would prevent an impartial settlement of the dispute. Second, he feared that an acceptance of arbitration was tantamount to an explicit recognition of British claims to at least some part of the territory. Taking such a position would have put him at odds with

slavery and sectional differences into internal party conflicts that had been temporarily swept aside by the powerful personality of Jackson. Southern Democrats long hostile to Van Buren and desirous of extending slavery to Texas used swelling public interest to force Van Buren to pledge his support for their project or be stripped of the nomination. Knowing that it would throw his political future into doubt, Van Buren announced his opposition to annexation three weeks before the convention. This announcement created a new internal struggle with such figures as John Calhoun, James Buchanan, Lewis Cass, and Richard Johnson challenging Van Buren for the nomination. Over the first two days of the convention, seven ballots failed to secure the nomination of a candidate capable of finding support from two-thirds of the nominating delegates. Seeing that his enemies had the strength to continue blocking Van Buren's nomination, George Bancroft helped broker a compromise that allowed Polk to emerge as the nominee the next day on the ninth ballot.

many members of his Democratic Party who argued that the United States possessed a righteous claim to the entire disputed territory up to 54°40′.

By early January of 1846, continual American rejections of arbitration along with what appeared to be increasing public support for the entire territory led Aberdeen and Peel to decide that a change in negotiating tactics was necessary. Aberdeen alerted the American representative in London, Louis McLane, that Britain would be increasing defenses in Canada and moving portions of its navy to North America.[4]

Throughout the crisis, Polk had sought to adopt a strong bargaining position in the hope of extracting concessions from Britain. This shift in the British position along with an emerging sectional conflict within the Democratic Party increased his urgency to resolve the conflict. His annual address in December had asked Congress to prepare a resolution giving Britain notice of American intention to abrogate the joint occupation of the territory. For the next four months, Congress debated the terms of this notice. While western senators wanted to include an American claim for the entire territory in the notification, southern and northeastern senators blocked these resolutions fearing that a bold congressional message would heighten the prospects for war. Instead, they wanted the resolution to include some statement indicating an American intent to settle the disagreement on peaceful terms.

As the debate in the Senate in March and April wore on, Polk eventually signaled his willingness to compromise with the British. Informal communications among business officials, diplomats, and members of the American cabinet and the British government had led both Polk and Aberdeen to believe that a compromise could be reached by dividing the territory along the 49th parallel up to Puget Sound and then granting Britain all of Vancouver Island. Polk was unwilling to grant free navigation to the British on the Columbia River in perpetuity but was willing to grant it for some transition period. Once Polk had expressed to legislators his willingness to compromise, a resolution announcing American abrogation of the treaty of 1827 passed both houses of Congress.[5] When news of this notice reached Britain, Aberdeen and McLane quickly constructed an agreement dividing the territory along the 49th parallel and granting Vancouver Island to the British. After receiving a British proposal for these terms in June, Polk submitted it to the Senate where it passed. News of the American acceptance

4 Aberdeen to Pakenham, February 3, 1846, Aberdeen Papers 43123.

5 Western annexationists realized that Polk was abandoning their interests and the proponents of peace stopped blocking the resolution knowing that a compromise averting war was nearly at hand.

of this treaty reached Britain on the same weekend that Peel's conservative ministry fell from power after repealing the Corn Laws.

American Interests in Oregon

Similar to other great policy debates in the United States in the nineteenth century, domestic political divisions over the Oregon territory broke down along sectional lines. Much of the Democratic Party had adopted broad annexationist goals in response to the economic depression of the late 1830s.[6] Western Democrats were the most belligerent with respect to Oregon. From 1842 until 1844, western senators – like Lewis Linn (MO), Edward Hannegan (IN), and Thomas Hart Benton (MO) – stepped up the pressure on President Tyler to defend American claims to all of the disputed territory up to 54°40′, which includes a sizable portion of present-day British Columbia. As trade opportunities began to open in Asia, these expansionists in the United States saw Oregon as the commercial link between the Pacific and the continental United States. Missionaries and settlers had already begun a steady migration to the territory. The prospect of free land offered relief for agricultural interests facing a recession-inspired period of declining prices from 1839 until 1842. Furthermore, these senators were concerned that the British might be tempted to annex California if they could occupy the entire Oregon territory.

Although generally supportive of annexation, particularly in the case of Texas, southern Democrats adopted a more moderate position on Oregon. Led by John Calhoun and his policy of "masterly inactivity," they argued that rapid migration of American settlers to the territory was altering the local political situation on the ground. The United States could afford to avoid provoking Great Britain. Once American settlers possessed the numerical strength in the territory to revise local institutions, they could then freely join the United States. This preference for patience was also shaped by strong commercial links with Great Britain. Southern politicians hated to risk the loss of cotton's primary export market in a war over Oregon.

Focused on the internal consolidation of federal power, the Whig Party opposed the annexation of new territories. One of its key constituencies, the merchant classes of the Northeast, had long developed a political affinity for Great Britain and its institutions. These groups favored a peaceful compromise in the dispute. Worried about the commercial losses associated with

[6] The discussion in this paragraph relies on Hietala (1985).

war, they continually sought to block efforts by northwestern Democrats to push through legislation – for the establishment of local governments or frontier protections – in the disputed territories that could worsen relations with the British.

The domestic battle among these contending groups grew more intense following the president's annual address in December 1845. Attempting to negotiate a settlement over Oregon, Polk asked Congress to pass a resolution giving Great Britain the one-year notice that the United States was required to terminate the joint occupation of the disputed Oregon treaty. He hoped that Congress would simply agree quickly on any form of notice.[7] Instead, this hope was thwarted as the debate dragged on for four months. While testing the patience of Aberdeen and Peel and thus raising the risk of war, this debate also revealed a growing split within the Democratic Party that threatened to undermine Polk's larger political agenda, which also included substantial tariff reform. Competing factions within Congress saw the notice not as an intermediate step toward the president's successful conclusion of negotiations but instead as a device to tie Polk's hands in favor of either a conciliatory solution or a maximalist resolution supporting American claims to all the disputed Oregon territory.

Reminding Polk of the Democratic Party platform he had committed to fulfilling at Baltimore in the summer of 1844, western senators like Cass from Michigan and Hannegan from Illinois sought a bold statement of American intent to possess all of the disputed territory. These senators pushed for maximum territorial claims while fully aware that they heightened the risk of war with Great Britain.

An alliance between northeastern and southern commercial interests played a critical role in blocking the adoption of aggressive resolutions favored by western senators and thus preventing the further deterioration of relations between the two countries. Their desire for peace and an amicable agreement was strongly driven by economic interests. The most vocal advocate for peaceful merchant interests from the Northeast was Senator Daniel Webster from Massachusetts.[8] Webster disagreed with Polk's request for any notification of termination. Instead, he preferred delay so as to prevent the notification from including any proclamation of American claims to the entire Oregon territory.

[7] During March and April, his periods of highest anxiety over Oregon, Polk (Polk and Quaife 1970) fretted in his diary that the crisis could have been amicably settled long ago if Congress had only acted quickly to give notice.

[8] Some of his fellow Whigs felt that Webster was too heavily influenced by financial circles on Wall Street and simultaneously risked the party's interests by siding so strongly with Calhoun (Sellers 1966, p. 364).

Polk's annual address in December 1845 expressing clear title to Oregon and referencing the Monroe Doctrine had worried commercial and financial circles on the East Coast.[9] Apart from pressuring Webster to block attempts by western senators to force through a belligerent resolution, these economic groups also sought out the support of Senator Calhoun to help prevent the United States from falling into war with Great Britain (Sellers 1966, p. 357). A long-time supporter of free trade, Calhoun also worried that the execution of Polk's recommendations on Oregon would mean war with Britain (Sellers 1966, p. 363). Recognizing the pacific preferences of the Whigs, the British identified Calhoun and his faction as the key to a peaceful resolution of the Oregon controversy.[10] If Calhoun could generate sufficient support from Southerners and then combine this faction with northern Whigs, together they could block any congressional attempt to force Polk into adopting a more belligerent policy. Calhoun held regular meetings with the British representative, Pakenham, apprising him of the progress of the Senate debates. While arguing that the United States could afford to be patient until American settlers had fully occupied much of Oregon, Calhoun also worried that delay of the settlement combined with the threat of war was imposing severe costs on the American economy (Sellers 1966, p. 389). Perhaps most importantly, many southern Democrats had planned on fulfilling their bargain struck with western Democrats at Baltimore to support annexation of the entire Oregon territory in exchange for western support for annexation of Texas until Calhoun changed their minds (Sellers 1966, p. 371).

Walker, Polk, and American Moderation of Its Territorial Claims

The capacity of southern politicians favoring both free trade and peace to facilitate accommodation with Great Britain is perhaps best reflected by Polk's treasury secretary, Robert Walker. His policy preferences and arguments show how economic interests supporting free trade tempered the demand for territorial annexation among southern interests. The crisis over Oregon created a real policy dilemma for Polk and his closest advisor, Walker. By the spring of 1846, they both came to believe that the goals of tariff reform and securing the entire disputed Oregon territory had become mutually exclusive. When forced to choose, Walker pushed Polk to pursue tariff

[9] Pakenham wrote to Aberdeen on December 13, 1845, that the address "disclosed so completely the animus with which the government of the United States approached negotiations." He also noted that the combination of Polk's message and news from Britain of new defense construction created a fall in the stock market. FO 5/430.

[10] Pakenham to Aberdeen, December 13, 1845 FO 5/430. See also Everett to Aberdeen, January 28, 1846, Aberdeen Papers, 43123.

reform and territorial compromise with Britain. The prospective benefits of free trade would push them both to opt for peace.

Previously a senator from Mississippi, Walker had long been an ardent supporter of territorial annexation. He played a critical role in securing support from most northern Democrats for the annexation of Texas and the extension of slavery to the new territory.[11] During this campaign, Walker published a widely circulated letter extolling the virtues of the annexation of Texas. Texas offered new market opportunities for the industrial North and more territory to the slaveholding South. Fearing British market penetration into Texas and its promotion of abolition, Walker's arguments also displayed a strong opposition to growing British influence in North America (Pletcher 1973, p. 140). When Martin Van Buren, the likely Democratic nominee in 1844, publicly declared his opposition to the annexation of Texas, Walker helped first to block his presidential nomination at the Democratic Convention in 1844 and then to secure the nomination of Polk. Perhaps most importantly for the dispute with Oregon, Walker helped to unify the northern and southern sections of the party by authoring a pro-annexationist platform that committed Polk to annexing Texas and reoccupying Oregon.

Along with supporting American territorial aggrandizement, Walker ardently opposed protection. His annual Treasury report of 1845 offers multiple arguments favoring tariff reductions (Walker, R. 1893[1845]). His attack on protectionist tariffs reflected the economic interests of the beneficiaries of free trade, like merchants, agriculture, and consumers. These critiques centered on the consequences of protection on domestic economic equality. Tariffs redistributed income in the United States to the benefit of only a few manufactures. He wrote, "The present tariff is unjust and unequal . . . It distributes in favor of manufactures, and against agriculture . . . and against the merchant . . . and against the ship-building and navigating interest . . . It discriminates in favor of the rich, and against the poor, by high duties upon nearly all the necessaries of life (Walker 1893[1845], p. 8). By increasing the prices of consumption goods, most of the revenues derived from tariffs were paid not to the treasury but to the protected classes (Walker 1893[1845], p. 9). Apart from diverting revenues to the already

[11] Walker argued that the extension of slavery to Texas would disperse the population of slaves and freed slaves in the United States and prevent their migration north into free states. For these claims see Hietala (1985, pp. 26–40). Paul (1951) casts Walker as the political mastermind behind the annexation of Texas jointly working with Tyler and members of his party to ensure that the nominating convention of 1844 produced a candidate supporting his policy. Walker also held strong personal economic interests at stake in Texas as he had engaged in considerable land speculation. Polk's friends warned the president not to tie his political fate too closely to Walker fearing potential scandals.

wealthy, the reduction of tariffs would also increase government revenues. High tariffs on some articles had choked off imports and simultaneously eliminated government opportunities to tax this exchange.

This report also reveals connections between Walker's views on economic policy and what he felt should be the broader global interests of the United States. He thought that a unilateral reduction of tariff barriers would promote reciprocity on the part of other countries around the world. As will be discussed shortly, Walker held similar views about the foreign-policy benefits of trade reform as Britain's foreign secretary, Lord Aberdeen. Both saw their own government's efforts at tariff reform as a device to shift the domestic balance of power in the other country toward groups that favored more friendly political ties between the two governments. While Aberdeen thought British trade reform would temper western annexationists in the United States by offering them new market outlets in Europe, Walker argued that the elimination of tariffs in the United States would alter the domestic balance of power in England in favor of those groups that sought to eliminate the Corn Laws. He wrote, "If we reduced our tariff, the party opposed to the corn laws of England would soon prevail, and admit all of our agricultural products at all times freely into her ports, in exchange for her exports" (Walker 1893[1845], p. 11). As trading partners responded by eliminating their own tariff barriers, market opportunities for American products would expand and the system of double taxation, whereby agricultural interests faced higher prices at home and closed markets abroad, could be eliminated.

Walker also argued that tariff reduction would promote peace. On this score, his arguments clearly reflected his southern political interests and the central role of cotton in America's trade portfolio. He wrote, "The cotton planting is the great exporting interest, and suffers from the tariff in the double capacity of consumer and exporter . . . It is the thus the source of two-thirds of the revenue, and of our foreign freight and commerce; upholding our commercial and marine and maritime power. It is also a bond of peace with foreign nations, constituting a stronger preventive of war than armies or navies, forts or armaments . . . at present prices, our cotton crop . . . furnishes profits abroad to thousands of capitalists, and wages to hundreds of thousands of the working classes; all of whom would be deeply injured by any disturbance, growing out of a state of war, to the direct and adequate supply of the raw material" (Walker 1893[1845], p. 6).

In the spring of 1846, Walker's support of free trade and annexation created a real policy dilemma that forced him to choose one over the other. The bold policy of expansion in the Oregon territory – that he had helped to include in the Democratic platform of 1844 – heightened the possibility of war with Great Britain. War not only risked closing off the market so crucial to southern agricultural interests, it also threatened to make tariff reform impossible by consuming all of the government's attention (Shenton 1961, p. 78). The growing tension over Oregon within the Democratic Party between northern and southern factions compounded these difficulties by hindering tariff reform. As Whigs also represented many manufacturing interests of the Northeast, they supported protection. Consequently, Walker needed unity in the Democratic Party supporting free trade to overcome Whig opposition to tariff reform. As the Oregon dispute lingered, it threatened to undermine this unity by splintering the party into northern and southern factions. In the critical months of March and April of 1846, Walker tempered his traditional support for annexation and instead favored peaceful compromise to achieve tariff reform. His biographer writes (Shenton 1961, p. 79), "The settlement permitted Walker to concentrate upon his major concern: the construction of a new tariff law. He had admitted before a Washington Day dinner his wish to settle the Oregon controversy on reasonable terms, for without a settlement all tariff reform was impossible. Alex Gardiner, a guest at the dinner observed, 'Walker would naturally desire to see the dispute arranged for he is engrossed with the tariff, and of course jealous . . . of any other question.'"[12]

Contemporary observers felt Walker possessed the dominant influence within Polk's cabinet.[13] His policy views were thus critical in internal deliberations about how to settle the Oregon dispute with Britain. This imbalance was partly attributable to the disagreement among Polk, Walker, and the secretary of state, James Buchanan, over tariff reform. Like Walker, Polk desired tariff reform and was concerned that war with Great Britain would render that goal impossible.[14] Buchanan frequently vacillated on Oregon.

12 Interestingly enough, in the case of Oregon, Walker also envisioned a long-run harmony between his support for free trade and expansion. By authorizing a series of reciprocal trade agreements, Walker thought his tariff reform would increase trade with Canada that would then stimulate support for political union between the two. Consequently, the United States would ultimately be able to annex all of the Oregon territory through this political union (Shenton 1961, p. 82).

13 In a letter to the Governor Letcher of Kentucky on March 9, 1846, Senator Crittenden (D-Ky) writes in reference to Polk's cabinet: "It being understood and agreed here that Walker is the ruling spirit in that council" (Coleman 1871, p. 236). For a similar view of Walker's influence in the cabinet, see also Shenton (1961, p. 85).

14 In a rare moment of candor at the start of his term, Polk identified four key goals he wished to accomplish during his single term in office: the settlement of the Oregon question, the acquisition of California, the reduction of the tariff to a revenue basis, and the establishment of an independent treasury (Sellers 1966, p. 213).

Possessing strong political ties with manufacturing interests from his home state of Pennsylvania, he pushed a tougher negotiating line with the British at the end of the crisis to protect high tariffs.

Polk's concerns that the lingering of the Oregon dispute would sidetrack tariff reform appeared in his diary entries during Senate deliberations in late February and early March 1846 – a period that represented to him the high point of the crisis. He had recently received notice that his rejection on January 3, 1846, of the British proposal for arbitration had stimulated new defense preparations by Britain.[15] Moreover, Senate deliberations revealed a growing split within the party. In March, Polk grew increasingly concerned that a party split over Oregon would prevent him from accomplishing the rest of his political agenda. His diary during these months records a steady stream of meetings with Democratic senators that shed light on the party's internal politicking. Polk writes of a conversation with Senator Lewis on March 4:

> I urged harmony in the Democratic Party, and expressed the hope that the notice would not be lost in consequence of differences of opinion as to the form the resolution of notice should assume. I told Mr. Lewis that if the notice was lost the Democratic Party were in danger of being so distracted and divided in Congress that my recommendations for reduction of duties on the tariff and all my other measures would be lost also. I expressed an anxious desire to effect a reduction of the tariff, and again urged harmony on the Oregon question. (Polk and Quaife 1970, p. 263)

Similarly in a conversation with his close friend, Senator Haywood (NC) on March 7, Polk noted that his "administration and its usefulness to the country would be destroyed" thereby enabling the Whigs to take advantage of the situation unless harmony could be achieved within his party (Polk and Quaife 1970, p. 276). Like Walker, Polk was aware that both the continuing disagreement within the Senate over the nature of the resolution and war itself would prevent tariff reform. Shortly thereafter, he strove to break this deadlock by signaling to the Senate, through Senator Benton of Missouri, his willingness to compromise.[16]

[15] Aberdeen received official notice of Polk's rejection on January 29. Shortly thereafter, he held a meeting with the American ambassador and informed him that Britain would be forced to "prepare for the worst." Aberdeen to Peel, February 3, 1846. Aberdeen Papers 43123.

[16] Polk records in his diary a long conversation with Benton over Oregon on March 11, 1846 (Polk and Quaife 1970, pp. 284–7). In this entry, he tells Benton confidentially that he was willing to compromise with Britain on the following terms: the 49th parallel to the sea would serve as the border in the territory and all of Vancouver Island would be ceded to Britain. Polk was unwilling to grant perpetual free navigation on the Columbia River

Buchanan, Protection, and "54°40′ or Fight"

Apart from illustrating the links between tariff reform and support for compromise and peace, internal cabinet deliberations during this period also reveal that some protectionists were quite willing to go to war to acquire all of the Oregon territory. These forces found voice in James Buchanan. By March of 1846, Buchanan had already undergone two significant revisions in his views on Oregon since the crisis first began. While in the Senate, Buchanan had acquired a reputation for being an Anglophobe.[17] As recently as March 1844, he supported American claims for all of Oregon up to 54°40′ in Senate debates over termination of the joint occupation agreement (Pletcher 1973, p. 215). Later, his promotion to secretary of state led him to quickly disavow these political views upon his first meeting with the British ambassador, Pakenham.[18] As secretary of state until February of 1846, Buchanan had long counseled Polk to adopt a conciliatory stance relative to Britain.[19]

As Walker's movement toward tariff reform gained momentum and news of the imminent Corn Law repeal in Britain reached the United States, Buchanan again reversed his position on Oregon. He went from being one of the most dovish members of the cabinet – advocating settlement at 49 degrees and continually trying to get Polk to tone down what could be interpreted as aggressive public statements – to being its most hawkish member – supporting claims to the entire disputed territory. Upon receiving Aberdeen's final proposal for the resolution of the dispute that was ultimately accepted by the United States, Buchanan unilaterally dissented in the cabinet and resisted submitting the proposal to the Senate. He argued that the western annexationists were the "true friends of the administration" (Polk and Quaife 1970, p. 453).

From Pennsylvania, Buchanan had long supported industrial protection. In cabinet debates, he resisted Walker's initiative to move away from protective tariffs and toward revenue tariffs by seeking to maintain specific duties on certain goods, like iron, produced in Pennsylvania.[20] By March of 1846, it appears that Buchanan had come to believe that an aggressive stance on Oregon, which heightened the risk of war, could defeat Walker's plan for

but was willing to offer a limited period of free navigation, perhaps seven to ten years. In early April, Benton broke the deadlock in the Senate by proclaiming his support for compromise. The implication of his speech was that the president was ready to compromise as well (Sellers 1966, pp. 396–7).

17 Pakenham to Aberdeen, March 29, 1845. FO 5/428, No. 33.

18 Pakenham to Aberdeen, March 29, 1845. FO 5/428, No. 40.

19 See for example, Polk and Quaife (1970, pp. 101–2, 106–8, 122–3).

20 Polk and Quaife (1970, pp. 94–5).

tariff reform.[21] A conversation in early March between President Polk and Senator Speight of Mississippi reveals the connections between tariff and war in Buchanan's vacillating position. Through Senator Cameron, also a supporter of protection from Pennsylvania, Speight learned that individuals from manufacturing districts in Pennsylvania had lobbied Buchanan to prevent any tariff changes. Buchanan subsequently began to organize opposition to tariff reform. More importantly, these manufacturing interests had informed Buchanan that they would prefer a war by insisting on all of the Oregon territory rather than see a reduction in the tariff.[22] Support for this link between protection and war also shows up in a letter written from Senator Crittenden of Kentucky to Governor Pletcher of his home state describing Buchanan's role in the emerging conflict within the Democratic Party over Oregon and its implications for tariff reform. He wrote:

> They quarrel about what the President's sentiments and purposes are in relation to Oregon... If he don't settle and make peace at forty-nine or some other parallel of compromise, the one side curses him; and if he yields an inch or stops a hair's breadth short of fifty-four degrees forty minutes, the other side damns him without redemption. Was ever a gentleman in such a fix?... But all this is not enough; our friend Buck not only comes in for his share of these common troubles, but has his own particular grief besides. He is for all Oregon – he would not yield an inch "for life or death," and he is quite careful to have it told and known that he stands fixed on the north pole, right at the point of fifty-four forty... But what comes next? Why, he is charged with wishing to have war in order to save the tariff for Pennsylvania and defeat his colleague, Mr. Walker, depriving him of all the glory of his free-trade bill lately submitted to Congress. If war comes, all know we can't think of reducing the tariff (Coleman 1871, pp. 235–6).

This domestic struggle reveals important theoretical mechanisms by which the distributional pressures associated with globalization shape foreign policy interests and decisions for war and peace. The commercial peace literature has tended to focus on the role played by advocates of strong trading links and peace while ignoring the possibility that such domestic lobbying efforts will not necessarily be successful. Buchanan's political maneuverings illustrate that the beneficiaries of economic closure can facilitate war by countering lobbying efforts for peace. He responded positively to

21 A recent biography notes that Buchanan had become particularly sensitive to the growing call supporting claims to all of Oregon within the Pennsylvania Democratic Party (Binder 1994, p. 88) but does not link this switch to the tariff question.

22 Polk and Quaife (1970, pp. 261–2). Illustrative of Polk's growing concern that the Oregon controversy would halt tariff reform, he stressed the need for party unity and the risks that discord posed to tariff reform in a meeting with Senators Yulee (FL) and Lewis (AL) right after his conversation with Senator Speight.

lobbying from manufacturing interests for protection and territorial expansion by trying to block an amicable settlement with Britain. Just as Walker saw tariff reform as creating a path to peace with Great Britain, Buchanan promoted an expansionist program that heightened the risk of war to preserve the tariff.[23] The outcome of this domestic conflict between free traders and protectionists critically shaped American territorial interests in Oregon and Polk's willingness to go to war to defend them. Once the risk of war with Great Britain threatened to derail tariff reform, Polk pushed the United States toward a peaceful compromise by restraining the demands from his own party for territorial expansion in Oregon.

Free Trade and Peace in Britain

On June 29, 1846, in his last act as foreign secretary, Lord Aberdeen announced that the United States had accepted the British proposal to settle the Oregon controversy. The timing was not merely a coincidence. This internal struggle in Great Britain over globalization that was eventually settled by the repeal of the Corn Laws influenced the peaceful resolution of the Oregon dispute in three key ways. First, Aberdeen consistently argued to his colleagues that the opening of the British economy could promote support for conciliation in the United States. Second, free-trading interests within the Whig opposition prevented the formation of a new cabinet in December of 1845 that was likely to pursue a much more aggressive stance against the United States. Third, Lord Russell's public political support for free trade and a peaceful accommodation with the United States granted Aberdeen the necessary breathing space to make concessions for such an agreement. The same coalition dynamics that brought about repeal enabled Robert Peel, the British prime minister, to compromise with Polk over Oregon.

The Politics of Repeal

By the time Polk reasserted American claims to all of the Oregon territory in his inaugural address, Robert Peel's grip on power in Great Britain was eroding. His gradual moves toward free trade in the spring of 1845 had riled

[23] This willingness of protectionist interests in the United States to pursue war with Great Britain was also reflected in a letter from Edward Everett, McLane's predecessor as American ambassador to Britain, to Lord Aberdeen. Agreeing with Aberdeen's suggestion that the elimination of the Corn Laws would pacify western annexationists and promote a peaceful compromise, he wrote, "Your Corn law has been the greatest obstacle with which our free traders have had to contend and the best ally of our Manufacturers . . . The Manufacturers of the North would suffer least by a war." Everett to Aberdeen, January 28, 1846, Aberdeen Papers, 43123.

the protectionist bloc of his Conservative Party. While the Conservatives held a substantial majority in the House of Commons, his loyal Peelites who supported more liberal trade policies numbered only one-third of this Conservative coalition. Peel could only find sufficient support to eliminate the Corn Laws by drawing on votes from the opposition. This tactical option threatened his government by splitting his Conservative party into two factions – Peelites and Protectionists – neither of which possessed the votes necessary to sustain a governing coalition. The potato famine in Ireland accentuated these divisions by inciting a food crisis that seemed solvable only by repealing the high tariffs on foreign grains. Eventually this food crisis provoked the resignation of two governments, a failed attempt at an alternative government, and the repeal of the Corn Laws. These political developments shaped the settlement of the Oregon dispute with the United States by first preventing a government hostile to the United States from taking power and then creating the domestic political freedom necessary for the Peel government to make territorial concessions to the United States.

Peel faced a series of difficult political choices as news of the potato crop failure began to circulate in the fall of 1845.[24] Given the Conservatives' long-time support for the Corn Laws, Peel's government resisted repeal and reacted slowly to the crisis in the fall of 1845. The supporters in the cabinet for repeal were relatively limited, including only Peel, Lord Aberdeen, James Graham, and Sidney Herbert. Opponents of repeal, including the Duke of Wellington, Lord Stanley, and Lord Lincoln, doubted the extent of the crisis and sought instead to acquire more information on the extent of the damage to that summer's crop or postpone the debate over repeal for a year. Unable to find consensus, the cabinet debated such options as temporary repeal, a fixed tariff, and the government purchase of foreign grains in November of 1845.

Peel's political options narrowed substantially when the opposition leader, Lord John Russell, published a letter to the Electors of the city of London on November 22, 1845. In this letter, he publicly proclaimed his support for the elimination of the Corn Laws. Although written without consulting a number of his key political allies, this letter unified a fractured opposition coalition consisting of free-trade Radicals, Whigs, and Irish Nationals behind a policy of free trade and consequently heightened the public pressure on Peel's government to move closer to this policy proposal.

[24] Much of this discussion of the November cabinet debates relies on Chapter 15 of Gash (1972).

By the end of November, Peel had attempted to lay out a path of compromise within his cabinet. He circulated a memo advocating a lower sliding-scale tariff on the import of foreign grains with a duty that would progressively decrease until it was completely abolished in eight years. After three days of debate, it became clear that Peel's proposal would provoke resignations and thus fracture the cabinet. Consequently, on December 6, Peel resigned as prime minister.

His absence from government was short. Due to a disagreement over the allocation of cabinet posts within a Whig administration, Russell was unable to form a new government. The queen called on Peel to form another Conservative ministry. Although dissent remained in the cabinet toward abolishing the Corn Laws, its opponents realized that their political options had been severely constrained by the respective decisions of Peel and Russell to support free trade. Some change to the Corn Laws was inevitable. The choice to Conservative protectionists was either to remain in government or allow the party to be pushed into the opposition while this legislation passed. Apart from Lord Stanley, dissenting voices within Peel's potential cabinet chose the former.

After Peel presented a plan to eliminate the Corn Laws at the end of January, parliament spent the next six months debating this legislation.[25] Despite strong public support for repeal, Peel knew that his time in office was limited. Passage of his tariff revision required support from the Whig opposition – support that would only last until that legislative initiative was accomplished. Once his revision to the Corn Laws was passed at the end of June, this support was withdrawn along with that of protectionist Conservatives who sought to punish him for abandoning the majority of the party. Peel's conservative cabinet fell with his resignation on June 26 – a day after his Corn Law bill had passed the House of Lords.

Aberdeen, Economic Statecraft, and the Second Face of Hegemony

Throughout this internal political crisis, Aberdeen sought to utilize the elimination of the Corn Laws to create the foundation for peaceful compromise with the United States over the Oregon territory.[26] Accurately apprised of the sectional differences within the United States over the Oregon territory, Aberdeen believed that unfettered access to the British grain market would serve as an economic carrot to western senators and would temper their demands for the entire Oregon territory. For example, in the midst of the

[25] Peel's proposal would reduce the existing duties on corn and abolish them completely in three years. His plan included spending for rural highway development and public loans for agricultural improvements as compensation to landholders for lower grain prices.

[26] See for example Greville (1885, pp. 310–13).

December 1845 cabinet crisis that forced Peel to temporarily resign from office, Aberdeen leaked information to a newspaper reporter that the cabinet had reached an agreement abolishing the Corn Laws. He hoped that this news would reach the United States on the steamer leaving London the next day.[27] On the same ship, Aberdeen sent an optimistic dispatch to Pakenham, noting, "But many things may shortly occur to improve the prospect of affairs considerably. The access of Indian corn to our markets would go far to pacify the warriors of the Western States."[28]

One prominent study of the relationship between repeal and the Oregon settlement casts doubt on the success of Aberdeen's efforts to use the elimination of the Corn Laws to mollify Western annexationist pressures (Merk 1967, Ch. 11). It notes that such western supporters of claims to all of Oregon explicitly refused to limit their claims in exchange for greater access to the British market. All major Democratic newspapers that had supported claims to all of Oregon did not switch their opinions after news of the potential tariff reforms in Britain reached the United States (Merk 1967, p. 329). In a heated debate on the Senate floor over the termination of joint occupation notice, Senator Hannegan of Indiana stated, "The last steamer from Europe, it is said, puts this question in such a position, that for Oregon we can get free trade. Free trade I love dearly; but never will it be bought by me by the territory of my country. He who would entertain such an idea is a traitor to his country . . . Free trade for a surrender of the ports and harbors of the Pacific? Never, sir; never" (*Congressional globe* 1846, pp. 458–60).

This skepticism over the capacity of free trade to transform territorial demands in the United States unnecessarily limits the target constituency solely to Western extremists who were already unlikely to mollify their views. As the previous section argued, this transformative role of commerce was more important in tempering the expansionist interests of key politicians who were closer to the center of opinion on this issue – like Walker, Calhoun, and southern senators leaning toward supporting the compromise constructed at Baltimore in 1844 – and thus crucial to the final stage of compromise.[29] Walker's annual address identified how free-trade movements

[27] For his role in this public disclosure see Greville (1885, pp. 312–13).

[28] Aberdeen to Pakenham, December 3, 1845, Aberdeen Papers, 43123.

[29] Everett summarized these political dynamics in a letter to Aberdeen on November 15, 1845. He wrote, "I apprehend that the section of the Democratic party, which yields an unqualified support to the Administration, is disposed to insist upon the American title up to the Russian boundary. The Whigs or regular Opposition Party are willing to compromise the question on the basis of the 49th degree, leaving to you the whole of Vancouver Island, or they would agree to an Arbitration. In this state of things, M. Calhoun and his southern friends will hold the balance. They will have the power, if they choose to exercise it, to

in one country could strengthen similar pressures in others. Buoyed by the possibility that the repeal of the Corn Laws would make it easier to reduce tariffs in the United States, he was unwilling to sacrifice his own tariff initiative for the sake of claiming the entire Oregon territory.[30]

Blocking a Hostile Government

The political movement against the Corn Laws also pushed the governments toward peace by preventing Lord Palmerston from taking over as the head of the Foreign Office during the brief attempt by Russell to establish a Whig government in December of 1845 (Merk 1967, Ch. 9). Palmerston had consistently pursued an independent, hard-line foreign policy during his tenure in the Melbourne government that had preceded Peel. Throughout Europe and within the British Whig leadership, the return of Palmerston evoked concerns over the heightened prospect of war and the risks this posed to commercial interests. In January, Aberdeen received a dispatch from Vienna detailing a general despair there, "particularly among the commercial interests," at the possibility of a Russell government in Great Britain and its potential to upset the peace then existing in Europe.[31]

Such concerns over a potential belligerent British policy were most felt within Palmerston's party. Once Peel resigned in early December, Lord John Russell tried to form a cabinet that would respond to the current food crisis by eliminating the Corn Laws. Russell felt that the inclusion of Sir George Grey, an ardent supporter of free trade, was crucial to the success of his cabinet. Because support for repeal was relatively limited in the House of Lords, Russell needed Grey to lead the campaign in that body.

At the same time, Grey laid out a series of conditions for serving in the cabinet. Two were policy oriented and one directed at the allocation of cabinet posts. He argued that the cabinet should pursue two fundamental policy goals. The first was directed at eliminating the system of protection that was "essentially vicious and unjust." He also wanted the government to support religious equality in Ireland.[32] Even more importantly, Grey was willing to serve with Palmerston in the same cabinet if the latter did not hold the foreign ministry portfolio. When Russell decided to offer Palmerston

prevent the passage of any law for taking exclusive possession of the territory; and if the President were able and willing to come to any settlement by negotiation, they could, by joining forces with the Whigs, procure its ratification by the Senate, in spite of the ultra democracy." Aberdeen Papers, 43123.

30 For a discussion of how repeal in England helped to promote the Walker tariff reform see Lake and Scott (1989).

31 Aberdeen Papers, January 12, 1846, British Library, 43245.

32 Russell Papers, Grey to Russell, December 16, 1845, PRO 30/22/4E.

the position of foreign secretary, Grey refused to serve. Already facing an uphill battle with a minority government and an uncertain promise of support from Peel for repeal, Russell felt that he could not lead a government without Grey to champion the free-trade cause within the House of Lords. This failure led to the subsequent reestablishment of a slightly different Conservative government led by Peel. In a letter to Russell dated December 19, 1845, Grey explained his objections to Palmerston's appointment as foreign secretary. He wrote, "I could not but believe that the appointment to which I objected might very materially increase the danger of the country's being involved in all the calamities of war, and so believing I could not in conscience agree to it."[33] Grey's actions illustrate how the struggle over free trade shaped the composition of any cabinet and as a consequence, British foreign policy. Free-trade supporters, represented by Lord Grey, prevented the formation of a government likely to pursue a more hostile stance on Oregon.

Similar Domestic Coalitions for Repeal and Oregon Compromise

As opposition leader, Russell also played a critical role in the eventual settlement of the Oregon dispute. In November he publicly committed his party to full support of the abolition of the Corn Laws. Shortly thereafter he did the same for the Oregon question, publicly supporting compromise with the United States.

These policies reflected the growing influence of the free-trade Radicals in this political coalition. Led by Cobden, this group saw an intimate connection between the abolition of trade barriers and peace among nations. Russell had long been a supporter of pacific relations between the United States and Great Britain. While believing that Great Britain had conceded too much in the Webster–Ashburton negotiations, he felt that "it was not too great a price for peace" (Scherer 1999, pp. 140–41). Hoping to strengthen commercial ties and the political relationship with the United States, he attempted to tie Palmerston's political hands and prevent him from a strong denunciation of the treaty. In two speeches in January 1846, Russell made this connection between the elimination of the Corn Laws and peace with the United States explicit in his thinking. He stated:

> There is another advantage which I think would arise from the total abolition of the duties on the importation of grain – it would bind this country much more closely in the bonds of peace and amity with foreign states, and more especially with one – I mean the United States of America . . . If we are determined on this side to import

[33] Ibid., December 18, 1845.

the products of the United States, and if the United States are equally satisfied to do the same with the manufacturers of this kingdom, that they should feed us, and that we should clothe them, if no unhallowed legislation should stand in the way of these desirable results, then we should see two nations of the same race and same language united in the bonds of amity and peace.[34]

While his November speech committed Russell and his party to the mission of free trade, this speech committed his party to an amicable settlement with the United States. Unlike the Webster–Ashburton negotiations when Palmerston had strongly criticized British concessions, public criticism of the Oregon negotiations from the opposition would now threaten an open split in the party at a time in which it was preparing to retake power from a fractured Conservative Party. Even Palmerston was unwilling to do this when it was so apparent that a Whig government could quickly form after the elimination of the Corn Laws.

This public gesture and private assurances from Russell to Aberdeen gave political breathing space to the latter so he could offer concessions to the United States to reach an amicable settlement (Merk 1967, pp. 332–6). Peel and Aberdeen were concerned about the domestic political costs of conceding too much to the United States, particularly after the bold statements by Polk in his inaugural and annual addresses and the supportive responses these generated from expansionist press outlets. The precarious nature of their governing coalition compounded such worries. They wished to avoid the same public criticisms they faced from Palmerston following the Webster–Ashburton negotiations. Consequently, Russell's public proclamations supporting free trade and peace with the United States freed them from these concerns.

The emergence of nearly identical coalitions within Britain supporting repeal and compromise over Oregon in 1846 reveals the intimate connection between free trade and peace. Peel could not generate support for either policy initiative solely from his party. He needed additional backing from an opposition – that included Lord Russell and the free-trade Radicals – to enact both repeal and compromise over Oregon. The resolution of the internal struggle in Britain over repealing the Corn Laws thus played a critical role in facilitating a peaceful settlement with the United States.

Summary: Free Trade and Peace in 1846

A reexamination of the resolution of the Oregon dispute between the United States and Britain offers numerous instances to confirm how an invisible

[34] As quoted in Merk (1967, p. 317).

hand pushed the two governments toward peace. First, it illustrated how distributional conflicts over globalization influenced societal pressures for war and peace. Financial and merchant interests in the northeastern United States pressed Daniel Webster to prevent the Oregon dispute from disrupting commercial ties with Great Britain. Southern cotton growers pressed Calhoun to block western senators from pushing Polk into demanding all of the disputed territory. Protectionist forces in Pennsylvania were willing to countenance war with Britain and sided with western expansionists so that the industrial tariffs could be preserved.

Second, the domestic triumph of free-trade coalitions in both the United States and Britain facilitated compromise over Oregon that preserved peace. In Britain, Aberdeen saw the abolition of the Corn Laws as critical to shifting the balance of domestic power within the United States toward groups that favored peace. Unable to rely on support from their own Conservative Party, Peel and Aberdeen could not enact this strategy until being pushed by a political opposition that largely supported both repeal and peace. Even the opposition leader, Lord Russell, acknowledged this intimate connection between free-trade policies and peace when he noted that "unhallowed legislation" stood in the way of peace with the United States. As the dispute over Oregon lingered in the United States, Polk and Walker faced a stark trade-off between two policies that they had both previously embraced: free trade and territorial annexation. When forced to choose, they opted for free trade and peace, abandoning western Democrats and the campaign pledges made in Baltimore in 1844.

VENEZUELA, THE GOLD STANDARD, AND THE EMERGENCE OF A GLOBAL POWER

In the summer of 1895, President Cleveland and his secretary of state, Richard Olney, collaborated to pen a robust extension of the Monroe Doctrine. The particular issue that gave rise to this bold assertion of American hemispheric hegemony was a long simmering dispute between Great Britain and Venezuela over the delineation of the border between the latter and British Guyana. While asserting that the encroachment of British settlers into disputed territories where new gold supplies had been recently discovered constituted a threat to the independence of the Venezuelan government and thus a violation of the Monroe Doctrine, Cleveland demanded that the British government allow the dispute to be settled via third-party intervention. Recently returned to government and occupying the positions of prime minister and foreign minister, Lord Salisbury disagreed with the specific and general issues now in dispute between Great Britain and the

United States. While he believed that Cleveland was overplaying his hand and catering to jingoes unleashed by the Jacksonian politics characteristic of the United States, Great Britain could not risk establishing a precedent that would allow smaller countries to slowly whittle down its empire via arbitration. Salisbury's blunt rejection of American interference angered Cleveland and prompted a hasty December address to Congress that threatened war if Britain continued to stall the negotiations and be dismissive of the broader importance of Latin America to the United States. For a few days, the American public and Congress were whipped into a state of frenzy, broadly supportive of Cleveland's willingness to go to war. This war talk abruptly ended with a financial crisis that simultaneously threatened to drive the United States off the gold standard and activated a sizable commercial opposition to war. Cleveland responded by publicly signaling a willingness to find compromise. Even though it would take the United States and Britain nearly a year to reach an accord that would both honorably reaffirm the extension of the Monroe Doctrine and settle the border dispute between British Guyana and Venezuela, the possibility of war was largely confined to developments in the second half of December of 1895.

The domestic struggle in the United States over commercial and financial policies shaped the evolution of this conflict with Britain. The financial sector, supporters of free trade, and Cleveland saw the maintenance of the gold standard as critical to balance-of-payments stability and growth in American exports. One of the norms inherent in the gold standard – namely capital mobility, which protected the right of private traders to freely import and export gold – provided the institutional freedoms necessary for private economic actors to spark the broader financial crisis that forced Cleveland to rethink his aggressive posture. Cleveland's fervent belief in the need to protect the government's commitment to maintaining gold convertibility had long remained strong despite continual Populist pressures for bimetallism. Silver interests associated the gold standard with British global economic dominance and argued that the turn toward bimetallism provided the perfect mercantilist policy. Dollar devaluation would stimulate exports and depress imports. They explicitly advocated war as a device to drive the United States off the gold standard and free it from financial dependence on Britain. The silverites were joined in their advocacy of confrontation with Britain by protectionists like Henry Cabot Lodge, who hoped to integrate more territory into America's sphere of economic influence.

These arguments are presented in the following steps. First, I review the historical details of the dispute. Second, I review the treatment of this dispute by political scientists in the broader debate over the sources and strength of the liberal peace. I use this discussion to show how these applications have misdirected attention toward democracy as a critical force for peace and neglected important historical studies of American foreign policy during this period that can shed light on the broader debate over the liberal peace. Third, I show that domestic distributional cleavages over globalization shaped the course of this dispute. The chapter concludes with a brief discussion of the importance of this case to broader debates over the emergence of the special Anglo-American relationship that endures today along with the role played by economic interests in American foreign policy.

Background of the Dispute

Rival claims by both Venezuela and Britain to the territory surrounding the current border between Venezuela and Guyana date back to the period between 1811 and 1814. In 1811, colonial settlers broke from Spanish rule in the process of declaring an independent Venezuela. In 1814, Holland ceded territory to Britain that then became British Guyana. A sizable portion of territory along both sides of this unofficial border remained largely unsettled and subject to competing claims by both parties for decades following the initial establishment of these respective territories.

In 1841, the British government hired a botanist, Robert Schomburgk, who had been working in the area, to locate the border between the two territories. He constructed the Schomburgk line, which was later to provide a critical negotiating point. While continually pressed by both Venezuela and the United States to submit the entire disputed territory to arbitration, the British government would refuse until February of 1896 to subject any territory east of this line to arbitration.

The value of this disputed territory increased as time passed. British settlers continued to move west of the Schomburgk line, particularly after gold was discovered in the 1870s. Perhaps more importantly, Schomburgk had delineated the northern border of British territory at Point Barima along the Atlantic Ocean. This area sat at the mouth of the Orinoco River and thus gave Britain a base by which to control access to this important waterway that granted commercial access to the interior of the northern part of the continent.[35] In the 1890s, the suggestion that Britain could control trade in this region via this strategic piece of territory activated many American congressional officials to defend rival Venezuelan claims.

[35] For a discussion of the extension of the British claim to territory just inside the mouth of the Orinoco River and its importance to how the State Department viewed the crisis, see LaFeber (1998[1963], pp. 251–5).

In the summer of 1893, the Venezuelan government sent an envoy to Britain to reach some sort of settlement over the disputed territory. It continued to demand arbitration on all disputed territory, both east and west of the Schomburgk line. Dating back to the end of Lord Aberdeen's tenure as foreign secretary in 1846, most British governments refused to subject any territory east of the Schomburgk line to arbitration. Incompatible bargaining positions thus doomed these negotiations and led the Venezuelan government to enlist the United States in the dispute. It hired William Scruggs, the U.S. ambassador to Venezuela during the Harrison administration, as a lobbyist and representative for Venezuelan interests.

Scruggs' lobbying activities on behalf of Venezuela directed attention toward the role of Latin America in Anglo-American relations and stimulated public support for American intervention (Perkins 1937). He found a willing audience among many Republicans, such as Henry Cabot Lodge, who had traditionally favored high tariffs and a more assertive foreign policy in the hemisphere for economic reasons. In a rhetorically important article in October 1894, Scruggs tapped into both nationalist and anti-British sentiment in the United States by invoking the need to defend the Monroe Doctrine. He drew a parallel between the existing colonial struggles among European powers in Africa and future competition in Latin America. Shortly thereafter, multiple congressional officials openly advocated policies to limit British influence in both the Caribbean and Latin America. President Cleveland addressed these concerns in his December message that opened Congress. By February 1895, both houses of Congress had passed resolutions recommending arbitration of the dispute and asserting that American interests were at stake via the Monroe Doctrine.

By the summer of 1895, President Cleveland had also grown impatient with British diplomatic inaction that was enabling more settlers to move into disputed areas. British military intervention in Nicaragua in April of 1895 at the port of Corinto increased public pressure on President Cleveland to defend American interests in Latin America, particularly with respect to Venezuela (Blake 1942). He directed his secretary of state, Walter Gresham, to research the issue and prepare a message to the British government. The tone of this message changed with the transition at the State Department, necessitated by Gresham's death in May 1895. Cleveland appointed his attorney general, Richard Olney, to succeed Gresham. Olney sought a quick resolution and believed that an assertive declaration of American interests would shock the British out of complacency (Perkins 1937).

Sent in July 1895, Olney's letter to Salisbury invoked the Monroe Doctrine to justify American intervention in the dispute between Britain and Venezuela. He defined the Monroe Doctrine as denying the right of

European governments to "deprive an American state of the right and power of self-government and of shaping for itself its own political fortunes and destinies" (Perkins 1937, p. 156). He then went on to declare that any political union between a European and American state with three thousand miles between them to be "unnatural and inexpedient." This statement drew the attention of the British, particularly the Colonial Office, as it seemed to threaten directly the status of Canada in the British Empire. To determine whether or not Britain was challenging Venezuela's independence, Olney argued that all the parties involved needed more information regarding the delineation of the border. He offered arbitration as a means to acquire this information. However, Olney then requested an answer from Britain before Cleveland's opening message to Congress in December as to whether or not it would submit the entire dispute to arbitration. Perkins (1937, pp. 167–8) argues that the tone of the final paragraphs of the message constituted an ultimatum to the British, noting that "the United States would insist upon arbitration at all costs."

Salisbury's response arrived after Cleveland's annual message in the first week of December. He defiantly challenged Olney's declaration that the Monroe Doctrine was a part of international law and the accompanying assertion that Britain was extending its colonization of the area. Instead he argued that the dispute was over the determination of the frontier of an existing British possession (Perkins 1937, p. 175). He then rejected Olney's claim that a third party like the United States via the Monroe Doctrine possessed the right to demand the manner in which a dispute between two other parties would be settled. Instead Britain and Venezuela would settle their dispute via direct negotiations.

Cleveland's response was immediate, emotional, and harsh. After consulting with Olney, he decided to submit a second message to Congress. On Tuesday, December 17, he detailed Salisbury's rejection of the Monroe Doctrine in the Venezuelan case and asked that Congress appropriate the necessary funds so that a boundary commission could be established so as to ascertain the facts of the situation. Cleveland finished his message with an implicit threat to defend American interests with military force. He stated:

> When such report is made and accepted it will, in my opinion, be the duty of the United States to resist by every means in its power, as a willful aggression upon its rights and interests, the appropriation by Great Britain of any lands or the exercise of government jurisdiction over any territory which after investigation we have determined of right belongs to Venezuela. In making these recommendations I am fully alive to the responsibility incurred and keenly realize all the consequences that may follow (Perkins 1937, p. 192).

Historians, contemporary commentators, and politicians on both sides of the Atlantic recognized this message as a threat for war (e.g., Bertram 1992; LaFeber 1998[1963], p. 268; Bourne 1967, p. 319; James 1923, p. 121).[36]

For the next three days, the American public rallied behind Cleveland's threat. By Friday, and with almost no debate, both houses had passed appropriations bills to establish the boundary investigation committee. This tide, however, turned dramatically on Friday, December 20. Cleveland was forced to send another message to Congress, requesting authorization for a loan that would replenish the treasury's dwindling gold reserve. A substantial sell-off had already begun that day on Wall Street, precipitated by the withdrawal of substantial quantities of British capital back to London. This short-term financial crisis provoked a weekend of introspection across the United States, particularly among financial, commercial, and religious groups. By the end of the weekend, support for Cleveland's assertive posture had faded.

On the following Tuesday, Cleveland began to back away from his bold stand. His message of December 17 had already left open some diplomatic breathing room by declaring that the charge of the American commission was solely to investigate the facts behind the competing boundary claims. In a subtle, but important public suggestion meant to reemphasize solely the informational purposes of this commission, Cleveland's close friend and spokesman in the senate, George Gray of Delaware, stated:

> As I understand the position of this government in regard to the appointment of a commission, it is that facts may be ascertained for the information of the government... This information, as I understand it, is solely to inform the conscience of the government and the American people, and could not have been expected that its conclusions were binding upon either of the disputants... The United States does not assume to delimit a frontier for Great Britain, but to ascertain whether there is any design by Britain, under the pretext of a boundary dispute, to aggrandize her own territory at the expense of Venezuela (Bertram 1992, p. 67).

Bertram (1992) argues that many components of the British press interpreted this statement as a withdrawal by Cleveland from his belligerent tone of the previous week.

A personal letter from Cleveland to the American ambassador, Thomas Bayard, on December 29 also illustrates the former's decision to stand

[36] For example, Senator Mills (D-TX) stated on the Senate floor on December 20, "But the President of the United States, and the Government of the United States through our Executive, and the Government of Great Britain have arrived at the point, after a long discussion, where both say they will not yield, and the President says that we ought to resist with all the means in our power the establishment as proposed by Great Britain. Surely we are standing face to face on the very edge of battle..." (U.S. Congress, 54, 1, p. 258).

down from veiled threats of war made on December 17. Given Cleveland's close relationship with Bayard, historians have described this letter as an attempt to explain his motivations for a policy that Bayard clearly opposed. Referring to the continued British refusal for arbitration, he writes, "We do not threaten nor invite war because she refuses it – far from it . . . So instead of threatening war for not arbitrating, we simply say, inasmuch as Great Britain will not aid us in fixing the facts, we will not go to war, but do the best we can to discover the true state of facts for ourselves, with all the facilities at our command" (Nevins 1930, p. 419).

During these weeks of crisis, Salisbury followed a quiet strategy of nonresponse (May 1961, p. 48). While he and the rest of Britain had been caught off guard by the breadth of anti-British sentiment existing across the political spectrum in the United States, he avoided escalating the conflict. He chose to consult informally with cabinet ministers and did not call a full cabinet meeting until January 11 to avoid creating speculation in the media about British reactions. Although Salisbury continued to refuse to submit the entire disputed territory to arbitration and threatened to resign at this meeting if the rest of the cabinet pushed him to do so, widespread support existed then in the cabinet behind some sort of compromise with the United States. By this point, Salisbury and Chamberlain had opened multiple diplomatic channels through newspaper editors and "amateur diplomats" like Lord Playfair to try and reach this compromise.

Cabinet opposition to escalating the conflict with the United States was given a push by a new crisis in Anglo-German relations. On January 3, the kaiser sent a congratulatory telegram to the president of the Transvaal, Paul Kruger, for having defeated the Jameson raid initiated at the end of December. The kaiser's interference provoked widespread opposition in Britain and reaffirmed the need to find a peaceful compromise with the United States over Venezuela. Although it is important to evaluate the Anglo-American dispute in the context of the Kruger telegram, the trend toward peace in both the United States and Britain had already emerged (e.g., Bertram 1992).

With both the United States and Britain committed to some form of peaceful compromise by the middle of January, the diplomats were then charged with constructing a bargain that allowed both sides to protect their prestige and the broader interests that were at stake. Apart from the burst of domestic support that emerged behind Cleveland from commercial interests that sought to block British access to Latin America and silver interests that wished to drive the United States off the gold standard, there was also an important moral component of Cleveland's pronouncements of December.

He sought to ensure both the sanctity of the Monroe Doctrine and the rights of small and weak states in the Americas from political manipulation by European powers (Welch 1988). The use of third-party arbitration offered a legal means to help protect these weaker states.

Conversely, both Salisbury and Chamberlain were concerned by the long-term damage posed by establishing a precedent that threatened to expose every disputed portion of the British Empire to arbitration. Salisbury also sought to protect the right of British settlers who had moved into the territories that his government had long claimed as part of British Guyana. Salisbury's long refusal to subject any territory east of the Schomburgk line was undermined by the release of a report in late January showing that Lord Aberdeen did not regard this line as the permanent demarcation of British territory when he had first commissioned it.

The compromise that eventually emerged over the summer from these developments subjected all the disputed territory in the region between British Guyana and Venezuela to arbitration except those areas where permanent British settlements had existed for fifty years. By the time the dispute officially ended with the signing of an accord in November of 1896, it had fallen completely out of public attention. War had been averted. The right of the United States to intervene in Latin American relations with Europe via the Monroe Doctrine had been reaffirmed. And the groundwork for a much broader cooperative relationship between the United States and Britain had been established. In the midst of negotiations over Venezuela, they began negotiating a general treaty that would subject all their remaining territorial disputes to arbitration.

Venezuela and the Liberal Peace Debate

This Venezuelan case has played an important role in debates over the existence, strength, and causes of a democratic peace among states. Owen (1994, 1997a) argues that perceptions of liberal values in other states and domestic institutional constraints, created by competitive elections and a free press, jointly explain the peace among democratic states. Societies within democratic political systems generally oppose going to war against other societies that they perceive to be governed by democratic rules and norms. By promoting American perceptions that Great Britain was a democracy, British political reforms in 1867 and 1885 created the foundation for an active American resistance against war to emerge when the dispute over Venezuela erupted. Even though the aggressive stance of Cleveland and Olney risked war, this public opposition then raised the political costs to

Cleveland for continuing this policy line. Moreover, pro-American feelings in Britain helped push Salisbury at the crucial cabinet meeting of January 11 into making concessions to the United States.

Like Owen, Layne (1994) points to this cabinet meeting as critical to the end of this crisis. To illustrate that geostrategic interests and concern over the balance of power instead account for the absence of war between democracies, he argues that the resolution of this crisis hinged on the British decision to reverse its policy over Venezuela in January 1896. The cabinet had initially supported Salisbury's rejection of the Olney note in November. Why the change? Layne points to the rapid decline in the British position, sparked in part by the crisis precipitated by the kaiser's telegram to Kruger, and the risks associated with moving substantial components of its navy out of Europe to fight the war against the United States. He also notes that "it does not appear . . . public opinion affected policy on either side of the Atlantic" and suggests that the American public would have supported Cleveland, if war occurred (Layne 1994, p. 26).

Concurring with Layne's broader arguments, Rock (1997) dismisses the role of democracy in the peaceful resolution of the Venezuelan dispute. Like Owen and Layne, he begins by asking why Britain retreated. He then points to Britain's growing strategic vulnerabilities as reason behind this policy reversal. Rock directly challenges Owen by arguing that shared liberal values did little to alter the decisions from the British cabinet. After pointing to several potential sources of public opposition to war in both countries, he writes, "There is little evidence that public pressure had a pacifying effect on government policy in either Britain or the United States during the most acute phase of the crisis, which ended with Britain's retreat" (Rock 1997, p. 130).

While these three studies reach different conclusions about the relative role of democracy and traditional realist variables like the balance of power in resolving this dispute, they possess multiple similarities in their interpretations of the historical record. I briefly examine some of these similarities to set up an alternative explanation for the peaceful settlement that focuses on the role played by economic interests benefiting from free trade.

First, these three studies all highlight the central role of the January meeting of the British government in which a cabinet led by Chamberlain pushed Salisbury to negotiate a peaceful compromise with the United States. This focus then leads these studies to set up their analysis with the same historical puzzle: Why did Britain concede? If Cleveland's forceful extension of the Monroe Doctrine had precipitated the crisis, British concessions enabled the two governments to escape it.

These studies overlook the possibility that the real danger of war had faded before both the Jameson raid that sparked the crisis in Anglo-German relations and the subsequent January meeting of the British cabinet. The financial crisis of December 20 provoked sharp financial and religious opposition to the war in the United States. Bertram (1992) argues that Cleveland had already stepped down from his bellicose message of December 17 via the public comments made by his spokesman in the Senate, George Gray, on December 24.

Additionally, Salisbury's own letters suggest that a recession in tensions can be dated prior to the January 11 cabinet meeting. In a letter to his colonial secretary, Joseph Chamberlain, on Monday, December 23, Salisbury noted the dramatic change in American opinion over the weekend writing that "the American squall seems to be blowing out."[37] This sentiment expressing Salisbury's confidence in achieving some sort of immediate peaceful settlement is confirmed in a letter to the chancellor of the exchequer, Sir Michael Hicks Beach, on January 2. While acknowledging that the Venezuelan conflict had increased the probability of war with the United States in the future, Salisbury simultaneously rejected the idea that this would occur in 1896 (Campbell 1960, p. 31). He indicated to the queen on January 9 that the United States was ready to make concessions (May 1961, p. 49).

If the critical stand-down in this diplomatic crisis lies with Cleveland rather than Salisbury, then the reexamination of British strategy sparked by the Kruger telegram played a smaller role in the subsequent peace simply because it had not been sent yet. These possibilities suggest the need to consider the possibility that the brief period in which the threat of war loomed was both started and stopped within the United States. Furthermore, this shifts the motivating question surrounding the peaceful settlement from "Why did Britain concede?" to "Why did Cleveland retreat from his message of December 17?" and necessarily raises the importance of the financial panic in the resolution of the crisis.

Second, these studies evaluating the role of democracy in shaping the outcome of the Venezuelan crisis also focus more on how the dispute ended rather than how it started. This choice leads these studies to neglect important components of the broader historiographical debate over American foreign policy during this critical period in which the United States transitioned from being a hemispheric to a global power. Owen, Layne, and Rock

[37] Chamberlain Papers, JC 5/67.

suggest that realist concerns over the balance of power in the Americas led Cleveland and Olney to confront Britain. Rock (1997, p. 127) writes that the United States "was fearful that European powers might expand their influence in the Western Hemisphere." Layne largely concurs with this analysis but adds that the United States was concerned about European political *and* commercial intrusion in the Western Hemisphere (italics added). Owen (1994, p. 114) writes that "Cleveland and Olney... saw a boundary dispute between British Guiana and Venezuela as an opportunity to assert U.S. power in the New World." Owen (1997a) acknowledges that Cleveland faced domestic pressure to confront Britain because he had failed to do so over the Corinto affair. He notes that this domestic support "was based on the claim that Britain was trying to spread monarchism in the Western Hemisphere" (Owen 1997a, p. 165).

Apart from Layne's brief mention that Cleveland feared European commercial intrusion, these analyses do not confront a key historical question over this crisis. How did the long depression in the United States from 1873 to 1896 and domestic demands for foreign markets shape the American decision to confront Great Britain and the broader imperial project upon which it was embarking? Multiple historians (e.g., LaFeber 1998[1963]; Crapol 1973) direct attention to economic factors as a critical source for American expansion during this decade.[38] This research carries implications for the debate over whether liberal institutions in the United States shaped its foreign policy during this period for two key reasons. First, given the centrality of domestic interests and institutions to the democratic peace, they examine how the variety of domestic interests within the United States influenced decisions to both confront Britain and then retreat. Second, this historical research program has been used to build and support broader arguments linking the internal development of capitalist economies to expansion and war (e.g., Grandin 2006).

The next sections confront these questions that have been overlooked by examinations of liberal peace arguments in the Venezuelan case that direct attention primarily toward the role played by democracy in the resolution of the crisis. It makes three shifts from existing liberal peace research. First, it draws on the Wisconsin school to examine some of the economic foundations for domestic support of Cleveland in his confrontational policy toward Britain. In particular, I focus on arguments made by imperialists like Henry Cabot Lodge and silver interests opposed to the British-dominated

[38] For reviews of this literature, see Fry (1996), Crapol (1992), and Field (1978). For a recent discussion of the Wisconsin school of history, see Gardner and McCormick (2004).

gold standard. Leaders of both groups saw a bold posture in Latin America as critical to creating economic opportunities for their constituents particular groups. Second, by shifting responsibility for the end of the war scare associated with this confrontation from the January 11 British cabinet meeting to Cleveland's subtle retreat on December 24, I place the causes and consequences of the financial crisis at the center of my interpretation of the resolution of this conflict. Third, I examine the financial crisis in the broader context of Cleveland's commitment to the gold standard and its role as a supporting institution of capitalism in the United States at the end of the nineteenth century.

Economic Interests and Territorial Expansion

LaFeber (1998[1963]) traces how economic motivations, largely left out of previous historical debates, shaped American foreign policy during this critical period. Policymakers, the media, and businesspeople came to embrace the idea that a crisis of overproduction had gripped the American economy. Well into the transition to an industrial economy, the mechanization of production had decreased the need for labor and enabled manufacturers to increase dramatically the scale of production. Declining demand for labor heightened unemployment and contributed to social unrest. This crisis of overproduction accentuated the deflationary trends long associated with the gold standard. LaFeber argues that a global policy of naval, territorial, and commercial expansion came to be seen as a device to cure many of the nation's economic ills. Access to foreign markets would help relieve this crisis by creating outlets for surplus goods and capital. This access required a more assertive foreign policy – one that embraced a stronger navy to defend commercial interests and a willingness to confront European governments in South America and the Pacific to ensure that American businesses would not be excluded from such economic opportunities.

LaFeber (1998[1963], p. 242) places the crisis over Venezuela alongside the war with Spain in 1898 and the economic consequences of the depression as critical to the development of the American Empire. He argues that Cleveland's decision to press Britain on the Venezuelan boundary dispute stemmed in large part from the fear that European states would deprive the United States from the foreign markets in South America it desperately needed to stave off the economic pressures associated with the depression. These concerns accelerated with the Corinto incident in Nicaragua and the British construction of a railway line in 1894 that terminated at the northernmost point of the Schomburgk line just inside the mouth of the

Orinoco River. If Britain controlled the mouth of the Orinoco River, it could control commercial access to the northern interior of the continent.[39]

As part of the broader argument linking commercial pressures to territorial expansion, LaFeber (1960, 1961, 1998[1963]) uses the Venezuelan case to challenge arguments that business interests uniformly opposed expansion during this period of American history. He shows that a split between business interests emerged over the content of Cleveland's bold statement of December 17. Although banking interests of New York and Chicago along with commercial interests that relied heavily on business with Britain opposed Cleveland's stance, numerous business groups throughout the United States supported him. In particular, industrial groups and western Populist interests rallied behind the president. This immediate support for the president was quite unusual in that these groups had traditionally opposed many of the president's policies.[40] LaFeber (1960, p. 401) writes:

> But many business journals, especially those published in industrial and in iron and steel centers supported the President. The *American Manufacturer*, published in Pittsburgh, was usually not a pro-Cleveland paper since it advocated high tariffs. But in discussing the Venezuelan situation this journal reasoned that England refused to submit her case to arbitration because "Her commercial supremacy is being threatened on all sides. The markets of the world are being wrested from her," and so she "seeks to extend her commercial influence in South America." ... The United States had to stand firm against this commercial infiltration even if it led to "blood and iron."

In short, LaFeber notes that many groups that had traditionally favored high tariffs also supported challenging Britain.

Although LaFeber does not explore the causes of these differences among business opinion, the split he identifies falls largely along the lines predicted

[39] LaFeber (1998[1963], pp. 250–51) cites an exchange with close friend Don Dickinson as demonstrating Cleveland's support for these ideas. Dickinson gave an important speech in May 1895 in which he stated, "We are a nation of producers; we need and must have open markets throughout the world to maintain and increase our prosperity... our material interests today depend upon the markets abroad... our diplomacy should be alert to secure and protect favors and advantage from all peoples that buy and sell or have a port our ships can enter." At the end of July, Cleveland wrote to Dickinson noting his pleasure at the latter's speech.

[40] The actions of these groups have been used to challenge claims, like those of Blake (1942), which suggest that Cleveland initiated the crisis simply to prop up declining public support. Such arguments are problematic because the immediate public backing Cleveland garnered for his Venezuelan policy came from groups, like supporters for high tariffs and silver, that had long opposed him. Consequently, their support was likely to be short-lived and thus incapable of sustaining a longer term growth in Cleveland's domestic coalition.

here, emphasizing a link between reliance on government intervention in the economy and support for expansionist foreign policies. Business groups, like iron and steel, which depended on tariffs to reduce competition within the domestic economy also sought government aid to prevent British commercial activity in South America. Such groups responded immediately and favorably to the bold statement of December 17 that heightened the risk of war.

Henry Cabot Lodge: Advocate of Protection, Territorial Expansion, and Confrontation with Britain

The strongest link within the Republican Party between support for high tariffs and a bold foreign policy relative to Britain over Venezuela can be seen best in the policy views and political activities of Henry Cabot Lodge.[41] A political historian by training, a close friend of Theodore Roosevelt, and a true believer in Alfred Thayer Mahan's arguments about the importance of naval power, Lodge first helped rally domestic opposition against Cleveland's foreign policy over the summer and fall of 1895 and then rushed to support the confrontational line adopted against Britain in December 1895.[42] At the opening of the 54th Congress in early December, Lodge introduced a bill to enshrine the Monroe Doctrine as a component of American law. Then in January, after the crisis had receded, Lodge reportedly authored a bill later introduced on the Senate floor by Cushman Davis, which advocated an even more confrontational line against Britain (Bertram 1992, p. 85; Perkins 1937, pp. 227–31). The bill sought to delineate all conditions associated with the Monroe Doctrine and included the Caribbean Islands within its reach. While quickly condemned by public opinion, the bill antagonized the British at a time when negotiations were just commencing.[43]

41 For discussions of the evolution of Lodge's foreign policy views over the 1890s see Grenville and Young (1966, pp. 201–38), Garraty (1953, pp. 146–65), and Widenor (1980).

42 In a complete about-face, Lodge rushed to support the president in congressional debates over appropriating the money for a boundary commission in the days following Cleveland's message of December 17. On the Senate floor he stated, "[I] think it is of the utmost importance that there should be absolutely no division whatever in the Senate on any question involving the support of the President in the position he has taken . . . I desire to give the President all that he asks and the utmost latitude" (*Congressional record* 54, 1, p. 259).

43 The British ambassador in Washington, Julian Pauncefote, closely monitored these deliberations in the Senate. FO 5/2289.

Lodge's support for confrontation over Venezuela fit with a broader vision for a bold policy of commercial, naval, and territorial expansion in South America, the Caribbean, and the Pacific. Great Britain generally served as the chief obstacle to this grand strategy. A speech given on the Senate floor in a debate over naval appropriations in March of 1895 in which Lodge reaffirms his support for annexing Hawaii illustrates these views:

> This country is the rival and competitor of England for the trade and commerce of the world . . . She has always opposed, thwarted, and sought to injure us. She desires to keep her control of the great pathways of commerce. She desires to put us in a position where we cannot fight, if we wish, except at a great disadvantage . . . to neglect our Navy and the outlying islands which ought to belong to us puts us in the position where all the advantage is on her side and none on ours. The control of these great points in the highways of commerce is the control of sea power (*Congressional Record* 53, 2, p. 3084).

Lodge relied on traditional Republican principles, traced back to Washington, Monroe, and Hamilton, in espousing these views (Lodge 1891, 1893, 1895a). In the economic realm, he supported protection for infant industries to increase wages and facilitate the entry of American firms in both domestic and foreign markets.[44] In foreign policy, he sought to defend the corollary of Washington's farewell address, the Monroe Doctrine.

Lodge publicly waged a joint campaign against both the weak foreign policy of Cleveland and British encroachment in key strategic areas for the United States in two key policy statements in 1895 (Lodge 1895a, b). He wrote these essays, in part, to set the stage for a congressional confrontation with the president when the new session convened in December.[45] Like Olney's letter to Salisbury, Lodge's piece in the *North American Review* cast British pressures on Venezuela as challenging the Monroe Doctrine. He accused Britain of primarily seeking to gain control of "one of the great river systems of South America" (Lodge 1895b, p. 653). This aggrandizement

[44] In late 1891, Lodge (1891) assessed the economic consequences of the protectionist McKinley tariff of 1890. He first critiqued the doctrine of free trade and then defended protection, particularly for infant industries. He claimed that the McKinley tariff had not led to any general rise in prices and that it had stimulated the entry of many new American enterprises.

[45] Lodge admitted in a letter to Henry White that the article in *North American Review* sought to prepare the public for a congressional debate over the Monroe Doctrine in December. Describing his own essay he wrote, "I wanted first to call attention to the facts but little known here, and second, to pave the way for a stiff declaration of the Monroe Doctrine by the next Congress. You know that has never been done. The next Congress will do it, and we shall serve notice on the world that we shall regard an infringement of the Doctrine as an act of hostility" (Nevins 1930, p. 108).

directly left the United States with two stark choices. The Cleveland administration could choose to defend or surrender this principle. A choice for the latter would signal to the rest of Europe that South America was open for colonial competition just as Africa had been.[46]

Earlier that year, Lodge penned another critique of Cleveland's foreign policy that reveals more of his thinking about the intimate link between protecting American industry and protecting American territorial interests in South America. Citing multiple foreign-policy failures in Hawaii, Samoa, the Far East, Canada, Armenia, and Venezuela, Lodge characterized Cleveland's foreign policy as too willing to make concessions. Lodge attributed this weakness to the pervasiveness of the free-trade doctrine in the making of Cleveland's foreign policy. He wrote:

> It has grown to be the fashion of late to neglect our foreign relations and to treat them as of little or no consequence, and this unfortunate tendency has been greatly stimulated in recent years by the tariff reform or free trade agitation. The economic doctrines which the tariff reformers have been urging were of course borrowed from England . . . the theory of the Manchester school in its fullest development was not merely that free trade was economically correct, but if universally applied it would prove to be a panacea for all human ills, that it meant universal peace, and that all such things as armies, navies, war, territorial extension, or national expansion must be stopped because they were likely to interfere with the complete freedom of trade . . . our free traders, not content with urging their economic views, have undertaken at the same time to break down the American spirit and to prevent our defending our own interests in other parts of the world (Lodge 1895a, pp. 13–14).

Perhaps most interestingly, Lodge then draws a direct connection between free trade and satisfaction with the territorial status quo. While chiding the Cleveland administration for abandoning traditional Democratic support for territorial expansion, he attributes this transformation to free-trade influences that "Cobdenized" the party (Lodge 1895a, pp. 14–15). Lodge concludes the essay by claiming that America's commercial interests necessitate territorial expansion in Canada, Cuba, the Caribbean, and Hawaii (Lodge 1895a, pp. 16–17).

Together, these essays reveal an intimate connection among protection, commercial expansion, and territorial expansion in Lodge's politics.[47] The

[46] Lodge again drew this parallel to Africa over the possibility of colonial competition in South America in a long letter to Arthur Balfour in February 1896 after the crisis had begun to recede. Balfour papers, MS 49742.

[47] In his defense of the McKinley tariff, Lodge draws a direct connection between protection and enhanced competitiveness of American industry in global markets. He writes (Lodge 1891, p. 657), "The general policy of the United States has been to give encouragement to the domestic producer and manufacturer, and maintenance to high rates of wages, by

adoption of free-trade policies fostered submissiveness in foreign policy that exposed American interests, particularly commercial, to challenges from around the globe. Both protection and a robust resistance to British expansion in South America facilitated the creation of economic opportunities for American industry in foreign markets. Just as the American government had long intervened in the domestic economy via protection to heighten industrial competitiveness, the long-term health of the American economy again demanded active government intervention to defend commercial expansion around the globe. Intervention in the Venezuelan boundary dispute could prevent the European powers from parceling out the continent, to the exclusion of the United States, as they had done in Africa. Similarly, a strong navy, a Nicaraguan canal, and coaling stations in the Caribbean and Pacific would facilitate the government's capacity to defend American commercial interests outside of North America. These ideas played a critical role in the Venezuelan dispute because Lodge first helped to heighten public pressure on Cleveland to confront Britain throughout 1895, then rallied to support the bold message of December 17, and finally sought to maintain this pressure via the Davis resolution in January of 1896.

Silver and Confrontation: The Gold Standard and Venezuela

While disagreement over protection and free trade shaped domestic support for confrontation with Britain over Venezuela, domestic conflict in the United States over the gold standard played perhaps an even larger role in the evolution of this conflict. A decades-long struggle with deflation, particularly in agricultural products, coupled with the depression of 1893, brought the currency issue to the fore of American politics. This debate centered on American adherence to the gold standard, the deflationary tendencies this commitment engendered, and its consequences for the distribution of income within American society. While eastern financial and industrial interests generally supported gold and the concomitant government commitment to anti-inflationary monetary policies, western mining and farming interests opposed such monetary restrictions imposed by the gold standard. Believing that the infusion of silver would expand the domestic money supply, they advocated a bimetallist approach in which both silver

laying duties in such a way as to discriminate in their favor against those outside. The result, speaking broadly, has been to put the *United States* as a competitor into countless lines of new industries. The effect of the competition of the United States, added to that already existing in the rest of the world, has been to reduce the world's prices in the products of those industries according to the well-known laws of competition" (italics added).

and gold circulated. Inflation would ease the debt burdens of farmers and stimulate foreign demand for American agricultural exports. This domestic struggle over monetary policy in the United States became central to the Venezuelan boundary dispute because the gold standard had long been associated with subservience to British financial power.[48] Silverites advocated confrontation and sometimes war against Britain over Venezuela to break this economic yolk.

Adherence to the gold standard in the first era of globalization obligated governments to enact a number of monetary policies.[49] Governments set a fixed rate at which the national currency could be converted to a given quantity of gold, then adjusted the domestic money supply in response to changes in its gold reserves, and maintained on demand convertibility of the currency into gold by private actors at that fixed rate. These policies were designed to reduce inflation expectations and convince private actors that the risks of holding currency rather than gold were minimal.[50] These rules also possessed important international implications. First, the joint maintenance of these commitments created a fixed exchange rate regime among those economies that adhered to the gold standard. Second, governments were supposed to uphold their pledge to maintain convertibility irrespective of the nationality of the private actor demanding gold. In theory, private individuals could freely import or export gold.

The absence of barriers on the import or export of gold constitutes the key link between the gold standard and the theoretical focus here on free trade.[51] Whereas discussions have so far concentrated on the presence or absence of political barriers that alter the flow of goods across national boundaries, capital mobility – or the absence of restrictions on capital

48 Crapol (1973, p. 192) writes, "During the last two decades of the nineteenth century the free silver issue came to represent all of America's grievances against England. The remonetization of silver promised to liberate the American farmer from the grip of the English market, to open alternate markets in South America and Asia for his agricultural surplus, and to end the nation's humiliating reliance on foreign capital with its attendant evils of alien ownership and bond issues."

49 This discussion of the gold standard relies on Bordo and Kydland (1995), Eichengreen (1994, 1996), and Simmons (1994).

50 Contemporary economists have described this policy choice as a device by which governments could solve the time inconsistency problem associated with assuring private actors that it would not adopt inflationary policies in the future (e.g., Bordo and Kydland 1995).

51 The gold standard has long symbolized the laissez faire capitalism believed to characterize this first era of globalization. For example, Jeffry Frieden (2006, p. 6) writes, "The gold standard became the most powerful organizing principle of global capitalism during the nineteenth century." For similar views, see Polanyi (2001[1944]).

flows – creates similar competitive pressures in financial markets.[52] By allowing private actors to divest themselves of financial assets and then move gold out of an economy, governments in the nineteenth century necessarily exposed their commitments to adjust domestic monetary supply in response to these reserve changes. This commitment required governments to adopt deflationary policies in response to gold outflows. Deflationary policies, like interest-rate hikes, create further political costs by slowing domestic economic activity (Simmons 1994). Capital mobility, when it existed, enabled private financial actors to penalize governments by moving their assets to another country.[53] This withdrawal challenged governments attempting to maintain either the gold standard, or more generally a fixed exchange rate, to respond with politically unpopular policies that further slowed economic activity.[54]

The struggle over silver threatened to split the Democratic Party into western and northeastern factions. Moreover, even though the Republicans generally favored the gold standard, plenty of their congressional officials were perfectly willing to countenance policy delays if it facilitated serious rupture within the Democratic Party. Western agitation had already led to the construction of a compromise bill in 1890, the Sherman Act, which obligated the government to make regular purchases of silver at a premium above market prices through the issuance of new treasury notes that expanded the money supply. Cleveland believed this policy to be disastrous and a principal cause of the depression in 1893.[55] It threatened to drive gold out of circulation by encouraging citizens to hoard gold purchased at a discount. By draining gold reserves, it challenged the treasury's capacity to maintain gold convertibility. He also believed that the continuation of silver agitation weakened business confidence by encouraging even more gold exports.

Shortly after the financial panic of May 1893, Cleveland called a special summer session of Congress to repeal the Sherman Act and break this cycle

52 As the Bretton Woods era demonstrated, capital controls facilitated the capacity of governments to shape domestic interest rates, namely by allowing them to diverge from world interest rates (e.g., Eichengreen 1996).

53 This capacity to punish via withdrawal of financial assets is the same as Hirschman's (1970) discussion of how exit through competitive markets pushes organizations to reform.

54 For a discussion of these structural constraints created by capital mobility on government macroeconomic policy, see Andrews (1994). Extensions of commercial liberalism have already linked capital mobility to peace between states (Gartzke, Li, and Boehmer 2001; Gartzke 2007).

55 This discussion draws on Welch (1988).

of uncertainty over the course of American monetary policy. He prevented the passage of compromise bills short of complete repeal by threatening to withhold all patronage appointments for congressional officials that would not support repeal. By the end of October, Cleveland finally achieved his political victory. The Sherman Act had been repealed. The costs for this legislative victory, however, were steep. It had set the stage for a split in the summer of 1896 between the eastern and western factions of the party over the party's presidential nomination.

This struggle over the distribution of domestic income between western farming interests and eastern banking interests played a critical role in shaping the battle over the gold standard and American foreign policy toward Britain. Tight money policies had deflated agricultural prices and simultaneously exacerbated the credit burdens faced by all farmers. Inflation held out the possibility of raising prices and reducing the real costs of servicing debt in the agricultural sector. In short, inflation via bimetallism carried the potential to shift wealth away from eastern banking circles closely allied with British financial interests and back to western farmers.

Although this struggle has often been characterized as an internal one between farmers and bankers, open-economy approaches (Crapol 1973; Frieden 1997) have demonstrated that silver supporters saw gold's collapse in a broader international context. Frieden (1997) argues that Populists advocated silver as a way to engineer a devaluation of the dollar. Bimetallism could then stimulate exports in classic mercantilist fashion. A declining dollar in foreign exchange rate markets would stimulate greater foreign demand for American exports and simultaneously slow imports by reducing the purchasing power of the American consumer (Frieden 1991).

Crapol (1973) identifies multiple international motivations behind western support for silver. Western farmers charged that adherence to the gold standard in the United States helped banks and British consumers. Apart from protecting the financial assets of creditors, reduced agricultural prices benefited the world's largest food importers, namely Britain. By increasing the world's money supply, bimetallism would inflate world prices for wheat, cotton, and corn and break the price monopoly in London and Liverpool commodity markets. Finally, a shift toward silver in the United States would grant American exporters a competitive advantage in emerging markets in South America and Asia already on a silver standard. As falling world silver prices relative to gold raised the price of imports from gold-standard economies in these markets, American adoption of bimetallism would counteract this trend.

This economically motivated antagonism from Populists played a critical role in the dispute over Venezuela. Silver interests supported a bold policy against Britain and some even announced their willingness to countenance a war to achieve the larger goal of driving the United States off the gold standard. Perhaps the most famous statement along these lines comes from a leading Senate supporter of silver from Nevada, William Stewart. He declared, "War would be a good thing even if we get whipped, for it will rid the country of English bank rule" (Perkins 1937, p. 193). Similarly, William Allen, a Populist senator from Nebraska, suggested during a Senate debate over Cleveland's policy of December 17 that it might be "[w]ise to pursue such a policy as would cause the withdrawal of English capital from this country and the transaction of business upon our own money" (*Congressional record*, 54, 1, p. 262).[56] Along these lines, LaFeber notes (1960, p. 400), "It was to be expected that many Western organs under the control of Populists and silver forces would applaud any policy which could conceivably lead to a financial or diplomatic crisis which, in turn, would necessitate an enlargement of the amount of paper and silver money in circulation."

Finally, a long letter written by Lodge to Sir Arthur Balfour, Lord Salisbury's nephew and the Conservative leader in the House of Commons, in February 1896 also illustrates the importance of the domestic struggle over silver in the United States to the outbreak of the crisis. In the letter, Lodge tries to dissociate himself from the war movement while explaining the public antagonism in the United States over Venezuela that had clearly surprised all of Britain. He writes:

> Last and deepest of all present causes is the money question. The times have been very bad, and there has been much suffering. The Silver question is widely believed to be at the bottom of it all. The Bimetallists know that England alone stands in the way of an agreement. The Free Silver men, and they control many states, believe that England not only prevents international bimetallism, but that her influence is largely responsible for the resistance of the North and East to Free Silver – I am not concerned to discuss the correctness, or the justice of their feelings. All I desire to point out is that they exist. When the President suddenly took a stand which the country thought right in Venezuela, the materials were ready and the explosion followed.[57]

Like struggles over tariff policy, domestic distributional pressures over globalization drove Populist support for war against Britain. This

56 Allen also argued that the crisis necessitated immediate silver coinage in financial preparation for war (*Congressional record*, 54, 1, p. 254).

57 Lodge to Balfour, February 1, 1896, MS 49742.

distributional struggle differed slightly in that exchange rates, rather than tariffs, shaped competing foreign policy lines. Bimetallist groups favored confrontational policies, which included war, to drive the United States off the gold standard, reduce the financial and commercial power of Britain, reduce the political power of banks and eastern creditors in the United States, and stimulate agricultural exports. Their antipathy toward the gold standard is important because this regulating institution of the global economy in the nineteenth century has long been associated with a laissez faire political stance toward market exchange.[58] Like high-tariff Republicans, silver supporters sought to limit the pressures associated with competitive global markets and demanded active government intervention to enhance their ability to penetrate global markets.[59] A devaluation of the dollar was a classic mercantilist policy in that it both stimulated exports and depressed imports. Most importantly for the arguments here, this demand for active government intervention in foreign exchange markets influenced the willingness of such groups to support aggressive foreign policies that heightened the danger of war with Britain.

Financial Panic and a Diplomatic Opening

This domestic struggle over exchange rates and the gold standard elevates the importance of the financial panic on December 20 in the resolution of the Anglo-American conflict over Venezuela. Since the repeal of the Sherman Act in October of 1893, Cleveland had already thrice instructed the treasury to issue bonds so as to shore up the nation's gold reserves. Cleveland's message of December 17 sparked the withdrawal of British capital from the American economy and the export of gold. In the face of this declining reserve position, Cleveland again sent a message to Congress on the morning of Friday, December 20, requesting action to bolster the nation's gold supply. The financial panic, sparked jointly by this declining reserve position and Cleveland's threat for war, provoked a weekend of sober reflection that turned the domestic tide in the United States against war and toward some

[58] When governments tied the size of the domestic money supply to the quantity of gold reserves held, market actors would facilitate the adjustment to balance-of-payments deficits or surpluses via normal market transactions (Eichengreen 1996).

[59] By drawing this comparison between western support for currency devaluation and Republican support for tariffs, Frieden (1997) suggests that they could be treated as policy substitutes. He writes (1997, p. 387), "Populist monetary policies were indeed usually framed as policies to help primary producers in ways analogous to trade protection's support for manufacturers."

peaceful compromise. Cleveland had long demonstrated his commitment to maintaining the gold standard. When faced with the choice of preserving this commitment or continuing the confrontation with Britain, he chose the former.

The norms associated with the gold standard, namely the capacity of private individuals to export and import gold, enabled financial interests to alter the course of Cleveland's foreign policy. British financiers began liquidating financial assets, exchanging these dollars for gold, and exporting gold back across the Atlantic following Cleveland's implicit threat for war on December 17. This withdrawal threatened a weak reserve position and directly challenged Cleveland's commitment to the gold standard.

These pressures intensified with the broader financial crisis of December 20. Selling was no longer confined to British capitalists. The nation's gold reserve lost more than $4 million on this Friday alone.[60] These losses prompted the following plea from the assistant treasurer at the New York Treasury, Conrad Jordan: "'The Philistines are upon us' – in other words private hoarding has begun – and we must stand both foreign and interior drains... Whatever action is had should be pursued quickly – because we can't stand both drains" (Barnes 1931, pp. 405–6).

The withdrawal of British capital following the message of December 17 was coordinated among some of the largest financial players in London. This effort by British financiers to alter the course of American policy became the subject of Congressional debate on December 20 (*Congressional record*, 54, 1, p. 261). Senators used this opportunity to disparage British financiers and argue that American policy would remain steadfast in the face of such financial threats.[61] The debate also illustrates that financial interests from New York lobbied Congress to find some compromise solution. On the Senate floor, Senator Chandler (R-NH) remarked of this coordinated British attack: "[i]t has had its influence today in Wall Street and State Street, and telegrams are being sent in here now by the score, warning the Senate not to protect the honor of the United States for fear that stocks may go down a little" (*Congressional record* 54, 1, p. 262).

60 The gold reserve fell by $20,000,000 during December 1895 to stand at $63,000,000 at the end of the month (Barnes 1931, p. 408).

61 Lodge stated on the Senate floor, "I want the action of the Senate to say plainly to those people in London who are undertaking to make a scare in this country by selling stocks and calling loans in the American market, that the American people are united on this question, that they propose to stand by the Monroe Doctrine, and the attempt to create a panic in Wall street, to call loans and drain our gold, is not the road to an honorable and peaceful settlement (*Congressional record* 54, 1, p. 259).

For the broader arguments here linking liberal economic institutions to peace, it is important to note that this financial panic was initiated by private actors rather than the British government.[62] Evidence from Salisbury's private papers suggests that he did not direct British citizens to withdraw capital from the United States so as to pressure Cleveland to step away from his bold posture of December 17. Market expectations grew in the week of December 23 that the treasury would again have to issue bonds to shore up the gold reserve. Upon hearing speculation that part of this loan would be floated in London, British financial interests queried Salisbury as to the position of the British government on such a loan. A memorandum from his private secretary on December 28, 1895, notes, "Mr. G. Harvey, the comptroller of the national debt office called today to say that the Americans are going to try and float a loan in London, that Daniel the Govt broker repeated that there was a strong feeling amongst a certain section on the stock exchange against taking it up in view of the President's attitude, but that matter was hanging in the balance and a hint from you would turn it one way or the other." Salisbury's reply was brief: "No affair of ours."[63]

This exchange illustrates two key elements critical to the arguments presented here. First, after already seeing markets punish Cleveland's bold stance, Salisbury chose not to accelerate these pressures when faced with an opportunity to do so. This supports the position here that both sides were already standing down from the crisis by the end of December, before both the Kruger telegram was sent and the British cabinet meeting of January 11. Second, this exchange underscores the critical role played by private actors, rather than the British government, in pressuring the American government to back away from its confrontational policy. If Salisbury declined to encourage British financial interests from withdrawing their assets from the United States in the week following December 20, it is unlikely that he would have done the opposite in the week leading up to the financial crisis.

While there is no smoking gun saying Cleveland began the deescalation on December 24 because of the financial panic and the threat it imposed on the American commitment to the gold standard, substantial circumstantial evidence suggests that it was critical in his decision. Over the weekend, financial leaders felt that the United States was in a dire crisis. A letter to Whitelaw Reid, a newspaper editor and vice-presidential candidate in 1892,

[62] Chapter 7 will examine how government control of capital markets contributed to the origins of World War I.

[63] Salisbury Papers, Volume 96.

described this mood prevailing after the stock market crash of Friday. It notes, "I dined on Saturday night with a lot of financiers, among them Morgan, Lanier, and Sturgis, President of the Stock Exchange, and they all believed on Monday that the frightened English investor and European holders of our securities would be tumbling them across the Atlantic at a rate which would take all the gold from the Treasury to pay for them; that they would find no market here capable of buying them, and so they would sell for nothing; that they would cramp the banks; that the loans would all be called in and no new ones made; that everybody owing money would fail in business, and that we were on the eve of a financial cataclysm the like of which had never been witnessed" (Cortissoz 1921, pp. 201–2).

Moreover, these private pressures found a willing representative in the secretary of the treasury, John Carlisle. He had objected both to the sending of the Olney letter in the summer and again to Cleveland's message of December 17 because of the threat they posed to the nation's finances and its ability to maintain the gold standard (Barnes 1931, p. 409). News of his disagreement with Cleveland had even reached Salisbury. Pauncefote relayed intelligence on December 20 indicating that Carlisle was upset with the president's policy because the treasury would face more difficulties in issuing new bonds to shore up the gold reserve.[64]

The effectiveness of these pressures must be weighed alongside Cleveland's long-demonstrated commitment to maintaining the gold standard. He had already paid substantial political costs with the repeal of the Sherman Act. By withholding patronage to those that opposed repeal, he set the stage for a later party conflict over the presidential nomination of 1896 (Barnes 1931). This split in the Democratic Party had doomed Cleveland's efforts at substantial tariff reform in 1894 (Welch 1988). Despite their growing political strength, Cleveland remained unwilling to compromise with the silverites throughout his second term. He vetoed a concession bill to this group in March 1894 that would have coined all the remaining silver bullion at the treasury. He increased the federal debt by $262 million in four bond offerings between February 1894 and February 1896, specifically designed to replenish the treasury's dwindling gold reserves.

These instances of politically defying a significant portion of his own party illustrate the depth of his commitment to the gold standard and must be remembered when thinking about the pressures facing Cleveland on Friday, December 20. His veiled threat of war to Britain and dwindling gold reserves had jointly created a financial crisis that once again placed

[64] Pauncefote to Salisbury, Salisbury Papers, December 20, 1895, Volume 139.

this commitment at risk. With this background, Cleveland's withdrawal of December 24 becomes less puzzling. The continuation of a tough line over Venezuela risked a policy that he had long spent substantial political capital to maintain – America's commitment to the gold standard.

OREGON, VENEZUELA, AND THE LIBERAL PEACE

The evolution of the Oregon and Venezuelan crises illustrates how the distributional pressures associated with globalization often create contradictory foreign-policy pressures. The debates over abolishing the Corn Laws in Great Britain and the Walker tariff in the United States played a critical role in the peaceful resolution of the Oregon dispute. American merchant interests and southern cotton interests combined to block attempts by western senators to pressure President Polk into forcibly annexing all of the disputed Oregon territory. At the same time, the possibility of a substantial and simultaneous reduction of tariffs in both the United States and Great Britain forced politicians like Polk and his treasury secretary, Robert Walker, to choose among competing political goals – territorial expansion and free trade. For these key decision makers, the latter won out over the former. In Great Britain, Robert Peel and Lord Aberdeen sought to use the abolition of the Corn Laws to mollify expansionist sentiment in the United States and construct an agreement whereby their government could escape war and withdraw from part of the Oregon territory with honor. Moreover, the hope of eliminating the Corn Laws also played a critical role in the behavior of their Whig political opposition. It first sparked a cabinet crisis that prevented a new aggressive foreign minister that had openly talked of challenging American interests in North America from coming to office. The possibility of repeal then motivated the opposition to offer domestic political cover for Aberdeen and Peel by publicly supporting peaceful compromise with the United States.

Cleveland's veiled threat of war in December of 1895 to extend the Monroe Doctrine to the Venezuelan dispute briefly rallied widespread public support. Mercantilist pressures in the United States, associated with strong support for tariffs and devaluation, valued a confrontational policy against Britain to promote American commercial independence from Britain and market access in South America and Asia. These pressures met strong opposition from groups that depended heavily on trade with Britain and the financial community. Financial interests sought to preserve America's commitment to the gold standard, an institution long associated with capitalism in the nineteenth century. When the financial crisis of December 20 threatened this commitment, Cleveland retreated from his implicit threat for war and signaled his willingness to compromise. Within a year, the two parties had negotiated a general arbitration treaty that provided a means for settling all outstanding disputes.

This evidence carries important implications for the broader liberal peace debate. First, it substantiates multiple claims made in this book, particularly the key argument associating liberal economic institutions with peace. It moves beyond the correlational evidence presented in the previous chapters to confirm multiple subsidiary causal mechanisms linking both free trade to peace and protection to war. These cases also illustrate that this capacity of liberal economic institutions to promote peace is not restricted to the post–World War II era. The pressures associated with competitive global markets also pushed the United States and Great Britain toward peace in the nineteenth century.

Second, these findings also suggest that liberal economic institutions, not democracy, played a larger role in the outbreak of peace between the United States and Britain in these two disputes. A significant component of this larger pacifying role for economic institutions rests on the relatively mixed record of democracy to promote peace. During critical phases of the disputes, democratic institutions may have even intensified pressures toward war.

The Oregon dispute reveals at least two possible mechanisms by which democracy may have heightened the Anglo-American political conflict. The first mechanism relates to the adoption of the annexationist platform by the Democratic Party in 1844 and the large role played by Congress in the negotiations over the Oregon treaty. Growing sectional conflict between the northeastern, northwestern, and southern factions of the party foreshadowed the subsequent deadlock over the party's presidential nominee at the convention. Robert Walker played a critical behind-the-scenes role by first making support for the annexation of Texas a litmus test for the nomination prior to the convention and then securing a two-thirds voting rule at the start of the convention. These moves effectively blocked Martin Van Buren, who publicly opposed Texas annexation, from being the party's nominee and threw the entire nominating process into disarray by splitting the northwestern and southern sections of the party. Worried about this emerging split, northwestern Democrats and southern Democrats struck a bargain whereby each would support the respective expansionist goals of the other region. Western Democrats would support the annexation of

Texas and southern Democrats would support the annexation of Oregon. This broad expansionist platform, constructed to create a consensus among all factions of the party, then set the stage for the conflict with Britain.[65] In this case, the democratic process itself facilitated a logrolling dynamic within the party that both generated an expansive definition of the national interest and heightened the risk of war.

Second, Polk frequently attributed aggressive stances on Oregon by members of his party to their presidential ambitions (e.g., Polk and Quaife 1970, I, p. 265). Two stood out in particular – Senator Cass from Michigan and Polk's secretary of state, Buchanan. Polk believed these ambitions explained Buchanan's policy flip on the Oregon settlement and his desire to stand with western Democrats in advocating war to acquire all of the territory. Referring to Buchanan in his diary on March 22, 1846, he noted, "Within a few days past it is pretty manifest to me, that Mr. Buchanan has manifested a decided change in his position, and a disposition to be warlike. His object, I think, is to supersede Gen'l Cass before the country, and to this motive I attribute his change of tone and the warlike character of his draft of my proposed message. I think he is governed by his own views of his chances for the Presidency" (Polk and Quaife 1970, I, p. 297). In these cases, electoral pressures led politicians to adopt aggressive foreign-policy positions to distinguish themselves from their adversaries and generate support for their campaigns.

Finally, it is important to note that even if democratic institutions facilitated peace in these cases, material interests motivated by the level of competitiveness in the broader global economy animated these societal pressures both for war and peace. The application of democratic peace arguments to these cases generally focuses on the capacity of society to facilitate peace by restraining a political leadership focused on traditional realist concerns like the global balance of power. Societal interests in the United States did not uniformly try and constrain a political leadership from going to war. Instead, domestic society in the United States was split over how best to respond to British challenges in the Americas. While southern cotton and northeastern financial interests generally lobbied for peace, groups that needed the state to remain competitive in global markets – whether through tariffs or devaluation – helped create these disputes by pushing for territorial aggrandizement and war.

65 These logrolling dynamics are similar to those described in Snyder (1991) and Irwin (2002).

CAPITALISM AND PEACE? AMERICA'S EMERGENCE AS A GLOBAL POWER

The Venezuelan dispute looms particularly large in broader historical debates over the emergence of the United States as a global power in the closing decade of the nineteenth century and the emergence of the Anglo-American special relationship. This decade saw the United States dramatically broaden the scope of its interests in Latin America, the Caribbean, and the Pacific by resisting British and German encroachments in these regions, inflicting a costly military defeat on Spain, and taking control of the Philippines, Cuba, Puerto Rico, and Hawaii.

Revisionist arguments suggest that capitalism played an important role in the emergence of the United States as an imperial or global power. In a fashion similar to Lenin, such arguments point to how the crisis of overproduction in the United States generated demands for a more robust foreign policy that included a strong navy and territorial expansion to promote commercial interests in an increasingly competitive but fractured global economy. The claims presented here suggesting instead that capitalism facilitated a peaceful resolution of this crisis challenge the broader implications of such approaches.

Part of the disagreement between these arguments lies in the definition of capitalism. The pressures associated with capitalism cannot solely be captured by such alternative concepts as industrialization, economic growth, or growing integration in the global economy. This book focuses on the institutions regulating domestic economic activity, and especially those institutions that increase the capacity of private actors to interact on equal terms through competitive markets, to understand the process by which capitalism shapes a state's foreign policies. It posits that as economies become increasingly governed by private property and competitive markets, the governments overseeing such social interactions become less likely to employ military force to settle their political disputes. In the United States at the end of the nineteenth century, the anticapitalist sectors of the domestic economy, like the protected manufacturers of the northeast, pressed their political officials not only for territorial and naval expansion but for confrontation with Britain. However, the beneficiaries of open competitive markets, namely merchant and financial interests, sought to pursue both further liberalization of the domestic economy and peaceful foreign policies that would stimulate even more international trade.

Moreover, by showing how similar distributional pressures over globalization also shaped the evolution of the Oregon dispute, these cases suggest continuity in American foreign policy over the nineteenth century. Free trade helped promote peace in 1846 and 1895. The long postbellum depression – critical in LaFeber's account for generating the crisis of overproduction, the demand for territorial expansion, and a break in American foreign policy – did not alter this trend. Protectionist interests pushed for territorial expansion in both 1846 and 1895.

Chapter 7 will explore these broader arguments within the context of the case that first gave rise to Lenin's claim that capitalist development necessarily generates imperialist expansion and war among the great powers – the outbreak of World War I. It adopts a line similar to the points raised in the conclusion here. Rather than equating globalization with capitalism, it will examine how variation in market competition and property rights regimes during this first era of globalization shaped national interests and government responses to the growing security challenges in the decade before the July crisis.

SEVEN

The Achilles' Heel of Liberal International Relations Theory?

Despite thousands of monographs, governmental inquiries, and nearly a century of intense research, scholarly controversy still surrounds the outbreak of World War I. This body of work has generated literally hundreds of explanations for those ominous political decisions made in July 1914. It is not difficult to look at the enormity of this literature, conclude that the outbreak of this war was overdetermined, and decide that any further research offers little intellectual leverage in understanding both this particular conflict and its place in the broader study of war. European leaders had been sitting on a powder keg and narrowly sidestepping war for nearly a decade. Even if some political compromise, like the kaiser's "Halt in Belgrade" solution, had been reached at the end of July, an incredibly unstable political situation on the continent in which leaders increasingly viewed war as inevitable made it unlikely that the diplomats would repeatedly be able to steer peacefully out of each new crisis.

The tendency to point to this case as the most glaring weakness of liberal international relations theory necessitates revisiting its origins in light of the arguments raised here. Rather than asking why globalization failed to prevent war, I build on the discussion from prior chapters that illustrated how the dramatic expansion in international trade during this period occurred despite extensive government constraints on private economic activity. I show how these political barriers to market-driven commerce played a critical role in the outbreak of World War I. Apart from supporting the broader arguments here linking liberal economic institutions to peace by showing how government efforts to limit private economic activity can contribute to war, this focus creates the opportunity both to pose and to answer critical but neglected questions of this central event in twentieth-century world history. Although consistent with many elements of the emerging consensus in the historiography of this war, this reexamination breaks from it in at least one critical point. Instead of arguing that German interests, institutions, or position in the European balance of power played the critical causal role in the outbreak of war, I argue that domestic institutions in Russia created the fundamental strategic dilemma that caused war in July 1914.

This discussion of the origins of World War I examines the three war-generating mechanisms identified at the end of Chapter 2. A focus on government attempts to contain markets via tariffs, capital controls, and the nationalization of private assets sheds light on the political interests motivating the competing alliance blocs; the capacity of governments to sustain the requisite domestic political strength at home to embark on confrontational foreign policies; and the failure to reach a diplomatic resolution to the July crisis.

Tariffs and capital controls helped generate and sustain political conflict between Germany and the Franco-Russian alliance. Although tariffs facilitated the construction of the iron and rye coalition that enabled Weltpolitik and stoked political conflict via a naval race with Britain, these tariffs also poisoned relations with Russia. An emerging trade war loomed large in the critical Russian decision in July 1914 to reverse nearly a decade-long practice of foreign-policy restraint and capitulation.

The direction of French private savings to the Russian government along with substantial quantities of public property in Russia played critical roles in cementing the tsarist regime's hold on domestic power in the period from 1905 until the start of World War I. Russia repeatedly backed away from diplomatic crises during this period until its leaders felt that internal economic recovery from war and revolution was complete. The tsar's principal advisors feared that active military intervention abroad would provoke political instability at home. This domestic weakness threatened the viability of Russia's alliance commitments to France. Capital controls enabled the French government to divert massive quantities of private savings to the Russian government, which helped to restore the tsarist regime's domestic strength following the revolutionary threat of 1905. Moreover, large quantities of public property in Russia created even more financial autonomy for the government. Unlike in France and Germany, the possession of such resources insulated the tsarist regime from substantial domestic political opposition to military spending and freed it to accelerate the arms race on the continent after 1910.

The dramatic recovery of Russian military power after 1905 frustrated efforts to reach a peaceful compromise between the Triple Entente and the

Triple Alliance during the July crisis.[1] Historians and political scientists alike have long recognized that preventive war logic played a critical role in internal deliberations within Germany from 1912 up to the outbreak of World War I (e.g., Mommsen 1973; Fischer 1975; Hillgruber 1981; Lieven 1983; Snyder 1984; Van Evera 1984; Fearon 1995; Copeland 2000; Mombauer 2001). Once Russia's grand rearmament campaign was completed around 1917, Germany's capacity to protect its interests and play a decisive role in European politics would be substantially constrained. The successful use of German military threats in political negotiations depended on the presumed effectiveness of the Schlieffen Plan, which in turn depended on the snail-like pace of Russian mobilization and the concomitant hope of defeating France before Russia could bring the full weight of its numerical advantage in troops to the battlefield. New strategic railways in western Russia would shrink Russia's mobilization time and erase Germany's hope for victory. Most importantly, as Russia had discovered in the 1908 Bosnian annexation crisis, the inability to credibly threaten the use of military force left a government with little choice other than to make critical political concessions in diplomatic confrontations. Fearing a future of political impotence, Germany launched a preventive war to preserve its influence within the existing European balance of power.

Given strong historical evidence attaching such preventive war motivations in Germany to the outbreak of World War I, the rapid rise of Russia's strength begs an important series of questions that remain understudied. How was Russia able to escape the fiscal constraints on military expenditures that were crippling other European powers? More importantly, how could Russia suffer domestic revolution, the loss of its Great Power status through military defeat in the Far East, and near bankruptcy only to stage such a quick and dramatic recovery that threatened Germany, Austria–Hungary, and even its entente partner, Great Britain?[2] Public property and capital

[1] This example illustrates how the inability of states to make credible commitments not to exploit future bargaining advantages encourages preventive wars that forestall unfavorable shifts in the balance of power. This is one of three causes of bargaining failures and war (Fearon 1995; Powell 2006).

[2] British officials, particularly in the Foreign Office, worried that a victorious Russia would set its sights on the most valuable component of the British Empire, namely India, after defeating Germany, taking control of the Straits, and consolidating its sphere of influence in the Balkans. For example, George Buchanan wrote to Arthur Nicolson on April 16, 1914, "Russia is rapidly becoming so powerful that we must retain her friendship at almost any cost. If she acquires the conviction that we are unreliable and useless as a friend, she may one day strike a bargain with Germany and resume her liberty of action in Turkey

controls helped vault the Russian government to financial preeminence within Europe and freed it from the rapidly tightening political constraints on armament spending faced by all other European governments. By 1913, political leaders in Germany, Britain, and Russia all believed that Russia possessed the financial capacity to accelerate the arms race on land, which would eventually leave it sitting atop the continental balance of military power. Their inability to keep pace in the arms race and Russia's inability to commit not to exploit its related financial and military advantages in the future prevented a peaceful compromise in the summer of 1914.

The rest of this chapter explores these arguments in the following fashion. I begin by examining how protective trade policies contributed to a critical political dispute between Germany and Russia. I then examine the fiscal foundations of Russia's post-1905 recovery in two parts. The first discusses how capital controls helped the French government aid Russia's escape from revolution in 1905. The discussion then shifts to the role played by these capital controls and public property in Russia's financial recovery. A final section examines how the financial foundations of Russian military power hindered a peaceful compromise by pushing both Russia and Germany toward war during the July crisis.

SETTING THE STAGE FOR WAR: IRON, RYE, AND THE RUSSO-GERMAN CONFLICT

The publication of Fritz Fischer's (1967, 1975) two key books, *Germany's Aims in the First World War* and *War of Illusions*, rekindled the debate over the relative role played by German political motivations in the origins of World War I.[3] Fischer's work shook the German historical community by challenging a tacit agreement on the role of World War II in German history,

and Persia. Our position then would be a very parlous one" (Gooch and Temperley 1938, pp. 784–5). Nicolson shared these concerns. Two weeks later he noted, "[I] do fear . . . that if we do not try to tighten up the ties with Russia she may become weary of us and throw us overboard. In that case we should be in an exceedingly awkward position, as she could cause us an infinity of annoyance, to put it mildly, in the Mid and Far East, without our being in any way able to retaliate . . . She could, without being hostile or even if you like unfriendly, cause immeasurable damage to our prestige and seriously shake our political position in India and the adjoining countries. This to me is such a nightmare that I would at almost any cost keep Russia's friendship" (Gooch and Temperley 1938, p. 786). For a broader discussion of these fears within the Foreign Office and how they shaped the British decision to enter the war on the side of Russia see Wilson (1984).

3 For reviews of the Fischer controversy and its central role in the historiography of World War I, see Geiss (1966), Langdon (1991), and Mombauer (2002). For a relatively recent response by Fischer to this controversy, see Fischer (1988).

one that had cast Hitler as an aberration. He argued that Germany's internal sociopolitical structure had long served as an incubator for National Socialism and for an aggressive foreign policy. Hitler's bid for world supremacy was a manifestation of the same internal pressures that had created a similar expansionist program in the years leading up to World War I. The German political elite, led by Chancellor Bethmann von Hollweg, had deliberately embraced the possibility of war after the second Moroccan crisis to pursue an expansionist foreign policy.[4] A defense of the empire from foreign invasion would rally nationalist support for traditional institutions like the monarchy and shift the internal balance of power away from socialists and toward conservative groups like large landowners. The seizure of new colonial markets in the Near East and Africa would tie industrial interests to the German state by providing new sources of raw materials and markets for their finished products.

While multiple components of the Fischer thesis remain controversial, such as his focus on expansive German interests as a key cause of World War I and the relative importance of domestic pressures in the construction of these foreign-policy interests, the debate inspired by his arguments has left a new historical consensus that shifts disproportionate responsibility for the outbreak of war on Germany.[5] This consensus helps make German policies in the decade before and actions during the July crisis crucial to the analysis here. I will not delve into the broader historical disagreement over the relative scope of Germany's political aims and the role these interests played in the German decision for war. Nor will I argue that the broader policy of Weltpolitik alone caused the war. However, Germany's pursuit of colonial markets bears on the arguments here linking liberal economic institutions to peace for two reasons.[6] First, as has been demonstrated amply by historians

[4] Bethmann's culpability in the German decision for war remains the subject of controversy. Fischer's more sinister characterization of him has been challenged by many who instead argue that he was a conservative reformer who had long restrained the military and the kaiser from war before eventually succumbing in the summer of 1914. For a recent review of Bethmann's place in the historiography of World War I see Jarausch (1988).

[5] Annika Mombauer (2002, pp. 223–4) concludes her review of the Fischer debate, "Is there a consensus at the end of so much debate? The Fischer controversy of the 1960s has itself become history... Some consensus has been reached, and most historians would no longer support Lloyd George's dictum of the European nations slithering into war accidentally... The current consensus is thus that Germany bore the main share, or at least a very large share of the blame, but the policies of other European governments also need to be considered for a fair judgment."

[6] The bargaining framework suggests that this debate over German political goals carries implications for the first stage of the war-generating process. However, even if we accept the arguments of those like Fischer (1975), Kaiser (1983), Pogge von Strandmann (1988),

and political scientists, the domestic coalitional dynamics that resulted in this global policy illustrate how government direction of internal markets can be utilized to build domestic support behind an aggressive foreign policy (Gordon 1974; Fischer 1975; Kaiser 1983; Snyder 1991; Berghahn 1993[1973]). Second, the implementation of Weltpolitik generated substantial political conflicts with Great Britain and Russia that pushed the continent closer to war.

The consequences of Weltpolitik on Anglo-German relations have received substantial historical attention.[7] Industrialization and urbanization created a looming political crisis in Germany following unification. By fueling demand for an urban labor force, industrialization fostered the emergence of a growing political tension between a socialist electorate in the cities and the conservative agrarian class whose waning political influence was propped up by a constitution that protected rural representation and the rights of the individual states. These pressures loomed throughout the 1890s as the kaiser and conservative elements in his cabinet and the army contemplated a coup d'état to disband the Reichstag and rewrite the electoral laws to minimize socialist representation. Moreover, Caprivi's liberalizing tariff reforms of the 1890s had provoked a sharp backlash from conservative landowners, a key government coalitional mainstay.

The launching of the German naval program created an opportunity for the government to counteract these pressures and reestablish the alliance between conservatives and industrial interests. While Tirpitz trumpeted the strategic benefits of a navy that challenged Britain's commercial supremacy and could be used as an instrument of coercive diplomacy, the opportunity to consolidate the government's support coalition without threatening civil war was crucial in the passing of the Navy Laws of 1898 and 1900

Rohl (1995), and Lieber (2007) and adopt the view that Germany went to war in July 1914 as part of larger political program designed to establish global hegemony, an answer to the question "Why war in 1914?" must include an investigation of the factors that prevented a bargain that would have enabled Germany to achieve its political and economic program without suffering the costs of war. Bethmann's repeated attempts to construct a global compromise with Britain demonstrate his willingness to view Weltpolitik as complementary with British interests (Kaiser 1983). A focus on the commitment problem thus directs attention away from explanations that rely solely on conceptions of conflicting national interests to account for the outbreak of war. The adoption of this framework carries important implications for the relative role played by Weltpolitik in the decision for war. This discussion here thus does not claim that the domestic coalitional dynamics behind Weltpolitik, which then generated political conflict with both Britain and Russia, provide a complete explanation for war in July 1914.

7 See for example Steiner (1977), Berghahn (1993[1973]), Kennedy (1980), Kaiser (1983), Snyder (1991), and Ferguson (1998).

(e.g., Berghahn 1993[1973]; Gordon 1974; Kaiser 1983). Industrial interests favored the construction of a navy because it offered strategic protection to international commerce if the global economy were to break apart into trading blocs, as Joseph Chamberlain's campaign for imperial preference in Great Britain suggested. Additionally, in light of the long depression from which Europe had only recently emerged, steady government demand for new battleships also created protection against downturns in the business cycle.

Arguing that Germany was necessarily a continental power, agrarian interests preferred that the resources devoted to the navy instead would have gone to the army.[8] However, the decision to pay for the navy by reestablishing a broad set of agricultural tariffs that reduced grain imports from its American, Argentine, and Russian competitors solidified agricultural support behind Weltpolitik. While it was believed that these tariffs would generate the necessary revenue to pay for this naval buildup, they also increased the incomes of the agricultural class. The imposition of the tariffs thus allowed the government to generate side payments for conservative support of its navy and divert the massive armament costs to the left wing of the electorate.

Most importantly, the international ramifications of these domestic pressures were immense. By utilizing naval construction and the agricultural tariffs as means to solidify domestic support, the German government initiated a policy that challenged fundamental British interests. Despite repeated attempts to convince the British government of its benign intentions, the navy program and Germany's unwillingness to slow construction until 1912 threatened British commercial interests and its reliance on naval supremacy to protect the British Isles (e.g., Kennedy 1980; Steiner 1977).

Even though Weltpolitik escalated tensions between the two countries, its role in the respective decisions by Britain and Germany to go to war against each other in 1914 remains less established. Their relationship had been marked by scattered cooperation in the decade before World War I. Both Bulow and Tirpitz viewed Weltpolitik as a policy designed to secure small foreign-policy concessions, not risk a broader war with England (Kaiser 1983). German hesitation over going to war over Morocco both in 1906 and in 1911 illustrates this. By the fall of 1912, Germany had begun shifting national defense resources away from naval construction and had accepted defeat in the naval arms race. Moreover, Bethmann repeatedly courted

[8] For a good discussion of the relative breakdown of economic and political interests within Germany and England during this period, see Chapter 17 in Kennedy (1980).

colonial cooperation with Britain, resulting in the conclusion of the Baghdad railway agreement in July 1914.

The consequences of Weltpolitik, and in particular the use of tariffs to construct its domestic foundation of political support, bear more directly on the origins of war in 1914 in the context of Russo-German relations. Prospects of an ensuing tariff war and the risks associated with growing German influence in the Ottoman Empire over the first six months of 1914 contributed to Russian decisions to implement retaliatory tariffs, adopt a less conciliatory approach in foreign policy, and ultimately to recommend a partial mobilization against Austria–Hungary during the July crisis.

Russo-German relations were marked by ambivalence after Bismarck pushed Russia closer to France with the closure of the German money market in 1887. On the one hand, the two governments repeatedly, but irregularly, demonstrated a capacity for cooperation with each other.[9] Monarchical ties between Wilhelm and Nicholas kept alive the potential rebirth of the Three Emperors' League or a continental grouping among Germany, France, and Russia directed against Britain. Although subsequently aborted as the extent of Russia's financial predicament following its war with Japan became clear, the two emperors signed an alliance pact at Björkö in July 1905 (Taylor 1954, pp. 432–4). Hoping to secure German opposition to further Austro-Hungarian expansion in the Balkans, Russia agreed to German participation in the Baghdad Railway in the summer of 1910. However, growing German dependence on its alliance with Austria–Hungary pushed the two powers apart, particularly over any development in the Balkans. German military threats supporting Austria–Hungary in the Bosnian annexationist crisis provided a humiliating reminder to Russia of the diplomatic shackles imposed by its post-1905 military weakness.

The deterioration of relations following the Liman von Sanders crisis effectively ended any hope of reconciliation between the conservative powers. The tsar, along with many Russian leaders, had long coveted the straits at Constantinople and regarded unrestricted passage of merchant ships through them as critical to the Russian economy. The appointment of a German general, Liman von Sanders, in December 1913 to command the Ottoman garrison at Constantinople fueled Russian fears about the broader threat posed by Germany to these economic interests. Still an agrarian economy, more than 60 percent of exported grains, Russia's key export and source of hard currency, flowed through the Bosphorus Straits

[9] A sizable component of the tsar's court and multiple advisors, including Sergei Witte and P. N. Durnovo, continued to favor closer ties with Germany up to the outbreak of war. For a discussion of this group see Lieven (1983, pp. 65–83).

(Fischer 1975, p. 330). The tsar worried that Germany was exploiting the Ottoman Empire's weakness following the Balkan Wars and leveraging security responsibilities at Constantinople for political influence there. When the British ambassador, Buchanan, queried the tsar in April of 1914 about the possibility of a rapprochement with Germany, the tsar dismissed the idea by pointing to growing German influence at Constantinople. He expressed a concern that Germany sought to "shut Russia altogether in the Black Sea" and said he would be willing to prevent this by going to war if necessary.[10]

These concerns were reinforced as Russia and Germany began posturing for negotiations over a successor agreement to their commercial treaty of 1904. Since Bismarck had constructed the famous iron and rye coalition, a series of trade wars had marked often-tense commercial negotiations between Russia and Germany. While Germany traditionally maintained high agricultural tariffs and subsidies to appease landowners and maintain the domestic coalition supporting the kaiser, Russia protected its nascent industrial base.[11] This earlier accord – negotiated while Russia was at war with Japan and in need of access to the German money market – had provoked a sharp backlash from Russian agricultural interests. High protective tariffs had shielded the German market from Russian grain. Russian rye exports to Germany in 1912 were approximately 30 percent of their level in 1902 (Fischer 1975, p. 367). Despite Russia's abundance of land, agricultural subsidies made Prussian grains competitive in western Russia and had paradoxically turned Russia's large agricultural interests into an import-competing sector. In response to these agricultural pressures, the Russian government instituted sharp tariff hikes on rye, wheat, barley, oats, peas, and beans in June of 1914 (before the assassination of Franz Ferdinand).

This growing economic conflict during the first six months of 1914 increased Russia's willingness to face larger risks of war while defending vital national interests, particularly following the removal of Vladimir Kokovtsov as the chairman of the Council of Ministers in February of 1914.[12] While remaining committed to a system of industrial protection that disadvantaged agriculture, Kokovtsov had long sought to diminish the risks of war and the potential for another domestic revolution after 1905. A growing

[10] Buchanan to Grey (Gooch and Temperley 1938, p. 781).

[11] Writing about the transition in Russian foreign policy as the Three Emperors' League expired and Russia moved closer to France in the late 1880s, Geyer (1987, p. 152) notes, "Protectionism was clearly the Achilles' heel of the Russo-German Entente . . . There was an inevitability in the mounting economic antagonism because neither Germany nor Russia could renounce protectionism."

[12] For a discussion of how Kokovtsov's removal reoriented Russian foreign policy, see McDonald (1992).

desire to reverse this course, which had contributed to perceptions of Russian weakness following the Bosnian annexation crisis and during the Balkan Wars of 1912–13, emerged in the Russian cabinet during the Liman von Sanders crisis. Just before a peaceful compromise was reached, Russia's foreign minister, war minister, naval minister, and chief of the general staff voiced support for occupying parts of the Ottoman Empire (McDonald 1992, pp. 194–5).

This willingness to confront Germany grew as A.V. Krivoshein, the minister of agriculture, emerged as the de facto leader of the new cabinet. He played the central role in the key meetings of July 24–5 that set the stage for Russia's entry into World War I.[13] During these meetings, Russian leaders took the most resolute steps aimed at reversing the decade-long tendency toward restraint in foreign policy. They decided to ask Austria–Hungary for a delay in the ultimatum to Serbia and to mobilize the army in districts bordering Austria–Hungary. Bark, the minister of finance whose notes provide the key historical record of these deliberations, commented that Krivoshein's arguments not to abandon Russia's Balkan interests were critical to the cabinet's decisions (Lieven 1983, pp. 142–3). Krivoshein argued it was time for Russia to show "that we had come to the end of the concessions we were prepared to make," believing that caution and restraint had simply heightened German aggression (Lieven 1983, p. 143).

Perhaps most importantly, the ongoing economic conflict with Germany contributed to Krivoshein's readiness to defend Russia's interests with actions that heightened the risk of war. As a key leader of the conservative bloc behind Kokovtsov's removal, Krivoshein wanted to redress the long imbalance between the agricultural and industrial sectors in the Russian economy. These policy goals had already been reflected in the June 1914 tariff hikes directed against German agricultural exports. However, these policy goals also influenced Krivoshein's arguments during the July crisis. Spring (1988a, p. 68) writes, "[t]he stand he took at the Council of 24 July was symptomatic of the decline of the pro-German lobby amongst the

[13] Williamson (1988, p. 813) writes of the decisions made at the July 24–5 meetings, "Simply put, the Russians initiated a series of military measures well in advance of the other great powers, although Austria–Hungary's partial mobilization came shortly after the Russian initiative. These measures, moreover, were the equivalent of partial mobilization and accelerated the crisis far more than recent historiography has usually conceded." Lieven (1983, p. 146) concurs with the importance of these decisions for the outbreak of war noting, "Russia's key decision was the one taken on 24/25 July to support Serbian independence even at the risk of war." For a discussion of Russian decision making and mobilization measures between July 24 and July 30 that blames the war's outbreak on Russia, see Turner (1968).

landowning interests... But by 1914 an awareness was growing of the conflict of agrarian interests with those of Germany... Krivoshein considered a robust stand should be taken for the protection of agriculture."

The simmering economic conflict between Russia and Germany assumed great importance in the first six months of 1914. German agricultural protection led to demands within Russia to restrict imports of German grain and to institute a shift in foreign policy. A trade war loomed as Germany indicated that it would be unwilling to make concessions in the 1904 agreement and Russia instituted significant new agricultural tariffs in June of 1914. These tariffs were large enough that groups in Germany feared they would act as an import ban (Fischer 1975, p. 367). As the tsar stated to the British ambassador, George Buchanan, Russia could no longer eschew the risk of war while defending vital interests like its position in the Straits. The need to defend these economic interests by adopting a tougher line vis-à-vis Germany played an important role in the cabinet deliberations that placed Russia on a path to war in 1914.

CAPITAL CONTROLS, THE FRANCO-RUSSIAN ALLIANCE, AND THE BEGINNING OF RUSSIA'S POST-1905 RECOVERY

The emergence of this Russo-German conflict following the Liman von Sanders crisis bears on another significant storyline in the origins of World War I. Fears of growing Russian military power dominated internal strategic debates in Germany in the two years before July 1914 and bolstered arguments favoring a preventive war in 1914.[14] How did Russia emerge so quickly over the previous decade from the depths of domestic revolution, financial bankruptcy, and defeat in war against Japan to become the most threatening military power in Europe? Two recent histories of the European arms race in the decade before World War I underscore the importance of these developments in the history of this war's origins. David Stevenson (1996, p. 146) writes, "Developments in Russia between 1908 and 1912 undermined the military equilibrium not only in Eastern Europe but in Europe as a whole: in the land arms race the government in St. Petersburg can most justifiably be said to have fired the starting shot." David Herrmann (1996, p. 7) concurs, noting, "The history of the balance of military power in Europe in the decade between 1904 and the outbreak of the First World

[14] Wolfgang Mommsen (1973) writes, "The military leaders were seriously worried about the reappearance of Russia as a first-rate military power – *and as we know now beyond doubt* – they were harboring the idea of a preventive war against Russia and France, for within a few years the Schlieffen Plan would no longer work."

War was in large measure the story of Russia's prostration, its subsequent recovery, and the effects of this development upon the strategic situation."

The next two sections detail the sources of this Russian phoenix and its relationship to the start of World War I. This section focuses on French efforts to restore the military capability of its alliance partner following the revolutionary year of 1905. This discussion illustrates two critical theoretical components of this book. Capital controls helped the French government cultivate domestic support for its key foreign-policy goal – the preservation of the alliance with Russia. Moreover, the domestic financial autonomy of the Russian government in 1905–6, created by these capital flows, strengthened it at home despite widespread societal opposition and a calamitous defeat at war. The Russian government's escape from chaos was a critical first step to the reconstitution of its military power that would take place over the next nine years. A following section then examines how Russia's comparative financial power enabled it to surge ahead in the arms race on land.

France's alliance with Russia had long served as a cornerstone of its national security policy, particularly in the decade before World War I.[15] The key military components of the agreement were ratified in 1894. The alliance was designed to protect France's position relative to Germany and Italy, and to preserve Russia's position relative to Germany and Austria–Hungary, particularly in the Balkans. Russian military strength would help offset a military balance that favored Germany over France. The French hoped that the specter of fighting simultaneously on its eastern and western fronts against Russia and France would deter a German attack. Substantial economic ties bound these two states even closer together than other alliances.[16] Large quantities of French capital flowed into Russia to finance industrialization and frequent government budget deficits after Bismarck closed the German money market to the Russian government in 1887. Russia's enormous appetite for foreign investment and the paucity of surplus capital outside of British, French, and German money markets limited its bargaining power relative to creditors. The French government repeatedly used capital controls that required its approval for sovereign lending to direct private capital to Russia in exchange for important political concessions that reaffirmed the latter's alliance commitments.

The Russian government stood on the brink of complete disaster in 1905. The failing war against Japan had provoked a domestic revolution, left the

[15] For discussions of the importance of this alliance to French security, see Keiger (1983), Krumeich (1984), Langdon (1991), and Joll (1992[1984]).

[16] For discussions of the links between these capital flows and the alliance, see Crisp (1960/61), Long (1968), Sontag (1968), Collins (1973), and Spring (1988b).

government on the verge of bankruptcy, and undermined its ability to play a significant role in European politics. Apart from suffering a tremendous defeat that resulted in the almost complete destruction of its navy and a dangerous shift of much of its army from the western portion of the empire to the east, the war had provoked a violent backlash against the tsarist regime. A series of strikes had paralyzed industrial production in the winter of 1904–5 and forced the diversion of large components of the Russian military to internal policing duties. Eventually to stave off revolution, the tsar capitulated to popular pressure and allowed the creation of a popularly elected legislative body, the Duma, in October 1905.

The financial costs of war and labor and railway stoppages in the fall of 1905 pushed the Russian government to the verge of bankruptcy. The war was initially paid for by injecting more paper rubles into the domestic money supply. Because the government possessed a surplus of gold reserves at the start of the war, it could do so without endangering its legal commitments with respect to the gold standard. This breathing space was eliminated by war's end as the number of paper rubles in circulation had doubled in less than two years' time. In fact, a financial survey within the government in 1905 determined that gold reserves would fall below the statutory minimum after making a series of interest payments on its debt in January of 1906 (Long 1968, pp. 121–4). These financial difficulties were compounded in the fall of 1905 as opposition politicians attacked the government's commitment to the gold standard by encouraging private citizens to withdraw gold deposits from state banks.[17] Having already exhausted the supply of domestic credit, government officials worried that the collapse of the gold standard would eliminate its ability to borrow in international markets, necessary to both liquidate the financial obligations from the war and ensure industrial investment critical to economic growth.[18]

Shortly after the war's outbreak, Russia's Finance Minister Vladimir Kokovtsov constructed a plan to fund the war through foreign loans, domestic loans, previous budget surpluses, an expansion of the money supply in the Far East, and reduced government expenditures on nonmilitary items.[19] In the initial phases of the war, his plan succeeded. He secured a loan of 300 million rubles (800 million francs) from French banks in April 1904 and another loan of 230 million rubles (500 million marks) from German

[17] State banks lost at least 16% of their deposits, mostly in gold, from August 1905 to January 1906 Long (1968, pp. 118–19). See also Chapter 8 in Kokovtsov (1935).

[18] See for example Geyer (1987, p. 230).

[19] For a discussion of this plan, see Kokovtsov (1935, pp. 14–18).

banks in January 1905.[20] As the tide turned steadily against the Russians in the war, the French government grew increasingly skeptical that its alliance partner could still effectively fight in Europe and became much less willing to approve the loans that were necessary to continue the war. This shifting position manifested after the Russian defeat at the Battle of Mukden (February–March 1905). Kokovtsov initially successfully negotiated another loan with a French banking syndicate in March 1905 for 225 million rubles (600 million francs). The French banks then quickly withdrew from this deal after the French Finance Minister Maurice Rouvier informed them that he opposed the loan.[21]

The Battle of Mukden changed the public and official mindset in France toward Russia.[22] Seeing the price of Russian bonds fall, French banks hesitated at extending more credit to finance the failing military venture. French officials in the foreign ministry and Rouvier also began to discuss how to pressure Russia to withdraw from the war against Japan so that its capacity to fight in Europe would not be diminished any further. Although hesitant to offend Russia, they recognized that cutting off Russia from more credit was likely to give the latter little choice but to push for some peace settlement.[23] These financial pressures levied by the French government, internal concerns about the state of domestic finances, and increasing fear over the heightening instability within Russia together pushed the tsar to enter peace talks with Japan in May 1905.[24]

The peace settlement negotiated by Theodore Roosevelt at Portsmouth did not end the acute political crisis facing the tsarist regime. Even though Witte used these peace talks to begin negotiations over a large international loan that would simultaneously dispose of the war's costs, bolster internal gold reserves, and reduce Russia's credit dependence on France, domestic instability within Russia increased the reticence of foreign creditors to extend capital in the midst of such a crisis. The general strike in October 1905 dramatically contracted economic activity and, consequently, shrank normal sources of government revenue. French banks became increasingly

[20] To put these numbers in some perspective, the ordinary Russian budget was approximately 1.89 billion rubles in 1903 (Apostol, Bernatzky, and Michelsen 1928, p. 65).

[21] Geyer (1987, p. 233).

[22] Working in the British Embassy in St. Petersburg, Cecil B. Spring Rice felt that this battle also played critical role in German decision to initiate the Moroccan crisis. FO 800/177, February 20, 1906.

[23] These conversations are discussed in Long (1968, pp. 87–90); and Paléologue (1924).

[24] Both Kokovtsov and Witte lobbied the tsar extensively to withdraw from the war for financial reasons. For a discussion of these considerations and the meeting at which the tsar announced his decision to enter into peace talks, see Geyer (1987, p. 235).

sensitive to growing domestic support in France for the Russian opposition and to the real possibility that a revolution in Russia would threaten more than 10 billion francs invested there. These fears were compounded by at least two more developments. The first Moroccan crisis and the possibility of a European war right after Russia's defeat caused a run on French banks that held large amounts of Russian securities. Moreover, French banks also wished to preserve domestic access to credit to fund a potential war against Germany. Second, opposition parties in Russia threatened not to fulfill any loan obligations entered into by the tsar prior to the meeting of the newly created Duma.

By the end of December 1905, Russia stood on the brink of financial bankruptcy and revolution. The tsar sent Kokovtsov to Paris with instructions to make the French aware that he would trade diplomatic support at the Algeciras conference[25] for a loan.[26] Kokovtsov began his visit in January by opening talks with leaders of the largest banks in France. Their representatives initially expressed doubt over the benefits of preserving the gold standard in Russia and, as a consequence, the necessity of extending new loans to Russia. These hesitations changed dramatically after Kokovtsov sought assistance from Rouvier. At an initial meeting, Kokovtsov shared the tsar's willingness to follow direction from France at Algeciras if the French capital markets were again opened to Russia. Unwilling to approve a large loan that would end Russia's financial predicament until the completion of the conference, Rouvier promised Kokovtsov to pressure French bankers to grant a short-term loan to Russia that would end its immediate liquidity pressures. The following day Kokovtsov found the bankers more agreeable to a short-term loan of 100 million rubles. Kokovtsov writes of Rouvier's subsequent meeting with the bankers, "According to Netzlin the Credit Lyonnais had attempted to object and to argue that the French banks did not need a gold standard in Russia. Rouvier brushed aside the rejection, however, and rebuked the sponsor by saying that a stable monetary system in Russia was necessary to France and her government. His rebuke silenced all opposition, and the representatives of the group announced that they were ready to start negotiations with me . . ." (Kokovtsov 1935, p. 97).

Upon the successful completion of the Algeciras conference, the Russian government entered into negotiations for a giant loan of nearly 850 million

[25] The international conference convened at Algeciras brought the first Moroccan crisis to a peaceful conclusion. Sensing an opportunity to weaken either the newly formed Anglo-French entente or the Russo-French alliance, Germany had challenged French interests in Morocco in 1905.

[26] For the details of his negotiations in France, see Kokovtsov (1935, pp. 90–97).

rubles (more than half of which was eventually subscribed to in France) that ended the financial crisis in Russia.[27] Perhaps just as important, British participation in the loan helped lay the groundwork for the Anglo-Russian Entente. Although German banks had initially planned on subscribing to the loan, the German government forbade their participation after observing Russia's support for France at the Algeciras conference. These developments effectively ended the brief flirtation between Russia and Germany initiated at the Björkö meetings. These developments even pushed Witte away for a time from his traditional pro-German tendencies. The French government had successfully leveraged its control over its capital market and Russia's financial difficulties to secure multiple foreign-policy victories that included stabilizing its alliance partner.

This episode in Russian history and Franco-Russian relations bears on multiple aspects of the links here between government constraints on markets and war. First, capital controls enabled the French government to manipulate jointly its own domestic financial sector and the Russian government in service of its critical foreign-policy goal – the preservation of Russia's capacity to fulfill its alliance obligations. Its refusal to approve loans forced French bankers to withdraw from negotiations with the Russian government in the spring of 1905. This financial vulnerability in turn led the tsar to halt the war against Japan. Kokovtsov's plan to prosecute a war largely through access to foreign credit was effectively thwarted when the French government eliminated this access. Rouvier then used the lure of renewed access to French capital markets in January 1906 to ensure Russian support at Algeciras. Perhaps most illustrative of the French government's power over the holders of private capital, Rouvier convinced them to extend credit to Russia when they appeared most unwilling.[28]

Second, it is highly unlikely that the dramatic recovery staged by Russia in the ensuing decade as it recaptured its lost Great Power status would have been possible had Russia collapsed into a state of political and financial anarchy in 1905 and 1906. The withdrawal from war and international politics during the 1917 revolution powerfully suggests that Russia may have followed a similar course in 1905 had the tsarist regime collapsed. French loans played a critical part in helping the government escape from revolution

[27] Because elections to the Duma had just been held in March, the French were still concerned that Russia still might default on all of its obligations incurred during the war. Poincare demanded that the tsar issue an *ukaz* (which the latter subsequently did on April 10) stripping the Duma of any control over credit operations.

[28] Similarly, Kokovtsov argues that Poincare was critical to the success of the loan negotiations of April 1906.

and bankruptcy while preserving the gold standard. Whereas the split with Germany over Morocco effectively closed the German capital market to Russia, the French were quite willing to replace this lost capital. With the help of another loan in 1909 from France, the Russian treasury possessed a surplus by 1910. In the period between 1908 and 1913, government ordinary revenues skyrocketed, growing more than 42 percent (Apostol et al. 1928, p. 222).[29] French capital paved the way for the broader and dramatic recovery of the tsarist regime and the Russian economy in the ensuring decade.

Third, the ability to secure credit was critical to the tsarist regime's ability to avoid bankruptcy, remain in office, and limit the Duma's role in Russian politics. Sergei Witte, the tsar's chairman of the Council of Ministers, described the April 1906 loan as "the one that saved Russia."[30] Mehlinger and Thompson argue that this loan played an important role in the long-run political history of Russia by limiting the power of the Duma relative to the tsarist regime.[31] They describe Witte's strategy as one of strengthening the political independence of the government relative to the Duma by preventing the latter from using this financial weakness as leverage. Witte remarked of this strategy in his memoirs, "My intention was to conclude the loan before the opening of the Imperial Duma. As I felt sure that the First Duma would be unbalanced and to a certain extent revengeful, I was afraid that its interference might thwart the loan negotiations and render the bankers less tractable. As a result, the government, without the funds, would lose the freedom of action, which is so essential during a period of upheaval."[32] This relative importance of the loan to the preservation of the

[29] This expansion was larger than the level of growth for the entire Russian economy during this period, which was approximately 34% (Gregory 1982).

[30] Interestingly, the tsar referred specifically to the importance of this loan to the regime and the critical roles played by Witte and Kokovtsov in weathering this crisis when he relieved them of their duties in April 1906 and February 1914, respectively. He wrote to Witte, "The successful completion of the loan forms the best page in the history of your ministerial activity. It is for the Government a great moral triumph and a pledge of Russia's undisturbed and peaceful development in the future" (Mehlinger and Thompson 1972, p. 237). To Kokovtsov, the tsar wrote, "Ten years ago I entrusted you with the administration of the Ministry of Finance. Having entered upon the execution of these duties, always intricate and responsible, but especially so during a time of war, followed more by a period of internal disorder, you carried out the task imposed on you, notwithstanding all its difficulties, with distinguished success. Owing to your real and characteristic economy the Budgets of the State for a number of years have shown a surplus of revenue over expenditure, and the Treasury 'free balance' has reached unprecedented proportions." Nicholas to Kokovtsov, FO 371/2091 February 15, 1914.

[31] See Chapter 7 of Mehlinger and Thompson (1972).

[32] As quoted in Mehlinger and Thompson (1972, pp. 238–9). They (p. 239) comment on Witte's strategy, "This paragraph holds they key to the problem: it was not so much a

tsarist regime can also be seen in the opposition of the centrist and leftist parties to the loan during its negotiations. V. A. Maklakov, a member of the Kadet Party in Moscow, traveled to Paris and lobbied French government officials, including Clemenceau, not to approve the loan to the tsarist regime. Maklakov argued that the loan would strengthen the tsar relative to the Duma, enabling him to dissolve it if necessary, and halt the potential for democratic reform in Russia.[33]

The intervention by the French government in the loan negotiations coupled with the internal struggle between the tsar and Duma also led to an important clarification and constraint on the Duma's powers. The Social Democratic and Socialist Parties in Russia had both issued warnings to the French government that any loans agreed to by the tsar in the period of revolutionary activity would be repudiated when the tsarist government fell. These warnings were coupled with those from more centrist parties challenging the legality and thus obligation to repay any loans completed between the October Manifesto of 1905 and the convocation of the First Duma.[34] These clear signals of opposition worried both the French government and banks about the safety of any new loans extended to Russia. The French government demanded a guarantee from the Russian government that it possessed the legal right to conclude a loan without the Duma's approval. Shortly thereafter at an April 1906 meeting of the State Council, Witte convinced this body to issue an *ukaz*, or new state law, that effectively stripped the Duma of any power to determine the credit operations of the Russian government. Given the historical importance of foreign loans in normal fiscal procedures of the Russian government, this law strengthened autocratic control over the purse strings and set an important precedent by eliminating an important source of popular, budgetary control over the tsar's policies.

These loans fulfilled Kokovtsov's financial goals initially set at the outset of the Russo-Japanese War. The scale of these loans with respect to normal

question of strict legality concerning who had control over financial matters as it was a desire by the government not to be dependent on the Duma. Therefore Witte's success in negotiating the loan contributed ultimately to undermining his own efforts to introduce civil freedom and political reform into Russia, because the autocracy, given considerable financial independence, was able to operate with less regard for the wishes of the representatives of the people in the Duma that might otherwise have been the case. A bankrupt government would inevitably have been far more beholden to the Duma."

33 For a discussion of Maklakov's visit and pleas see Crisp (1960/61) and Chapter 10 in Long (1968).

34 Aware that it would need access to foreign credit to undertake its reform program, the centrist Kadet Party eventually announced its willingness to fulfill the obligations of any loan entered into the tsarist government. It, however, continued to criticize the loan.

government revenues and the total cost of the war were enormous. The two loans issued in 1906 comprised nearly 50 percent of ordinary government revenues in that year. The total cost of the war against Japan was more than 3 billion rubles. More than 80 percent of these expenditures were met through foreign borrowing (Apostol et al. 1928, p. 68)! Kokovtsov had succeeded in financing a war without increasing the burden of taxation on the Russian people.

The relationship among these financial concerns, the tsarist regime's ability to hold on to power, and the decision to end the war correspond with the discussion of the links among financial autonomy, regime survival, and decisions for war from Chapters 2 and 3. While these earlier discussions pointed to public property as a critical source of both financial and policy autonomy for government officials, access to French credit offered similar political benefits during and after the war against Japan. Like public property, this resource relieved the government from limiting current private consumption by raising taxes or expropriating private assets to fund the war effort.[35] Access to foreign capital, which was controlled by the French government, influenced Russia's decision for peace and its capacity to weather the storm of domestic revolution following the war. More importantly, as Sergei Witte would later acknowledge, access to French credit strengthened the position of the autocracy relative to the Duma. This episode thus possesses remarkable similarity to the story told by Locke (1988), North and Weingast (1989), and Pipes (1999) among others about the emergence of parliamentary constraints on monarchical authority in seventeenth-century England. Unlike in England, however, access to French capital freed the Russian government from having to make critical political concessions to the newly organized Duma in the midst of a financial emergency and helped it remain in power despite losing a disastrous war.

PUBLIC PROPERTY AND THE RUSSIAN PHOENIX

Along with access to French capital, substantial quantities of public property helped the tsarist regime to recover from the financial and political crises

[35] Bueno de Mesquita et al. (1999, 2003) describe this basic dilemma faced by governments when setting optimal tax rates. While high tax rates secure public access to larger portions of aggregate economic activity, they also encourage private citizens to work less – which then shrinks total economic activity – because they reap smaller portions of their economic activities. The use of credit operations, like public property, frees the government from making this difficult choice at least in the short term. Recall also the quote by Ricardo that initially motivated this discussion in Chapter 3. Ricardo pointed to constraints on a government's ability to secure credit for wartime expenditures as a critical source of peace.

of 1905. Before the turn of the century, most European governments relied on some mix of tariffs, consumption taxes on such sin products as alcohol and tobacco, and loans to fund most public expenditures including those for the military. An accelerating arms race at sea and on land in the decade before World War I tested the political foundation of this financial paradigm for all participants. Most governments were confronted with the twin challenge of finding new sources of revenue to offset exploding defense budgets without undermining traditional political coalitions that rested on the exclusion of the far left. Between 1906 and 1913, Russia moved from a position of near financial destitution to being the financial powerhouse of Europe.[36] This fiscal fitness would insulate the Russian government from domestic resistance to military spending, lead it to abandon the foreign-policy restraint that was a legacy of 1905, and rapidly shift the balance of military power on the continent in its favor.

The first symptom of Russia's financial power was an incredible growth in government revenues during the decade prior to World War I. This upward trend is displayed in Table 7.1. Between 1908 and 1913, ordinary government revenues skyrocketed, growing more than 42 percent from 2.4 billion rubles to 3.4 billion rubles (Apostol et al. 1928, p. 222). The treasury consistently ran annual surpluses during this period, but they grew in size following the immediate financial recovery from the Russo-Japanese War. These surpluses averaged approximately 200 million rubles in the five years prior to 1914. The government also accelerated its debt repayment during this period.[37]

How did this radical change in the balance of financial power and thus the future balance of military power in Europe come about in the span of only a decade? Undoubtedly, two economic factors loomed large in this recovery. First, Kokovtsov embarked on a dramatic program of financial retrenchment in the aftermath of the Russo-Japanese War. Poincare's insistence that Russia not borrow in foreign credit markets as a condition of the giant 1906 loan partly forced this strategy to ensure that Russia's revenue needs could be met internally.[38] Ultimately, Kokovtsov's steadfast devotion to these spending constraints would shorten his career in government. A widespread revolt

36 In a study of British military observers in Russia, Keith Neilson (1985, p. 207) writes of this dramatic turnaround, "As far as the British were concerned, Russia had clearly remained in the first division of European great powers, at least in financial terms."

37 The government put a halt to this early debt repayment in 1912 to help pay for growing armaments costs. British Foreign Office, Russia – Annual Report, 1913, FO 371/2092.

38 Long (1968, p. 233).

Table 7.1. *Russian government revenues and expenditures before World War I*

Revenues	1903	1908	1913
Spirit Monopoly	542.2 (26.7%)	718.8 (29.7%)	899.2 (26.3%)
Railways	453.3 (22.3%)	567.9 (23.5%)	813.6 (23.8%)
Other Public Property	117.1 (5.8%)	140.3 (5.8%)	229.9 (6.7%)
Customs	241.4 (11.9%)	274.3 (11.4%)	352.9 (10.3%)
Remaining Revenue Sources	678 (33.3%)	716.7 (29.6%)	1119.4 (32.8%)
Total Ordinary Revenue	2,032	2,418	3,415

Expenditures	1903	1913
Administration	327.4	495.2
Debt Service	288.7	424.3
Other Expenses	213.7	526.2
State Enterprises (Railway and Spirits)	586.9	821.7
National Defense	466.3	825.9
Total Ordinary Expenses	1883	3093.3

Note: All figures are in millions of rubles. Numbers in parentheses indicate the proportion of total annual revenues derived from that source.
Source: Apostol et al. (1928, pp. 43, 61, 64–5).

within the tsar's Council of Ministers led to his dismissal in February 1914 largely because of his repeated unwillingness to approve more spending for each of the ministries.[39] Second, robust economic growth facilitated by surplus harvests also increased the size of the pool of potential economic resources at the government's disposal.[40] From 1908 to 1913, the size of the Russian economy increased by approximately 34 percent (Gregory 1982, p. 59).

Most importantly, the Russian government harnessed this growing economic capacity for the arms race more effectively than its European counterparts did. As a percentage of gross domestic product (GDP), Russia spent more on defense than Germany (Ferguson 1994, p. 164). Over the period from 1903 to 1913, Russian aggregate increases in defense spending were three times those of French increases and six times those of Austro-Hungarian and British increases (Apostol et al. 1928, p. 66). Defense expenditures as a percentage of total government spending increased from

[39] Buchanan to Grey, February 12, 1914; February 15, 1914; FO 371/2091.

[40] Neilson (1995) argues that the above-average harvests were critical to the growing pool of national resources for defense.

23.2 percent in 1908 to 28.3 percent in 1913 (Neilson 1995, p. 102). The Balkan Wars dramatically increased these pressures. British observers estimated the total military expenditures in Russia, including normal and emergency expenditures for the partial mobilizations, increased from approximately 586 million rubles (62 million pounds) in 1912 to 945 million rubles (100 million pounds) in 1913.[41]

The institutional structure of the domestic economy enhanced the capacity of the Russian government to utilize its nation's economic resources for national defense more effectively than other Great Powers.[42] The Russian government did not face the same set of political constraints that existed in France, Germany, and Britain. While these governments were forced to upset traditional support coalitions and integrate the political left – a group that had clearly signaled opposition to future increases in defense outlays – as the price of property or income taxes necessary to fund military expansion, the Russian government could increase defense spending as necessary to continue the arms race without facing similar domestic political resistance. This financial autonomy came from two critical sources – access to foreign capital markets facilitated by capital controls in France and a system of public revenue procurement that relied heavily on public property.

First, French loans played a critical role in the recovery of Russia's military and financial position. Previous sections have already examined how the loans of 1906 helped Russia stave off bankruptcy and revolution. In 1913 and 1914, this privileged financial access would enhance Russia's military capability by enabling it to begin a massive strategic railway construction program that could decrease its mobilization time at the start of a war. In the midst of internal discussions over its Great Program of military spending, Russian officials began negotiations with French bankers to obtain capital for railway construction. When the French government learned of these talks, they informed the French syndicate in charge of the negotiations that government approval depended on an increase in the size of

41 British Foreign Office, Russia – Annual Report 1913, FO 371/2092. The report quotes all figures in pounds. The pre-war conversion from rubles to pounds was 9.45 to 1 (Bidwell 1970, p. 43).

42 While some of the political insulation generated by relative fiscal strength can be attributed to the autocratic institutions of the tsarist regime that enabled the Russian government to disband the Duma until it was populated by more pliant representatives, there are at least two reasons to doubt explanations of relative Russian fiscal strength that rely solely on differences in regime type. First, it must be remembered that French capital played a critical role in propping up the troubled Russian autocracy in 1905 and 1906. Second, similar fiscal constraints faced both by democratic France and autocratic Germany underscore the need to look beyond regime type to understand differences in relative fiscal capacity in the European arms race.

Russia's standing army and the use of these funds to build strategic railways that would decrease mobilization times.[43] Despite some internal haggling within Russia that delayed the agreement over the course of 1913,[44] a deal was eventually completed in December of 1913. Russia could receive up to five annual disbursements from the Paris bourse of up to 500 million francs (187.3 million rubles) for railway construction. In return, Russia would fulfill the agreements made at the August 1913 staff talks in which more than 5,000 kilometers of new track would be laid in western Russia. The French government had once again successfully utilized its control over access to domestic money markets to leverage its alliance partner into protecting French national interests. Heightened mobilization times in Russia could force Germany to divert more troops to its eastern border and simultaneously enhance the ability of the French army to achieve victory in its struggle for security.

Second, the Russian state held vast assets throughout its country, even prior to the Communist Revolution of 1917. Apart from the tremendous base of natural resources that included land used for agriculture, mines, timber, and oil, a program of nationalizing private railways had been initiated in the 1880s. By 1912, 67.7 percent of the total railway mileage in Russia was owned by the state (Apostol et al. 1928, p. 56). As shown in Table 7.1, railway revenues usually accounted for nearly a quarter of annual ordinary receipts from 1903 to 1913. A state monopoly on the sale of vodka provided a second lucrative public holding. Beginning in 1893, the government began taking over this industry by forcing distillation to occur under government supervision or in state-owned distilleries. All retail sales were conducted through state shops at prices set by the treasury. Over the same period, the vodka monopoly provided more than a quarter of the state's

[43] These negotiations are detailed in Chapter 6 of Krumeich (1984) and Stevenson (1996, pp. 323–6).

[44] While preferring that railways be built for commercial rather than military purposes, Kokovtsov initially approved of these conditions believing that he had signed off on the General Staff agreement of September 1912 for 900 kilometers of new track in Russia. He sought to renegotiate these terms in the fall of 1913 when learning of a new General Staff agreement reached in August of 1913 for 5,000 kilometers of new track. However, Kokovtsov's political leverage, and thus ability, to change the deal were limited. His desire to spend the budgetary surplus on the Great Program meant that the government needed to obtain foreign loans for the railways. Moreover, the tsar favored the military's preferences for the larger construction plans, which were made even more important by an army reorganization that had redeployed substantial quantities of troops to the country's interior. Kokovtsov's resistance was completely undermined by the Liman von Sanders crisis and the decisive shift within internal debates toward adopting a more assertive foreign policy.

revenue.[45] The two primary illiberal components of public revenue, state property and customs duties, dominated government receipts, consistently constituting two-thirds of public revenues throughout this period. More importantly, these assets would allow the Russian government to continue to locate new monies for heightened defense spending while simultaneously avoiding the domestic political backlash facing other European governments that sought to meet these challenges by imposing new taxes on property and income.[46]

The 1913 Annual Report on Russia compiled by the British embassy in St. Petersburg and submitted to the Foreign Office in March 1914 described Russia's unique financial position.[47] During the first nine months of 1913, public revenues had increased by more than 25 million pounds (236 million rubles) from the prior year. The two principal sources for this gain, accounting for 6.8- and 4.5-million pound increases (64.2 and 45.5 million rubles), respectively, were the vodka monopoly and state railways.[48] Total defense expenditures from 1912 to 1913 had increased by more than 60 percent from approximately 62 million pounds to nearly 100 million pounds. The report, however, noted, "The continual expansion of Russian ordinary revenues . . . enabled her to bear this burden without any perceptible strain on her finances."

These trends showed no signs of slowing. The report noted that the 1914 budget submitted to the Duma projected that Russia's revenues would grow by approximately 30 million pounds (283.2 million rubles) from 1913 "without fresh taxation." Ordinary defense expenditures for 1914 were scheduled to increase by another 12 percent from levels in 1913. Revenue growth continued to leave large budget surpluses that relieved the government from having to impose any new taxes. Russia was financially prepared to accelerate the arms race.

[45] The vodka monopoly was much more profitable than state railways. In 1913, expenditures on the vodka monopoly totaled 234.9 million rubles while revenues were 899.2 million rubles. In the same year, expenditures for state railways totaled 586.8 million rubles while revenues were 813.6 million rubles (Apostol et al. 1928, p. 65).

[46] A study on Russian finances commissioned by the Carnegie Endowment for Peace (Apostol et al. 1928, p. 72) before and during World War I completes its survey of the pre-war period by noting, "The foregoing epitome of the state of Russian public finances reveals how rapidly Russia had been able to recover from the blows dealt to her national economy and finance by the unsuccessful war with Japan, and how vigorous had been her economic progress . . . These favourable results were achieved, moreover, by means of light taxation, contrasting with the heavy burdens imposed in the countries of Western Europe."

[47] British Foreign Office, Russia – Annual Report 1913, FO 371/2092.

[48] The Carnegie report attributed the tremendous growth of government receipts after 1897 to the state railways and the state's monopoly on spirits (Apostol et al. 1928, p. 15).

At least two points from this report deserve special emphasis. First, Russia's growing financial resources facilitated a dramatic expansion of military spending in the period right before World War I. Second, substantial quantities of public property helped Russia accelerate the arms race without increasing the taxation burden on its society. This financial autonomy thus reduced domestic opposition in Russia to the arms race.

RUSSIA AND THE ARMS RACE

Russia used its financial power to surge ahead in the armaments race on land in Europe that accelerated after the second Moroccan crisis in 1911.[49] The political capacity to finance this arms race shaped the action and reaction dynamic of this competition as well as its relationship to the outbreak of war. Political and military leaders alike worried about their respective abilities to find the money necessary to maintain this race so that the military balance of power on the continent could be either preserved or shifted to their advantage. The Russian government exploited huge public property holdings and privileged access to French capital to assume a position of relative financial preeminence among the Great Powers. This financial power freed the Russian government from making domestic concessions that were simultaneously constraining other European governments from matching any future arms increases. Concerns over financial collapse felt as recently as 1906 had been replaced by a Russian confidence and a simultaneous German fear that the former possessed an endless supply of both troops and financial resources. This German fear and Russian confidence both contributed significantly to their respective decisions for war in July 1914.

Key Armaments Programs

Germany's capitulation in the second Moroccan crisis helped reorient it away from naval construction and colonial competition and back toward

49 While the naval arms race between England and Germany has received substantial attention in the historiography of World War I, the outcome of this battle had been largely determined by 1912. The exploding costs of dreadnought construction coupled with the British willingness to meet these financial burdens through income taxes propelled them forward in the race at sea (D'Lugo and Rogowski 1993). By 1912, the kaiser had essentially admitted defeat in the naval race and shifted attention back to continental interests and army improvements. Many historians have characterized this as one of the crucial implications of the famous War Council meeting in December 1912 (Rohl 1973, p. 31; Mombauer 2001, p. 142). The end of this naval arms race coincided with a brief and intense arms race on land in which the participants built railways, increased the sizes of their standing armies, and modernized their artillery. Two important studies of this arms race are Herrmann (1996) and Stevenson (1996).

Europe. Knowing that the continuation of the naval arms race threatened to undermine his long-term political goal of bringing Britain closer to Germany, Bethmann sought to shift German military spending away from the navy and toward the army (Herrmann 1996, pp. 161–72). He found support from worried army leaders, such as Moltke, who believed that naval conflict with Britain would simply heighten the likelihood of their intervention on the side of the Entente and shift the balance of military power to Germany's disadvantage in a continental war. In a series of secret consultations with the kaiser, Wermuth, the finance minister, and Heeringen, Germany's war minister, in the fall of 1911, Bethmann laid the foundations for this shift in national security strategy.

While capitulation in the Moroccan crisis heightened public fears over growing German weakness and inspired broader support in the Reichstag for the bill, the shifting balance of military power on the continent due to the recovery of Russian military capabilities and finances was significant as well.[50] The following passage from the general tasked with drafting the 1912 legislation to augment the army illustrates these concerns:

> The information that has newly become public concerning the course of political events last summer makes Germany's military position appear in a substantially different light from when the last peacetime strength law was introduced. At the time we expected only France as a definite enemy. Although Russia was attached to it, one could nevertheless assume... in view of the military weakness of Russia at the time, that it would take part only half-heartedly... But we know now that the number of our likely enemies has grown... It seems beyond doubt that Russia is working with gigantic financial resources on the reconstruction of its army and, now that it is no longer hampered by the worry of complications in the far east, will be inclined to give vent to the ever-growing anti-German mood through active participation in war.[51]

The 1912 army bill passed the Reichstag in May of 1912. It increased the peacetime strength of the German army by more than 28,000 troops, from 515,000 to more than 543,000.

The Balkan Wars of 1912 and 1913 only heightened these German fears and need to offset a declining military balance by bolstering its army.[52]

[50] Russia reorganized its mobilization plans in 1910. It shifted to a system of territorial recruitment and moved the principal locations of mobilization to the interior of the country. It also increased naval and army spending by 1.3 billion rubles in 1911 with the "Small Program."

[51] As quoted in Herrmann (1996, p. 167). For the concerns held by Moltke and the kaiser with respect to Russia in these discussions see Stevenson (1996, pp. 202–3).

[52] David Stevenson (1996, p. 212) writes of the pressures this crisis unleashed, "It took the new Balkan crisis at the end of the year to open the floodgates to material expenditure and a much larger manpower increase... " The kaiser had initially approached Moltke and

Serbian gains in southeastern Europe at the expense of the Ottoman Empire threatened the increasingly fragile Austro-Hungarian Empire and heightened German concern that its alliance partner would be forced to divert its military strength toward the Balkans and away from the larger struggle against the Triple Entente. When Russia increased its short-term readiness and capacity to intervene in the Balkans by retaining its conscript class in the fall of 1912, Germany responded with its army bill of 1913. This initiative increased the size of its standing army by one-sixth or 136,000. Many of the arguments used to support the bill in the spring of 1913 echoed those that had been made in the fall of 1911. For example, Heeringen focused on the dramatic improvements made by Russia in its standing army, noting, "The situation of Germany in comparison with 1912 had become much more difficult . . . in the future these troops would no longer be sufficient. Russia was not yet ready for war . . . But in a few years this would be different. Russia had enough men and money and a willing parliament. Already today it had 400,000 more men than in 1912."[53] The bill approving the largest army expansion in German history passed the Reichstag in July 1913 (Herrmann 1996, p. 190).

As the French government became aware of German plans for this army bill in January 1913, they initiated similar discussions over how to respond to this new challenge.[54] French generals worried that a larger German standing army would enhance its ability to inflict tremendous losses on France's covering troops, whose primary responsibility lay in repelling the initial invasion while the rest of the country mobilized for war. This immediate advantage could thus tempt Germany to try and score a decisive victory at the very outset of war. The augmentation of the German army also threatened to undermine the effectiveness of its existing offensive strategy.[55] In March of 1913, the French political leadership agreed to propose extending the length of conscription from two to three years. While the initial proposal possessed multiple amendments to ensure clearing the legislative hurdle,

Heeringen about further army expansion in October 1912 and was rebuffed. They quickly changed their minds in the aftermath of the first Balkan War (Stevenson 1996, p. 285).

53 As quoted in Herrmann (1996, p. 183).

54 This discussion of the Three-Year Law in France relies heavily on Krumeich (1984).

55 Both Krumeich and Stevenson distinguish between the public and private arguments made by the French government for the Three-Year Law. In private, the leadership worried that the technical argument of needing army expansion to ensure the effectiveness of Plan XVII (its military strategy to launch an offensive strike against Germany at the outset of war) would be insufficient to garner enough public support to ensure legislative passage. Consequently, the public rhetoric of the political and military leadership highlighted the apparent emergency need to bolster the strength of the cover troops so as to prevent an initial German breakthrough at the start of war. See Chapter 2 in Krumeich (1984) and Stevenson (1996, pp. 309–10).

the government secured passage in August 1913 for a bill that would raise the size of the French standing army from 545,000 to 730,000 by 1916.[56]

The German army bill of 1913 also contributed to the largest pre-war armaments program of them all – the Great Program in Russia. Russia had already initiated multiple reforms in the aftermath of the Bosnian annexation to enhance its military power. The reorganization of 1910 moved the principal staging area for Russian mobilization to the interior of the country so that mobilization would not be disrupted by an initial invasion and the military could respond more easily to threats in Europe or Asia. While the French were initially concerned that these reforms would slow a Russian offensive against Germany, they along with the Germans soon came to believe that reorganization would decrease mobilization times.[57] The small program of 1910 allotted more than 1.3 billion rubles over a ten-year period to the army and the navy to strengthen fortresses in western Russia and augment both the Baltic and Black Sea navies. The Great Program, initiated by the tsar in February 1913 and ultimately approved by the Duma in June of 1914 after substantial revisions, dwarfed these internal programs and all other European initiatives.[58] Scheduled for completion in 1917, the Great Program would expand Russia's peacetime army by more than 460,000 men or 40 percent of its current force. It also extended the term of service for every conscript class by releasing them in April rather than the previous October. This had the effect of increasing the size of Russia's peacetime standing army by more than 800,000 men during the winter. Russia simultaneously pursued railway construction to reduce mobilization times and fulfill promises made during general staff talks with France in the summer of 1912.

Political Constraints on Financing the Arms Race

This arms race on land posed enormous financial and political challenges to ruling coalitions in both France and Germany. Governments were confronted with the twin challenge of finding new sources of revenue to offset exploding defense budgets without undermining traditional political

56 These size estimates are taken from Stevenson (1996, p. 303).

57 Russia also moved to a system of territorial recruitment that reduced the time needed to get reserves to the principle staging areas once mobilization was ordered. For a discussion of the military reorganization of 1910, see Fuller (1992, pp. 423–33). For a discussion of how these reforms were seen in Germany, France, and Britain, see Stevenson (1996, pp. 159–63).

58 This discussion of the Great Program relies on Stevenson (1996, pp. 315–28).

coalitions that rested on the exclusion of the far left. The construction of political support behind any new armaments spending generally necessitated excluding leftist parties for two key reasons. First, these parties tended to oppose conscription and its concomitant defense burdens because of the costs they imposed on the working classes.[59] The financial burdens were generated by existing taxation policies that distributed the costs of public finance disproportionately on those classes that spent large portions of their income on consumption and the opportunity costs of years of lost wages necessitated by conscription. Second, any turn to the left jeopardized traditional support from centrist and rightist parties unwilling to work with parties from the left. Socialist gains in the German elections of 1912 and the French elections of 1914 simply accentuated the challenges faced by governments seeking to construct stable legislative coalitions that would support the existing pace of the arms race.

Similar to the domestic political strategy adopted by the British government in 1906 to prosecute the naval arms race, the French and German governments compromised with the left to garner the finances necessary to pay for their respective army bills of 1913.[60] These compromises, which had been politically unthinkable in previous decades, came in the form of tax reform that shifted the financial burdens of armaments policy away from working classes. Leftist parties in both France and Germany supported the respective army bills of 1913 because they were paid for primarily through property and income taxes, whose burdens fell on the supporters of bourgeois parties in the political center and wealthy landowners on the right. These groups traded arms for tax reforms that ultimately held out the promise of more fiscal democracy.

A public commitment by French Prime Minister Barthou in May 1913 to finance the Three-Year Law with new taxes on capital and income assisted its passage later that summer.[61] This gesture helped sway many Radical legislators who were committed to financial reform but unsure about whether the current security situation constituted an emergency that required the Three-Year Law. Barthou, however, balked at fulfilling this commitment in the fall of 1913 when submitting the government's budget for 1914. His

[59] For a discussion of the domestic political costs associated with conscription and how globalization accentuated these, see Rowe (1999, 2005) and Rowe, Bearce, and McDonald (2002).

[60] On the British case and how taxation reform propelled it ahead of Germany in naval construction, see D'Lugo and Rogowski (1993).

[61] For a discussion of the political battle over how to finance the Three-Year Law, see Krumeich (1984, pp. 137–48, 236).

government proposed to finance a large portion of the upcoming deficit, due in large part to the Three-Year Law, with a large state loan. More importantly, the government reversed an initiative from 1909 that had eliminated the traditional tax-exemption status given to profits accrued from holding government bonds. In short, the government sought to placate the financial interests of the wealthier segments of French society by eliminating taxes on investments in government bonds. When this bill extending tax exemption failed to pass the legislature in December 1913, the Barthou government fell. This episode illustrates the fragility of the domestic coalition supporting the Three-Year Law and the critical role that the finance question played in these internal domestic political struggles. Not passed until the summer of 1914, the finance bill included both a progressive income tax and taxes on movable financial assets, like government bonds. The political left had secured these political concessions as the price for supporting army expansion (Herrmann 1996, pp. 193–4).

A similar dynamic unfolded in Germany as Bethmann sought to find the funds for the German army law of 1913. While he secured political support for the expansion of the army with a coalition from the center and right, he faced numerous hurdles in financing the bill. Tight credit markets and the closure of French capital markets ruled out extensive borrowing. The federal division of political authority limited Bethmann's capacity to raise revenue via income taxes as this instrument had traditionally been the domain of state governments. Any move to impose new income taxes threatened to generate a backlash from state political officials. Finally, the coalition mainstay of the government, namely the conservative aristocracy, opposed new income taxes even though their proceeds would be spent on a policy they strongly supported.[62] Bethmann thus faced a series of bad political options.

While the competitive arms race in Europe necessitated more troops, Germany's unique federal structure and coalitional alignment threatened to derail its implementation. Bethmann ultimately chose to draw on the political left and meet the military's demands with the imposition of new property taxes. While the Socialist left supported the bill, the conservative party voted against it. Bethmann had set a dangerous precedent by reversing the government's traditional coalitional base to meet the demands of the arms race. Given that the Socialists had long opposed growing militarism, their support for the military in the future was anything but certain.

[62] For a discussion of the fiscal constraints generated by the unique structure of Germany's political system, see Ferguson (1994).

Herrmann (1996, p. 191) writes of this decision, "By the standards of the anti-progressive Reich leadership, it was an act of desperation that showed how much the military crisis had traumatized the government." Similarly, Stevenson (1996, p. 298) writes of this situation, "Like its counterpart in Vienna, the Government was nearing its borrowing limits, but by trying to raise taxes it was breaking up its parliamentary base and forfeiting the Conservative support coveted both by Chancellor and Emperor." By helping to alienate the traditional base of the emperor, the arms race on land had thus pushed Germany to its financial limits and threatened the government's capacity to sustain it.

The Russian government enjoyed more insulation from these internal challenges posed by the financial demands of the arms race. By 1913, observers within and outside Russia agreed that it had emerged as the strongest financial power in Europe and was thus in the best position to sustain the arms race. In April 1913, the tsar expressed this confidence while discussing the German army bill of 1913 with George Buchanan, the British ambassador in St. Petersburg. Buchanan described this conversation in a letter to Edward Grey, the British foreign secretary:

> He (the tsar) quite understood the reasons which had prompted the proposed increase of the German army; but the German Government must be aware that they were setting an example which other States would be bound to follow. They would probably have no difficulty in finding the men, but whether the country would for long be able to bear the increased taxation was another question. Russia, on the other hand, had unlimited resources to draw on, both regards men and money . . . [63]

Buchanan repeatedly concurred with the tsar's optimism. Writing to Nicolson in April 1913, he wrote, "She (Russia) can bear the strain far easier than Germany, as finances are flourishing and her supply of men almost inexhaustible" (Neilson 1985, p. 207). In March 1914, Buchanan described to Grey how Russia's relative financial strength was contributing to a greater assertiveness in foreign affairs and shifting the European balance of power. He wrote:

> Russia is determined to place her house in order and to ensure it against the danger of any attacks from without by a large increase of her army. With a population, which is now estimated at about 180,000,000, she has almost unlimited resources to draw on, while her finances are on such a satisfactory footing that they will hardly feel the strain of the additional expenditure which these military measures

[63] Buchanan to Grey, April 14, 1913, FO 418/52.

will entail... Unless therefore Germany is prepared to make still further financial sacrifices for military purposes, the days of her hegemony in Europe will be numbered.[64]

This Russian confidence was matched by German trepidations about their fiscal difficulties. In the famous War Council meeting of December 1912, Moltke expressed his concern "that the army would be getting into an increasingly disadvantageous position, because the enemies are increasing their armies more than us, since we are very financial restricted."[65] Falkenhayn, Germany's war minister, opposed Moltke's requests for even more troops in July 1914 right before the delivery of the Austrian ultimatum to Serbia largely because of these financial constraints.[66] Because Russia had the capacity to match any numerical increases, Germany had to preserve its quality advantage by giving the troops added by the 1913 bill more time to be trained and thus effectively integrated into the force structure. Moreover, he claimed that neither the Bundesrat nor the Reichstag would sanction even more spending on the army so shortly after the 1913 bill. While acknowledging the existence of these financial constraints, Moltke argued that they simply had to be overcome. In light of recent Russian and French increases, he pressed the kaiser to move Germany to universal conscription.[67]

On the eve of the assassination of Franz Ferdinand, widespread changes across Europe – linked in multiple ways to the financial and military recovery of Russia – had unsettled the continental balance of power and contributed to a fatalistic belief that war loomed near. The Balkan Wars had both fueled a new arms race on land among the Great Powers and redistributed the regional balance of power in southeastern Europe to the detriment of the Austro-Hungarian Empire. While the growth of Serbia created opportunities for the extension of Russian influence in the Balkans, it simultaneously heightened both the external military threat to Austria–Hungary and its domestic nationalities problem. These pressures in turn increased German fears about the declining power of its key alliance partner. The arms race taxed the political and financial capacity of both France and Germany to

[64] Gooch and Temperley (1938, p. 767).
[65] As quoted in Mombauer (2001, p. 140).
[66] The discussion of this exchange draws on Mombauer (2001, pp. 174–81).
[67] Mombauer (2001, p. 181) argues that this exchange with Falkenhayn played a critical role in Moltke's decision to press for a war against Russia in the summer of 1914. Falkenhayn's resistance suggested to Moltke that he would continue to face opposition at home to his requests for further increases while Russia and France augmented their armies. Consequently, Germany's position would deteriorate over the next few years, making the summer of 1914 the most opportune point for Germany to still achieve victory.

keep up with each other and with Russia. Socialist legislative gains in the French elections of April and May 1914 broke up the center–left governing coalition and cast doubt on any government's capacity to preserve the Three-Year Law.[68] Moltke's demands for universal conscription in May 1914 went unfulfilled in part because of a perceived legislative unwillingness to finance more army increases so shortly after the huge increase of 1913. Financial recovery and frustration with Kokovtsov's miserly ways helped eliminate a critical source of foreign-policy restraint within the Russian government. Russia's financial resources and the domestic political benefits these conferred contributed to the view held across both alliance blocs that it would shortly be sitting atop the hierarchy of European politics. Over the course of 1914, even Britain grew concerned about the threats to its interests in Central and South Asia, the most important of which was India, posed by a reconstituted Russia.[69] These dim prospects of a deteriorating balance of military power left German leaders believing that its window for protecting national interests on the battlefield was closing and willing to embrace the next favorable opportunity for war.

RUSSIA AND GERMANY'S DECISION FOR PREVENTIVE WAR

This chapter has utilized the framework of neoclassical liberalism presented in Chapter 2 to examine how government efforts to control commerce contributed to the origins of World War I. Up to this point, the discussion has largely focused on how tariffs, capital controls, and public property shaped the first two of these conditions – the political conflicts between the alliance blocs that gave rise to war; and the relative domestic political strength of leaders that shapes expectations about their ability to remain in office during and after a war.

Russia's recovery also looms large in the inability of the alliance blocs to reach a political solution short of war. Preventive wars reflect commitment problems, which are one of the three causes of war in Fearon's bargaining

[68] Krumeich (1984) argues that these fears both raised Russian concerns over France's commitment to the alliance and, as a consequence, France's willingness to follow a policy course during the July crisis that heightened the risk of war. After the Socialist electoral victory and their leader's (Jaures) public support for overturning the Three-Year Law, Russia conveyed multiple warnings to France during June and July that the elimination of the Three-Year Law threatened military coordination within their alliance (pp. 213–14). Consequently, Poincare compensated for these growing doubts by signaling France's commitment to the alliance via support for Russia's decision to defend its Balkan interests in the July crisis (p. 241).

[69] See for example Wilson (1984).

framework. The logic proceeds as follows: Governments opt for war to prevent the future deterioration of their capacity to protect national interests. A declining power chooses war because the rising power is unable to commit to forego the political advantage created by its enhanced bargaining power in the future. Fearon (1995, p. 406) writes of this situation: "[t]he declining state attacks not because it fears being attacked in the future but because it fears the peace it will have to accept after the rival has grown stronger." Powell (2006) shows how rapid shifts in the balance of power among states exacerbate such preventive war incentives.

This section examines two aspects of how a rapidly shifting balance of military power on the continent from 1905 to 1914 generated such a commitment problem that prevented peaceful compromise during the July crisis. The first draws on the prevailing historiography of the war to illustrate the widespread German belief that a decisive shift in the military balance had rendered preventive war the best means to preserve its political position in Europe. Such concerns dominated German debates over military strategy and war in the period between the outbreak of the first Balkan War and July 1914. Both civilian and military leaders repeatedly argued that Germany possessed a greater chance to achieve military victory in 1914 than in 1917, by which time Russia's Great Program would have been completed. The second examines how Russia's relative financial strength freed it from many of the domestic constraints on military spending faced by other powers. Germany launched a preventive war in July 1914 because it could not procure the financial resources necessary to keep pace with an accelerating arms race that was rapidly shifting the balance of military power on the continent to its detriment.

The July Crisis

Before examining the preventive war consensus in Germany and the role played by the arms race in provoking war, I first briefly present here the details of the July crisis. The assassination of Franz Ferdinand, the heir to the Austro-Hungarian throne, by a group of Bosnian Serb terrorists on June 28 sparked the July crisis. Given that he was the immediate successor to the aging Franz Joseph, it raised significant questions about the political future of the empire. Perhaps more importantly, Serbian complicity would constitute an act of war. Given the growth of the Serbian threat in the aftermath of the Balkan Wars, a failure to respond aggressively to this challenge would not only invite more challenges by demonstrating weakness but undermine

German confidence in its alliance partner.[70] Austria–Hungary's leaders decided that the maintenance of its Great Power position depended on crippling Serbia through war. They believed that a diplomatic victory would not sufficiently contain the centrifugal forces unleashed by growing Southern Slav nationalism. They agreed that such action could not be taken without consulting Germany and being assured of its support. Strong Russian ties with Serbia and its ongoing efforts to construct a grouping of Balkan states to check Austria–Hungary's influence in the region heightened the risk of Russian military intervention in support of Serbia. Consequently, Austria–Hungary dispatched Count Hoyos to Berlin for meetings on July 5 and 6 to gauge German support for action against Serbia given the risks of a broader continental war. This meeting resulted in the famous so-called blank check in which both the kaiser and Bethmann, aware of potential Russian intervention, encouraged Austria–Hungary to strike at Serbia as soon as possible. Despite this firm promise of support, internal political haggling in Austria–Hungary prevented the emergence of a political consensus behind a strongly worded ultimatum to Serbia backed by the threat of war until July 19.[71]

The delivery of this ultimatum at 6:00 P.M. in Belgrade on July 23 violently woke the rest of Europe to the real possibility of a larger continental conflict. It consisted of a series of demands and threats that challenged Serbian sovereignty. Failure to comply with these demands within forty-eight hours would be followed by the severing of diplomatic relations between the two countries and war. Austria–Hungary strategically timed the delivery of this ultimatum to prevent Russo-Franco consultations over support for Serbia. The French President Poincare and Prime Minister Viviani were just that afternoon concluding a visit to St. Petersburg to review and reaffirm the status of their alliance. By waiting until Poincare and Viviani had departed St. Petersburg to present the ultimatum, Austria–Hungary may have limited French restraint on Russia in the next stage of the crisis. Poincare and Viviani were out of regular communication with both Paris and St. Petersburg during their return to France over the next six days. Their absence left

[70] For the internal discussions in Austria–Hungary on how best to respond to the assassination and the Serb threat, see the documents found on pp. 66, 67, 78, 80–87 in Geiss (1968).

[71] Hungarian Prime Minister Tisza, concerned about the diminution of Hungarian power within the empire, opposed the annexation of Serbian territory. He eventually was won over by arguments that the failure to respond harshly to Serbia would further aggravate the internal nationalities problem within the empire by signaling weakness to ethnic groups, like the Romanians, poised to challenge Austria's political control in the future (Williamson 1991, p. 200; Stevenson 1996, p. 369).

Paléologue, France's ambassador to St. Petersburg, with an unusual amount of independence to shape French foreign policy. A staunch supporter of the alliance, he deliberately withheld information from Paris about Russia's military preparations and encouraged Russia to stand firm in its support of Serbia.[72]

Upon receiving official notification of Vienna's ultimatum on the morning of July 24, the tsar convened two critical meetings of his chief advisors that afternoon and the following morning.[73] These meetings broke decisively with the dominant trends in Russian foreign policy over the previous decade and moved the continent closer to war. Russia would no longer shrink from the risks, namely defeat and internal revolt, exposed by the experiences of 1905. Led by Sazonov, the foreign minister, and Krivoshein, the agricultural minister, the Council of Ministers decided that a failure to stand by Serbia would signal weakness and simply encourage future challenges by the central powers. Although Russia's rearmament was incomplete, its military strength was growing rapidly and the recent press war with Germany suggested that public opinion would be frustrated by further foreign-policy impotence. Aware that a willingness to stand firm could escalate the conflict, the tsar and his advisors laid out a course of actions to take if circumstances deteriorated. These included the mobilization of military districts in Kazan, Moscow, Kiev, and Odessa, the withdrawal of financial assets from Berlin and Austria, and the decision on July 26 to order the Period Prepatory to War.

The Serbian government's conciliatory rejection of the Austrian note on July 25 generated responses that seemed to both push the Great Powers closer and further away from war. On the one hand, it initiated a short wave of optimism that a peaceful compromise could be reached. Upon seeing the text of the Serbian response on July 28, the kaiser described the note as a capitulation. Edward Grey, the British foreign secretary, offered to host mediation talks among Britain, France, Italy, and Germany. However, the Austro-Hungarian ambassador had been instructed to break relations immediately if Serbia did not unconditionally accept all provisions in the ultimatum. Shortly thereafter, Austria–Hungary began mobilization for war against Serbia. The Russians also increased their military readiness on July 26 with the tsar's order for a partial mobilization that would be directed primarily at Austria–Hungary.

[72] In a meeting with Sazonov and Buchanon on the morning of July 24 Paléologue reaffirmed all of France's alliance commitments.

[73] This discussion of the meetings of July 24–5 relies heavily on Lieven (1983), Spring (1988b), and Stevenson (1996, pp. 379–84).

The shift in Russian foreign policy first hinted at in the aftermath of the Liman von Sanders crisis and reaffirmed in the meetings of July 24–5 led St. Petersburg to escalate the crisis following the Dual Monarchy's declaration of war against Serbia on July 28. Encouraged by military leaders who viewed partial mobilization as a logistical nightmare that would make Russia more vulnerable and now convinced that war was inevitable,[74] Sazonov pushed the tsar to order general mobilization in all military districts. In the midst of exchanging notes with the kaiser that seemed to augur some peaceful compromise, Nicholas initially resisted these pressures knowing that full mobilization would likely mean war with the central powers. His wavering led to a panicked crisis in Russian decision making from July 28 to July 30 as orders for full mobilization were first ordered, then countermanded with partial mobilization orders, and finally reinstated in the afternoon of July 30. Sazonov ultimately convinced the tsar that war with Germany was inevitable and any further delays in mobilization would leave their military at a distinct disadvantage at the start of the conflict.

Some argue that Russia's full mobilization on July 30 effectively played into the trap set by a German leadership already long resolved for war (e.g., Fischer 1975; Pogge von Strandmann 1988; Rohl 1995; Copeland 2000). Most segments of the German leadership had recognized throughout the crisis that Austro-Hungarian action against Serbia carried significant risks of Russian and French intervention. Germany's position could be improved on at least two political fronts if Russia was successfully cast as the aggressor. It would heighten the domestic political obstacles for any attempt by the British government to secure public approval for aiding an autocrat who had started the war. This tactical goal corresponded with Bethmann's historical goal of achieving British neutrality. While German efforts at British neutrality failed when Bethmann's diplomatic bumbling revealed his broader political program to use the crisis to secure German colonial gains,[75] Russian mobilization facilitated a second key element of Bethmann's political program for conducting the war. At home, Bethmann sought to quiet potential Socialist opposition and prevent a general strike in protest of war. This meant rallying national support to defend against a

[74] Stevenson (1996, pp. 384–5).

[75] Bethmann's final proposal for British neutrality committed Germany to respect French territory on the continent. His unwillingness to extend this guarantee to French colonial possessions was interpreted by Grey and the Foreign Office as evidence of a broader German program to upset the global status quo. Bethmann's failure to secure British neutrality triggered his panic on July 29 as he sought for a short time to restrain Austria–Hungary and secure some form of the "Halt in Belgrade" strategy proposed by the kaiser.

Russian invasion, which would be difficult if Germany were cast publicly as the aggressor in the crisis. Bethmann thus resisted military pressures on July 29 and July 30 to order full mobilization until Russia had done so.

The Russian mobilization on July 30 thus gave Germany the political cover it needed to launch the Schlieffen Plan. Charging that Russian mobilization constituted a direct threat, Germany demanded that Russia halt its military preparations. When this ultimatum passed without a Russian reversal, Germany ordered general mobilization of its army and declared war on Russia on August 1. Germany was the only country in which mobilization meant war. The success of the Schlieffen Plan depended on rapid German troop movements through the low-lying areas of Belgium. Its activation thus led to an immediate assault on the Belgian fort of Liege so that German troops could move more easily into a flanking position on Paris and secure a quick victory on the western front. While the declaration of war against Russia had already guaranteed French intervention, the violation of Belgian neutrality pushed a divided British cabinet, then debating the scope of British obligations to France and Russia, toward intervention on the side of the Triple Entente. On August 6, the cabinet voted to send the British Expeditionary Force to Belgium.[76] The Balkan conflict had been transformed into a world war.

Preventive War Consensus in Germany

While the final stages of the July crisis suggest that military arguments focusing on mobilization pressures created a vortex that pulled Europe into war,[77] political and military leaders on both sides of the conflict had proceeded into this predicament with eyes wide open. Shortly after the assassination, the Austro-Hungarian government decided that only war, not a diplomatic victory, would be sufficient to crush the growing Serb threat in the Balkans. Following the Liman von Sanders crisis, Russian leaders repeatedly expressed their willingness to remove the shackles imposed by 1905 and utilize their growing military strength to defend their interests in the Balkans and the Near East. Most importantly, German policy had already been narrowed by the emergence of broad consensus in favor of a preventive

[76] For a discussion of the internal cabinet debate in Britain see Wilson (1995) and Ferguson (1998).

[77] This is one of explanations for war generated in the offense–defense literature. See for example Van Evera (1984); Snyder (1984); and Lieber (1998).

war against the Triple Entente.[78] The scheduled completion of Russia's Great Program in 1917 created widespread fears among both military and civilian officials that Germany faced a future of political impotence in Europe unless its momentary military advantage was seized to defeat the Triple Entente. This "now or never" logic dominated German considerations in favor of war in July 1914.

Moltke has long been pointed to as the primary proponent of such claims. Aided in internal political struggles by his close friendship with the kaiser, he consistently offered a supportive voice for war in the diplomatic crises following his succession of Schlieffen as the chief of the general staff in 1906. Uncertain of Russia's recovery, he encouraged Austria's chief of staff, Conrad, to exploit Russia's weakness and to go to war against Serbia in 1909 (Mombauer 2001, p. 114). He supported Kiderlen's efforts to secure colonial concessions in Africa during the Agadir crisis in 1911, arguing again that the crisis provided offered a favorable opportunity to defeat England. Following the Moroccan crisis, Moltke advocated army increases to counter growing Russian strength from the reorganization of 1910.

His fears over an ascendant Russia grew noticeably after the start of the first Balkan War in October of 1912. Moltke supported the bellicosity of the kaiser in the famous War Council meeting of December 1912, arguing that Germany was beginning to lose the arms race relative to its enemies.

[78] Historians of World War I have used different definitions of preventive war. These distinctions are similar to the distinctions made by Levy (1987) between preemptive and preventive wars. In a preventive war, a state attacks in a present period to avoid having to fight later when its relative military power has declined or to avoid a period of peace in which it has diminished bargaining power. Levy (p. 89) writes, "Preventive war is more concerned with minimizing one's losses from future decline than with maximizing one's gains by fighting now." In a preemptive war, a state initiates an attack because it believes that an attack by the adversary is imminent. Levy (pp. 90–91) notes that a preemptive strike is a tactical response to a short-term threat while a decision for preventive war is a strategic response to a long-term decline in relative power. The discussion here, because it emphasizes how expectations of the distribution of military power in 1917 shaped decisions for war in 1914, focuses on preventive war. Hillgruber (1981) emphasizes this focus on the two- or three-year time horizon that characterizes the preventive logic in his discussion of German decision for war in 1914. He writes (pp. 33–4), "The most important points of accord between the political leadership and the general staff concerned the steadily increasing Russian threat and the assumption, by now axiomatic, that in a few years Germany would be brought to its knees in a politically and strategically hopeless position without a drop of blood being shed . . . In other words, the political leadership knowingly ran such a great risk in the July crisis because it was convinced that should the other side choose war, the odds for military victory by the Central Powers were better than they would be several years hence."

Such calls for war grew as his repeated demands for universal conscription went unfulfilled and the details of Russia's Great Program emerged. In May 1914, Moltke met with Conrad and voiced concern over further delays to war, noting "every delay signified a reduction in our chances; one cannot undertake a competition in numbers with Russia."[79] Shortly thereafter, Moltke reiterated these fears of Russia's armament campaign to Jagow, Germany's foreign minister, and encouraged him to create the conditions for war. Jagow recalled of the meeting:

> The military superiority of our enemies would then be so great that he (Moltke) did not know how we could overcome them. Today we were still a match for them. In his opinion there was no alternative to making preventive war in order to defeat the enemy while we still stand a chance of victory. The Chief of the General Staff therefore proposed that I should conduct a policy with the aim of provoking a war in the near future.[80]

On July 26 in the midst of the July crisis, Moltke concurred with Falkenhayn's preference for war noting "[t]hat we shall never hit it again so well as we do now with France's and Russia's expansion of their armies incomplete."[81]

Utilizing new documents returned to Germany in 1988 after being seized by the Soviets after World War II, Mombauer (2001) places Moltke at the center of the German decision for war in 1914. Even though Moltke had repeatedly made such arguments in the crises of 1909, 1911, and 1912, his exhortations gained new traction in 1914 because he had altered the strategic debate within Germany and pushed civilian leaders closer to his views.[82] Prince Lichnowsky, Germany's ambassador to London, believed that Moltke had convinced Bethmann of the need to go to war in 1914 rather than in 1916 or 1917 (Rohl 1995, p. 32). The latter shared Moltke's fears about how Russia's rapidly growing military strength would constrain Germany's future. Kurt Riezler, Bethmann Hollweg's personal secretary, notes that the Chancellor remarked on July 6, "[t]he future belongs to Russia which grows and grows and weighs upon us as an ever more terrible nightmare."[83] Two weeks later on July 20, Riezler's diary records more evidence of Bethmann's thinking, "Again the topic is the entire situation. Russia's increasing demands and amazing potential. In a few years no longer

[79] As quoted in Geiss (1968, pp. 46–7).
[80] As quoted in Mombauer (2001, p. 172).
[81] As quoted in Berghahn (1993[1973], p. 203); see also Fischer (1975, p. 493).
[82] Hillgruber (1981) agrees that a consensus between civilian and military leaders on the nature of the Russian threat had emerged in Germany.
[83] As quoted in Fischer (1975, p. 469).

possible to fend off, especially if current European constellation remains."[84] Even Bethmann himself acknowledged in 1917 the paramount role of Russia in German calculations for war in 1914, noting, "Yes, by God, in a way it was a preventive war. But if war was in any case hovering above us; if it would have come in two years' time, but even more dangerously and even more unavoidably, and if the military leaders declared that then it was still possible without being defeated, in two years' time no longer! Yes, the military!"[85]

These fears extended to the foreign office and the kaiser. In the middle of June 1914, the kaiser expressed his concerns over Russian armaments to his friend Max Warburg. The latter wrote of this conversation, "Russia's armaments, the big Russian railway constructions were in his view preparations for a great war which could start in 1916 . . . He complained that we had too few railways at the western front against France; oppressed by his worries he even considered whether it might not be better to attack than wait."[86] At the foreign ministry, Jagow shared these views and decided shortly after the assassination not to try and restrain any push for war inside Germany (Geiss 1968, pp. 65–6). He wrote to Lichnowsky on July 18:

> Russia is not ready to strike at present. Nor will France or England be anxious for war at the present time. According to all competent observation, Russia will be prepared to fight in a few years. Then she will crush us by the number of her soldiers; then she will have built her Baltic Sea fleet and her strategic railways. Our group, in the meantime, will become ever weaker . . . I do not desire a preventive war, but if the fight does present itself, we must not run away.[87]

The assassination of the Austrian archduke coincided with the emergence of a broad consensus within Germany among both political and military officials about the need to address their long-term security problem posed by Russia's leap forward in the arms race. This conception of Germany's strategic situation created a relatively clear policy solution: their momentary military advantage must be exploited at the next favorable opportunity. The assassination provided such an opportunity because it necessarily engaged the Austro-Hungarian Empire and the Entente's large programs of military improvements were not yet complete. Germany would not have to fight France, Russia, and England by itself and it could exploit the temporary advantage created by its massive army increase of 1913.

[84] As quoted in Mombauer (2001, p. 189).
[85] Ibid., p. 189.
[86] As quoted in Fischer (1975, p. 471).
[87] As quoted in Geiss (1968, p. 123).

The Russian Phoenix, the Arms Race, and War in 1914

Russia's related surge in both financial capacity and the arms race generated intense pressures for war inside and outside Russia. Inside Russia, the growing availability of financial resources reordered its internal balance of power away from those forces that had long counseled foreign-policy moderation (Stevenson 1996, p. 319). The memories of 1905 exerted a strong influence on Russian foreign policy until the Liman von Sanders crisis in December 1913. Stolypin, the chairman of the Council of Ministers from 1906 until his assassination in 1911, and Kokovtsov consistently pushed for a conciliatory foreign policy so as not to risk repeating the period of domestic upheaval stemming from the Russo-Japanese War.[88] This foreign-policy restraint could be seen in the capitulation in the Bosnian crisis of 1909, Russia's attempts to restrain the Balkan League in the fall of 1912, and its compromise with Austria–Hungary to stand down from the mobilization measures in the spring of 1913.[89] By the end of 1913, Kokovtsov's repeated arguments about the need for financial moderation and his unwillingness to appropriate funds for the respective ministries had provoked a widespread revolt against him, led by Krivoshein and Sukhomlinov, within the Council of Ministers.[90] His departure in February left Krivoshein as the most influential member in the tsar's cabinet.

This shift in the internal balance of power, sparked by financial recovery and an internal bureaucratic fight over access to these resources, altered the foreign-policy interests of Russia. The Liman von Sanders crisis catalyzed this shift. Throughout this crisis, Kokovtsov thwarted the efforts by Krivoshein, Sazanov, and Sukhomlinov to adopt a more confrontational

[88] See in particular McDonald (1992) for a discussion of Kokovtsov's long-held view that threats posed by domestic instability, like those seen during the near collapse of 1905, necessitated assuming a compromising foreign policy line. These dynamics also reflect the insights of the selectorate model discussed in Chapter 3. Fears of being removed from office because of the decision to enter war push political leaders not to go to war in the first place. In Russia's case, the fear of domestic revolution sparked by 1905 consistently led Kokovtsov and Stolypin to argue that internal stability demanded foreign-policy concessions to avoid war. Once the regime's internal position had been solidified via the recovery of its finances, these arguments within the Council of Ministers possessed less traction. Shortly thereafter, the tsar became much more willing to face all the risks associated with war.

[89] The Balkan League was an alliance formed initially between Bulgaria and Serbia and then extended to include Greece. Shortly after it was formed, this grouping went to war against Turkey to strip it of territorial possessions in Europe. In the fall of 1912, Kokovtsov told the Serbian ambassador that "Russia under no circumstances would go to war. Rather would he resign as minister-president than sanction such a policy" (McDonald 1992, p. 181).

[90] McDonald (1992); Buchanan to Grey, February 15, 1914, FO 371/2091.

policy vis-à-vis Germany over the Straits. However, his dismissal in its aftermath removed the last critical domestic hurdle within the tsar's small coterie of advisors to diplomatic postures that heightened the risks of war. By the spring of 1914, the tsar, Krivoshein, and Sukhomlinov all believed that the recovery from the internal crises of 1905 was complete. Consequently, they would no longer shrink from the possibility of war to defend Russia's interests in Europe.[91] For example, the tsar discussed with Buchanan in April 1914 his willingness to go to war if Germany used its increasing influence in the Ottoman Empire to close the Straits to Russian trade.[92] Similarly, while aware that Russia's military reforms were not complete, Krivoshein and Sukhomlinow both cited, in the crucial Council of Ministers meeting on July 24, 1914, the tremendous progress in domestic recovery efforts after 1905 while arguing that Russia both could and should adopt a more confrontational policy line in response to the Austro-Hungarian ultimatum (Lieven 1983, p. 142–3).

Russia's growing financial and military power also caused war by tempting Germany and Austria–Hungary to strike so they could avoid the political and economic costs of keeping pace in the arms race to maintain the continental balance of power.[93] In this variant of the commitment problem, Russia could not promise to restrain its military spending and exploit the attendant bargaining advantages, and its adversaries rationally chose war to escape the political and financial burdens of maintaining their military deterrents (Powell 2006). Such pressures, observed by decision makers on both sides of the alliance blocs, emerged in the period of militarized diplomacy after the second Moroccan crisis.

The growth of Russian revenues enabled it to accumulate substantial surpluses that created staying power or resolve in crisis situations.[94] On January 1, 1914, Russia's treasury held a discretionary reserve (the free balance) of 514 million rubles. The government utilized this reserve during the Balkan Wars of 1912 and 1913 to cover the costs of the partial mobilization and the retention of the conscript classes past their normal release

[91] Buchanan to Grey, March 18, 1914, Gooch and Temperley (1938, pp. 766–7).

[92] Gooch and Temperley (1938, p. 780).

[93] The general logic of preventive war suggests that the fear of political impotence upon the completion of Russia's Great Program in 1917 tempted Germany and Austria–Hungary to go to war. This mechanism is different in that it examines the role played by relative financial capability in the arms race that was shifting the balance of military power. For this distinction see Powell (2006).

[94] For the discussion of how resolve shapes games of brinkmanship and the outbreak of war, see Powell (2003).

dates in the fall of 1912.[95] This financial ease by which Russia could mobilize her reserve forces needs to be contrasted with the relative difficulties faced by Austria–Hungary during the same crises. Following the outbreak of the first Balkan War in October of 1912, Austria–Hungary called up reserve troops in response to Serbian territorial gains and the retention of the Russian conscript class that was bolstering its strength in Poland. Austria–Hungary maintained these heightened troop levels for nearly a year. However, the costs of retaining these troops led to internal arguments from the finance minister, Bilinski, that war might be cheaper than mobilization. By the end of the second Balkan War in the summer of 1913, Conrad, the chief of the general staff, shared similar concerns, noting that Austria–Hungary could not afford the cost, measured in public opinion or money, of maintaining high readiness levels without going to war (Stevenson 1996, p. 275).

British and French observers shared similar concerns that the financial pressure on the Triple Alliance inflicted by Russia's surge in the arms race would lead Germany to choose war as its only policy option.[96] Delcasse, France's ambassador in St. Petersburg, saw Bethmann's decision to finance the German army bill of 1913 with the tax on property as one of financial desperation that indicated determination for war in the near term (Buchanan 1923, pp. 186–7). Buchanan worried that the financial pressure levied by Russia on Germany via repeated army increases might tempt Germany into fighting. He raised these concerns in a discussion with the tsar in April 1913[97] and in a dispatch to Grey in March 1914. Buchanan wrote to Grey, "In the race for armaments Russia has more staying powers than Germany; and as Germany is aware of the fact, there is always the danger that she

[95] While the budgetary surplus in 1913 was nearly 8 million pounds (76 million rubles), Britain's Annual Report on Russia noted that it would have been closer to 20 million pounds (189 million rubles) without supplementary spending bills. Nearly two-thirds of this supplementary or emergency spending paid for the partial mobilization on the Austro-Hungarian frontier in 1913. British Foreign Office, Russia – Annual Report 1913, FO 371/2092.

[96] Ferguson (1994) argues that the inability of Germany to keep up with Russia in the financing of the arms race contributed to its decision for war in 1914. Another indicator of Russia's comparative financial strength (and thus of its capacity to sustain the arms race) was much lower per capita taxation rates than all other European powers. Russia's per capita taxation rate in 1911 was 11.23 rubles. The respective figures for Germany, Austria, France, and Great Britain were 27.38, 24.61, 41.66, and 48.54. Russia's reliance on direct taxation was also much lower than all its European counterparts. Its per capita direct taxation (including local and imperial taxes) rate in 1911 was 3.11 rubles while those for Germany, Austria, France, and Great Britain were 12.97, 10.19, 12.35, and 26.75, respectively. These figures were taken from Apostol et al. (1928, pp. 24–5).

[97] Buchanan to Grey, April 14, 1913, FO 418/52.

may be tempted to precipitate a conflict before Russia is fully prepared to meet it."[98]

Perhaps most importantly, this conversation between Buchanan and the tsar reflects the reality of the commitment problem generated by the financial burdens of the arms race and its role in the outbreak of war in 1914. The tsar – along with Buchanan, the British Foreign Office, Moltke, the kaiser, and Falkenhayn for that matter – believed that Russia possessed the relative financial capacity to outpace Germany in any arms race. Once Buchanan had raised the possibility of how this reality could lead Germany to fight, we can be sure that the tsar was definitely aware of the risks that his continued military spending posed to peace. However, at the time of his conversation with Buchanan, the tsar had already chosen to accelerate the arms race by initiating the Great Program despite these risks. He could not help but exploit this growing military resource. As the continental balance increasingly shifted in Russia's favor, the tsar could look forward to a future in which he could extract more political concessions from Germany, Austria–Hungary, and even Great Britain in the Balkans, the Middle East, and Central Asia. Consequently, any promise made by him to restrain military spending created an intractable credibility problem. Faced with being unable to locate the economic resources to maintain its military deterrent and preserve its political freedom in European politics, Germany opted for war in July 1914.

This argument bears important similarities with both Ferguson (1994) and Mombauer (2001). In a recent biography of Moltke, Annika Mombauer (2001) argues that a debate in the middle of July crisis – before the delivery of the Austrian ultimatum – between Moltke and Falkenhayn over the race for more soldiers reinforced Moltke's belief in the necessity of a preventive war and pushed him to actively support war in July 1914. The minister of war's refusal to grant new army increases until at least 1916 had further shrunk Moltke's time horizons and killed any hope of keeping pace in the arms race. Mombauer (2001, p. 181) writes of this exchange, "Moltke's resolve in the crucial days of July stemmed at least partly from his growing awareness of the future limitations of Germany's military power, and was a direct result of the arguments between the Minister of War and the Chief of the General Staff."

In exploring the relative financial capacity of Germany and Russia to prosecute the arms race, Ferguson instead focuses on the domestic constraints on military spending within Germany created by its federal system.

[98] Gooch and Temperley (1938, p. 768).

Whereas the German central government generated revenues via consumption taxes and tariffs, the empire's component states possessed the capacity to levy taxes on income and property. Once the arms race had exhausted the central government's financial resources, it failed to wrestle the power to impose new direct taxes from the states. This left the German government unable to maintain the pace of the arms race set by Russia. He argues that peace might have been preserved if the central German government could have seized from state governments the right to impose income taxes and engineered another round of army expansion. This analysis informs only part of the dilemma facing Germany in 1914. Germany still faced the long-term problem of competing with an adversary that was free of an even more foundational institutional constraint. The predominance of private property in an economy forces a government to undertake a broader renegotiation of its contract with society whereby national resources held by citizens are turned over to the state for use in the public sector. If Bethmann had wrestled the right to levy income taxes from federal governments, he then would have had to renegotiate the tax contract with all the citizens holding private property in Germany. The army bill of 1913 had already demonstrated the political costs of such a renegotiation, as that bargain required Bethmann to make substantial concessions that threatened the sustainability of his ruling coalition. Extensive quantities of public property in Russia freed the Tsar from having to renegotiate the domestic tax contract between state and society to locate more financial resources for military expansion. War occurred in July 1914 because these assets prevented the Tsar from thinking about or committing to any form of arms control that could have preserved Germany's long term position within the continental balance of power and tempered its desire for a preventive war.

In his presentation of the now classic formulation of the bargaining approach to war, Fearon (1995, pp. 406–8) uses this dilemma facing the German government in 1914 to illustrate how commitment problems can undermine negotiations and lead to war. Powell (2006) extends this analysis by showing how arms races and rapid, sizable shifts in the global distribution of military power generate the commitment problems that create incentives to launch a preventive war. The near collapse and then dramatic recovery of Russian military power between 1905 and the onset of the July crisis, documented both by historians of the arms race and contemporary observers, exemplifies such a dramatic power shift. German civilian and military leaders believed that the military advantage of the Triple Alliance relative to the Triple Entente was fleeting. Any promise by the Russian government not to exploit this growing bargaining strength in the future, such as by limiting its influence in the Balkans or by cutting its military spending, was simply not credible. Once the Great Program was complete, Russia could increase its support for Serbian expansion at the expense of Austria–Hungary or increase pressure on the Ottoman Empire for control of the Straits. The dramatic growth of Russian power led Germany to opt for war in 1914 to avoid a future of impotence in European politics.

CONCLUSION

Because it followed a sustained period of globalization, critics of liberal international relations theory have long pointed to the outbreak of World War I as powerfully contradictory claims that commerce or capitalism promotes peace. This exploration of the origins of World War I challenged these theoretical characterizations of it as the Achilles' heel of liberal international relations theory by recasting the nineteenth-century era of globalization as one in which governments still maintained important mechanisms of control over economic activity.

Neoclassical liberalism identifies three key mechanisms that shape the outbreak of war among states – the presence of conflicting national interests; the relative capacity of governments to wage war and maintain their hold on domestic power; and the failure of pre-war bargaining. Tariffs and capital controls stimulated political conflict between the two blocs on at least two fronts. First, Germany's policy of Weltpolitik poisoned relations with both Britain and Russia. German colonial expansion and its accompanying program of naval construction threatened British dominance in global markets and at sea. Perhaps more important for the outbreak of World War I, the protective policies necessary to pay for naval construction and ensure conservative support for Weltpolitik created a sharp backlash from Russia that increased its willingness to confront Germany in 1914. Second, capital controls helped the French government co-opt its domestic financial sector in support of a key foreign-policy interest in the decade before World War I: the military recovery of its alliance partner. The French government used this control over credit to pressure Russia into withdrawing from its war against Japan in 1905, to facilitate its escape from bankruptcy in 1906, and to fund a massive railway construction program that heightened German fears of imminent military decline.

I then built upon important points of consensus in the historiography of the war to explore a question that has received less attention but which nonetheless carries important implications for the failure of the two sides to reach some negotiated compromise that avoided the costs of war. Most historians agree that Germany bears disproportionate responsibility for the outbreak of the war and that its fears of growing political impotence in Europe caused by Russian military expansion led it to launch a preventive war in July 1914. Given the centrality of Russia's growing military power in the German decision for war, I examined how Russia emerged from the depths of domestic revolution and defeat in war so quickly. Enormous quantities of public property and preferential access to the vast private savings pool of French citizens granted Russia unique financial and political advantages in the arms race that destabilized the balance of military power in the continent. While Germany, France, and Britain all faced similar domestic constraints that upset traditional political coalitions and appeared to cap future increases in military spending, Russia's financial capacity to accelerate the arms race appeared endless. By the spring of 1914, even its quasi-alliance partner, Britain, grew increasingly worried over the challenges posed by Russia's financial and military strength. Germany launched a preventive war in July 1914 because it could not keep pace with an accelerating arms race that was rapidly shifting the balance of military power on the continent to its detriment.

A failure to examine the domestic institutions that underpin commercial exchange within and across countries has strengthened a conventional wisdom skeptical of the capacity of globalization to promote peace. Rather than asking why globalization failed to prevent war in 1914, this chapter has sought to build on the historiography of World War I to examine how government controls over capitalism contributed to its outbreak. Tariffs, public property, and capital controls shaped the character of the arms race that ultimately led German political and military leaders to believe that war offered the best means to preserve their position in Europe. Chapter 8 extends this examination of the links between government controls on commercial exchange and questions of war and peace to a critical case for liberal international relations theory in the contemporary period of globalization – cross-Strait relations between China and Taiwan.

EIGHT

Peace Across the Taiwan Strait?

Just as World War I has often been held out as the archetypal failure of globalization to prevent war in the nineteenth century, the recent history of confrontation across the Taiwan Strait appears to be a similarly confounding case for claims linking trade and peace. Many contemporary studies of current relations between China and Taiwan begin with an apparent paradox.[1] Just as similar reform initiatives in both China and Taiwan began to unleash a torrent of trade, travel, and investment across the Strait by the end of the 1980s, a brief thawing in cross-Strait relations gave way to the return of substantial political tension between the two by 1995. The visit of Taiwan's president, Lee Teng-hui, to Cornell University in 1995 provoked a military standoff in which the People's Liberation Army test-fired missiles around Taiwan under the guise of multiple military exercises. U.S. President Clinton responded by sending two aircraft carrier groups to the region to deter further military action. Diplomatic crises again broke out after Lee characterized relations between China and Taiwan in 1999 as that between two states and during the campaigns for Taiwanese presidential elections in 2000 and 2004, which were conducted with the threat of independence looming.

Despite a dramatic reorientation in Chinese foreign policy in the era of economic reform whereby Beijing has embraced multilateralism and globalization, settled numerous outstanding territorial disputes, and eschewed support for revolutionary movements around the world, Taiwan appears to have remained relatively exempt from these demonstrations of restraint.[2] A simple focus on the simultaneous growth of macro trade levels and political

[1] See, for example, Bush (2005a, b) and Tian (2006).

[2] On Beijing's shift in grand strategy and willingness to settle outstanding conflicts, see Johnston (2003), Goldstein (2005), and Fravel (2008).

conflict between China and Taiwan seemingly supports realist skepticism of commercial liberalism that sees extensive trading ties as a source of asymmetrical dependence, contempt, and discord rather than peace (e.g., Waltz 1979).

This chapter explores the recent history of this dispute with the theoretical arguments made here.[3] Its conclusions are more tentative because, unlike previous disputes examined, the conflict over Taiwan's political status relative to the mainland remains unresolved. Although the most recent elections in Taiwan that created a dramatic victory for the more pro-mainland Kuomintang (KMT) Party augur well for peace, a final political compromise still seems to be far off. However, both sides appear to be increasingly willing to live with a status quo that avoids military conflict and exploits joint opportunities for economic growth created by Taiwanese investment on the mainland.

Even though this dispute possesses an uncertain future, the last decade offers numerous opportunities to trace the causal mechanisms identified here associating liberal commercial policies with restrained national interests. This chapter shows how cross-Strait ties illustrate at least four components of these broader arguments. First, the period of economic reform in China has corresponded with a decisive shift toward a more accommodating and restrained grand strategy. This suggests that economic liberalization has helped transform Chinese national security interests. Second, recent examinations of cross-Strait developments that challenge the relevance of commercial liberalism focus on the concept of economic dependence, which highlights the macroeconomic implications of such ties. I discuss the weaknesses of such an approach to illustrate how the distributional pressures associated with globalization have reinforced an internal conflict over identity within Taiwan and made domestic struggles over commercial policy a critical component in the larger national debate over independence. Third, I discuss how critics of commercial liberalism in this case overlook the *ceteris paribus* nature of the claim linking trade to peace. Over the last two

[3] This chapter draws on approximately fifty hours of interviews in Beijing, Shanghai, and Taipei in 2005 and 2006. The interview subjects were promised confidentiality. In Beijing and Shanghai, I talked with academics from universities and think tanks, business entrepreneurs from both the mainland and Taiwan, representatives of American and Taiwanese commercial organizations in China, and a legislator from Taiwan. In Taipei, I interviewed academics in universities and think tanks; party officials from the KMT and the DPP; members of the Legislative Yuan from the KMT, the DPP, and the TSU parties; government officials from the National Security Council, the Ministry of Economic Affairs, the Mainland Affairs Council, the Ministry of Foreign Affairs, and the Taipei Mayor's office; and representatives of commercial organizations.

decades, however, all else is not equal across the straits. Just as commercial exchange has exploded between China and Taiwan, democratization in Taiwan has unleashed electoral dynamics that have rewarded confrontational foreign-policy positions. Political and economic liberalization in Taiwan have created opposing foreign-policy tendencies. These dynamics illustrate a claim raised in Chapter 5 that will be reinforced in Chapter 9: Markets have historically played a larger role than elections in promoting international peace. Fourth, this case also helps to illustrate important similarities across the two eras of globalization. Just as Britain sought to use greater access to its consumers to tilt the domestic balance of power in the United States toward groups that favored accommodation in the Oregon dispute, the mainland is similarly using access to its economy to alter the domestic balance of power within Taiwan in favor of the Pan-Blue Coalition that seeks to preserve the status quo.

This chapter proceeds in four parts. The next section offers a brief history of this dispute. The second section examines the foreign-policy implications of the recent period of economic reform in China. A third section examines the domestic struggle in Taiwan over growing commercial ties with the mainland. A fourth section examines how democratization in Taiwan has influenced its relations with the mainland.

THE CROSS-STRAITS DISPUTE

The contemporary dispute between the two political entities known as China and Taiwan has gone through multiple phases over the past century.[4] During this struggle, sovereignty, both de jure and de facto, over Taiwan has shifted among at least three parties – mainland China, Japan, and Taiwan itself. Following nearly three centuries of Chinese rule, Japan set up a colonial administration over Taiwan in 1895 after defeating the Qing Dynasty in the Sino-Japanese War. Taiwan was then transferred back to China in 1945 after Japan's defeat in World War II.[5] Throughout the Cold War, its status was shaped both by the internal struggle between the Communist and KMT Parties to rule China and the larger global struggle waged by the United States against communism.

The Chinese Civil War continued after the leader of the KMT, Chiang Kai-shek, fled to Taiwan in 1949 to set up an alternative government. Despite his departure, the KMT still held territory in the southern and western

[4] This section draws heavily on Romberg (2003), Bush (2005a), and Wachman (2007).

[5] In the peace treaty signed in 1952, Japan did not specify to which political entity (i.e., the Communists or the Nationalists) it was ceding Taiwan.

regions of the mainland. Chiang used Taiwan as a base to continue military operations on the mainland. Throughout 1949 and 1950, Mao Zedong, the leader of the Chinese Communist Party (CCP), pressed his military advisors to invade Taiwan and defeat the Nationalist resistance. However, the outbreak of the Korean War in 1950 effectively thwarted this political and military goal. Seeing Taiwan as a geostrategically important base in East Asia and hoping to prevent any further communist territorial gains, President Truman sent the Seventh Fleet to the Taiwan Straits and blocked any invasion plans that Mao may have had. The military campaign between China and Taiwan continued sporadically until 1979, primarily in the form of artillery attacks by the mainland against the offshore islands of Quemoy and Matsu still held by the KMT government in Taiwan. The most serious of these confrontations occurred in 1954–5 and 1958.

The larger superpower confrontation, motivated by the underlying ideological struggle between democratic capitalism and communism, drove American policy toward Taiwan during the Cold War. America's commitment to Taiwan waxed and waned according to shifts in the relationship between the People's Republic of China (PRC) and the Soviet Union. After deterring an invasion by Mao in 1950, the United States extended its military commitment to Taiwan by signing a mutual defense treaty in 1954. This responsibility for protecting Taiwan went so far as to include threats of a nuclear attack against the mainland during the crisis of 1954–5. The emerging Sino-Soviet split later led Nixon to reorient American policy away from the clear commitment to defend Taiwan and toward the position of ambiguity that exists today. Seeing that closer ties with the PRC would strengthen America's position relative to the Soviet Union, Nixon laid the groundwork for the formal recognition of the PRC as the rightful government of China. President Carter completed this process by ending official diplomatic relations with Taiwan, removing all American forces from Taiwan, and recognizing the PRC's bid to assume China's seat at the United Nations.

The United States though did not surrender all responsibility for the security of Taiwan. While improving ties with the mainland, Carter also sought to protect the continuation of arms sales to Taiwan so that it could assume more responsibility for its physical security. Upset with the administration's apparent abandonment of a critical Cold War ally, Congress used these negotiations with the administration to pass the Taiwan Relations Act. This bill asserted America's interest in seeing a peaceful resolution to any political dispute between the mainland and Taiwan and seemed to reaffirm a quasi-commitment to the latter.

America's formal recognition of the PRC altered the relationship between the mainland and Taiwan. Mao's successor as the leader of the CCP, Deng Xiaoping, responded with a diplomatic offensive designed to reintegrate Taiwan with the rest of China. He halted the shelling of Quemoy and Matsu. He also proposed the "One China, Two Systems" framework, granting Taiwan substantial autonomy in local matters. Taiwan initially responded to these overtures by holding firm to its traditional policy toward the mainland: no contact, no negotiations, and no compromises. Preparations to ease martial law and begin democratization in 1987 later led Chiang Kai-shek's successor Chiang Ching-kuo to relax restrictions on travel to the mainland and on foreign direct investment there.

This opening unleashed an explosion of travel and commerce and a relative flurry of diplomatic exchanges designed at reaching some type of settlement. The mainland continued to use the "One China, Two Systems" approach that guided talks with the Great Britain over Hong Kong as its negotiating benchmark. Chiang Ching-kuo's successor Lee Teng-hui originally seemed receptive to these preliminary discussions.[6] His willingness rested on his political weakness at home. Born in Taiwan, he was distrusted by the mainlander – officials that had followed Chiang Kai-shek to Taiwan after 1949 – faction of the KMT. Hoping to continue the process of political reform that Chiang Ching-kuo had initiated, he sought a relaxed external situation to quell any revolt by this faction within his own party that still sought some form of unification. Lee renounced the use of force to achieve unification, surrendered the KMT's territorial claims on the mainland, and established the National Unification Guidelines that were designed to protect the interests of the Taiwanese people in a democratic China. These initial discussions yielded at least one modest breakthrough: a 1992 agreement whereby each party recognized that there was only "One China" while allowing the other side their own interpretation of what "One China" meant. This allowed Taiwan to define "One China" in cultural and ethnic terms while the mainland could define "One China" in political terms. Beijing though refused one of Lee's critical demands, namely to treat Taiwan's government on equal terms in any diplomatic exchanges. Beijing insisted on characterizing any negotiations as those between a central and local government. It feared that any formal or informal recognition that conveyed equal political standing on Taiwan's government would obviate its claims to be the legitimate government over Taiwan.

[6] On Lee's foreign policy see Bush (2005a, b) and Jacobs and Liu (2007).

Mainland fears of losing Taiwan via a declaration of independence reflect multiple domestic and foreign policy interests. Taiwan poses a political, rather than a direct physical, security threat to the mainland (Bush 2005a). The current leadership in Beijing sees the maintenance of the legitimacy of its claims over Taiwan as central to regime stability (e.g., Shirk 2007). The emergence of a strong Chinese nationalism during the period of reform has fueled a popular belief that Taiwan is part of China. Consequently, any break for independence could be greeted at home as a dramatic policy failure, potentially stoking a much broader revolt against the regime. Moreover, Beijing also worries that a successful Taiwanese bid for independence could encourage other separatist movements within China, such as in Tibet.

The domestic risks posed by Taiwanese independence are compounded by the mainland's broader regional and global interests, including its relationship with the United States. The mainland has long maintained that its relationship with Taiwan is a domestic matter and accordingly bridled at American interference. Because Taiwan sits in the center of critical shipping lanes, America's ability to block the Straits and inflict substantial damage to the Chinese economy constitutes a key national security threat that underscores the mainland's need to keep Taiwan within its broader sphere of influence.[7] Recently though, democratization in Taiwan has slightly reoriented the mainland's position on American intervention. As democratization has created a new institutional vehicle by which supporters of independence can insert their preferences into the policy-making process, the mainland has come to recognize that American intervention can influence domestic debates in Taiwan and help publicly undermine extremist politicians.

Cross-Strait ties stand out as the critical policy cleavage inside Taiwan. The Pan-Blue Coalition, led by the KMT, seeks to exploit the economic opportunities on the mainland while preserving Taiwan's capacity to negotiate peacefully some compromise over its political status. The Pan-Green Coalition, led by the Democratic Progressive Party (DPP), has adopted a more confrontational approach to Beijing. Fueled in part by an emerging Taiwanese identity and a belief that the United States could not risk its broad set of external commitments throughout Asia by abandoning Taiwan, the DPP has taken steps to increase the island's autonomy from the mainland. It has limited investment on the mainland to reduce Taiwan's economic dependence and Beijing's influence with the business community. More importantly, it has pursued a series of constitutional measures, such as

[7] Wachman (2007) argues that these geostrategic concerns, rather than worries over domestic stability, play a larger role in Beijing's calculations with respect to Taiwan.

popular referenda, and international initiatives, like membership in the United Nations and the World Health Organization, to strengthen Taiwan's legal claims for political independence.

Since the end of the Cold War, the American policy of strategic ambiguity has helped to cap the escalation of tensions between the mainland and Taiwan in a series of crises that have possessed significant risks of war.[8] The uncertain nature of the American commitment has simultaneously deterred military action by Beijing and a declaration of independence by Taiwan. Accordingly, the United States has tilted back and forth between the two parties during these crises over the past decade, shifting implicit support away from whichever side it deemed to be trying to alter unilaterally the peaceful status quo that has existed since 1979.

The first of these crises occurred in the aftermath of President Lee's visit to Cornell University in 1995. Because the mainland had repeatedly blocked Lee's efforts to gain external recognition for Taiwan in international organizations, Lee sought to improve its status via a series of high-level trips to other countries. He used support for Taiwan in the U.S. Congress to pressure the Clinton administration into granting him a visit to Cornell. American approval of his trip reaffirmed fears on the mainland that Lee ultimately sought to move Taiwan closer to independence. The PRC responded with a series of military maneuvers in the summer of 1995 and then again in March 1996 before Taiwan's presidential elections. The Clinton administration intervened with its own military displays, sending two aircraft carrier groups to the region. Tensions dropped shortly thereafter as the mainland's exercises finished on March 23, the same day that Lee was elected and one of the U.S. carrier groups arrived.

Lee again challenged Beijing's political claims over Taiwan in the summer of 1999. He publicly characterized the relationship between Taiwan and the mainland as that between two states in an attempt to establish an international legal basis for Taiwanese sovereignty. This declaration provoked another brief conflict in which Beijing heightened military activity in the Straits.

The United States has adopted a tougher line toward Taiwan during the tenure of Lee's successor, Chen Shui-bian. Like Lee, Chen has sought to raise Taiwan's international profile, particularly through membership in international organizations. He has also sought constitutional revision, provoking worries in Beijing that he was pushing Taiwan closer to a formal declaration of independence. Many of these efforts during 2002 and 2003

[8] For a recent discussion of this policy of strategic ambiguity, see Tucker (2005).

were geared to mobilizing the base of the DPP in anticipation of the 2004 presidential elections. This older segment of the party has traditionally supported independence. These provocations led U.S. President Bush to issue a stern warning to Chen in December 2003 at a joint press conference with China's premier Wen Jiabao. Bush reaffirmed America's commitment to a one-China policy and its opposition to any unilateral alteration of the status quo. He continued, "And the comments and actions made by the leader of Taiwan indicate that he may be willing to make decisions unilaterally to change the status quo, which we oppose."[9] Strong American criticism of Chen continued in the spring of 2006 when he violated his 2000 inauguration promise not to abolish the National Unification Council. This policy-making body in Taiwan was created in 1990 to oversee cross-Strait negotiations. It partially symbolized earlier cooperative efforts to dampen tension between the two parties.[10] These public criticisms by President Bush have bolstered stability in the region by reassuring the mainland that the United States was willing to oppose any move toward independence. This American posture simultaneously reduces domestic pressure, particularly from the military, on the government in Beijing to signal with military force its opposition to independence.

Recent American statements have also encouraged the PRC to show more restraint, patience, and confidence relative to Taiwan. Although scholars differ over the exact timing of this important shift in Chinese foreign policy, the administration of Hu Jintao has refrained from reciprocating provocations by Chen (e.g., Medeiros and Fravel 2003; Chu 2005; Gill 2005). In part, Beijing has learned that Chen has exploited its hard-line policies, like the 2000 declaration that "independence means war" or the 2005 anti-secession law, for his own political benefit. Such threats simply grant greater credence to fears among staunch supporters of independence (the Deep-Green faction) within the DPP's coalition over the mainland's true intentions. For example, China has either remained relatively quiet or let the Bush administration lead the condemnations of recent Chen initiatives like the abolition of the National Unification Council. Moreover, the mainland has simultaneously used growing economic integration across the Strait to signal to constituencies across the political spectrum in Taiwan that a relaxation of

9 This press conference is available online at http://www.whitehouse.gov/news/releases/2003/12/20031209–2.html. Accessed February 11, 2008.

10 This council also reflected a period in the KMT's history in which it was split between mainlander and Taiwanese factions. Lee created the National Unification Council to allay concerns of mainlanders within the party that he was not committed to eventual reunification with the mainland.

tensions between the two governments would create significant economic opportunities. This growing array of mechanisms to influence Taiwanese domestic political struggles has increased Beijing's confidence that time is on its side and a peaceful, negotiated compromise that protects its sovereignty over Taiwan is possible so long as the small group of staunch independence supporters on the island is politically marginalized.

ECONOMIC REFORM AND FOREIGN-POLICY RESTRAINT IN CHINA

Joseph Schumpeter (1951[1919]) argued that capitalist development destroys imperialist interests within states responsible for war by democratizing, individualizing, and rationalizing society. By focusing individual attention on economic survival within competitive labor markets and shifting the primary path to social ascendancy away from military glory, capitalism pushes a country to eschew territorial conquest and embrace peace. This transformative capacity of capitalism to alter the national interests of a state can be seen in China during the period of economic reform initiated by Deng Xiaoping in 1978 that continues today.

Economic Reforms

Deng's emergence in the post-Mao power struggle deemphasized ideological struggle and catapulted economic reform and development to the top of Communist Party policy priorities.[11] Deng sought to move beyond the economic failures of Mao's tenure – marked perhaps most dramatically by rural collectivization and its induced famine in the late 1950s as part of the Great Leap Forward – through a series of economic reforms that enabled greater individual initiative and entrepreneurship.[12] A decade before the reforms began, the Chinese economy was the antithesis of capitalism, dominated by the public sector and largely insulated from the competitive pressures of global markets. Twelve state-owned corporations held monopolies over all external trade, which was oriented toward importing capital goods for industrialization. The RMB, its currency, was not convertible and the economy was closed to foreign sources of capital or technology. Today, a large and dynamic private sector has emerged alongside a reforming public sector. China is a member of the World Trade Organization (WTO) and one

[11] For a discussion of this internal struggle and domestic political transformation, see Harding (1987).

[12] This brief review of economic reform in China relies on Naughton (1995, 2007).

of the world's most important destinations for foreign direct investment. This period of economic reforms, marked by both privatization and globalization, has generated more than twenty-five years of consistent economic expansion with annual growth rates regularly hovering around 10 percent.

Gradualism, experimentation, and the devolution of economic authority from the state to local enterprises and then to individuals have characterized the reform process. The first programs began in the agricultural sector. The government created more discretion for collectives to innovate by freeing them to sell surplus production to the market after meeting reduced production quotas. Collectives then continued this strategy of experimentation by giving individual farmers control over plots of land. This effective transfer of ownership over agricultural surpluses from the public to the private sector enhanced rural productivity and created important spillover effects in local industry by freeing up more resources for township and village enterprises.

This devolution of authority to local governments for economic policy continued with the broader policy of ending China's economic isolation and embracing the global economy. Perhaps the most well-documented example of this political innovation was the creation of special economic zones in Shenzhen, Zhuhai, Shantou, and Xiamen in 1979 that later spread to the remaining coastal regions.[13] Local governments in these regions were allowed to create export processing zones, in which capital equipment and other inputs used to assemble final goods destined for global markets could be imported free of tariffs. These processing zones were encouraged to seek foreign investment by offering incentives like land concessions and reduced corporate taxes to multinational corporations. The central government supported these local initiatives by lowering tax obligations owed to Beijing and creating a special bureaucratic agency responsible for protecting the economic needs of these regions with respect to the rest of the central planning apparatus (Shirk 1994, p. 36). The economic success of these zones then unleashed intense competitive pressures within China as other provincial authorities began demanding similar rights and concessions from the central government so that they too could seek infusions of foreign capital critical for economic growth.[14]

[13] In addition to Naughton (2007), see Lardy (1992, 2002) and Shirk (1994) for discussions of the reforms that facilitated China's integration in the global economy.

[14] For a theoretical discussion of how the competitive political pressures associated with federal structures of economic policy making promote economic growth, see Weingast (1995).

Changing National Interests

Having now gone through multiple stages and spread throughout the entire economy, this overarching strategy of economic reform carries important implications for the national priorities of the CCP, Chinese foreign-policy interests, and Chinese grand strategy in the post-Mao era. Deng and his successors have clearly placed economic development atop the hierarchy of Chinese national interests and subordinated competing party goals, like political mobilization and transformation, income equity, and the expansion of military power (Naughton 1995, pp. 93–4).[15]

Deng's reforms have also transformed the foundations of legitimacy for Communist Party rule. The maintenance of high economic growth rates now stands as the critical means to deal with a number of internal challenges – like growing income inequality, corruption, environmental distress, urbanization, and the threat of political instability more generally – facing the CCP.[16] Rather than being able to rely on a communist ideology promising future gains in social equality, political leaders in the reform era increasingly rely on practices and behaviors long associated with capitalism – like foreign direct investment, private ownership, and competitive markets – to propel economic expansion. Perhaps most illustrative of the dramatic political implications of this economic transition, local growth rates and foreign direct investment inflows now serve as two of the most important performance benchmarks for promotion and raises within some local branches of the Communist Party.[17]

This priority of economic growth carries important foreign-policy implications because it has reversed China's relationship with the broader global economy. China has embraced globalization and exploited foreign capital and technology to stimulate exports and economic growth. Consequently,

[15] For example, when opening the Twelfth National Congress of the CCP, Deng (1982) stated, "The 1980s will be an important decade in the history of our Party and state. To accelerate socialist modernization, to strive for China's reunification and particularly the return of Taiwan to the motherland, and to oppose hegemonism and work to safeguard world peace – these are the three major tasks of our people in this decade. Economic development is at the core of these tasks: it is the basis for the solution of our external and internal problems."

[16] Describing a wide range of challenges to internal stability, Shirk (2007, p. 30) writes that growth rates of at least 7% are necessary to generate sufficient job creation in the Chinese economy.

[17] Tian (2006, p. 136) provides some examples of this dynamic. A member of a local chamber of commerce in Shanghai also described this practice to me. Author interview, Shanghai, December 2005.

China has cut off support for revolutionary movements in the Third World, sought to settle outstanding territorial disputes, and reassure regional neighbors of its peaceful intentions to stimulate even more economic integration and development.[18] Deng's belief that the current era of world history is defined by both peace and development and recent extensions of these principles manifested in debates about China's Peaceful Rise illustrate this intimate connection between the growth imperative and China's national interest in actively promoting a peaceful external environment.

In addition to implementing market-oriented reforms, Deng reversed China's Maoist orientation to the international system that emphasized autarky, an inherent struggle with capitalist world, and the expansion of military power.[19] In 1985, he justified the continuation of his economic reform program by pointing to two key trends in China's external environment, that of peace and development. Believing that the danger of superpower war had subsided, Deng argued that China could look forward to at least two decades of peace. While arguing that this global situation enabled the pursuit of domestic reform, he simultaneously emphasized that China had a strong interest in both peace and the broadening of cooperative ties with Western economies to exploit the opportunities created by the favorable external environment and to ensure that it continued. These overarching principles that guided China's grand strategy were also used to deemphasize the importance of military modernization.

The recent debate surrounding China's Peaceful Rise illustrates that these ideas continue to guide Chinese national interests today.[20] This term was coined by Zheng Bijian, a prominent intellectual in the CCP with strong ties to Hu Jintao, in the fall of 2003.[21] A trip to Washington in the fall of 2002 led Zheng to believe that many American officials remained concerned that the existing pace of economic growth in China would create internal pressures for military expansion.[22] Following a year of study and internal

[18] For recent discussions of Chinese foreign policy in the era of reform, see Yahuda (1993), Goldstein (2005), and Chu (2004).

[19] This discussion of Deng's characterization of China's external environment as marked by peace and development relies on Finkelstein (2000).

[20] See for example the introduction by John Thornton in Zheng (2005).

[21] Although public references to the concepts associated with Peaceful Rise are now characterized instead by the term Peaceful Development, Glaser and Medeiros (2007) argue this is really just a shift in terminology, not in purpose. The strategic principles for contemporary Chinese policy remain the same. For a collection of speeches by Zheng on China's Peace Rise, see Zheng (2005).

[22] The initial formulation of this concept also illustrates the awareness of China's senior leaders of the security dilemma and its potential to frustrate the implementation of their policies. Goldstein (2005) discusses this strategic learning in China. Military disputes over

debate, Zheng gave a speech at the Bo'au Forum in 2003 that invoked the term *Peaceful Rise.* He emphasized that China sought to exploit globalization to develop. China would continue to implement reforms that opened its economy while being attentive to domestic problems associated with growing inequality. Moreover, China would not follow the development strategy of previous rising powers – like Germany and Japan – that ultimately destabilized the international system through territorial expansion and colonialism. He argues that open global markets made this new path possible by enabling China to acquire the inputs, like foreign capital and raw materials, necessary for growth through peaceful means (Zheng 2005, p. 52). Zheng emphasizes that China is following its new security concept, which seeks to build mutual trust and mutually beneficial cooperation with other states.[23]

While Peaceful Rise and its next incarnation, Peaceful Development, can be cast as rhetorical devices designed to reassure the world and thus worthy of skepticism as accurate reflections of contemporary Chinese national interests in both international peace and economic growth, this official policy has been matched with important instances of cooperation over the past decade. China has settled numerous outstanding territorial disputes and made substantial progress in ameliorating border tensions with great powers like India and Russia (Fravel 2005). It pushed North Korea to the negotiating table in recent six-party talks to end the stalemate over North Korea's nuclear program. China chose not to destabilize further the regional economy during the Asian financial crisis by devaluing its currency so as to retain the competitiveness of its export profile (Moore and Yang 2001; Goldstein 2005, pp. 128–30). It has strengthened ties with international organizations like the WTO, the Association of Southeast Asian Nations (ASEAN), and the Shanghai Cooperation Organization.[24] China signed an

the Spratly Islands and with Taiwan in the 1990s created fears in the international arena that China would seek to revise the international status quo once it had completed programs of economic development and military modernization. The Jiang administration decided that the adoption of a confrontational foreign-policy line could threaten China's development by provoking a counterbalancing coalition that sought to contain its rise. Consequently, China began to participate actively in international organizations while launching a broad diplomatic effort to strengthen ties with other great powers, like the United States.

23 On the new security concept see Gill (2007). He (pp. 10, 21) writes that three overarching goals guide China's new security diplomacy. First, it seeks to promote regional stability and peace so that it can focus on internal development. Second, it wants to increase its wealth and influence in a way that reassures, rather than threatens, its neighbors. Third, it seeks to balance the American influence in the region without provoking any confrontation.

24 See Chapter 2 in Gill (2007) for a discussion of this reorientation of Chinese foreign policy toward greater participation in regional organizations.

agreement for a peaceful resolution of the South China Sea disputes in 2002. It then signed the ASEAN Treaty of Amity and Cooperation in 2003. In short, China is acting like a status quo state possessing national interests that are both consistent with and furthered by the existing international order (Johnston 2003).

Multiple scholars have noted a growth of confidence in China's foreign policy over the past decade or so (Medeiros and Fravel 2003; Chu 2005; Gill 2005).[25] This shift has helped push Chinese leaders to embrace the role of responsible Great Power (e.g., Goldstein 2005) while moving away from characterizations of their national identity as that of colonized victim. China has also actively promoted stability in Asia by enhancing its participation in regional institutions and cementing its central role in the region's increasingly tight economic division of labor (e.g., Ohashi 2005; Gill 2007).

Although the mainland's policy relative to Taiwan is often viewed as separate from its broader foreign-policy orientation, there is some evidence that its preferences for restraint and the status quo are beginning to shape cross-Strait relations as well. The inability of the Jiang Zemin's administration over the 1990s to push Taiwan closer to unification has helped cause a reorientation in the approach of his successor, Hu Jintao.[26] The Chinese leadership recognized that the use of military coercion in the Straits crises of 1995–6 and 1999 had backfired by strengthening independence forces on Taiwan. Hu has adopted a longer-term view of cross-Strait relations. Realizing that the chances of securing unification during his tenure are slim, he has sought to downplay the pursuit of this traditional foreign-policy goal while focusing on the maintenance of the status quo and the preservation of peace in the Straits. Hu's public statements during the visits of Lien Chan and James Soong, two leaders of Taiwan's Pan-Blue Coalition, to the mainland in 2005 help demonstrate this reorientation. Hu intentionally omitted any mention of unification in his scripted remarks.[27] Beijing has a strong interest in peace because war with Taiwan would generate too many uncertainties – like domestic instability, a surge in nationalism, a military stalemate, a potential war with the United States – that could threaten development and regime stability. Consequently, so long as Taiwan does not force Beijing's

[25] These discussions focus more on identifying this trend and its implications rather than examining its causes. Medeiros and Fravel (2003, p. 29) provide one exception. They point to increasing economic integration as a source of the mainland's increasing confidence and patience with respect to Taiwan.

[26] A senior DPP legislator timed this shift in the mainland's approach to the promulgation of the anti-secession law in 2005. Author interview, Taipei, March 2006.

[27] A Beijing academic pointed to this carefully worded statement as evidence of Hu's shift. Author interview, Beijing, December 2005.

hand by declaring independence, the current leadership is willing not to press for unification while living with a peaceful status quo that at least leaves open the possibility of unification at some indefinite, even distant, point in the future (Chu 2005, pp. 246–7).

Changing Tactics

Apart from altering China's national interests, reform and global economic integration have also moderated China's foreign policy by expanding the range of tools it deploys when interacting with other states. In this causal pathway, growing commercial integration enhances China's bargaining leverage by creating a wide range of economic incentives that can be used to induce other governments to make concessions at the negotiating table. This expanded statecraft toolkit augurs well for peace in the region by raising China's willingness to rely more on economic carrots rather than military sticks as instruments of foreign-policy influence. More importantly, the current leadership in China has gotten increasingly sophisticated and adept at deploying these instruments at the micro level so as to alter the domestic balance of political power in its targets, like Taiwan.

China's negative experience with coercive diplomacy relative to Taiwan during the 1990s, its continued focus on economic modernization as the chief policy goal, and its growing economic clout have all heightened the importance of economic tools of statecraft relative to military instruments. Lampton (2005) argues that the Soviet legacy and Asian regional economic integration have both pushed Beijing to reorient its strategic approach. While the Soviet comparison is often made to illustrate the risks associated with simultaneously pursuing political and economic reforms, Lampton notes that the Soviet experience also demonstrates the long-term costs of relying too heavily on military strength to achieve strategic objectives. The current leadership in Beijing has moved to focus more on what he calls remunerative power to promote its interests.

The decisions by many Asian countries to orient their own economic policies around Chinese economic growth have created even more opportunities for Beijing to exert political influence in the region.[28] Any conflict carries the risk of disrupting the increasingly tight regional supply chain whereby China imports intermediate products from such countries as

[28] For example, China now stands as the most important export destination for goods from both Taiwan and South Korea. China is Japan's second-most important export market. These statistics were for 2006 and are available on CIA World Factbook Web site: https://www.cia.gov/library/publications/the-world-factbook/. Accessed on February 2, 2008.

Taiwan, South Korea, and Indonesia before final assembly in China. Chu (2005) argues that this regional economic integration has enhanced the stake of other states in the continuation of the status quo in the Taiwan Straits. He points to the support shown from ASEAN, France, Japan, and Germany for President Bush's strong criticism of Chen Shui-bian in December 2003 as evidence of this global interest in peace.

The mainland's shift in preference for deploying economic carrots carries important implications for cross-Strait relations because it coincides with a greater confidence in Beijing that has lengthened its time horizons relative to the question of unification with Taiwan. Therefore, as long as Beijing believes that forces for independence can be checked on Taiwan, they are willing to embrace a peaceful status quo that at least leaves open the possibility of unification at some undefined point in the future. Undoubtedly, recent American willingness to chastise Taiwan publicly has helped to reassure China that the United States is committed to preserving the status quo by politically undermining independence forces on Taiwan.[29] However, the rapid deepening of economic integration with Taiwan has also helped to strengthen confidence on the mainland that it possesses both the policy levers and the time to construct a political deal whereby it maintains some form of sovereignty over the island (Medeiros and Fravel 2003; Chu 2005). Accordingly, Beijing hopes that economic integration will alter the internal balance of power in Taiwan toward the Pan-Blue Coalition. These possibilities bear important similarities to British efforts in the 1840s to utilize targeted economic incentives to shift the domestic balance of power inside the United States toward groups that supported cooperation over Oregon.

For example, in a very public signal in the summer of 2005, the mainland eliminated tariffs on many types of fruit imported from Taiwan. Taiwanese agriculture has been hit particularly hard following accession to the WTO in 2002. This initiative was designed to signal to Taiwanese farmers that the mainland could help to compensate them for their recent income losses.[30] It followed two key visits to the mainland by opposition leaders Lien Chen and James Soong earlier that year. Aware that the DPP opposed more fruit exports to the mainland in part because it was likely to increase local prices, both Lien and Soong pushed the mainland to offer this relatively

[29] For example, President Bush, with Wen Jiabao at his side, publicly blamed Chen Shui-bian for unilaterally trying to alter the status quo in November 2003. Similarly, the Bush administration criticized Chen Shui-bian for abolishing the National Unification Council in spring 2006.

[30] Author interview, December 2005, Beijing.

low-cost political gesture.[31] Because fruit production is concentrated in southern Taiwan, a traditional political stronghold for the DPP and pro-independence forces, the mainland and the KMT hoped that new outlets for these products would encourage farmers to support greater economic exchange and political accommodation with the mainland.[32]

A senior KMT legislator pointed to this agricultural trade initiative as evidence of how the mainland had shown increasing diplomatic skill in the precision by which it targeted key constituencies in Taiwan to receive such economic carrots.[33] He noted an important strategic break between Jiang and Hu. While comparing Jiang's economic diplomacy to that of a shotgun blast – relying heavily on rhetoric and being too broad – he likened Hu's approach to that of a rifle shot aimed directly at strategically important constituencies in Taiwan. Apart from the green-leaning agricultural sector, he also pointed to tuition waivers for students from Taiwan, tourism initiatives, and incentives for bankers as all evidence of Beijing's growing ability to use economic carrots to influence cross-Strait relations by altering internal political struggles within Taiwan.

In short, economic integration is helping to promote peace in the Straits by altering Beijing's approach to the region, including Taiwan, in at least two critical ways. First, a strategy of national development oriented around economic reform and globalization has moved China's foreign-policy interests in a more cooperative direction. A decreased willingness to threaten economic growth has led Beijing to embrace territorial restraint and multilateral cooperation.

Second, globalization has altered the relative priority of means that China uses to realize these interests by reducing the appeal of military coercion. Economic integration offers new levers by which China can shape the internal balance of power within its trading partners, including Taiwan, and the foreign policies these trading partners then adopt relative to China. In the language of the commitment problem, economic integration across the Straits has promoted peace by reducing the PRC's need to launch a preventive war to forestall Taiwanese independence. Wolford (2007a, b) shows how leadership turnover in one state can alter the likelihood of war by altering another state's incentives to launch a preventive strike. Fearing that a potential successor in a target regime might be more resolved than an incumbent

31 Author interview, March 2006, Taipei.

32 DPP legislators told me in March 2006 that they could already detect a decline of support from agricultural constituents because of this initiative. Author interview, March 2006, Taipei.

33 Author interview, Taipei, March 2006.

to escalate or continue an existing dispute, a government may rationally launch a war in the present to avoid facing this successor in the future. This analysis implies that the possibility of facing a less resolved opponent in the future facilitates restraint in the present as a government waits for a more conciliatory bargaining partner to come to office. Along these lines, the lengthening of Beijing's time horizons relative to Taiwan reflects this willingness to wait for the KMT to return to power. Globalization promotes peace in the Straits by creating mechanisms by which Beijing can hasten this domestic transfer of power in Taiwan. This ability to influence Taiwanese domestic political outcomes has reduced Beijing's need to deploy military force in the Straits by providing reassurance that the Pan-Green Coalition can be blocked from pushing closer to independence.

CHINA'S ECONOMIC ORBIT AND THE DOMESTIC POLITICS OF CREATIVE DESTRUCTION IN TAIWAN

As economic liberalization has altered Chinese foreign-policy interests and tactics, it has simultaneously stabilized cross-Straits relations by empowering groups within Taiwan possessing a strong material stake in the peaceful status quo. Critics of the proposition that globalization is promoting peace in the Straits (e.g., Bush 2005a; Tian 2006) often overlook the domestic political consequences of trade that are the focus of the arguments here by focusing on the national security implications of asymmetric dependence.[34] The rapid opening of trade and investment across the Straits since 1987 has shifted the distribution of income within Taiwan, fueling a battle over commercial policy between the groups that benefit and are hurt by this exchange. These distributional pressures have reinforced the existing struggles over identity and independence between the Pan-Blue and Pan-Green Coalitions (Chen 2004). Moreover, the Taiwanese government has actively sought to shape these economic flows to support its foreign-policy goals relative to the mainland. The rest of this section provides multiple examples of the causal mechanisms linking globalization to peace discussed in previous chapters. The capacity of globalization to promote peace in the Straits depends critically on the balance of political influence between protectionists and free traders in Taiwan, and the relative capacity of the governments in Beijing and Taiwan to influence this balance.

[34] For a recent study that compares the relative explanatory power of different variants of commercial liberalism in the cross-Straits case, see Kastner (2006).

Post-1987 Economic Integration

Chiang Ching-kuo's decisions in 1987 to end martial law and reverse the KMT's long-standing policy limiting all contacts with the mainland unleashed massive economic flows that have reoriented the Taiwanese economy.[35] The primary instrument of economic integration has been Taiwanese direct investment on the mainland. Recent estimates from Taiwan's central bank that include capital flowing through third parties, like the British Virgin Islands, indicate that the total value of Taiwanese capital invested on the mainland now stands around $70 billion (Tian 2006, p. 70). This accounts for more than 60 percent of Taiwan's total stock of foreign direct investment (nearly $114 billion) and is equivalent to approximately 10 percent of its GDP in 2006 (CIA World Factbook 2008). This investment has occurred in three waves. The first occurred during the late 1980s and was confined to small and medium enterprises in labor-intensive sectors. Larger, publicly listed firms joined the movement to the mainland after 1993. The information-technology sector led a third movement to the mainland after 1998 and concentrated mostly around the Shanghai region. A dramatic expansion in flows of people and goods has followed these capital movements. More than 50,000 Taiwanese enterprises on the mainland employ at least 500,000 Taiwanese citizens (Cheng 2005, p. 108). The mainland now stands as Taiwan's top export market, accounting for more than 28 percent of its total exports in 2006.[36] Most of these exports are intermediate products sent to the mainland for final assembly.

A mix of economic and political incentives has drawn Taiwanese investment to the mainland. In the late 1980s, rising labor costs, stronger unions, and an appreciating currency hurt the competitiveness of Taiwanese exports and encouraged smaller businesses to shift labor-intensive manufacturing to the mainland in pursuit of lower wages. Later, tighter environmental regulations in Taiwan, the dotcom bust in the United States, the lure of the Chinese market, and the need for greater proximity between intermediate goods suppliers and their mainland partners in an increasingly tight supply chain brought even more waves of investment. At the same time, local governments in China have actively courted Taiwanese investors with such incentives as reduced taxes, cheap land, and relaxed environmental

[35] For recent descriptions of these economic ties see Ash (2005), Bush (2005a), Cheng (2005), Ohashi (2005), and Tian (2006).

[36] Mainland Affairs Council (2007).

regulations. Taiwanese investors are often given preferential access to these incentives over local entrepreneurs.[37]

Blues v. Greens Over Commercial Policy

The debate in Taiwan over the scope and pace of economic integration across the Straits has mirrored the larger one between the Pan-Blue and Pan-Green Coalitions over Taiwan's political status with the mainland. The Pan-Blue Coalition has sought to accelerate trade with the mainland for economic and political reasons. The lure of a large consumer market and the opportunity to push down costs offers the possibility of restoring a strong trajectory of growth in Taiwan. In particular, the KMT has trumpeted the business community's most frequently demanded change – easing restrictions on the three links with the mainland (direct communication, trade, and transportation). A focus on economic issues also allows the KMT to downplay the role of identity in Taiwanese politics that carries with it connotations of independence that necessarily provoke the mainland. Apart from offering a pragmatic means by which the PRC and the ROC can interact with each other, this economic concentration is also an attempt to move the internal debate away from an agenda pro-independence forces have successfully utilized for political gain.

Business groups have been particularly active in lobbying the KMT to liberalize trade with the mainland, improve the broader political relationship, and minimize the role of identity in Taiwanese politics. For example, Bush (2005b, p. 77) argues that business lobbying of Lee pushed him in 1991 to renounce the use of military force while laying out a clear process to achieve unification. When Lee later marginalized mainlanders within the party and moved away from supporting unification, he sought to divert trade to southern Asia because he feared that the growing political clout of this business constituency would generate popular support for political accommodations with the mainland that he did not want to make (Bush 2005a, pp. 40, 47; Chu 2004, pp. 499–500).[38] Business groups successfully lobbied Chen Shui-bian to relax many of Lee's restrictions on outward

[37] Author interviews, Beijing, December 2005. These business officials talked frequently about the absence of any government restrictions on their business activities on the mainland. They claimed that local PRC officials preferred Taiwanese investment because it also brought technology transfers and marketing skills that were in shorter supply on the mainland.

[38] See Cheng (2005) for business criticism and lobbying against Lee's "Go Slow" policy implemented in 1996.

investment to the mainland in 2001 (Tian 2006, p. 114). As a mayor and a presidential candidate for the KMT, Ma Ying-jeou actively courted the support of this constituency, regularly meeting with business leaders and making the acceleration of trade with the mainland a centerpiece of his campaign.[39]

Business interests also lobby mainland officials for political cooperation between the PRC and the ROC. Cheng (2005, p. 109) notes that the business community protested to the Beijing government its handling of the 1995–6 Straits crisis. When Lien Chan and James Soong led Pan-Blue delegations to the mainland in 2005, lobbying by the Taiwanese business community helped alter the agenda for those meetings. Although initially reluctant to discuss a free-trade zone between the mainland and Taiwan, Hu Jintao changed his mind after consultations with Taiwanese business interests.[40]

Just as globalization has created new opportunities to limit the political tensions between the PRC and ROC, it has unleashed pressures in southern and central Taiwan that reinforce this larger conflict. These regions of the country, where employment in labor-intensive manufacturing, agriculture, and the nontradable sector is concentrated, have been hit particularly hard by the recent surge of capital outflows to the mainland and agricultural liberalization (Chu 2004, p. 510; Keng, Chen, and Huang 2006, pp. 38–9). These regions also contain many of the staunchest independence supporters within the Pan-Green Coalition. Capital account liberalization and the accompanying offshore movement of jobs to the mainland create a strong economic incentive for these constituencies to oppose further liberalization in cross-Straits exchange. The DPP not only has opposed economic liberalization to limit the domestic political influence of the large businesses with interests on the mainland, it is also representing the economic interests of its core constituents. Accordingly, this economic conflict between the winners and losers from globalization has reinforced the larger struggle over identity in Taiwan between the Pan-Blue and Pan-Green Coalitions.

The role of these southern economic interests in the Pan-Green Coalition helps explain the mainland's efforts to woo this constituency with the 2005 measure to eliminate tariffs on fruit imports. Officials on the mainland were aware that the gesture was likely to have limited effects. The fruits' comparative advantage lay in their quality, rendering then more expensive and a luxury item for the majority of consumers on the mainland. The

[39] Author interview with advisor to Ma, Taipei, March 2006.

[40] One academic in Beijing pointed to this example as evidence of the growing influence of Taiwanese businesses with political officials on the mainland. Author interview, Beijing, December 2005.

policy was symbolic in nature, designed to signal to the agricultural sector in Taiwan that the PRC was willing and capable of initiating policies designed to offset some of the adjustment costs from globalization that had fallen on them.[41]

Government Intervention

The Pan-Green Coalition has utilized government barriers to trade to strengthen its domestic political position and pursue its preferred foreign-policy interests, namely moving Taiwan closer to independence. In particular, both Lee and Chen have enacted constraints on economic exchange to prevent the mainland from utilizing such ties for political leverage over Taiwan. The rationale for greater economic nationalism often takes one of two forms: the PRC can impose severe macroeconomic costs on Taiwan by holding its investment on the mainland hostage through either strict regulation or expropriation; or it can use such ties to strengthen groups inside Taiwan that both oppose the DPP and independence.[42] These policy initiatives are often discussed in the context of diversifying Taiwan's investments away from the mainland.

As Lee marginalized mainlanders within the KMT and began to push back against the "One China" framework proposed by Deng, he simultaneously sought to minimize the influence of Taiwanese business interests on cross-Straits policy. Worried that the growing power of these groups would limit his bargaining leverage relative to Beijing, he sought to reduce economic ties with the mainland through two key policy initiatives. His "Go South" strategy pressed businesses with close ties to the KMT to invest in public infrastructure projects in the Philippines, Vietnam, Thailand, Malaysia, and Indonesia. He hoped infrastructure development in these economies would encourage other Taiwanese investors to move there rather than the mainland. Formulated in 1993, these economic initiatives were also designed to encourage "vacation diplomacy," visits by Taiwanese officials to other countries to increase international recognition of Taiwan. This broader effort to diversify Taiwanese investment was largely unsuccessful though, hampered

41 Author interview, Beijing, December 2005.

42 Deindustrialization in Taiwan is also often cited as a third concern associated with increasing economic dependence on the mainland. I leave it out of the discussion here because the political implications of this macroeconomic effect are less clear. There is still an ongoing internal debate within the DPP over electoral consequences it would face from a further liberalization of their economy. Some legislators that I talked to challenged the claim that the DPP necessarily loses domestic support via liberalization. They pointed to Chen's initial economic policies as evidence that the DPP could do well politically through economic liberalization. Author interview, Taipei, March 2006.

by the lower transaction costs, stemming largely from language and cultural similarities, of doing business on the mainland.[43] Similarly, Lee instituted the policy of "go slow, be patient" in August 1996 after investment surged following the end of the military confrontation with the mainland that year. The policy led to the cancellation of many planned infrastructure projects by requiring the need for government approval on any investment over $50 million and limiting investment in public infrastructure and information technology (Tian 2006, pp. 82–3).

Upon assuming the presidency, Chen initially adopted a friendly stance relative to expanded cross-Straits trade. In part, this policy of "active opening, effective management" was hoisted on him by his limited electoral mandate, an economic downturn, pressures from the business community, and fears that the DPP possessed limited capacity to govern effectively, particularly with respect to economic policy. This policy eased restrictions on investment by limiting regulatory hurdles and restricting the list of prohibited sectors for investment. However, by the beginning of his second term, the Board of Foreign Trade at the Ministry of Economic Affairs was actively trying to slow the growth of exports to the mainland.[44] It hoped to do this in part by actively promoting exports to new markets with more trade missions and government partnering with private investment in alternative markets. For example, some legislators in the DPP have pushed for government subsidies to outward investment in places like Central America that already have duty-free access to the American market.[45]

Chen's maintenance of restrictions on the three links slowed the growth of trade with the mainland. Businesses and their representatives have repeatedly lobbied the government to ease these restrictions in part to exploit tightening supply chains and so multinationals can set up corporate headquarters in democratic Taiwan. The absence of travel restrictions would allow management to move freely back and forth to the mainland on a daily basis. More recently, these groups contented themselves with hoping for a return of some Pan-Blue Coalition to power following the 2008 elections, as many of its members have promised to reform these constraints on trade.

43 Author interviews with Taiwanese entrepreneurs, Beijing, December 2005.

44 Author interview, Taipei, July 2005.

45 This policy was frequently discussed when I visited Taipei in March 2006. There was real disagreement within the Pan-Green Coalition on this issue. One legislator from the Taiwanese Solidarity Union described the initiative as stupid. Other DPP legislators described plans for the government to serve as a silent partner on investment initiatives in Central America, potentially putting up 49% of the initial capital outlay.

The Invisible Hand?

Despite these government restrictions on trade designed to both preserve the domestic political position of the DPP and limit Taiwan's macroeconomic dependence on the mainland, scholars of cross-Strait relations and politicians within Taiwan readily agree that the government is fighting a losing battle and becoming increasingly irrelevant relative to the market when it comes to economic outcomes (e.g., Tian 2006).[46] Efforts by Lee Teng-hui and Chen Shui-bian to divert trade away from the mainland have largely failed. Taiwanese investors have simply used third-party countries or territories to skirt restrictions on capital movements to the mainland. The lure of a huge internal market, the need to drive down costs in an increasingly competitive global economy, and the unique advantages created by cultural and language similarities have pulled Taiwanese businesses irrevocably into the mainland's economic orbit.

The seeming inevitability of deep economic integration augurs well for the political stability in the region for at least two reasons. With a government increasingly incapable of restraining it, the invisible hand, once freed in 1987, has created vested interests in Taiwan seeking to maintain this peaceful status quo. Second, these economic ties have increased Beijing's confidence that such constituencies are capable of flourishing politically within Taiwan's democracy.

ALL ELSE IS NOT EQUAL IN THE STRAITS

Multivariate statistical analysis allows a researcher to examine the relative importance of many causal factors across multiple observations of a class of events, like the outbreak of military conflict. It estimates the effect of a single causal variable, like economic liberalization, by "holding constant" all other potential causes. This *ceteris paribus* clause allows the researcher to estimate the effect of one causal variable when all other potential confounding variables, like democratization, have no effect on the outcome observed. This analysis requires multiple observations that create sufficient variation across all the potential causal variables in a regression model.

When examining the role played by globalization in a single case, like cross-Strait relations over the past decade, it is critical not to overlook

[46] One senior DPP legislator noted that it was "meaningless to speak of the Taiwanese government as capable of controlling trade." One senior KMT politician argued that the "huge economic ties across the Straits had made Chen Shui-bian an anachronism. The Taiwanese people care about prosperity and want politics to reflect that." Author interviews, Taipei, March 2006.

these implications of the *ceteris paribus* clause. All else has not been equal during this period in which Taiwan has embraced trade and investment with the mainland. It has simultaneously undergone a successful democratic transition. Democratization has created institutional mechanisms by which independence advocates in Taiwan have been able to influence cross-Straits relations. Their political lobbying and influence within the DPP have created fears in Beijing that Taiwan has moved closer to declaring independence. The mainland has responded both militarily and diplomatically to these threats. The electoral season in Taiwan over the past decade has been particularly destabilizing. Many politicians have embraced Taiwanese nationalism and more confrontational policies relative to Beijing to cultivate votes.

Economic liberalization and democratization have pushed the mainland and Taiwan in opposite directions. While economic liberalization has helped restrain China's foreign policy and created vested interests in Taiwan hoping to freeze the peaceful status quo, democratization has unleashed popular pressures that have actually led to displays of military force and heightened the risk of war. These dynamics explain the simultaneous upward trend of both commerce and conflict in the Straits and help illustrate one of the broader claims of this book. Competitive markets have historically played a larger role than competitive elections in promoting peace between states.

The theoretical mechanisms identified by Mansfield and Snyder (1995, 2002a, b, 2005) to show how democratization can stimulate military conflict and war characterize many electoral dynamics inside Taiwan during the presidential elections in 1996, 2000, and 2004. They argue that stalled democratic transitions can heighten the risks of military conflict when state institutions are weak. In changing institutional environments like this, elites may use nationalism and external threats to generate popular support and legitimacy. Despite popular elections, weak institutions in a democratizing state – such as the absence of the rule of law, the absence of a free press, or nascent parties – inhibit public accountability for pursuing such aggressive foreign policies. Such internal dynamics heighten the risks of war by encouraging overconfidence in battle, making it difficult for newly elected populist leaders to back down in an international crisis, and tempting the external targets of this nationalist rhetoric to strike first.

The period of democratization has facilitated a dramatic change in identity on Taiwan with increasing use of nationalist appeals for domestic political purposes. Over the last fifteen years, surveys reveal a sharp decline in the number of people that self-identify as Chinese and a dramatic increase in the number of people that self-identify as Taiwanese.[47] The emergence

[47] A third grouping is that of people who self-identify as both Taiwanese and Chinese.

of this national identity has had a long incubation period, given a strong boost in the immediate years after 1945 with harshly repressive actions by the KMT but then contained during the period of martial law (Bush 2005a; Phillips 2005). Mainlanders, party elders within the KMT who had fled with Chiang Kai-shek after 1949 or those who identified themselves as Chinese, continued to dominate politics on the island until Chiang Ching-kuo began to initiate reforms late in his tenure.[48] More recently, Presidents Lee Teng-hui and Chen Shui-bian have actively encouraged this shift by revising textbooks in public schools, allowing judicial action against the government for civil rights' abuses during the period of martial law, casting Taiwan as a distinct political entity from the mainland, and emphasizing a Taiwanese consciousness in public statements (Bush 2005b, p. 47; Jacobs and Liu 2007). Given that elite efforts to cultivate this identity could strengthen popular support for national self-determination, the mainland has viewed these developments with increasing alarm.

Lee, in particular, promoted a distinct Taiwanese identity to alter the internal balance of power within the KMT. Born in Taiwan, Lee's ascendancy to the presidency after the death of Chiang Ching-kuo in 1988 was treated with some suspicion within the party. His weak internal position initially led him to avoid escalating tensions with the mainland so as not to alienate the mainlander faction and consolidate his own domestic position within the party. He secured election in 1990 by compromising with mainlanders and nominating their candidate, General Hau Pei-tsun, to be vice president.

Soon he sought to exploit popular pressures for democratic reforms by limiting the influence of mainlanders within the party. Senior legislators that had been serving in permanent seats since the 1940s were forced to retire. Lee changed the internal makeup of key positions within the KMT by appointing Taiwanese to cabinet posts and the Central Standing Committee (Jacobs and Liu 2007, pp. 379–80). Lee also responded to electoral gains made by DPP in legislative elections in 1992 by attempting to co-opt some of their positions, such as pressing for a seat at the United Nations. These efforts to cultivate the DPP, strengthen a Taiwanese identity, and shift the internal balance of power within the KMT alienated him from the mainlander wing of the party until a formal rift occurred in August 1993. Conservative mainlanders broke with the KMT to form the Chinese New Party.

[48] He calculated that democratic reforms could improve Taiwan's deteriorating relationship with the United States in the wake of its formal recognition of the mainland in 1979.

Bush (2005a, b) argues that the opening of the political space created by democratization helped cause an important shift in Lee's foreign policy around 1993. This formal split consolidated his hold over a trimmed party membership and freed him to pursue a more confrontational approach with the PRC. Lee moved closer to the DPP, stepped up his criticism of the one-China, two-systems framework, began a diplomatic campaign to visit countries that included his controversial 1995 trip to Cornell, and repeated public calls for the mainland to treat Taiwan as an equal political entity. Bush (2005b, p. 78) writes of this posturing: "... democratization had an instrumental value as well. Lee believed increasingly that he could strengthen his leverage vis-à-vis Beijing by releasing populist forces on Taiwan." Moreover, Bush (2005a, p. 47) argues that Lee utilized this populism to counter the rising domestic influence of Taiwanese business interests. Lee feared that it would grow more politically difficult to reject the calls of this group for a more cooperative political relationship with the mainland as economic integration grew deeper.

Taiwan's electoral institutions have rewarded politicians seeking to exploit the increasingly salient identity cleavage for domestic political purposes.[49] Before reforms in 2004, legislators sat for terms of three years and the president was elected every four years. With local elections regularly mixed in, parties and their leaders have faced perpetual campaign pressures. This has often pushed both Blue and Green Coalitions from the political center as they mobilize core supporters within their respective parties. Complicating this perpetual election cycle, the national legislature, until the most recent election in 2008, was elected through a system of single, nontransferable voting (SNTV) in multimember districts. Because multiple members were elected from single electoral districts, some legislators have held their seats with less than 10 percent of the popular vote in heavily populated districts. This system limited party discipline and encouraged politicians to cultivate small but stable pockets of support through political patronage. Moreover,

[49] See Rigger (1999) for a discussion of Taiwan's political institutions before and after democratization. She also examines how Taiwan's electoral system has rewarded politicians for taking extreme positions. This electoral system bears the imprint of both the Japanese colonial era and the KMT regime of mobilizational authoritarianism. During the nearly forty-year period of martial law, elections were used to sustain at least some measure of legitimacy. The KMT traced its ruling principles to Sun Yat-sen, focusing on the rhetoric of democracy and unification with the mainland. Over time, these elections, while having little substantive influence on policy, became a plebiscitary device whereby popular dissatisfaction could be partially expressed. Chiang Ching-kuo and Lee initiated a series of reforms, including lifting martial law and allowing new parties to form, that ushered a period of democratic transition and the popular election of Lee in 1996.

it allowed some politicians to remain in office while championing extreme policies, like political independence from the mainland.[50]

Recent electoral cycles in Taiwan have corresponded with heightened political conflict across the Strait and even threats of war. Following Lee's visit to the United States in 1995, the PRC conducted an extensive campaign of military coercion right up until presidential elections in March 1996. It hoped to shape the outcome of the election and deter any winner from pursuing independence.[51] A split within the KMT between Lien Chan and James Soong in 1999 facilitated the election of the DPP's candidate, Chen Shui-bian. Until his defeat in the Taipei mayoral race in 1998, Chen had long been an advocate for independence. The mainland responded to the possibility of a pro-independence president with the public threat by its premier, Zhu Rongji, in 2000 that "Taiwanese independence means war."

Wu (2005) examines the effects of three broad trends – the rapid development of a distinct Taiwanese identity, democratization, and globalization – in Taiwanese politics and concludes that presidential election cycles have played the largest role in destabilizing relations among the mainland, Taiwan, and the United States.[52] The run-up to the 2004 presidential election in Taiwan was particularly tense.[53] The incumbent President Chen Shui-bian embraced policies, like constitutional revision through public referenda, UN membership, and changing Taiwan's official name, geared toward independence. Concerned that Chen was establishing a legal precedent that could later be used to ratify independence and aware that adopting a confrontational approach relative to Taiwan during the campaign season would rally domestic support for him, the mainland pushed the United States to

50 For recent discussions of survey research showing that the majority, and thus the center of the political spectrum, of Taiwan's voters prefer the existing status quo and adopt quite pragmatic views with respect to independence see Chu (2004) and Chu and Nathan (2007–8). Lin and Chu (2008) examines how party activists in Taiwan have pushed elected officials into adopting positions that diverge from the median voter.

51 Ultimately, this military action by the PRC backfired as it strengthened independence forces on Taiwan and heightened domestic support for Lee (e.g., Jacobs and Liu 2007, p. 386).

52 Referring to the 2004 presidential election, Wu (2005, p. 59) writes, "[t]he change in the mass psychology touched off a race to embrace referenda and a new constitution. Elections stir up popular emotions and turn politicians into populists... Electoral competition continues to fuel identity debate and to poison cross-Strait relations."

53 A senior KMT legislator described 2004 as the most dangerous year in recent cross-Strait relations. He went on to argue that Beijing's concerns over Taiwanese independence were not reduced until legislative elections in December granted a majority to the Pan-Blue Coalition of the KMT and the PFP. Author interview, Taipei, July 2005.

intervene with Taiwan. President Bush responded with the sharp and public criticism in December of 2003 at a joint press conference with China's premier, Wen Jiabao. By pointing to Taiwan as unilaterally destabilizing the status quo, President Bush implied that the United States was unlikely to support it with military assistance if necessary.

Chen pushed a bolder policy line relative to the mainland as his domestic position weakened. He initially adopted a moderate stance relative to the mainland during the first two years of his presidency.[54] This partial retreat from traditional DPP policies and the mainland's unwillingness to reciprocate such gestures hurt Chen's position within his coalition.[55] These intra-coalition political difficulties were compounded when Lien and Soong agreed to run on a single presidential ticket in February 2003. While their political disagreements allowed Chen to win in 2000 by splitting the Pan-Blue Coalition, their conciliation left Chen to face a unified Pan-Blue opposition in 2004. At the same time, Lee Teng-hui, now the leader of the deep-Green party, the Taiwan Solidarity Union, organized large public demonstrations to rally popular support for independence while asserting that Taiwan should declare independence prior to 2008.[56] Growing domestic support for Lee threatened to siphon off Pan-Green support from Chen. Chen made the tactical decision to move away from the political center and closer to Lee's policy line by publicly championing a national referendum and laying out a timetable that would give Taiwan a revised constitution by 2006.

Chen also exploited a second destabilizing dynamic during this campaign season (Phillips 2005; Tian 2006, pp. 49–50). Aware that a hard-line approach from Beijing would rally voters to support a tougher line against

54 Aware that the DPP's long support for independence had created widespread doubts within Taiwan about its ability to govern and that the mainland stood ready to respond sharply to any bold policy shift, Chen sought to allay such concerns early in his term. His inaugural speech laid the groundwork for this approach by promising not to declare independence, not to alter Taiwan's name from the Republic of China to the Republic of Taiwan, not to promote a referendum on independence, and to preserve the National Unification Council. Moreover, he was initially receptive to expanding economic integration across the Strait.

55 Wu (2005), for example, times Chen's shifting approach to the mainland to the decision in July 2002 by the government of Nauru to pull its diplomatic recognition of Taiwan.

56 During a visit to Taiwan in the summer of 2005, the possibility that the mainland would become much more aggressive after 2008 was a frequently relayed concern on both sides of the political aisle. The logic went as follows. For fear of any potential international sanction that could lead to a massive boycott or cancellation of the Olympics, Beijing had to be restrained relative to Taiwan until after the summer 2008. After that, Beijing would be freer to utilize military force against Taiwan if necessary.

the mainland, Chen sought to shift the electorate closer to the policies that he was embracing by provoking the PRC with the constitutional referenda. In short, Taiwan's electoral dynamics and the incentives they created to embrace extreme positions destabilized cross-Strait relations during this period by encouraging Chen to pursue policies that heightened tension with the mainland.[57]

Rigger (1999, 2005) argues that Taiwan's democratic consolidation is incomplete, plagued by both too many elections and electoral rules that create incentives for politicians to move away from the center. Mansfield and Snyder (2005) show how such incomplete democratic transitions can unleash appeals to nationalism, limit public accountability, and heighten the risk of military conflict. Democratization in Taiwan has clearly altered domestic political competition in Taiwan and its broader relationship with the mainland. It has opened political competition, encouraged appeals to a rapidly emerging Taiwanese identity, and eliminated the political dominance of the KMT by enabling the independence-leaning DPP to capture the presidency. Taiwan's electoral system has rewarded politicians for pursuing pro-independence policies that the PRC views as threatening its capacity to govern the mainland.

At the same time, deeper economic integration has acted as a stabilizing force in cross-Strait relations. The period of economic reform has promoted a more moderate foreign-policy orientation from Beijing while creating a series of mechanisms by which it believes it can influence domestic political outcomes in Taiwan. In the language of the commitment problem, economic integration is promoting peace in the Straits by increasing Beijing's confidence that future leaders of Taiwan will be less anxious to pursue independence. The growth of Taiwanese investment on the mainland has created a powerful political lobby that benefits from the status quo. Moreover, the PRC can target economic incentives at politically important constituencies, such as farmers in Taiwan, to bolster support for politicians that Beijing sees as embracing policies consonant with its interests. Globalization has thus promoted peace by shifting domestic political interests within Taiwan and allaying the mainland's fear that democratization has enabled separatists to achieve formal independence.

[57] Similar dynamics were at work in February 2006 when Chen violated his 2000 inaugural promise not to abolish the National Unification Council. Chen's popularity was declining due to low economic growth and corruption scandals. During interviews in March 2006, both KMT and DPP legislators alike pointed to this violation of his 2000 inaugural promise as an effort by Chen to slow the decline of his domestic position by rallying support from staunch independence advocates.

CONCLUSION

This chapter has challenged critiques of commercial liberalism that point to the upward trend of both trade and political conflict during the previous fifteen years in cross-Straits interactions as strong reason to doubt the capacity of economic liberalization to promote peace. The broad program of economic reform in China initiated by Deng Xiaoping has caused a critical reorientation in Chinese grand strategy. During this period, the mainland has pursued more restrained national interests, particularly with respect to territory, and has embraced multilateral cooperation. Cross-Straits economic integration has also reduced the mainland's readiness to deploy military force against Taiwan by enabling it to use economic incentives to influence the internal balance of power within Taiwan. At the same time, democratization in Taiwan has encouraged some politicians to pursue independence and the risks it carries for greater conflict with the mainland. In short, this chapter has provided more support for the two central claims of this book. Economic liberalization has promoted peace in the Straits and helped to limit some of the conflict-heightening pressures unleashed by democratization.

NINE

The Invisible Hand or the Ballot Box?

If "capitalism" means here a competitive system based on free disposal over private property, it is far more important to realize that only within this system is democracy possible. When it becomes dominated by a collectivist creed, democracy will inevitably destroy itself.

– F. A. Hayek, *The Road to Serfdom*

Hayek's observation sets up an important question for international relations theory and contemporary debates over American grand strategy. A wide range of liberal thought and contemporary research claims that the emergence of democratic institutions depends on the presence of such factors as a robust middle class, economic development, market-based exchange, and international institutions that expose domestic economic actors to global competition. All of these possibilities suggest that democracy may be rooted in the emergence of capitalism. If this is true, then the tendency for democratic states to avoid military conflict with each other may be caused not by electoral restraints, but by competitive markets and the predominance of private ownership instead.

On top of the theoretical implications posed by the possibility that the democratic peace is nested in a larger capitalist peace, the relative role of markets versus elections in constraining war also carries important implications for contemporary American grand strategy. The United States has a long history of promoting democracy abroad to facilitate its foreign-policy goals, including peace in the international system. If liberal economic institutions play a larger role than liberal political institutions in promoting peace, perhaps the resources currently devoted to democracy promotion should instead be invested in efforts to extend the reach of globally competitive markets and to strengthen economic reform in other countries.

This question regarding the relative role of democracy and capitalism in promoting peace has received limited scholarly attention until recently within the broader liberal peace research program (e.g., Mousseau 2000, 2005; Gartzke 2007). The democratic and commercial peace research programs have remained focused primarily on three sets of research tasks: establishing whether democracy or commerce promotes peace; identifying causal explanations for such observed relationships; and responding to realist counterclaims asserting either that interdependence can also cause conflict or that the peace among democracies is caused by such structural factors as the balance of power among states (e.g., Layne 1994; Gowa 1999).

Three possible relationships among democracy, commerce, and peace are identified within the literature. First, the respective abilities of commerce and democracy to constrain war reinforce each other in a virtuous circle (Russett and Oneal 2001). Second, the emergence of the democratic peace is conditional on such economic factors as free trade or development (e.g., Weede 1995; Mousseau 2000, 2005; Mousseau, Hegre, and Oneal 2003). Third, the market-driven peace is instead nested in a larger democratic peace (e.g., Papayoanou 1999; Gelpi and Grieco 2003).

This chapter shows that the liberal economic peace identified here has played a larger role than democracy in restraining military conflict over the past two centuries. This claim rests on three pieces of evidence. The first builds on the work of multiple studies noting that the democratic peace was either less strong or nonexistent during significant portions of the nineteenth century (e.g., Gowa 1999; Oneal and Russett 1999; Mitchell et al. 1999; Blank 2000; Cederman 2001). I present statistical results that confirm and then extend these findings. The democratic peace does not emerge until after World War I. Perhaps more importantly, democratic states were more, not less, likely to engage in military conflict than authoritarian regimes prior to World War I. Along with the findings in Chapter 5 linking free trade to peace in the nineteenth century, these results show that liberal economic institutions, and not democracy, reduced the likelihood of military conflict during this period. Second, I show that the conclusion linking private property to peace shown in the dyadic research design employed in Chapter 4 also holds in a monadic framework. The same cannot be said for democracy. Liberal economic institutions generally pacify a country's foreign policy irrespective of the institutional traits of the country with which it is interacting. Third, I identify another condition that limits the capacity of democracy to promote peace: large quantities of public property in a domestic economy. I utilize the dyadic research design from Chapter 4 to show that the dyadic democratic peace in the post–World War II period holds only if both states in a dyad possess relatively liberal property rights regimes. Alternatively, the presence or absence of liberal political institutions does not condition the peace created by liberal property rights regimes. This version of the capitalist peace holds in autocratic, democratic, and mixed dyads.

The rest of this chapter proceeds in three more parts. The first section examines changes in the capacity of democracy to promote peace over the past two centuries by breaking up the sample into distinct historical periods. The second section examines the relative roles of property rights regimes and democracy in promoting peace in the post–World War II period. A final section concludes and discusses the implications of these empirical findings for democratic peace theory.

THE POST-WORLD WAR I EMERGENCE OF THE DEMOCRATIC PEACE

Multiple studies have noted that the absence of war and military conflict among democracies appears to be restricted to the twentieth century. These conclusions bear on the question of the relative roles of political and economic institutions in promoting peace given the findings presented in Chapter 5, identifying the latter as a source of peace in the nineteenth century. If democracy promoted war in the nineteenth century while free trade promoted peace, then the latter obviously possessed larger pacific effects during this period.

This section extends research tracing the historical evolution of a democratic peace. A democratic distinctiveness in foreign policy is generally discussed in either its monadic or dyadic variants. The dyadic version asserts that democratic states are only less warlike in their interactions with other democratic states. An important condition of the democratic peace is thus that it requires at least two democratic states.[1] The empirical strength of second variant, labeled the monadic version of the democratic peace, is less settled in the literature. This hypothesis asserts that democratic regimes should adopt more conciliatory foreign policies when interacting with all regime types. Democracies therefore should be less likely than authoritarian regimes to engage in military conflict with fellow democracies and autocracies as well.

[1] There is some evidence (e.g., Oneal and Russett 1997) that dyads composed of one democratic state and one autocratic state are more conflictual than both democratic–democratic and autocratic–autocratic dyads.

Using both of these variants, I show that democratic regimes displayed dramatically different proclivities for military conflict before and after World War I. As previous research has noted, the dyadic democratic peace does not emerge until sometime after the turn of the twentieth century. During the nineteenth century, dyads possessing two relatively liberal political regimes were more likely to engage in military conflict than dyads possessing one or no liberal political regimes. The monadic tests reveal an even larger challenge for democratic peace research. Before World War I, the autocratic regimes – not the democratic ones – were more peaceful!

Statistical Tests

Tables 9.1 and 9.2 illustrate how the relationship between regime type and military conflict has evolved over the past two centuries. I draw on two research designs. In Table 9.1, the unit of analysis is the dyad year, or a pair of two states in a given year. In Table 9.2, the unit of analysis is the state year. Each country possesses an observation for each year it is a member of the international system. The operationalization of each of the independent variables uses the same specifications from the dyadic models presented in Chapter 4 and the monadic models presented in Chapter 5 with one exception. Given the difficulties associated with finding economic data on gross domestic product (GDP) and trade across the entire sample, these economic variables are initially excluded from these results.

The changing relationship between democracy and military conflict over the past two centuries is illustrated by the flipping sign on the coefficient for democracy. These changes can be seen by scanning across the top row of Table 9.1 and Table 9.2. Three things are again important to keep in mind when examining these results. First, the sign attached to the democracy coefficient indicates how increasing levels of democracy alter the likelihood of military conflict. A positive coefficient indicates that more liberal political regimes are more likely to engage in military conflict. A negative coefficient indicates the opposite – more liberal political regimes are less likely to engage in military conflict than their authoritarian counterparts. Second, the number of asterisks attached to the democracy coefficient indicates the level of confidence associated with the coefficient estimates in this statistical model. The absence of any asterisks means that the coefficient estimates have not reached standard levels of statistical significance to be confident that the coefficient is different from zero. If the coefficient is not different from zero, we cannot be sure that the variable attached to it influences the likelihood of military conflict. Alternatively, if the coefficient is statistically

Table 9.1. *Dyadic tests, 1816–2001*

	1816–2001	1816–1914	1919–2001	1919–1939	1945–1989	1990–2001
DEMOCRACY$_L$	−0.031***	0.066***	−0.054***	−0.060***	−0.037***	−0.071***
	(0.006)	(0.013)	(0.008)	(0.012)	(0.011)	(0.011)
POWER-	−0.134***	−0.070	−0.198***	−0.273***	−0.201***	−0.282***
PREPONDERANCE	(0.030)	(0.058)	(0.030)	(0.066)	(0.039)	(0.053)
DISTANCE	−0.356***	−0.030	−0.491***	−0.369***	−0.443***	−0.762***
	(0.040)	(0.080)	(0.045)	(0.091)	(0.054)	(0.096)
INTERESTS	−0.912***	−0.670***	−1.174***	−1.487***	−0.987***	−2.263***
	(0.120)	(0.195)	(0.129)	(0.370)	(0.167)	(0.259)
CONTIGUOUS	1.885***	1.539***	2.020***	1.934***	2.258***	1.874***
COUNT	(0.118)	(0.262)	(0.121)	(0.275)	(0.155)	(0.484)
GREAT-POWER	1.537***	0.944***	1.854***	1.533***	1.891***	1.453***
	(0.106)	(0.238)	(0.111)	(0.326)	(0.142)	(0.188)
ALLIANCE	0.231**	0.032	0.192	0.201	0.072	0.649***
	(0.107)	(0.234)	(0.122)	(0.212)	(0.167)	(0.204)
CONSTANT	−0.573*	−3.043***	0.455	0.107	0.020	3.106***
	(0.330)	(0.674)	(0.364)	(0.803)	(0.449)	(0.797)
N	529,992	48,106	478,959	38,972	302,646	130,649
Log-Likelihood	12865.8	−2408.1	−9879.4	1017.6	−5524.9	−2212.8

Note: The top number in each cell is the estimated coefficient. Robust standard errors clustered on dyad are listed below in parentheses. Two-tailed estimates are conducted for all estimates. $^{***}p \leq 0.01$; $^{**}p \leq 0.05$; $^{*}p \leq 0.10$. Splines (not shown) are added to all models.

significant, we can be confident that it is different from zero and thus alters the probability that states engage in military conflict. Third, the statistical models displayed in these two tables utilize samples of different historical periods to examine how the effect of democracy on military conflict changes over time. These changing historical samples are indicated at the top of each column in the table.

The results in Table 9.1 draw on a dyadic research design. The dependent variable takes on a value of one when a new militarized dispute occurs between the two states in a dyad in a given year. For all other years, its value is zero. While the model specification remains the same across all six regression estimations, the composition of the sample changes by historical period. The first model includes all observations from the entire sample dating from 1816 to 2001. It conforms largely to what the conventional wisdom regarding the democratic peace expects. The negative and statistically significant coefficient on the DEMOCRACY$_L$ variable indicates that the likelihood of military conflict declines as the dyad becomes more democratic.[2]

[2] Once again, the construction of dyadic measurement from two state-level characteristics like regime type is done by drawing on the weak-link hypothesis. This hypothesis asserts

Across two centuries of history, it appears that democracy has possessed an important pacifying effect on the relations between states.

Decomposing this long historical era into distinct periods demonstrates that this relationship between regime type and military conflict changes in dramatic ways. The model displayed in the second column restricts the domain of cases to the period from 1816 until the outbreak of World War I in 1914. A radical change appears in the $\text{DEMOCRACY}_{\text{L}}$ term. Although highly significant, its sign is not negative but positive! Contrary to a large body of theoretical and empirical work, democratic dyads were more likely than all other dyads to engage in military conflict during the nineteenth century.[3] In other words, dyads composed of two states that incorporated more societal groups into the electoral process or possessed significant legal constraints on executive authority utilized violence more often to settle their political disputes.

Moving right in the table, we see why such a strong consensus supporting claims of democratic pacifism remains despite these puzzling results. The third column restricts the period under investigation to the period after World War I. Here the coefficient on $\text{DEMOCRACY}_{\text{L}}$ appears as expected. It is negative and highly significant, indicating that a separate zone of peace exists among liberal polities.

The final three columns illustrate that this negative effect is robust across the different international orders of the twentieth century. These regressions divide the period after 1918 into three groups, each distinguished by a dramatic change in the number of great powers presiding over the system. The fourth regression examines the interwar era. The fifth isolates observations from the bipolar Cold War period. The sixth examines the unipolar period that has been present since 1990. In all of these models, the coefficient on democracy is negative and significant. Across very different structures of polarity in the twentieth century, democracy still reduced the likelihood of conflict between states.

that the most weakly constrained member of the dyad drives the conflict potential of the dyad. Thus, this variable takes on the regime score of the most illiberal member of the dyad. As this score increases, the dyad is more democratic.

[3] I also conducted regression models that altered the manner in which the dependent variable was coded. The first variation only included militarized disputes in which force was used (a hostility score greater than or equal to four). In this regression, the coefficient on democracy was again positive and statistically significant in the pre–World War I period; and negative and statistically significant in the post–World War I period. In the second variation, the dependent variable included only wars (hostility score of five). In this regression, the coefficient on democracy was not statistically distinguishable from zero in the period prior to World War I. After World War I, the coefficient on democracy conformed to the conventional wisdom. It was negative and statistically significant.

Table 9.2. *Monadic models, 1816–2001*

	1816–2001	1816–1914	1919–2001	1919–1939	1945–1989	1990–2001
DEMOCRACY	0.015**	0.078***	−0.005	−0.026**	−0.003	−0.016
	(0.007)	(0.016)	(0.008)	(0.011)	(0.012)	(0.012)
MILITARY POWER	3.925***	3.375**	3.921**	3.828	6.994***	4.362
	(1.236)	(1.413)	(1.564)	(2.998)	(2.442)	(5.222)
INTERESTS	−0.158	−0.137	−0.049	0.603	−0.269	1.114***
	(0.138)	(0.218)	(0.199)	(0.526)	(0.227)	(0.324)
CONTIGUOUS COUNT	0.884***	0.071**	0.100***	0.099**	0.085***	0.091***
	(0.025)	(0.032)	(0.238)	(0.044)	(0.029)	(0.033)
GREAT-POWER	0.498**	0.746***	0.829***	1.146**	0.556*	0.710
	(0.241)	(0.259)	(0.221)	(0.486)	(0.318)	(0.521)
CONSTANT	−0.935***	−1.520***	−0.924***	−1.833***	−0.744***	−1.081
	(0.127)	(0.188)	(0.141)	(0.362)	(0.167)	(0.207)
N	11,613	3,133	8,319	1,281	5,069	1,704
Log-Likelihood	−4386.1	−1008.2	−3234.1	−397.1	−1935.1	−724.8

Note: The top number in each cell is the estimated coefficient. Robust standard errors clustered on dyad are listed below in parentheses. Two-tailed estimates are conducted for all estimates. ***$p \leq 0.01$; **$p \leq 0.05$; *$p \leq 0.10$. Splines (not shown) are added to all models.

A quick look at the six coefficients for DEMOCRACY, also illustrates why the aggressive nature of democracies in the nineteenth century has been obscured. The pre–World War I sample includes only slightly more than 48,000 observations whereas the post–World war I sample has more than 480,000 observations. Thus, the positive effect of democracy on conflict is vastly outweighed by its negative effects in the twentieth century and the dramatic explosion in the number of states (and cases) in this latter period. In short, the aggregation of data across different historical periods into a single sample does not come without cost.

A shift to a monadic research design that utilizes the state year as the unit of analysis produces a similar switching effect in the relationship between democracy and military conflict between the periods before and after World War I. These results are displayed in Table 9.2.[4] Because the focus is on a state's decision to participate in militarized conflict, I measure conflict by

[4] Each statistical model includes variables that control for a state's military power, its political relationship with the most powerful state in the international system, the number of states with which it shares common borders, and its great power status. This research design is not able to control for as many factors that might influence a state's propensity to engage in military conflict as the dyadic research design. Many of the factors identified in dyadic estimation of Table 9.1 are specific to dyads or pairs of states.

examining decisions to initiate military conflict.[5] The dependent variable receives a score of one when a state initiates a new militarized dispute in a given year.

Although less consistent, this table illustrates again that the relationship between democracy and conflict has changed substantially over the past two centuries. By splitting this larger collection of observations into smaller samples, we can see again how World War I provides the critical historical juncture for this result. The second model in Table 9.2 shows that the coefficient on democracy is positive, large, and highly significant during the nineteenth century. Democratic regimes were more likely than their autocratic counterparts to initiate military disputes prior to the outbreak of World War I.

Taken as a whole, the twentieth-century results correspond with the conventional wisdom positing no systematic relationship between regime type and the level of militarization in foreign policy. Shown in column 3, the coefficient on democracy is negative but fails to achieve statistical significance for the period after World War I. The disaggregation of the twentieth-century sample into three parts leaves this conventional wisdom strongest during the Cold War and post–Cold War periods (columns 5 and 6, respectively). The democracy coefficient was not statistically significant over the periods from 1945 to 1989 or from 1990 to 2001. A negative and statistically significant coefficient on democracy from 1919 to 1939 suggests that democracies were less likely than autocratic regimes to initiate military disputes for the interwar period.

While perhaps painful to slog through, these statistical results reveal an important limitation on claims elevating the democratic peace to lawlike status in international relations theory. Democratic states embraced very different strategies of conflict resolution in the nineteenth and twentieth centuries. Prior to World War I, democratic states were more likely to engage in military conflict than governments presiding over less liberal polities.

These results provide an important contrast with those presented in Chapter 5 linking free trade to peace over this same period. Whereas democracy heightened the risks of war in nineteenth century, free trade suppressed these risks. The invisible hand, not the ballot box, exerted a larger constraint on war prior to 1914. The next section continues this comparison between economic and political institutions by shifting the analysis to the

[5] For example, Rousseau (2005) argues that democratic constraints on war lessen when a democratic regime is the target of attack.

period in which the democratic peace has been strongest – after World War II.

PRIVATE PROPERTY, DEMOCRACY, AND PEACE AFTER 1945

Recent research utilizing dyadic research designs by Gartzke (2007), Mousseau (2000), and Mousseau, Hegre, and O'Neal (2003) shows that capitalism has played a larger role relative to democracy in promoting peace. Gartzke (2007) adds variables for capital flows, development, and similar political interests to standard statistical estimations of the likelihood of military conflict between states. By showing that the inclusion of these variables renders the coefficient on democracy insignificant, he concludes that democracy plays no role in reducing conflict once the effects of capitalism are modeled. Rather than saying that capitalism eliminates the pacific effects generated by democracy, Mousseau, Hegre, and O'Neal show that the democratic peace holds only among developed economies. This section extends these claims in two ways. First, I show that public property similarly conditions the capacity of democracy to promote peace within a dyadic research design. Democracy only promotes peace when both states possess relatively liberal property rights regimes. At the same time, democracy does not condition the capacity of private property to promote peace. Second, the capacity of private property to promote peace also operates in a monadic research design. Unlike democracy, the predominance of private property in an economy pacifies the foreign policy of a government irrespective of the institutional traits of the state with which they are interacting.

Dyadic Interaction Tests

The first model displayed in Table 9.3 replicates the dyadic test found in the first column of Table 4.2. The second model in Table 9.3 adds an interaction term to that baseline equation. This interaction term multiplies the variables for democracy (DEMOCRACY_{L}) and public property (PUBLIC_{H}). The inclusion of this additional variable enables an examination of whether democracy and property rights condition the capacity of each other to promote peace. In this iteration, the coefficients and standard errors for democracy and public property can vary according to the level of the other. In short, this model checks if the capacity of regime type to promote peace is the same if the dyad has either high or low levels of public property.

Table 9.3. *Dyadic tests, 1970–2001*

	CONFLICT	CONFLICT
$PUBLIC_H$	0.016***	0.024***
	(0.004)	(0.006)
$DEMOCRACY_L$	−0.035***	−0.065**
	(0.013)	(0.022)
$PUBLIC^*_H$		1.3^*10^{-3**}
$DEMOCRACY_L$		(6.9^*10^{-4})
$DEPEND_L$	−5.506	−5.990
	(5.382)	(5.198)
POWER-	−0.102*	−0.105*
PREPONDERANCE	(0.056)	(0.055)
GREAT-POWER	1.358***	1.377***
	(0.206)	(0.206)
INTERESTS	−1.072***	−1.094***
	(0.327)	(0.323)
ALLIES	0.681***	0.698***
	(0.208)	(0.207)
DISTANCE	−0.266***	−0.278***
	(0.088)	(0.092)
CONTIGOUS COUNT	2.364***	2.339***
	(0.273)	(0.275)
$DEVELOP_L$	1.5^*10^{-4**}	1.6^*10^{-4**}
	(6.8^*10^{-5})	(6.5^*10^{-5})
$DEVELOP^2_L$	-1.1^*10^{-8**}	-1.0^*10^{-8**}
	(4.7^*10^{-9})	(4.4^*10^{-9})
CONSTANT	−1.642*	−1.711**
	(0.853)	(0.869)
N	102,052	102,052
Log-Likelihood	−1490.03	−1488.22

Note: The top number in each cell is the estimated coefficient. Robust standard errors clustered on dyad are listed below in parentheses. Two-tailed estimates are conducted for all estimates. $^{***}p \leq 0.01$; $^{**}p \leq 0.05$; $^{*}p \leq 0.10$. Splines (not shown) are added to all models.

In the first model of Table 9.3, the constraints imposed by democracy on military conflict were estimated solely with the coefficient on $DEMOCRACY_L$. In the second model, the interaction variable (which is positive and statistically significant) allows the constraints imposed by democracy on military conflict to vary according to the level of public property. To estimate the effects of either democracy or public property on military conflict, some combination of the variables for democracy, public property, and their interaction term is now necessary.[6] The coefficients on DEMOCRACY_L and PUBLIC_H in the second model possess limited substantive meaning by themselves when this interaction term is included (Friedrich 1982; Braumoeller 2004). The coefficient on DEMOCRACY_L (−0.065) in model 2 now indicates the effect of regime type on military conflict only when PUBLIC_H equals zero. Because PUBLIC_H never equals zero across the entire sample, this coefficient possesses no substantive significance on its own. The coefficient on PUBLIC_H (0.024) indicates that high levels of public property heighten military conflict when the regime score equals zero. This regime score though only equals zero in 1.5 percent of the sample.

To aid the interpretation of this model, I constructed Table 9.4, which displays how the coefficients and standard errors for the coefficients on the democracy and public property variables change according to the level of the other variable. The changing coefficients and standard errors appear in the middle column. The top part of the table displays how the coefficient on democracy changes as the level of PUBLIC_H increases. The bottom part displays how the coefficient on public property changes as the regime score increases. As indicated by the positive coefficient on the interaction term, the conflict-reducing capacity of democracy decreases as PUBLIC_H gets larger. In other words, the capacity of democracy to promote peace shrinks if one member of the dyad possesses a relatively illiberal property rights regime. This coefficient on democracy remains negative and statistically significant ($p < 0.10$) only if PUBLIC_H is less than or equal to 31.6.[7] Slightly more than 86 percent of the sample meets this condition. At the same time, these results indicate that democracy possesses no statistically discernible influence on military conflict in the remaining 14 percent of cases in the sample. This limited sample includes dyads where at least one member includes such countries as Venezuela, Bolivia, Argentina, Cyprus, Romania,

[6] The first equation was estimated with the following form: MIDON = $\beta_1 * \text{PUBLIC} + \beta_2 * \text{DEMOCRACY} + \beta_x *$ control variable. The effects of public property and regime type on conflict were estimated with the coefficients β_1 and β_2, respectively. The equation with the interactive term takes the following form: MIDON = $\beta_1 * \text{PUBLIC} + \beta_2 * \text{DEMOCRACY} + \beta_3 * \text{PUBLIC} * \text{DEMOCRACY} + \beta_x *$ control variable. In the equation with the interactive term, the new coefficient on PUBLIC now equals $\beta_1 + \beta_3 * \text{DEMOCRACY}$. Thus the coefficient on PUBLIC changes as the score on democracy changes. Similarly, the new coefficient on DEMOCRACY now equals $\beta_2 + \beta_3 * \text{PUBLIC}$. It also varies as the level of public property of the least constrained member of the dyad changes.

[7] These results correspond with those of Mousseau (2000, 2005), which find that the dyadic democratic peace is conditioned by such economic attributes as development.

Table 9.4. *Conditional coefficients and standard errors for DEMOCRACY and PUBLIC from Model 2, Table 9.3*

$PUBLIC_H$	$\beta_{DEMOCRACY}$	% sample observations with $PUBLIC_H \leq n$
5	−0.059*** (0.019)	0.79
10	−0.052** (0.017)	15.86
15	−0.045** (0.015)	45.25
20	−0.038*** (0.013)	63.89
25	−0.031** (0.013)	75.00
30	−0.024* (0.013)	83.59
35	−0.017 (0.014)	88.83
40	−0.010 (0.016)	92.32

$DEMOCRACY_L$	β_{PUBLIC}	% sample observations with $DEMOCRACY_L \leq n$
−10	0.010** (0.004)	1.34
−5	0.017*** (0.004)	51.63
0	0.024*** (0.006)	63.75
5	0.031*** (0.009)	73.20
10	0.038*** (0.012)	100

Note: $^{***}p \leq 0.01$; $^{**}p \leq 0.05$; $^{*}p \leq 0.10$.

Nigeria, Congo, Ethiopia, Botswana, Iran, Egypt, Syria, Jordan, Bangladesh, Myanmar, and Malaysia.

Political regime type does not exert a similar conditioning role on the relationship between public property and conflict. Although the presence of autocracy reduces the positive effect of public property on conflict (as evidenced by the declining coefficient size on $PUBLIC_H$ as the level of $DEMOCRACY_L$ moves from 10 to −10), the coefficient on public property remains positive and statistically significant across all levels of democracy.

Public property heightens the likelihood of military conflict for all regime types.

Monadic Tests

While a consensus has yet to emerge, the bulk of empirical evidence suggests that the pacifying effects of democracy hold only when both interacting states are democratic.[8] When a democratic state engages an autocratic state, military conflict between those two states should occur at the same rate as in a dyad composed of two autocracies. Alternatively, the monadic version of the democratic peace holds that a democratic government should use military force less irrespective of whether it is interacting with a fellow democracy or an autocracy. In other words, the monadic version suggests that a dyad composed of one or two democracies should be less likely to engage in military conflict than a dyad composed of zero democracies. Another way to test this possibility is simply with a monadic research design that uses the state year as its unit of analysis. The utilization of a monadic research design provides another opportunity to test the relative role of democracy and public property on military conflict by examining whether the same interactive or dyadic constraint limits the commercial peace identified here.

The following monadic tests differ slightly from the previous dyadic tests. Because the unit of analysis is the state year, the operationalization and number of the independent and dependent variables change along with the estimation method. Most of the liberal peace variables rely on the same data sources and do not need the weak-link transformation necessary to move from state to dyadic characteristics. The model thus includes DEMOCRACY, DEVELOPMENT, and PUBLIC (all measured for each state at time *t-1*) on the right-hand side of the baseline regression.

Although the monadic research design here cannot control for such dyadic characteristics as bilateral trade, I include OPEN in the regression models to control for the effect of international trade on conflict. OPEN equals the total quantity of a country's exports and imports divided by its GDP. The data for OPEN are measured at time $t - 1$ using constant prices and are taken from version 6.1 of the Penn World Tables (Heston, Summers, and Aten 2002).

Because many of the control variables utilized in the dyadic design are traits describing pairs of states rather than single states, the number of

[8] For a recent study that presents strong empirical support for a monadic democratic peace see Souva and Prins (2006).

control variables falls in this design. I add controls for major power status and geographic contiguity. GREAT-POWER is a dummy variable that takes on a value of one when a state is defined as great power by the COW project. CONTIGUOUS COUNT counts the number of states that a given country directly borders by land or by water.[9]

Because many states participate in multiple militarized disputes in a given year, the dependent variable in this design (MIDSYR) counts the number of new military disputes a state enters in a year.[10] A state participates in at least one militarized dispute in more than 30 percent of the observations in the current sample. States participate in multiple disputes annually in approximately 10 percent of the cases.

The estimation strategy for these monadic tests draws on McDonald (2007a), which blends the choices of Benoit (1996)[11] and Reiter and Tillman (2002). Because the dependent variable cannot take on negative values, ordinary least squares estimation would be inappropriate. It would likely predict occasionally negative counts over the entire range of the independent variables. Like Benoit, I employ a regression model for event counts. I also adopt the general estimating equation (GEE) techniques followed in Reiter and Tillman (2002). GEE allows the modeling of multiple sources of correlation, including temporal and within panel (states in this case), common to time series–cross-sectional designs (Zorn 2001). The combination of these two research designs yields a GEE with a negative binomial functional link.[12] To account for the possibility that the count of disputes

9 The distance between two contiguous states via water must be less than 400 miles. The source of this definition and data is Stinnett et al. (2002).

10 Although not displayed in the tables, I also conducted three sets of additional regressions to ensure that the results were robust to different codings of the dependent variable. In the first, I simply counted the number of disputes that a state initiated in a given year. In the second, I restricted the coding of the dependent variable to include only new disputes in which the state under observation was identified as the target. In the third set of tests, I restricted the coding of the dependent variable to include only the most severe disputes (those with scores of either four or five on the MID hostility scale). The coefficient on the variable measuring quantity of public property was consistently positive and significant for all three alternative operationalizations of military conflict (initiation, targeted, violent disputes only).

11 Employing an events count model, Benoit argues that the limited empirical support for a monadic democratic peace lies in improper estimation techniques.

12 While event count models are often estimated by assuming that the dependent variable follows a Poisson distribution, such a technique is inappropriate here. Poisson regression models assume that the conditional expected mean of the dependent variable equals the expected conditional variance. When this assumption is violated and the conditional variance exceeds the conditional mean, a negative binomial regression is more appropriate. This technique also estimates a parameter, α, that measures the degree of overdispersion in the data. When α is statistically indistinguishable from zero, the negative binomial

Table 9.5. *Monadic results*

	1	2	3
PUBLIC	0.012***	0.009*	0.012***
	(0.004)	(0.005)	(0.004)
DEMOCRACY	−0.009	0.002	−0.016
	(0.013)	(0.011)	(0.014)
OPEN	−0.005**	$-3.6*10^{-3}$**	−0.005**
	(0.002)	$(1.4*10^{-3})$	(0.002)
CONTIGUOUS COUNT	0.119***	0.101***	0.119***
	(0.029)	(0.025)	(0.029)
GREAT-POWER	1.058**	1.110***	1.062**
	(0.447)	(0.427)	(0.441)
DEVELOP	$-3.8*10^{-5}$	$-6.0*10^{-5}$	$-3.7*10^{-5}$
	$(3.5*10^{-5})$	$(3.7*10^{-5})$	$(3.5*10^{-5})$
DEVELOP^2	$2.0*10^{-9}$	$2.7*10^{-9}$	$1.9*10^{-9}$
	$(1.3*10^{-9})$	$(1.6*10^{-9})$	$(1.3*10^{-9})$
CONSTANT	−1.453***	−0.497*	−1.177***
	(0.229)	(0.262)	(0.271)
N	2586	2592	2549
Log-Likelihood		−1346.6	

Notes: Models 1 and 3 estimated with GEE. The count of new militarized disputes entered in a given year by a state is the dependent variable. Model 2 estimated with logistic regression (splines not shown). Robust standard errors are clustered on country listed in parentheses. All *p*-values based on two-tailed tests of statistical significance: $^{***}p \leq 0.01$; $^{**}p \leq 0.05$; $^{*}p \leq 0.10$.

in one year affect the count in subsequent years, I model the data as following a first-order autoregressive process (AR1). Moreover, robust standards errors clustered by country were estimated and subsequently used for tests of statistical significance.

The monadic baseline model is displayed in the first column of Table 9.5.[13] The positive and statistically significant coefficient on PUBLIC in

estimator collapses to a Poisson estimator. For a general discussion of these differences see pp. 217–38 in Long (1997). For a discussion of a negative binomial estimator and an application to the democratic peace see Benoit (1996).

13 These models differ slightly from those found in McDonald (2007a) for two reasons. First, those regression results did not include controls for a squared development term. Second, the number of observations in McDonald (2007a) is approximately 10 percent larger than in this sample. While those models utilized data that combined versions 5.6 and 6.1 of the Penn World Tables, all of the models in this book utilize economic data from version 6.1 of the Penn World Tables. This smaller sample increases standard errors slightly without changing any substantive conclusions or tests of statistical significance.

column 1 confirms that the alternative research design generates the same substantive conclusion linking public property to conflict. Governments with larger quantities of public assets in an economy participate in more militarized disputes. Alternatively, as the size of the private sector increases (and PUBLIC declines), governments enter fewer military disputes annually.

The results for the traditional liberal peace variables – democracy and trade – are mixed. While the coefficient on DEMOCRACY is negative, it fails to achieve statistical significance. Democratic states are just as likely to engage in military conflict as other regime types.[14] The negative and consistently significant coefficient on OPEN confirms the findings of Domke (1988) and Souva and Prins (2006) that integration into the world economy also limits conflict. Despite the empirical literature's focus on dyads, the commercial peace generated by trade is not restricted to pairs of states. Greater quantities of imports and exports as a percentage of GDP reduce a state's participation in military disputes. Finally, the insignificant coefficient on development levels suggests that average income levels do not seem to influence military conflict in this monadic design.

The combination of these results and those found in Chapter 4 possess important implications for the larger question investigated in this chapter: Does democracy or capitalism play a larger role in promoting peace? These monadic findings show that democracies exhibit no difference from autocratic regimes in the extent to which they deploy military force against all states. Accordingly, the tests in Table 9.5 reaffirm a key limiting condition placed on the capacity of democracy to promote peace. Democracy only limits conflict when both states possess relatively open political systems. Alternatively, the same condition does not constrain the capacity of private property to promote peace. Private property limits the outbreak of military conflict in both the dyadic and monadic research designs. Whereas it takes two democracies within a dyad to reduce that pair's likelihood of engaging in military conflict, it only takes one state with a relatively large quantity of private property to reduce conflict within a dyad. The monadic results show that private property reduces the likelihood of a state engaging in military conflict irrespective of the economic institutions of the country with which it is interacting.

To ensure that these results are robust to alternative estimation techniques, model 2 alters the coding of the dependent variable to indicate

14 The insignificance of the coefficient for DEMOCRACY is not a function of the listwise deletion of cases due to missing economic data. I conducted regressions that progressively dropped all the economic variables. While the sample size steadily increased, the coefficient on DEMOCRACY remained insignificant in these regressions.

whether any level of military conflict is present and tests the relationship of PUBLIC on conflict with logistic regression.[15] Instead of counting the number of new disputes a state enters, the dependent variable here, MIDON, simply takes on a value of one if the state enters a new dispute in a year. If the state does not enter any new disputes, MIDON receives a value of zero. Apart from testing the effects of PUBLIC with a method of estimation that is more common to the recent liberal peace literature, this alternative specification offers another benefit. It ensures against the possibility that the significant results in the count models are driven by a small number of outlying cases in which a few states with high quantities of public property engaged in a large quantity of disputes in a year. Here these instances in which states enter a large number of disputes are treated the same as if a state entered a single dispute. The positive and significant coefficient on PUBLIC demonstrates again that greater quantities of state-owned assets increase the likelihood that a state will engage in military conflict in a given year.

Another potential criticism of these results stems from the potential presence of any relationship between public property and regime type. If democracies have lower quantities of public property, the statistical relationship between public property and conflict may result from indirect links between democracy and peace. Along these lines, democracy may promote peace by first encouraging economic liberalization. To ensure for the presence of an independent effect of public property on military conflict, I tested for this possibility by using residual rather than observed values for PUBLIC. I first used ordinary least squares to estimate the effect of DEMOCRACY (measured at time *t-1*) on PUBLIC (measured at time *t*). The predicted values for PUBLIC from this initial regression were then subtracted from the observed values for PUBLIC. These residuals were used to operationalize PUBLIC for another regression that appears in the third column of Table 9.5. This specification allows me to purge any indirect links between democracy and military conflict from the PUBLIC score and the subsequent regression. The remaining value can thus test for any direct link between PUBLIC and military conflict.[16] The positive and significant

[15] This model includes the Beck, Katz, and Tucker (1998) correction for autocorrelation in time-series cross-sectional designs with a binary dependent variable that adds a series of variables to the right-hand side of the equation that model the number of years since a country was last engaged in a dispute. These variables were not included in the table, but a log-likelihood test determined that they should be included in the estimation.

[16] Bueno de Mesquita et al. (2003) employ a similar strategy to separate the effects of the size of the winning coalition from Polity scores (taken to indicate level of democracy) on a series of dependent variables.

coefficient on PUBLIC strengthens confidence in the general result linking public property to higher levels of military conflict. The pacifying effects of private property are not solely explained by democracy's capacity to promote economic liberalization. Finally, it is important to note that although its significance improves slightly, the coefficient on democracy again fails to achieve standard levels of statistical significance.

CONCLUSION

To conclude, I wish to briefly review the primary claims generated by the statistical results found here along with those from Chapters 4 and 5. Together, they provide a wide range of evidence supporting the two primary conclusions of this book. First, liberal economic institutions promote peace. Second, these economic institutions have historically played a stronger role in promoting peace than democracy.

The strength of this domestic version of commercial liberalism lies with its presence across three critical dimensions – different institutional components; different historical periods; and different research designs. First, the statistical results in Chapter 4 showed that both institutional components of liberal economies (competitive market structures and private property) promote peace. Second, these results linking free trade to peace were not just limited to the post–World War II period. Chapter 5 presented multiple tests showing that free trade also promoted peace during the nineteenth-century era of globalization. Third, a monadic commercial peace was shown to exist in at least two sets of statistical tests – those linking free trade to peace in the nineteenth century; and those linking private property to peace in the twentieth century. Thus, liberal economic institutions generally pacify a government's foreign policy irrespective of the institutional traits possessed by other states.

These findings also possess three critical implications for democratic peace research. First, they illustrate that the democratic peace only holds up under a restrained set of circumstances. The democratic peace is a dyadic phenomenon; democracies exhibit no consistent pacific distinctiveness when interacting with autocratic regimes. The capacity of democracy to promote peace is limited to the period after World War I. The dyadic democratic peace in the twentieth century only holds when neither regime possesses substantial quantities of public property. Second, because the commercial peace identified here is not limited by any of these conditions, its capacity to promote peace has historically been larger than that of democracy.

Third, and perhaps most importantly, the historical tests presented in the second section of this chapter suggest an even broader theoretical problem for democratic peace research. Theoretical explanations for the democratic peace can be cast into two groups – what I label here as time-variant and time-invariant approaches. Time-invariant explanations, such as those that focus on institutional constraints, signaling, or domestic norms, suggest that the capacity of democracy should remain consistent throughout different historical periods. The tendency of democracy to promote military conflict before World War I directly challenges the validity of these explanations for the limited peace created by democracy after World War I. If the same set of domestic institutions promoted military conflict before 1914, how could they on their own produce opposite effects in the twentieth century?

Time-variant approaches (Mitchell et al. 1999; Cederman 2001; Cederman and Rao 2001; Kadera Crescenzi, and Shannon 2003; Lipson 2003; Cederman and Gleditsch 2004) face a different but related hurdle. They claim instead that the capacity of democracy to limit war has increased over time. While these theories can explain the emergence of the peace among democracies after World War I, they also struggle to explain the finding here linking democracy to conflict before then. Most time-variant approaches instead expect a null relationship, namely that democracies should behave just like autocracies during the pre–World War I period.[17] Apart from showing

[17] Two exceptions are Mitchell et al. (1999) and Cederman (2001). Mitchell et al. (1999) rely on Gleditsch and Hegre (1997) to account for the initial positive systemic impact of democratization on war. The latter argues that the inverted U relationship between systemic democratization and war follows logically by assuming two empirical regularities: that regime type has no influence on the likelihood that a state enters a war in a given year (the absence of a monadic peace) and that democratic dyads are less likely to go to war with each other than any other dyad. They defend these assumptions with evidence in support of these claims provided across the period from 1816 until 1994. However, the central conclusion of this time-dependent literature, namely that the effect of democracy on conflict changes over time provides ample justification to challenge these empirical assumptions and the logical propositions that follow from them. In particular, the evidence offered in the monadic design here explicitly challenges the assumption that democratic states are just as likely to engage in war as autocratic states. Instead, during the nineteenth century, democratic states were more likely to initiate war than autocratic states. Consequently, the hypothesis that the spread of democracy eventually decreases the level of war does not necessarily hold if the assumptions on which it is based are contradicted. Cederman (2001, pp. 22–3) briefly discusses the initial conflictual phase in the history of democratic evolution and is skeptical of the empirical strength of the positive result in the dyadic research design. He then suggests that if there was an initial democratic belligerence, it is likely to be explained by colonial competition that existed among France, Britain, and the United States in the nineteenth century. A simple check of this hypothesis was conducted by excluding these three countries from the pre–World War I era to see if the positive and significant coefficient remains in the rest of the sample (results not shown to conserve

that the capitalist peace has historically been stronger than that of democracy, these results linking democracy to conflict before World War I also suggest that the literature still lacks a valid explanation for why a limited democratic peace exists in the twentieth century. Chapter 10 begins to explore some of the broader policy recommendations implied by the relative strength of the capitalist peace.

space). Remembering that the baseline coefficient on democracy is 0.066 when the sample is restricted to the period before 1915 (model 2, Table 9.1), the coefficient decreases in size and remains statistically significant if the United States or the Great Britain is dropped from the analysis. If the sample excludes France, the coefficient increases in size and remains statistically significant. None of the three states are solely responsible for the positive link between democracy and conflict. The democracy coefficient for the period still remains positive and significant if both the United States and the Great Britain are excluded from the sample. While these results show that Great Britain and the United States had a tremendous impact on the size of the democracy coefficient and consequently are key cases to understanding democratic aggression, the puzzle persists as the positive and significant coefficient remains despite their absence from the sample. In short, the time-dependent approaches appear to be better positioned to explain the strengthening of democratic constraints – which suggest that the size of the negative and significant coefficient on the democracy term grows over time – rather than the initial aggression of democratic states – or its positive and significant coefficient in the nineteenth century.

TEN

Capitalism and America's Peaceful Market Power

The national security challenges facing the United States in the aftermath of September 11 have again exposed the historic struggle for the heart of American foreign policy. In *Diplomacy*, Henry Kissinger (1994) used the presidencies of Theodore Roosevelt and Woodrow Wilson to embody two sets of competing principles that have often pulled American foreign policy in opposite directions. On the one hand, America, since its independence, has drawn on and remained committed to a broad base of liberal ideas in its political, social, economic, and cultural life that have shaped its relationship with the world. Perhaps most dramatically, they guided Wilson's vision launched at the Versailles peace talks for a democratic global political order that would help the world to escape the plague of war. Both in practice and rhetoric, his legacy indelibly shaped the American century and guided the United States in its sustained political and military campaigns against fascism, communism, and now Islamic fundamentalism.

However, the pursuit of this liberal vision has often been reigned in by the competing conservatism of a cold-blooded realpolitik that Kissinger argued characterized the Theodore Roosevelt administration. This tradition would allow Franklin Roosevelt to overlook the tyranny of Stalin's communist regime to achieve victory in the larger struggle against Nazi Germany. Nixon could similarly exploit the split within the communist bloc and enlist China in the struggle against the Soviet Union. In addition, despite the opportunities to dramatically expand freedom in Eastern Europe, George H. W. Bush cautiously avoided "dancing on the Berlin Wall" as it crumbled in 1989 for fear of further destabilizing the increasingly conciliatory Soviet Union.

When President Clinton's national security advisor, Anthony Lake, coined the phrase "from Containment to Enlargement" that focused on the promotion of democracy around the world as the best means to strengthen

American interests and influence, it seemed as though Woodrow Wilson's vision had finally triumphed in the post–Cold War world. Unlike previous eras in which the pendulum of principle in foreign policy had eventually swung back to a more pragmatic realism, the administration of George W. Bush did little to reorient this liberal shift. If anything, it deepened America's commitment to this strategy of democracy promotion by fusing these often-conflicting traditions in a grand strategy that actively deploys military force to advance liberal ideals. This fusion can be seen in President Bush's 2006 State of the Union address when he noted:

> Abroad, our nation is committed to an historic, long-term goal – we seek the end of tyranny in our world. Some dismiss that goal as misguided idealism. In reality, the future security of America depends on it. On September 11, 2001, we found that problems originating in a failed and oppressive state 7,000 miles away could bring murder and destruction to our country. Dictatorships shelter terrorists, and feed resentment and radicalism, and seek weapons of mass destruction. Democracies replace resentment with hope, respect the rights of their citizens and their neighbors, and join the fight against terror. Every step toward freedom in the world makes our country safer – so we will act boldly in freedom's cause.

These claims argue that the proliferation of democracy around the world eliminates potential threats to American national interests and improves the lives of millions throughout the world because democracies embrace peace, tolerance, and the rule of law. Even if the policy failures associated with the war in Iraq have sparked a broader national debate over the strategies designed to promote democracy, American foreign policy still shows few signs of abandoning this fundamental goal, which is so intimately connected with the American experience.

This book confronts the fundamental intellectual rationale in support of democracy promotion as the raison d'être of American foreign policy. It does this by challenging the central conclusions of the contemporary liberal peace research program that has repeatedly confirmed the historical presence of a virtuous association among democracy, international trade, and peace. I reexamined this literature in light of a set of arguments often associated with liberalism and American foreign policy but rarely subjected to rigorous analysis within the context of these debates. Despite a strong conceptual correlation with both democracy and international commerce, an independent role for the domestic institutions that define liberal economic orders has been largely omitted from these debates. This is an important oversight given that variations in property rights regimes and domestic market structures shape the balance of power within domestic political orders. Because liberal theory has long held that a government's foreign policy and place in the international system depend greatly on the character of its internal order, this possibility suggested that these domestic institutions regulating domestic economic activity could also influence decisions for war or peace. The role of private property and competitive market structures in shaping relations between states carries broader implications for a whole range of arguments suggesting that capitalism promotes peace or war. Contemporary economists generally point to these two institutions as the foundations of capitalist economies.[1] Given this definition of capitalism, the wide range of empirical evidence presented here shows that capitalism has historically promoted peace between states. This evidence also demonstrated that the domestic institutions associated with capitalism have played a larger role than democracy in restraining war.

This concluding chapter summarizes these arguments, discusses a theoretical extension of them, and then examines their implications for current debates over American grand strategy. It suggests that a focus on promoting economic liberalization rather than democracy offers a similar opportunity to fuse the realist and liberal traditions of American foreign policy. However, this "economic fusion" offers a restraint and prudence that is more typical of the classic realism that Kissinger wrote of in *Diplomacy* than of the current neoconservative mix of liberal idealism and muscular realism.

CAPITALISM AND PEACE

This book broke with the contemporary liberal peace literature on at least two critical conceptual fronts. Both pushed its theoretical focus toward two domestic institutions – private property and competitive market structures – that economists have long associated with capitalism. The first challenged the centrality of democratic elections in characterizing variations in domestic political orders. Liberal international relations theory differentiates itself from the structural variants of both realism (Waltz 1959, 1979) and constructivism (Wendt 1999) by its theoretical concentration on the internal attributes of states to understand conflict and cooperation among states in the international system. The end of the Cold War and the bipolar competition between the United States and the Soviet Union has coincided with and propelled a new focus in international relations theory on such internal characteristics. Scholars of international relations have increasingly applied the theoretical approaches that specialists in American and comparative politics have long used to study domestic institutions to understand how

[1] See for example Kornai (1992, 2000) and Friedman (1962).

governments interact with each other in the international system (Milner 1998). Given that political science is distinguished from other social sciences by its focus on power and authority relationships to understand social behavior and organization, it is not surprising that political scientists generally turn first to such explicitly political institutions as competitive elections, the nature of electoral systems, the separation of powers between legislative and executive officials, or the differences between presidential and parliamentarian systems. In particular, international relations theorists, and not just those studying the democratic peace, have predominantly focused on the presence or absence of democracy when examining how characteristics internal to states shape their external relations.

A concentration on democracy has obscured important sources of economic institutional variation among states that shapes their internal distribution of political power. Locke long ago suggested how the concentration of wealth within the state and the absence of stable property rights constrained the liberty of individuals. An extension of this basic insight makes it possible to draw comparisons between the struggle for parliamentary oversight and democracy in seventeenth-century England and tsarist Russia. Similarly, an examination of such economic institutions as property rights creates opportunities to understand how politicians can utilize publicly owned assets to circumvent democratic constraints in countries like contemporary Venezuela and Russia. Perhaps most importantly, the growing resistance of these countries to American policy in both Latin America and the Middle East suggests that such domestic developments possess important foreign-policy implications. A focus solely on the presence or absence of democracy to explain the outbreak of war and peace would miss the critical institutional distinctions between autocratic Russia and autocratic Germany in the decades before World War I, distinctions that gave the former an enormous financial advantage in the arms race that preceded the outbreak of the July crisis. A focus only on democratic institutions in the United States and Great Britain overlooks how domestic economic disagreements over the extent to which the state should regulate international trade shaped the evolution of disputes over Oregon and Venezuela that nearly descended to war. Moreover, a focus on the political institutions associated with democracy would miss the recent foreign-policy reorientation by China following the period of economic reform.

The second conceptual break from the conventional liberal peace literature sought to treat international trade as one manifestation of the broader phenomenon known as capitalism. A definition of capitalism that relies on the institutions of private property and competitive market structures – domestic institutions that regulate internal and external trade – facilitated a critique of existing writings on trade and peace. While classical scholars argued that the natural dispersion of economic resources around the world created an opportunity for commerce to forge common interests among political societies, I showed how all international trade is not alike in its capacity to promote peace among states. Commercial flows can be driven by a number of factors, including alliances, transportation costs, differences in factor endowments, economies of scale, and political barriers to trade. Moreover, the adjustment process associated with integrating national economies into a single world economy can provoke an incredibly contentious struggle within and between societies over the extent to which globalization should be embraced or kept at arm's length. The capacity of trade to promote peace depends on the evolution of these domestic struggles. This break made it possible to reexamine an enduring puzzle for liberal international relations theory – the outbreak of World War I following a sustained period of globalization. It also shed new light on how the explosion of trade flows between Taiwan and China is shaping the domestic struggle within the former over the question of political independence.

The institutions of capitalism shape decisions for war by influencing three critical conditions associated with its outbreak: the presence of conflicting national interests between the participants; the capacity of a political regime to retain its hold on domestic power during and after a conflict; and the failure of disputants to reach a negotiated compromise that avoids the costs of war. I examined how large quantities of public property shape the second and third conditions. These resources relieve governments from having to make concessions that limit the scope of their authority when gaining access to the wealth of society. Leaders deploy these resources in multiple ways that shape the domestic distribution of power and policy outputs. They can use them to co-opt domestic political opposition by offering economic incentives in the form of higher budgetary allocations or direct payouts. Alternatively, they can use the threat of eliminating access to such resources to build loyalty among existing political supporters. When faced with the emergence of a new external security threat that requires more revenues to purchase additional military outlays, they can simply bypass the broader negotiation process with key political constituencies or some form of a legislative body that threatens to alter such spending levels or priorities. Most importantly, the control over such economic assets creates tremendous autonomy in the decision over how they are allocated. This fiscal autonomy generates domestic political security, which makes the outbreak of war more likely by reducing its attendant political risks.

The outbreak of World War I also provided an opportunity to examine how this financial power can exacerbate commitment problems by strengthening a regime at home. In possession of large quantities of public property and preferential access to French capital, the tsar was able to fend off internal challenges to his regime and replenish Russia's military power following the disaster of 1905. Germany chose to launch a preventive war in July 1914 because it could not secure the requisite financial resources to maintain the pace of the arms race set by Russia.

The scope of government barriers to international commerce shape both the level of competition in domestic markets and the domestic struggle over defining national interests, particularly with respect to territory. Firms that are competitive in international markets lobby their governments to eliminate political barriers to international commerce, like tariffs and capital controls, and to pursue restrained national interests. Such groups are unwilling to pay the costs – including higher taxes, trade embargoes, and death in battle – associated with using military force to secure new external markets. They can achieve this outcome peacefully within an open and competitive global economy. However, firms that rely on government intervention to remain competitive are more likely to support aggressive foreign policies. Their inability to penetrate foreign markets increases their willingness to pay some of the costs associated with territorial expansion. Accordingly, war and imperialism create opportunities to enlarge the size of the protected domestic market. Governments also use barriers to trade to construct domestic coalitions of support. The sale of market regulation thus creates opportunities for political leaders to pursue more aggressive foreign policies by first securing their hold on domestic power. Foreign-policy restraint, particularly with respect to territorial demands, emerges when the beneficiaries of open, global markets possess disproportionate domestic political influence and the state is deprived of this lever of domestic political influence.

The empirical sections of the book utilized quantitative and qualitative research methods to illustrate the validity of these claims. Because the capitalist peace has large implications for the contemporary democratic and commercial peace research programs, I initially examined my claims with the prevailing statistical techniques in this literature. This analysis established a strong relationship between the domestic institutions that constitute capitalist economies and peace among states in the international system. Multiple statistical tests found a consistent relationship between capitalism and peace across different institutional measurements of capitalism, different research designs, and different historical periods. The statistical analysis also showed that capitalist peace is stronger than the democratic peace. These conclusions rested on the following findings:

1. Higher quantities of private property reduced the likelihood of conflict between states during the Cold War and post–Cold War periods (dyadic).
2. Free-trade policies reduced the likelihood of conflict between states during the Cold War and post–Cold War periods (dyadic).
3. Free-trade policies reduced the willingness of governments to initiate military disputes during the first era of globalization (monadic).
4. Higher quantities of private property reduced the willingness of governments to initiate military disputes in the Cold War and post–Cold War periods (monadic).
5. Democratic states were more likely than autocratic states to initiate military disputes in the period prior to World War I (monadic).
6. The peace among democratic states does not emerge until after World War I (dyadic).
7. Even during the Cold War and post–Cold War periods, the peace among democratic states was conditioned by capitalism. This peace holds only if both states possess liberal property rights regimes (dyadic).
8. The capitalist peace operates independently of the characteristics of the political regime of the state. Higher quantities of private property lead to more peaceful foreign policies by both autocrats and democrats (monadic and dyadic).

The validity of these claims was further established through a series of in-depth case studies spanning both the nineteenth and twentieth centuries. Those cases were chosen to compare these conclusions with previous work on the democratic peace, confront some of the critical historical cases often held out as undermining liberal peace claims, and illustrate the political mechanisms by which the institutions of capitalism promote peace.

Despite limited qualitative research within the entire body of liberal peace literature, Anglo-American relations during the nineteenth century have repeatedly been utilized to either establish or challenge the role of democracy in promoting peace. Consequently, I utilized my theoretical framework to reexamine two critical cases in the evolution of this relationship. The dispute over Oregon in the 1840s illustrated how the resolution of internal conflicts over commercial policy in both the United States and Britain facilitated a peaceful compromise over the disputed territory. Free-trading interests in both countries opposed expansive territorial demands that heightened the risks of war. In the United States, southern cotton farmers and northeastern merchant interests repeatedly blocked efforts by western senators to push President Polk into demanding all of the Oregon territory. Western interests received a momentary burst of political support at the height of the crisis from protectionist interests in Pennsylvania. Ultimately though, President Polk and his closest counselor, Robert Walker, opted to limit their territorial demands and pursue peaceful compromise so as not to risk a broader split in the Democratic Party that would undermine their plan for tariff reform.

American pursuit of tariff reform and peace was facilitated by a similar struggle within Britain over the Corn Laws. While Aberdeen pushed repeal to shift the domestic balance of power within United States toward groups that supported compromise over Oregon, the goal of trade liberalization also prevented a more aggressive government, led by Russell and Palmerston, from coming to office at the height of the crisis. Furthermore, Russell's support for free trade led him to push Peel toward accommodation with the United States. The resolution of this internal struggle in Britain over tariff policy in favor of the interests associated with the Manchester school facilitated a peaceful compromise over Oregon with the United States.

The internal struggles within the Democratic Party in the United States during this period also possess implications for the relative role between democracy and capitalism in promoting peace. The Democratic Convention held in Baltimore in 1844 illustrates one mechanism by which democratic institutions heightened the risk of military conflict in the nineteenth century. The bold, expansionist program supporting the annexation of Texas and Oregon adopted by the Democratic Party emerged from the logrolling of northern and western factions of the party. Western interests supported the annexation of Texas with the expectation that southern Democrats would also support the annexation of all of Oregon. President Polk initially felt obligated to pursue this policy and only withdrew his political commitment when it risked his larger goal of tariff reduction. Although the democratic processes associated with selecting a presidential nominee at Baltimore in 1844 initially pushed Polk to confront Britain over Oregon, the emerging strength of free-trading interests later enabled him to move back from a military confrontation.

The dispute over Venezuela differed from that over Oregon as it began and ended with internal political developments in the United States. Protectionist interests, led by Henry Cabot Lodge, played an even greater role in the onset of this dispute. They quickly rallied to show public support for Cleveland's threat to prevent Britain from expanding its influence in South

America. Western congressional officials joined this coalition for confrontation, hoping that such a conflict would force the United States off the gold standard. Devaluation provided the perfect mercantilist policy by increasing the price of imports and reducing the price of exports. The threat of a collapsing gold standard, though, had the opposite impact that Westerners hoped. Rather than forcing the United States off the gold standard, Cleveland reaffirmed his commitment to maintaining it. During a financial panic at the height of the crisis in December 1895, Cleveland took public steps to back away from his public confrontation. He chose the preservation of the gold standard, a critical symbol of nineteenth-century capitalism, over the chance to expel Britain from disputed Venezuelan territory.

This case carries even more important implications for the role of American foreign policy in broader arguments about the relationship between capitalism and peace. It challenges arguments associated with the Wisconsin revisionist school that linked American territorial expansion with capitalism. While recognizing that economic interests per se can motivate some domestic groups to advocate territorial expansion with the aid of military force, this case illustrates that such sectors tend to rely on barriers that instead limit the capacity of capitalism to coordinate economic activity. These advocates for conflict tend to be proponents not of capitalism but of alternative economic systems, like mercantilism, that insulate their economic interests from the competitive pressures associated with capitalism.

Any modern claim linking globalization to peace has had to overcome the skepticism created by the failure of globalization to prevent war in July 1914. A focus on the domestic institutions associated with capitalism rather than aggregate trade flows among states facilitated a reexamination of the economic origins of this conflict and Russia's role in it. Expanding trade flows during this first era of globalization coexisted with significant political instruments – like capital controls, tariffs, and public property – capable of manipulating this exchange. These constraints on capitalism created and sustained some of the critical political conflicts between Germany and the Franco-Russian alliance. French capital controls helped rescue Russia from financial and political disaster in 1905. Russia's financial strength – derived largely from French capital and key state-owned assets – reduced the risks of domestic instability, enabled Russian leaders to pursue a more confrontational policy in the Balkans and the Near East following the Liman von Sanders crisis, shaped the arms race on land that preceded World War I, and fueled the German decision to launch a preventive war against Russia in 1914. Having reached their financial limits in the summer of 1914, German leaders knew that they could not sustain the existing pace of the arms race and match Russia's Great Program. The tsar chose to accelerate the arms race fully aware of the risk that this might provoke a German attack. Together, these arguments challenge an important point of consensus in the historiography of the war by pointing to domestic institutions in Russia, rather than in Germany, as a critical cause of World War I.

The case of cross-Straits relations between China and Taiwan illustrates how these same commercial pressures that shaped conflicts between Britain and the United States and between Russia and Germany in the nineteenth century operate in the current era of globalization. Like the case of World War I, recent developments in this relationship seem to challenge the conclusions associated with the liberal peace. As Taiwan has embraced democratization and trade has exploded with the mainland, the relationship has deteriorated with periodic military exercises and bold political statements that both raise the threat of war. A simple look at expanding trade flows suggests that they have had little capacity to promote peaceful reconciliation between the long-time political rivals. It is important to remember that this conclusion is often a *ceteris paribus* claim. It only holds when other potentially confounding causes can be eliminated. In the case of Taiwan, all else is not equal over the past decade. The pressures unleashed by democratization and electoral competition have encouraged Pan-Green politicians to use the threat of independence to solidify their own bases of domestic support, thereby contributing to political tension with the mainland. At the same time, the struggle over commercial policy in Taiwan, particularly over deepening economic integration with the mainland, is shaping the larger domestic battle over its ultimate political status vis-à-vis the mainland. By empowering domestic groups within Taiwan that oppose de jure independence from the mainland and the heightened risks of war such a policy is likely to bring, cross-Straits trade reassures Beijing that moderate political forces play a critical role in shaping current and future foreign policy in Taiwan. This reassurance, in turn, helps restrain the mainland's stance toward Taiwan. These developments suggest that capitalism rather than democracy is playing a larger role in the recent stabilization of this conflict.

THEORETICAL EXTENSIONS: TO GLOBAL MARKET STRUCTURE

This book has shown how the pursuit of wealth by private individuals interacting in competitive markets reduces the risks of war among states. By itself, this focus on the domestic institutions of private property and competitive market structures suggests that the emergence of the institutions associated with capitalism and peace depends primarily on developments internal to states. Long literatures on the politics of trade policy and world systems theory suggest important extensions to these claims.[2] They imply that the global structure of markets can either promote or impede internal economic reform and, therefore, can influence domestic pressures for territorial expansion. If open global markets strengthen the political influence of internationally competitive industries at home, they can also push states to adopt cooperative foreign policies. Alternatively, closed global markets can undermine the domestic political influence of free traders and strengthen protectionist calls for territorial expansion and war. This second possibility implies one condition when the argument made here linking the political dominance of free traders within a domestic political system to the adoption of peaceful foreign policies may not hold. The domestic ability of free-trade supporters to promote peace may be limited by closed global markets (Lobell 2003). This section examines how an extension of the broader theoretical framework employed here can be used to examine this potentially competing claim. This extension suggests that such arguments focusing on the broader structure of the global economy complement, rather than compete with, the primary arguments presented here. While leaving the empirical investigation for future work, it argues that the same underlying dynamic in both a domestic economy and the broader global marketplace, competitive market structures, promotes peace.

At least three key risks associated with opening the domestic economy to international competition can shape internal decisions for economic reform and territorial expansion. First, a strategy to invest and expand production oriented to global markets rests on the expectation that the good being produced for that external market can be sold to those outlets in the future. The closure of external markets for finished manufactured goods forces exporters to cut back production or market their products in the domestic economy. The reentry of this surplus production into the home market can spur deflation and put some market participants out of business. As discussed in Chapter 6, LaFeber (1998[1963]) argues that this need to find sales outlets for surplus manufacturing production played a critical role in American territorial expansion at the end of the nineteenth century. Because European markets were largely closed to American products, Republicans and Populists supported bolder foreign-policy initiatives, including confronting Britain, in both South America and Asia. Alternatively, open consumer markets in large economies around the world

[2] For recent reviews of the trade policy literature see Lake (1993) and Milner (1999). For an example of world systems theory see Wallerstein (1974).

can alleviate these pressures for territorial expansion by reducing the risks associated with reorienting domestic industry toward global markets. This logic played a role in American support for economic recovery in Europe and Asia following World War II (e.g., Layne 2006; Leffler 2007). Similarly today, as discussed in Chapter 8, China's foreign policy is predicated on the assumption that global markets are open. Zheng Bijian, Communist Party insider and source of the "Peaceful Rise" label for contemporary China's grand strategy, argues that this openness allows China to eschew the path of imperialism and war pursued by such countries like Japan and Germany when global markets were closed.

Second, just as the closure of markets for finished products can generate demands for territorial expansion, the closure of markets for key raw materials and inputs to the production process may create similar foreign-policy pressures. The decision to embrace open global markets carries significant risks because it simultaneously imposes specialization on the domestic economy. Attendant shifts in the industrial composition of the domestic economy displace inefficient industries and force the resources, namely workers, employed in them to redeploy to alternative sectors. As long as the inputs for the remaining domestic industries are readily available on global markets, the benefits of specialization can be significant as cheaper international sources replace more costly domestic sources. However, if the global supply chain for key imported products carries the potential to be regularly interrupted, governments may use both trade policy and military force to stabilize sourcing for the home market.

The use of trade policy generally entails adopting higher tariffs to protect inefficient domestic industries. Such policies accept the higher prices for home sourcing as a form of insurance that guarantees stability in supply. For example, opponents of the repeal of the Corn Laws worried that cheap imported grain would reallocate resources within the economy so that Britain would no longer be self-sufficient in food production. This dependence threatened to create significant influence opportunities for foreign governments controlling the supply of British food. Foreign governments could try to cut off the supply of food and drive up prices for a critical consumption good. Even though home production forced British consumers to pay higher prices, this sourcing decision could help to ensure political stability during times of political crises. These arguments continued to be made through the turn of the twentieth century when the brief crises with the United States over Venezuela provoked fears of American manipulation of British food supplies in a war and the concomitant risk that this could provoke riots and internal political instability (Rock 1989, pp. 44–5).

Governments have also historically utilized military force to solve such sourcing problems. The arguments here linking competitive markets to peace suggest that the global structure of these raw materials markets shapes both the present and future costs associated with orienting a domestic economy to global production and the incentives to utilize the military to mitigate these risks. When markets are competitive, buyers have access to multiple suppliers. This creates safety in numbers, so to speak. If any seller or group of sellers attempts to raise prices, the availability of multiple sources allows consumers simply to exit to lower cost producers. Similarly, consumers of raw materials meet other consumers of raw materials with equal power to secure these resources. Each consumer must pay the market price or he or she will not be able to obtain the desired good. Alternatively, when global supplies of key raw materials are owned by a few suppliers, like with oil, the opportunities to control output and prices grow. Apart from being able to extract monopoly rents from the sales of these goods, governments can also utilize them for political leverage by threatening to cut off access to other economies that are dependent on such resources (e.g., Hirschman 1969[1945]).

Consuming governments may respond to this vulnerability imposed by oligopolistic raw materials markets by extending political control, namely through conquest, over these assets. The extension of political control eliminates many of the risks associated with being manipulated via market power by simply replacing the exchange relationship with one based on coercive authority (Frieden 1994). The Japanese decision to embark on a program of territorial expansion throughout Asia during the interwar period was shaped by the potential and then actual closure of global markets, particularly an oil embargo by the United States (e.g., Iriye 1993). Similarly, the American decision to replace the French position in Vietnam in 1954 was partially shaped by the American commitment to rehabilitating the Japanese economy. To accomplish this, the United States sought to ensure that Japan had access to raw materials in Southeast Asia (Leffler 2007, p. 144).

A third key risk associated with reorienting a domestic economy to global markets stems from the possibility that other governments will not maintain current or future reciprocal commitments to open their domestic economy. This strategic decision by other governments to close their markets imposes real costs on home producers that lose access to foreign consumers while seeing their home market position erode. A related situation occurs when rival governments subsidize their own industries, which in turn allows firms to dump their goods in foreign markets. As discussed in Chapter 7, Germany subsidized Prussian farmers before World War I, thereby enabling them to export grain to land-rich Russia. German protection essentially transformed

Russian farmers from an export industry into an import-competing one. Russian farmers then pushed for both protection and a bolder foreign policy relative to Germany.

Hegemonic stability theory suggests at least one solution to the dilemmas associated with choosing a strategy of globalization when few other states do so. It argues that the concentration of global economic power in the hands of a single state increases the likelihood that global markets will be relatively open (e.g., Krasner 1976; Kindleberger 1981; Lake 1993). Because of its sheer economic size, the hegemon possesses multiple positive and negative tools that can be used to induce or compel smaller states to adopt free-trade policies. Moreover, open markets in the hegemon can mediate the risk that other states will renege on joint commitments to liberalize domestic markets. The hegemon acts as a consumer market of last resort and consequently reduces the costs to smaller economies of jointly reducing trade barriers with each other. Imagine a situation in which two small economies were considering whether to sign a trade treaty in which both states eliminated all tariffs. If either of the two smaller economies reneged on the deal, the other still has access to the large market of the hegemon. This can make both governments of the smaller economies more willing to sign trade agreements and maintain their commitments to them because of the marketing insurance provided by access to the hegemon's economy. For example, the United States implemented a number of policies following World War II – such as Marshall Plan aid, lower tariff barriers, and support for global institutions like the International Monetary Fund and the General Agreement on Tariffs and Trade – that helped to promote free-trade orientations by smaller economies.

This American embrace of globalization may have enabled open global markets to promote peace in at least two critical ways. First, by serving as a market of last resort for rebuilding economies in both Europe and Asia, the United States reduced many of the incentives for territorial expansion by ensuring market outlets for surplus manufacturing production. While relatively closed global markets promoted imperialism and territorial expansion at the end of the nineteenth century and during the interwar period, access to the large American market may have reduced the need to adopt similar policies after World War II. Second, by helping reassure states that third-party markets would remain open, American support of international openness may have helped prevent the escalation of trade conflicts into military disputes like that between Russia and Germany in 1914.

In sum, these risks associated with reorienting the domestic economy to global markets suggest at least three ways in which open global markets may promote peace. The first is a trait that focuses on the extent to which all of the local economies that constitute the broader global market have opened their own domestic markets to the pressures of foreign competition.[3] These unprotected markets reduce the risks associated with specialization for the broader world market and temper demands for territorial expansion by creating outlets for surplus goods. The second relies on globally competitive market structures in raw materials to prevent states from utilizing market power to penalize states that have opted to source critical resources for their domestic economy from abroad. States have historically acted on these fears of facing key supply shortages through policies of imperialism that substitute political control for exchange through markets to ensure access to these resources. The third suggests that the openness of global markets may prevent the escalation of trade disputes into military disputes by minimizing the dependence of any two trading partners on each other. Finally, it is important to note that the first two of these mechanisms complement, rather than contradict, a large portion of this book that focuses on how competitive market structures within states promote peace. They instead suggest that competitive global markets may also promote peace.

FROM THEORY TO POLICY IMPLICATIONS

The capacity of capitalism to promote peace along with the capacity of the American embrace of globalization after 1945 to facilitate economic liberalization in both Europe and Asia carries large implications for contemporary American foreign policy. In his book *Capitalism, Democracy, and Ralph's Pretty Good Grocery*, John Mueller (1999) argues that popular conceptions of the relative virtues and vices associated with democracy and capitalism should be reversed. While democracy often gets much of the credit for beneficial social outcomes, capitalism instead does much of the heavy lifting. In much the same way, this final section explores the policy implications of mistakenly giving democracy much of the credit for some of the recent positive revolutionary changes in the international system, including the peaceful collapse of the Soviet Union and its empire in Eastern Europe, along with the emergence of a robust peace in Europe. These possibilities imply that political capital and resources designed to promote

[3] This global openness can be created through multiple pathways – the adoption of free-trade policies by one large economy, the adoption of free-trade policies by a few large economies, or the adoption of free-trade policies by most of the small economies (e.g., Snidal 1985).

American foreign-policy interests and peace should be disproportionately devoted instead to liberalizing global markets.

Recent electoral developments around the globe in places like Venezuela, Bolivia, Germany, Spain, Russia, and the Palestinian territories where victorious politicians campaigned on anti-American platforms illustrate one of the challenges first exposed during the Cold War in relying too heavily on democracy promotion as a device to advance national interests. The institutions associated with democracy protect the process by which societies choose their political leaders. Democracy, however, does not protect the policy outputs resulting from this process. This risk partly explains the historically uneven American support for democracy around the world. For example, George Kennan would tell American ambassadors in South America in 1950, "It is better to have a strong regime in power than a liberal government if it is indulgent and relaxed and penetrated by Communists."[4] Just as the Bush administration effected regime change in Iraq for the sake of democratic reform in the Middle East while tolerating the repressive Saudi regime for the sake of American economic interests in the region, Cold War presidents supported the call for democracy in Europe but sanctioned the overthrow of democratically elected leaders in places like Chile given the larger struggle against Soviet-inspired communism.

The Palestinian election of 2006 illustrates this fundamental dilemma in the policy of democracy promotion. Although international observers certified the process as democratic, the election granted a political mandate to the organization Hamas, which has publicly taken credit for numerous terrorist attacks carried out in pursuit of its broader political goal – the destruction of a close American ally, Israel. Similarly, recent elections in Bolivia and Venezuela show that democracy simply does not guarantee the election of parties friendly to American interests. If anything, the recent mix of global frustration with the militarism of American foreign policy along with democratization has proven to be an effective recipe for ensuring the election of groups hostile to American interests.

Do these examples suggest that the United States should halt its current strategy of democracy promotion? Not necessarily. Yet they do clearly illustrate that a grand strategy centered on promoting institutional reform in other societies must simultaneously possess mechanisms beyond employing military threats to influence local politics in both democracies and autocracies so that common interests can be forged with the United States.

[4] As quoted in Pollard (1985, p. 212).

The capacity of capitalism to promote peace depends largely on its capacity to build such common political interests among governments. Over the last two centuries, the political leaders of large economies have recognized that controlling access to their domestic economy could prove to be a powerful political asset. Threats to cut off this access impose substantial costs on foreign economies by forcing their firms to seek alternative, smaller markets for their goods. Hope that these costs stimulate conciliatory policy changes motivates the belief that economic sanctions restricting trade can be an effective tool of contemporary statecraft. Similar logic currently prompts American policymakers to call for economic sanctions against such countries as Myanmar, Iran, North Korea, and Sudan.

Large economies – Great Britain in the nineteenth century, the United States after World War II, and China today – have also recognized the political benefits of employing economic carrots rather than economic sticks. The opening of their domestic markets enabled them to influence and transform the domestic balance of power in target states to strengthen groups friendly to the larger economy's broader global interests. Lord Aberdeen, the British foreign secretary, sought to use the elimination of the Corn Laws to resolve the Oregon dispute. In letters to Robert Peel, he argued that opening of the British market to grain exports from the United States would create a majority coalition of western and southern senators in support of a peaceful resolution of the crisis. As Chapter 6 noted, the hope of greater access to the British consumer market shored up support from southern leaders like Robert Walker.

The United States adopted a similar strategy throughout the Cold War. The opening of American markets to war-torn economies in Western Europe and Japan fostered economic recovery, stopped the spread of communism, and established firm economic foundations supporting stronger political ties in the Western bloc. As part of its broader economic strategy that included Marshall Plan aid, the United States tolerated discrimination against its exports in the form of undervalued currencies, the European Payments Union that liberalized intra-European trade, and delays on restoring current account convertibility in Europe to stabilize economic conditions in its allies.

Chapter 8 examined how China has also used such carrots to break the current stalemate that exists in the Taiwan Straits by influencing the domestic balance between Pan-Blue and Pan-Green forces. For example, in a very public signal in the summer of 2005, the mainland eliminated tariff restrictions on imported fruit from Taiwan. Because fruit production is concentrated in southern Taiwan, a traditional stronghold for the DPP, the mainland hopes that new outlets for these products in the mainland will lead farmers either to push the DPP toward greater accommodation with the mainland or defect to the Pan-Blue Coalition. In short, China is using access to its domestic economy to shape the internal political debate in Taiwan and foster greater support for its interests.

Finally, it is important to note that American promotion of open global markets in the post–World War II period has played a critical supporting role in China's recent economic transformation and, consequently, provides part of the underlying structure of U.S.–China relations today and in the future.[5] Access to the American consumer has fueled nearly three decades of staggering export-oriented growth in China with annual growth rates regularly hovering around 10 percent. Open markets have encouraged China to settle many outstanding territorial disputes as it seeks to reassure other states that its rise is an opportunity rather than a threat to the existing international order.

Many scholars and commentators invoke realist insights linking economic growth with territorial expansion and historical parallels with Wilhelmine Germany to suggest that China's rise is likely to generate conflict with the United States (e.g., Mearsheimer 2001; Kagan 1997). Such claims often point to the key insight of power transition theory, namely that declining military power can prompt a hegemon to launch a preventive war against a rising challenger to protect its position in the international hierarchy of influence (e.g., Gilpin 1981; Copeland 2000; Goldstein 2007). Accordingly, American's contemporary strategic situation relative to China is likened to Great Britain's relationship with Germany in the period prior to World War I. This historical analogy suggests that the United States may eventually go to war against China unless it contains the latter's ability to transform economic growth into military might.

The theoretical framework and evidence presented here imply that a better historical parallel for contemporary Sino-U.S. relations is instead the Anglo-American relationship at the end of the nineteenth century. This possibility suggests that the development of extensive economic ties between the two powers is creating vested economic interests on both sides of the Pacific Ocean that wish to preserve a status quo that has recently seen significant political accommodation between the two powers. Moreover, unlike at the end of the nineteenth century, open global markets are enabling China to sustain rapid economic growth while eschewing the imperialism of the past. At the very least, these possibilities suggest that maintenance

[5] For a similar argument see Ikenberry (2008).

of open consumer markets in the United States can temper, rather than exacerbate, demands within China for territorial expansion.

The Political Benefits of Unilateral Trade Liberalization

As these instances illustrate, liberal trade policies hold out the potential for creating important political dividends for American grand strategy. These benefits are not solely restricted to the capacity of trade to promote peace. Richard Cobden recognized these virtues while advocating the unilateral liberalization of British trade policies in the midst of the debate over the repeal of the Corn Laws. Unlike the promotion of democracy that has recently been shown to possess a limited capacity to build support for American policy outside of the West, the abolition of trade barriers helps stimulate common political interests among different societies by fostering economic specialization and integration into a global division of labor. Similarly today, the United States could extract numerous benefits by unilaterally eliminating trade barriers to create a series of free-trade areas with strategically important countries around the world.

The first real benefits associated with trade liberalization would accrue in the target economies. Expanding exports to the American market stimulate economic growth, encourage foreign direct investment, and promote further economic liberalization. Countries targeted to receive preferential access to the American market for national security reasons are likely to have the largest impact in two sectors – textiles and agriculture. In many cases, the reduction of subsidies to American farmers, like in cotton production, would help to raise world prices and stimulate new production in the developing world, particularly West Africa. The elimination of tariffs on textiles and agricultural products, like sugar and corn, would lead to a decline in prices paid by American consumers and increase imports into the United States.

American consumer appetites for clothing and textile imports are substantial. Annual textile imports to the United States totaled more than $95 billion in 2005.[6] More importantly, many of these imports come from battleground states in the broader war against terrorism. Indonesia, Pakistan, Bangladesh, the Philippines, and Turkey ranked sixth, seventh, tenth, fourteenth, and twenty-first, respectively, in textile exports to the United States in 2005.

[6] Data from NAICS Codes 313, 314, and 315. Data available online from U.S. Census Department at http://www.census.gov/foreign-trade/statistics/country/sreport/textile.html.

The textile sector accounts for a substantial amount of economic activity within these developing economies. In Pakistan and Bangladesh, textile production constitutes nearly 60 percent of their industrial base (Looney 2002; Gresser 2006, p. 76). Pakistan's textile exports to the United States were more than $3 billion in 2005, accounting for 3.3 percent of its GDP and more than 20 percent of its total export portfolio to all countries in all industries.[7] The relative importance of textile exports to the United States is even larger for Bangladesh. They totaled nearly $2.5 billion in 2005, making up 3.9 percent of its GDP and more than 26 percent of its total annual exports. With an estimated GDP of $63.5 billion in 2005, a $1 billion increase in textile exports to the United States (slightly more than 1 percent of total American textile imports) from Bangladesh would increase economic growth there by nearly 1.6 percent. In 2004, Pakistan's commerce minister estimated that every $1 billion in export growth yields 200,000 new jobs there (Bluestein 2004).

Free-trade areas with the United States would also enlist the global private sector as allies in support of sustainable development and democracy in strategically important countries. The elimination of trade barriers would stimulate foreign direct investment into these capital-scarce economies by entrepreneurs seeking to take advantage of preferential access to the American market.[8] For example, the Central American Free Trade Area has already created a push by the Taiwanese government to encourage their businesses to invest in places like Nicaragua and Honduras. Moreover, by encouraging greater exports to the United States, such a policy offers an important incentive for these targeted countries to pursue further liberalization of their economies, particularly with respect to foreign direct investment.[9]

These economic consequences hold out the potential for generating significant political benefits. Expanding economic opportunities created by preferential access to the American economy and higher levels of foreign direct investment also create opportunities for expanding individual freedom and political development. The architects of the Cold War order understood how difficult it would be to rely on democracy as a device to prevent Soviet expansion to Western Europe if the postwar recovery stagnated, industrial capacity remained underutilized, and unemployment

[7] Total exports and GDP statistics taken from CIA World Factbook.

[8] Duty-free textile exports to the United States might also serve to stimulate foreign direct investment in the textile industry in many African countries, like Ethiopia and Tanzania, which currently lack a developed manufactured base.

[9] For empirical support of the proposition that preferential trading arrangements stimulate foreign direct investment into developing economies see Buthe and Milner (2008).

rose. Very real fears of Communist Party electoral gains in France and Italy helped stimulate American cash infusions into these countries, including Marshall Plan aid. Recent research shows that development reduces the risk of democratic collapse into dictatorship (Przeworski et al. 2000). The encouragement of sustainable economic growth encourages democracy where it has yet to take hold and sustains it where it has.

Apart from the benefits accrued within these countries, such a policy holds opportunities for the United States to develop broad-based local support for its interests. As firm managers and employees come to depend on access to the American market for providing income growth and jobs, they could also develop a broader affinity for the United States. Surveys conducted in Beijing show that both higher income levels and support for free trade correlate with higher levels of amity toward the United States (Johnston 2003). This was Aberdeen's hope when advocating Corn Law repeal in the 1840s. Similarly, China today hopes to alter the balance of power within Taiwan toward groups that favor some type of peaceful accommodation with the mainland. Sparked by the American consumer, job creation extending broadly to all income levels and capital inflows could promote grassroots support for American interests in these countries.

This opportunity to stimulate popular support contrasts with economic carrots like the sale of military hardware or foreign aid. Rather than stimulating development, such resources are often spent on the instruments of military coercion and serve as lightning rods for nationalist or anticolonial forces. Moreover, the arguments made here with respect to the domestic political implications of financial autonomy and the case of Russia in the decade before 1914 suggest some of the risks associated with such aid-based strategies of economic engagement. First, literature on the resource curse suggests that the financial autonomy generated by such aid inhibits further political and economic liberalization, and all their attendant benefits, within the target country. Second, while such financial resources may strengthen a critical ally's hold on domestic power, these resources are likely to be spent narrowly to shore up a limited base of internal support. These spending decisions carry important implications for the long-term sustainability of common foreign-policy interests with the United States. What happens if the financial resources are insufficient to sustain the ally in the face of growing domestic opposition, as was the case with Russia in 1917?

If the benefits of such policies do not diffuse broadly across the target country, they have the effect of further tying the fate of American interests to that of the regime targeted to receive such aid. Unilateral liberalization of access to American markets alternatively creates more opportunities to develop broad-based support in developing economies. Given capital scarcity and relative labor abundance within these countries, these countries are likely to specialize in and thus export products made in labor-intensive industries. Consequently, American consumption of their agricultural and industrial products facilitates the diffusion of such economic benefits to holders of the abundant factor within these economies, namely labor.

Finally, unilateral liberalization of American markets provides another virtue, one long associated with liberal internationalism and the legacy of the post–World War II era. The unilateral relaxation of trade barriers also sends a powerful signal to the rest of the world that the United States is capable of imposing limits on its own power and was willing to cede the choice over whether to participate in a broader global order valuing democracy, prosperity, and peace directly to these countries. Because access to the American economy offers more consumers with disposable income than any other market, American trade negotiators have long been able to extract more concessions from other countries because of this bargaining leverage. In the round global trade negotiations initiated at Doha in 2001, representatives from Europe and the developing world charged that American negotiators, held hostage by domestic agricultural interests demanding greater access to European markets, prevented a comprehensive, multilateral bargain to liberalize global trade. Why surrender such leverage with a unilateral elimination of trade barriers, particularly if they protect the interests of American business? By agreeing to forego such economic gains, the United States would demonstrate a willingness to restrain its own power. This message of restraint would be particularly timely given rising doubts about American intentions and fears of a new American Empire in the Middle East.

Such fears have been fueled by the dramatic gap in military capabilities that has opened up between the United States and the rest of the world since the end of the Cold War and the expanding American position in the Middle East. Doubts about the genuineness of American support for democracy in Iraq and suspicions that the most recent intervention was part of a larger grab to secure oil interests grow as the United States strengthens ties with autocratic leaders in the region. By launching an initiative that would simultaneously impart significant opportunity costs on American business (in the form of lost reciprocal trade concessions) and promote sustainable economic development fueled by exports and integration with the global economy, the United States could demonstrate that its global economic interests were not driven by oil and limited to ensuring that political leaders possessing privileged access to this resource remained in power.

Finally, this invitation to deepen integration into the global economy would place the decisions over how best to generate development squarely in the hands of countries selected to receive such preferential treatment. By not attaching any terms or conditions to this initiative, the United States would allow these countries to choose for themselves whether they wanted to take advantage of such an economic opportunity. One of the most powerful sources of globalization backlash throughout the developing world over the last two decades has been the view that Western aid carries conditions – like government spending cuts, capital account liberalization, and trade liberalization – that only serve to widen the income disparity between the developed and developing world (e.g., Stiglitz 2002). These conditions imposed severe costs on developing economies as governments slowed social welfare spending, raised interest rates to contain inflation and protect the value of their currencies, and made local financial systems more vulnerable to exchange-rate crises sparked by rapid movements of short-term capital flows. The United States risks accentuating this backlash by tough bargaining that imposes harsh political or economic conditions in exchange for liberalizing the American market. One of the long-extolled virtues of the Marshall Plan was the decision to let Europeans in concert craft their own strategy to rebuild their economies after the war and independently determine how American aid would be spent. Similarly, the countries targeted to receive the unilateral elimination of trade barriers could choose whether to liberalize their domestic economy to foreign direct investment, allow rapid migration into cities to take advantage of new manufacturing jobs, or to implement an export-led growth strategy. These countries could gauge for themselves the costs and risks associated with globalization and determine the pace at which they chose to integrate their local economies into the American economy.

Such prominent critics of capitalism as Marx, Lenin, and Polanyi have pointed to this backlash to argue that the very nature of capitalist development contains the seeds of its own destruction. The impersonal nature of market competition and its tendency to move economic activities to their lowest cost location around the world necessarily alienates displaced individuals and groups. These groups often seek protection from the market by demanding and then supporting greater government capacity to provide insulation and protection from these pressures. This struggle thus carries the potential to strengthen the power of government relative to that of competitive markets in the allocation of economic resources.

The resurgence of free-market capitalism in the aftermath of the Reagan and Thatcher revolutions and the collapse of the Soviet Union challenges assertions that the success of capitalism necessarily breeds its own demise. However, the interwar period, contemporary developments in Latin America, and the global financial crisis in the fall of 2008 caution against ignoring the risks posed by such political resistance to capitalism. Efforts to reestablish the gold standard, the principle institution associated with capitalism prior to World War I, attempted to hoist a disproportionate burden of this policy on the newly emergent political left (Eichengreen 1996; Simmons 1994). Commitments to maintain overvalued exchange rates, as in Great Britain, were simply not credible because they required higher interest rates, which slowed economic activity. To defend the institutions associated with capitalism, governments tried unsuccessfully to slow domestic economic activity and ignore demands for greater social welfare spending in a political environment marked by intense societal demands for compensation after enduring all the costs associated with more than four horrific years of World War I. These efforts complicated postwar recovery and created conditions that facilitated a dramatic expansion in government powers to manipulate economic activity. The architects and their forebears of the post–World War II global economy, particularly Cordell Hull, understood how the collapse of the global economy into protectionist blocs had played a critical role in the outbreak of World War II.

Similarly, recent developments in South America, particularly the resurgence of leftist populism, suggest that widespread public support for globalization in the developing world may be tenuous. Heavy-handedness by the United States in promoting capitalism via institutions like the International Monetary Fund risks activating political resistance that alternatively strengthens the capacity of governments to control economic activity. The arguments of this book caution that such a strengthening of the state's capacity to control economic outcomes, created in part by the backlash against capitalism, risks heightening the chance of military conflict in the international system. The unilateral liberalization of American markets provides some insurance against this backlash by ceding choices over the pace at which the developing world embraces the institutions associated with capitalism to the governments in those countries.

These claims simultaneously recognize that American capacity to promote capitalism abroad depends critically on its ability to sustain it at home. Contemporary comparisons of the financial crisis of 2008 with the collapse of 1929 and the Great Depression show that periodic failures of capitalism to create sustainable and diffuse economic growth can create a backlash that facilitates greater government control of economic activity. This book has demonstrated some of the broader risks that widespread political restrictions on market-oriented exchange pose to international peace and stability. McDonald (2007b) examines how the United States can cushion some of the domestic backlash associated with the excesses of capitalism to ensure that globalization is capable to promoting American interests abroad. These arguments focus on promoting public investment at home to heighten American competitiveness both in the broader global marketplace and cushion some of the adjustment costs forced on domestic workers by globalization. However, such programs must possess finite durations to prevent the creation of vested interests – both in society and government – that push for their continuation in perpetuity.

The forbearance associated with unilaterally liberalizing American markets is not without important historical precedent in American history. The economic discrepancies between the United States and the rest of the world were even larger in the immediate aftermath of World War II. Yet the Truman administration recognized the dangers of shutting off American markets to paralyzed European and Japanese economies. Policies that would today be labeled as unfair trading practices by domestic interests favoring protection were countenanced then in light of the larger political struggle being waged against the Soviet Union.

The historical tendency of capitalism to promote peace and common political interests suggest that American grand strategy should shift its focus from democracy to market promotion in the hope of transforming societies at risk of plunging into war or in the process of escaping it. This strategy can bind great powers together with a common interest in exploiting the economic benefits created by unrestricted access to a global marketplace. Moreover, this strategy offers the opportunity to nudge many developing societies into gradually adopting liberal reforms that temper many causes of war. The deployment of the American consumer in this larger campaign to promote freedom simply builds on the enormous capacity of the invisible hand to promote development, democracy, and peace.

References

Primary Sources

Aberdeen Papers. British Library.

Balfour Papers. British Library.

Bush, George W. 2003. Remarks by the president in commencement address at the University of South Carolina. Columbia, South Carolina. May 9, 2003. Available at http://www.whitehouse.gov/news/releases/2003/05/20030509-11.html. Accessed February 8, 2008.

———. 2004. State of the union address, Washington, D.C. January 20, 2004. Available at http://www.whitehouse.gov/news/releases/2004/01/20040120-7.html. Accessed February 8, 2008.

———. 2006. State of the union address, Washington, D.C. January 31, 2006. Available at http://www.whitehouse.gov/stateoftheunion/2006. Accessed October 17, 2008.

Chamberlain Papers, Birmingham University (Britain).

Clinton, William J. 1994. State of the union address. *Public papers of the presidents of the United States.* Vol. 1. Washington, D.C.: GPO.

Deng, Xiaoping. 1982. Opening speech at the Twelfth National Congress of the Communist Party of China. September 1, 1982. Available at http://english.peopledaily.com.cn/dengxp/vol3/text/c1010.html. Accessed February 4, 2008.

Foreign Office [FO]. Public Record Office (Britain).

Gooch, G. P. and Harold Temperley. 1926–38. *British documents on the origins of the war, 1898–1914.* 11 volumes. London: Her Majesty's Stationery Office.

Greville, Charles. 1885. *The Greville memoirs (second part): A journal of the reign of Queen Victoria, from 1837 to 1852.* London: Longmans, Green, and Co.

Polk, James K. 1845. Inaugural address, March 4, 1845, in *House Executive Documents* 540, 82nd Congress, 2nd Session, 87–8.

Polk, James K., and Milo Milton Quaife. 1970. *The diary of James K. Polk during his presidency, 1845 to 1849.* New York: Kraus.

Russell Papers. Public Record Office (Britain): Foreign Office.

Salisbury Papers. Hatfield House. Hatfield, England.

U.S. Congress. 1846. *Congressional globe.* 29th Congress, 1st Session, vol. 15. Washington, D.C.: Blair and Rives.

———. 1895. *Congressional record.* 53rd Congress, 2nd session. Washington, D.C.: Government Printing Office.

———. 1895. *Congressional record*, 54th Congress, 1st session. Washington, D.C.: Government Printing Office.

Walker, Robert J. 1893[1845]. Report from the Secretary of the Treasury. In *State Papers and Speeches on the Tariff*, ed. F. W. Taussig. Cambridge: Harvard University Press.

Secondary Sources

Andrews, David. 1994. Capital mobility and state autonomy. *International Studies Quarterly* 38: 193–218.

Apostol, Paul N., Michael W. Bernatzky, and Alexander M. Michelsen. 1928. *Russian public finance during the war.* New Haven, CT: Yale University Press.

Ash, Robert F. 2005. China's regional economies and the Asian region: Building interdependent linkages. In *Power shift: China and Asia's new dynamics*, ed. David Shambaugh, 96–131. Berkeley: University of California Press.

Bairoch, Paul. 1989. European trade policy, 1815–1914. In *The Cambridge economic history of Europe*, eds Peter Mathias and Sidney Pollard. Trans. Susan Burke. Vol. 8, 1–160. Cambridge, U.K.: Cambridge University Press.

Barbieri, Katherine. 1996. Economic interdependence: A path to peace or a source of interstate conflict? *Journal of Peace Research* 33(1): 29–49.

Barbieri, Katherine, and Gerald Schneider. 1999. Globalization and peace: Assessing new directions in the study of trade and conflict. *Journal of Peace Research* 36(4): 387–404.

Barnes, James A. 1931. John G. Carlisle: Financial Statesman. New York: Dodd, Mead, and Co.

Barnett, Michael. 1990. High politics is low politics: The domestic and systemic sources of Israeli security policy, 1967–1977. *World Politics* 42: 529–62.

———. 1992. *Confronting the costs of war: military power, state, and society in Egypt and Israel.* Princeton, N.J.: Princeton University Press.

Bates, Robert H. 1981. *Markets and states in tropical Africa: The political basis of agricultural policies.* Berkeley: University of California Press.

Bearce, David H. 2003. Grasping the commercial institutional peace. *International Studies Quarterly* 47(3): 347–70.

Bearce, David H., Kristen M. Flanagan, and Katharine M. Floros. 2006. Alliances, internal information, and military conflict among member states. *International Organization* 60(3): 595–625.

Beck, Nathaniel, Jonathan Katz, and Richard Tucker. 1998. Taking time seriously: Time-series–cross-section analysis with a binary dependent variable. *American Journal of Political Science* 42(4): 1260–88.

Bennett, D. Scott, and Allan Stam. 2000a. EUGene: A conceptual manual. *International Interactions* 26: 179–204.

———. 2000b. Research design and estimator choices in the analysis of interstate dyads. *Journal of Conflict Resolution* 44(5): 653–85.

Benoit, Kenneth. 1996. Democracies really are more pacific (in general). *Journal of Conflict Resolution* 40(4): 309–41.

Berghahn, V. R. 1993[1973]. *Germany and the approach of war in 1914.* 2nd ed. New York: St. Martin's Press.

Bertram, Marshall. 1992. *The birth of Anglo-American friendship*. New York: University Press of America, Inc.

Bhagwati, Jagdish. 1988. *Protectionism*. The Ohlin lectures, 1. Cambridge, MA: MIT Press.

———. 1991. "Export-promoting protection: Endogenous monopoly and price disparity." In *Political economy and international economics*, ed. Douglas A. Irwin, 110–115. Cambridge, MA: MIT Press.

Bidwell, R. L. 1970. *Currency conversion tables: A hundred years of change*. London: Rex Collings.

Binder, Frederick Moore. 1994. *James Buchanan and the American empire*. London: Associated University Press.

Blake, Nelson M. 1942. Background of Cleveland's Venezuelan policy. *American Historical Review* 47(2): 259–77.

Blank, Joel Harold. 2000. *The decline of democratic imperialism and the rise of the democratic peace: Case studies in Anglo-American relations, 1800–present*. Ph.D. dissertation. University of California at Los Angeles.

Blattman, Christopher, Michael A. Clemens, and Jeffrey Williamson. 2002. Who protected and why? Tariffs around the world 1870–1938. Paper presented to the Conference on the Political Economy of Globalization, Trinity College, Dublin, August 2002.

Block, Fred. 1977. The ruling class does not rule: Notes on the Marxist theory of the state. *Socialist Revolution* 33: 6–28.

Blustein, Paul. 2004. U.S. free-trade deals include few Muslim countries. *Washington Post*, December 3, 2004, p. E1.

Boehmer, Charles, and David Sobek. 2005. Violent adolescence: State development and the propensity for militarized interstate conflict. *Journal of Peace Research* 42(1): 5–26.

Boehmer, Charles, Erik Gartzke, and Timothy Nordstrom. 2004. Do intergovernmental organizations promote peace? *World Politics* 57(1): 1–38.

Boix, Carles. 2003. *Democracy and redistribution*. Cambridge, U.K.: Cambridge University Press.

Bordo, Michael D., and Finn E. Kydland. 1995. The gold standard as a rule: An essay in exploration. *Explorations in Economic History* 32: 423–64.

Bordo, Michael D., Barry Eichengreen, and Douglas A. Irwin. 1999. Is globalization really different than globalization a hundred years ago? NBER Working paper 7195. Cambridge, MA: National Bureau of Economic Research. Available at http://www.nber.org/papers/w7195.

Bourne, Kenneth. 1967. *The balance of power in North America, 1815–1908*. Berkeley: University of California Press.

Braumoeller, Bear F. 2004. Hypothesis testing and multiplicative interaction terms. *International Organization* 58(4): 807–20.

Bremer, Stuart A. 1992. Dangerous dyads: Conditions affecting the likelihood of interstate war, 1816–1965. *Journal of Conflict Resolution* 36(2): 309–41.

Bremer, Stuart A. 1993. Democracy and militarized interstate conflict, 1816–1965. *International Interactions* 18(3): 231–49.

Buchanan, George. 1923. *My mission to Russia and other diplomatic memories*, vol. 1. Boston: Little, Brown, and Company.

Bueno de Mesquita, Bruce, James D. Morrow, Randolph M. Siverson, and Alastair Smith. 1999. An institutional explanation of the democratic peace. *American Political Science Review* 93(4): 791–807.

———. 2003. *The logic of political survival.* Cambridge, MA: MIT Press.
———. 2004. Testing novel implications from the selectorate theory. *World Politics* 56: 363–88.
Bueno de Mesquita, Bruce, and Randolph M. Siverson. 1995. War and the survival of political leaders: A comparative study of regime types and political accountability. *American Political Science Review* 89(4): 841–55.
Bueno de Mesquita, Bruce, Randolph M. Siverson, and Gary Woller. 1992. War and the fate of regimes: A comparative analysis. *American Political Science Review* 86(3): 638–46.
Bush, Richard C. 2005a. *Untying the knot: Making peace in the Taiwan Strait.* Washington, D.C.: Brookings Institution Press.
———. 2005b. Lee Teng-hui and "separatism." In *Dangerous strait: The U.S.–Taiwan–China crisis,* ed. Nancy Bernkopf, 70–92. New York: Columbia University Press.
Buthe, Tim, and Helen V. Milner. 2008. The politics of foreign direct investment into developing countries: Increasing FDI through international trade agreements? *American Journal of Political Science* 52(4): 741–62.
Buzan, Barry. 1984. Economic structure and international security: The limits of the liberal case. *International Organization* 38: 597–624.
Cain, Peter J. 1979. Capitalism, war, and internationalism in the thought of Richard Cobden. *British Journal of International Studies* 5(3): 229–47.
Campbell, Alexander E. 1960. *Great Britain and the United States, 1895–1903.* London: Longmans.
Cederman, Lars-Erik. 2001. Back to Kant: Reinterpreting the democratic peace as a macrohistorical learning process. *American Political Science Review* 95(1): 15–31.
Cederman, Lars-Erik, and Kristian Skrede Gleditsch. 2004. Conquest and regime change: An evolutionary model of the spread of democracy and peace. *International Studies Quarterly* 48(3): 603–29.
Cederman, Lars-Erik, and Mohan Penubarti Rao. 2001. Exploring the dynamics of the democratic peace. *The Journal of Conflict Resolution* 45(6): 818–33.
Chen, Ming-chi. 2004. Sinicization and its discontents: Cross-Strait economic integration and Taiwan's 2004 presidential election. *Issues and Studies* 40(3/4): 334–41.
Cheng, T. J. 2005. China-Taiwan economic linkage: Between insulation and superconductivity. In *Dangerous strait: The U.S.–Taiwan–China crisis,* ed. Nancy Bernkopf, 93–130. New York: Columbia University Press.
Chu, Yun-han. 2004. Taiwan's national identity politics and the prospect of cross-Strait relations. *Asian Survey* 44(4): 484–512.
———. 2005. The evolution of Beijing's policy toward Taiwan during the reform era. In *China rising: Power and motivation in Chinese foreign policy,* eds Yong Deng and Fei-ling Wang, 245–77. Lanham, MD: Rowman and Littlefield.
Chu, Yun-han, and Andrew J. Nathan 2007–8. Seizing opportunity for change in the Taiwan Strait. *The Washington Quarterly* 31(1): 77–91.
Chua, Amy. 2002. *World on fire: How exporting free market democracy breeds ethnic hatred and global instability.* New York: Doubleday.
CIA World Factbook. 2008. Published by the Central Intelligence Agency. Available at https://www.cia.gov/library/publications/the-world-factbook/.
Cobden, Richard. 1868. *The political writings of Richard Cobden,* vols 1–2. London: William Ridgway.

———. 1870. *Speeches on questions of public policy*, vols 1–2, eds John Bright and James E. Thorold Rogers. London: Macmillan and Co.

Coleman, Mary Ann. 1871. *The life of John J. Crittenden, with selections from his correspondence and speeches*. Philadelphia: J. B. Lippincott and Co.

Collins, D. N. 1973. The Franco-Russian alliance and Russian railways, 1891–1914. *The Historical Journal* 16(4): 777–88.

Copeland, Dale C. 1996. Economic interdependence and war: A theory of trade expectations. *International Security* 20(4): 5–41.

———. 2000. *The origins of major war*. Ithaca: Cornell University Press.

Cortissoz, Royal. 1921. *The life of Whitelaw Reid*. New York: C. Scribner & Sons.

Crapol, Edward P. 1973. *America for Americans: Economic nationalism and Anglophobia in the late nineteenth century*. Westport, CT: Greenwood Press.

———. 1992. Coming to terms with empire: The historiography of late nineteenth-century American foreign relations. *Diplomatic History* 16(4): 573–98.

Crisp, Olga. 1960/61. The Russian liberals and the 1906 Anglo-French loan to Russia. *Slavonic and East European Review* 39: 497–511.

Deutsch, Karl, Sydney A. Burrell, Robert A. Kann, Maurice Lee. Jr, Martin Lichterman, Raymond E. Lindgren, Francis L. Loewenheim and Richard W. Van Wagenhan. 1957. *Political community and the North Atlantic area: International organization in the light of historical experience*. Princeton, N.J.: Princeton University Press.

Dixon, William J. 1994. Democracy and the peaceful settlement of international conflict. *American Political Science Review* 88(1): 14–32.

D'Lugo, David, and Ronald Rogowski. 1993. The Anglo-German naval race and comparative constitutional "fitness." In *The domestic bases of grand strategy*, eds Richard Rosecrance and Arthur A. Stein, 65–95. Ithaca, N.Y.: Cornell University Press.

Domke, William Kinkade. 1988. *War and the changing global system*. New Haven: Yale University Press.

Dorussen, Hans. 2006. Heterogeneous trade interests and conflict. *Journal of Conflict Resolution* 50(1): 87–107.

Downs, George W., and David M. Rocke. 1994. Conflict, agency, and gambling for resurrection: The principle-agent problem goes to war. *American Journal of Political Science* 38(2): 362–80.

———. 1995. *Optimal imperfection: Domestic uncertainty and institutions in international relations*. Princeton: Princeton University Press.

Doyle, Michael W. 1983. Kant, liberal legacies, and foreign affairs: Part I. *Philosophy and Public Affairs* 12(3): 205–54.

———. 1986. Liberalism and world politics. *American Political Science Review* 80(4): 1151–69.

———. 1997. *Ways of war and peace*. New York: Norton.

———. 2005. Three pillars of the liberal peace. *The American Political Science Review* 99(3): 463–6.

Dunn, John. 1969. *The political thought of John Locke: An historical account of the argument of the "Two treatises of government"*. London: Cambridge University Press.

Dykstra, David L. 1999. *The shifting balance of power: American–British diplomacy in North America, 1842–1848*. New York: University Press of America.

Edwards, Sebastian. 1993. Openness, trade liberalization, and growth in developing countries. *Journal of Economic Literature* 31(3): 1358–93.

______. 1998. Openness, productivity and growth: What do we really know? *The Economic Journal* 108(447): 383–98.
Eggertsson, Thrain. 1990. *Economic behavior and institutions.* Cambridge, U.K.: Cambridge University Press.
Eichengreen, Barry J. 1994. *International monetary arrangements for the 21st century: Integrating national economies.* Washington, D.C.: Brookings Institution.
______. 1996. *Globalizing capital: A history of the international monetary system.* Princeton: Princeton University Press.
Ekelund, Robert B., Jr., and Robert D. Tollison. 1981. *Mercantilism as a rent-seeking society: Economic regulation in historical perspective.* College Station: Texas A&M University Press.
______. 1997. *Politicized economies: Monarchy, monopoly, and mercantilism.* College Station: Texas A&M University Press.
Fearon, James D. 1994. Domestic political audiences and the escalation of international disputes. *American Political Science Review* 88(3): 577–92.
______. 1995. Rationalist explanations for war. *International Organization* 49(3): 379–414.
______. 1997. Signaling foreign policy interests: Tying hands versus sinking costs. *The Journal of Conflict Resolution* 41(1): 68–90.
Feis, Herbert. 1930. *Europe: The world's banker, 1870–1914.* New Haven: Yale University Press.
Ferguson, Niall. 1994. Public finance and national security: The domestic origins of the First World War revisited. *Past and Present* 142(1):141–68.
______. 1998. *The pity of war.* New York: Basic.
______. 2005. Sinking globalization. *Foreign Affairs* 84(2): 64–77.
Field, James A., Jr. 1978. American imperialism: The worst chapter in almost any book. *American Historical Review* 83(3): 644–68.
Filmer, Robert, and J. P. Sommerville. 1991 [1680]. *Patriarcha and other writings: Cambridge texts in the history of political thought.* Cambridge, England: Cambridge University Press.
Finkelstein, David M. 2000. *China reconsiders its national security: The great peace and development debate of 1999.* Alexandria, VA: CAN Corporation.
Fischer, Fritz. 1967. *Germany's aims in the First World War.* New York: W. W. Norton.
______. 1975. *War of illusions: German policies from 1911 to 1914.* Trans. Marian Jackson. New York: Norton.
______. 1988. Twenty-five years later: Looking back at the "Fischer controversy" and its consequences. *Central European History* 21(3): 207–23.
Flam, Harry, and M. June Flanders. 1991. *Heckscher–Ohlin trade theory.* Cambridge, MA: MIT Press.
Flournoy, F. R. 1946. British liberal theories of international relations (1848–1898). *Journal of History of Ideas* 7(2): 195–217.
Fordham, Benjamin O. 1998. *Building the Cold War consensus: The political economy of U.S. national security policy, 1949–1951.* Ann Arbor: University of Michigan Press.
Fravel, M. Taylor. 2005. Regime insecurity and international cooperation: Explaining China's compromises in territorial disputes. *International Security* 30(2): 46–83.
______. 2008. *Strong borders, secure nation: Cooperation and conflict in China's territorial disputes.* Princeton: Princeton University Press.

Frieden, Jeffry A. 1991. Invested interests: The politics of national economic policies in a world of global finance. *International Organization* 45(4): 425–51.

———. 1994. International investment and colonial control: A new interpretation. *International Organization* 48(4): 559–93.

———. 1997. Monetary populism in nineteenth-century America: An open economy approach. *The Journal of Economic History* 57(2): 367–95.

———. 2006. *Global capitalism: Its fall and rise in the twentieth century.* New York: W. W. Norton.

Friedman, Milton. 1962. *Capitalism and freedom.* Chicago: University of Chicago Press.

Friedman, Thomas. 2005. *The world is flat: A brief history of the twenty-first century.* New York: Farrar, Straus, and Giroux.

Friedrich, Robert J. 1982. In defense of multiplicative terms in multiple regression equations. *American Journal of Political Science* 26(4): 797–833.

Fry, Joseph A. 1996. From open door to world systems: Economic interpretations of late nineteenth-century American foreign relations. *The Pacific Historical Review* 65(2): 277–303.

Fukuyama, Francis. 1992. *The end of history and the last man.* New York: Free Press.

Fuller, William C. 1992. *Strategy and power in Russia, 1600–1914.* New York: The Free Press.

Gardner, Lloyd C., and Thomas J. McCormick. 2004. Walter LaFeber: The making of a Wisconsin School revisionist. *Diplomatic History* 28(5): 613–24.

Garraty, John A. 1953. *Henry Cabot Lodge: A biography.* New York: Alfred A. Knopf.

Gartzke, Erik. 1998. Kant we all get along? Opportunity, willingness, and the origins of the democratic peace. *American Journal of Political Science* 42(1): 1–27.

———. 2007. The capitalist peace. *American Journal of Political Science* 51(1): 166–91.

Gartzke, Erik, Quan Li, and Charles Boehmer. 2001. Investing in the peace: Economic interdependence and international conflict. *International Organization* 55(2): 391–438.

Gash, Norman. 1972. *Sir Robert Peel: The life of Sir Robert Peel after 1830.* Totowa, N.J.: Rowman and Littlefield.

Gates, Scott, Torbjorn L. Knutson, and Jonathon W. Moses. 1996. Democracy and peace: A more skeptical view. *Journal of Peace Research* 33(1): 1–10.

Gawande, Kishore, and Bernard Hoekman. 2006. Lobbying and agricultural trade policy in the United States. *International Organization* 60(3): 527–61.

Geiss, Imanuel. 1966. The outbreak of the first world war and German war aims. *Journal of Contemporary History* 1(3): 75–91.

———. ed. 1968. *July 1914: The outbreak of the First World War: Selected documents.* New York: Charles Scribner.

Gelpi, Christopher, and Joseph M. Grieco. 2003. Economic interdependence, the democratic state, and the liberal peace. In *Economic interdependence and international conflict: New perspectives on an enduring debate,* eds Edward D. Mansfield and Brian M. Pollins, 44–59. Ann Arbor: University of Michigan Press.

Geyer, Dietrich. 1987. *Russian imperialism: The interaction of domestic and foreign policy 1860–1914.* Trans. Bruce Little. Leamington Spa, U.K.: Berg.

Ghosn, Faten, and Glenn Palmer. 2003. Codebook for the militarized interstate dispute data, version 3.0. Available at http://cow2.la.psu.edu.

Gill, Bates. 2005. China's evolving regional security strategy. In *Power shift: China and Asia's new dynamics*, ed. David Shambaugh, 247–65. Berkeley: University of California Press.

______. 2007. *Rising star: China's new security diplomacy.* Washington, D.C.: The Brookings Institution.

Gilpin, Robert. 1981. *War and change in world politics.* Cambridge, U.K.: Cambridge University Press.

Glaser, Bonnie S., and Evan S. Medeiros. 2007. The changing ecology of foreign policy-making in China: The ascension and demise of the theory of "peaceful rise." *The China Quarterly* 190: 291–310.

Gleditsch, Kristian Skrede. 2002. *All international politics is local: The diffusion of conflict, integration, and democratization.* Ann Arbor: University of Michigan Press.

Gleditsch, Nils Petter, and Havard Hegre. 1997. Peace and democracy: Three levels of analysis. *Journal of Conflict Resolution* 41(2): 283–310.

Goemans, H. E. 2000. *War and punishment: The causes of war termination and the First World War.* Princeton studies in international history and politics. Princeton, N.J.: Princeton University Press.

Goldstein, Avery. 2005. *Rising to the challenge: China's grand strategy and international security.* Studies in Asian Security. Stanford: Stanford University Press.

______. 2007. Power transitions, institutions, and China's rise in East Asia: Theoretical expectations and evidence. *Journal of Strategic Studies* 30(4): 639–82.

Gordon, Michael R. 1974. Domestic conflict and the origins of the First World War: The British and German cases. *The Journal of Modern History* 46(2): 191–226.

Gott, Richard. 2005. *Hugo Chavez and the Bolivarian revolution in Venezuela.* New York: Verso.

Gowa, Joanne S. 1994. *Allies, adversaries, and international trade.* Princeton, N.J.: Princeton University Press.

______. 1999. *Ballots and bullets: The elusive democratic peace.* Princeton, N.J.: Princeton University Press.

Grandin, Greg. 2006. *Empire's workshop Latin America, the United States, and the rise of the new imperialism.* The American Empire Project. New York: Metropolitan Books.

Gray, John. 1995. *Liberalism.* 2nd ed. Minneapolis: University of Minnesota Press.

Green, Donald, Soo Yeon Kim, and David H. Yoon. 2001. Dirty pool. *International Organization* 55(2): 441–68.

Gregory, Paul R. 1982. *Russian national income: 1885–1913.* Cambridge, U.K.: Cambridge University Press.

Grenville, John A. S., and George Berkeley Young. 1966. *Politics, strategy, and American diplomacy: Studies in foreign policy, 1873–1917.* New Haven: Yale University Press.

Gresser, Edward. 2006. Reviving Muslim economies. In *With all our might,* ed. Will Marshall, 69–83. Lanham: Rowman and Littlefield.

Grossman, Gene M., and Elhanan Helpman. 1994. Protection for sale. *The American Economic Review* 84(4): 833–50.

Gurr, Ted Robert. 1997[1989]. POLITY II: Political structures and regime change, 1800–1986 [Compute File]. Boulder, CO: Center for Comparative Politics [producer], 1989. Ann Arbor, MI: Interuniversity Consortium for Political and Social Research [distributor], 1990.

Haftel, Yoram. 2007. Designing for peace: Regional integration arrangements, institutional variation, and militarized interstate disputes. *International Organization* 61(1): 217–37.

Harding, Harry. 1987. *China's second revolution: Reform after Mao.* Washington, D.C.: The Brookings Institution.

Hayek, F. A. 1994[1944]. *The road to serfdom.* 50th Anniversary edition. Chicago: The University of Chicago Press.

Hegre, Havard. 2000. Development and the liberal peace: What does it take to be a trading state? *Journal of Peace Research* 37(1): 5–30.

Herrmann, David G. 1996. *The arming of Europe and the making of the First World War.* Princeton, N.J.: Princeton University Press.

Heston, Alan, Robert Summers, and Bettina Aten. 2002. Penn World Table, version 6.1. Center for International Comparisons at the University of Pennsylvania.

Hietala, Thomas R. 1985. *Manifest design: Anxious aggrandizement in late Jacksonian America.* Ithaca, N.Y.: Cornell University Press.

Hillgruber, Andreas. 1981. *Germany and the two World Wars.* Trans. William C. Kirby. Cambridge, MA: Harvard University Press.

Hirschman, Albert O. 1969[1945]. *National power and the structure of foreign trade.* Berkeley: University of California Press.

———. 1970. *Exit, voice, and loyalty: Responses to decline in firms, organizations, and states.* Cambridge: Harvard University Press.

———. 1997[1977]. *The passions and the interests: Political arguments for capitalism before its triumph.* 20th Anniversary Edition. Princeton: Princeton University Press.

Hiscox, Michael J. 2002. Commerce, coalitions, and factor mobility: Evidence from congressional votes on trade legislation. *American Political Science Review* 96(3): 593–608.

Hiscox, Michael J., and Scott L. Kastner. 2002. A general measure of trade policy orientations: Gravity-model-based estimates for 82 nations, 1960 to 1992. Working paper. Harvard University.

Howard, Michael. 1978. *War and the liberal conscience.* New Brunswick, N.J.: Rutgers University Press.

Huth, Paul K., and Todd L. Allee. 2002. *The democratic peace and territorial conflict in the twentieth century.* Cambridge, U.K..: Cambridge University Press.

Ikenberry, G. John. 2008. The rise of China and the future of the West. *Foreign Affairs* 87(1): 23–37.

International Monetary Fund. 2001. *Government finance statistics manual.* Available at http://www.imf.org/external/pubs/ft/gfs/manual/.

———. Various years. *Government finance statistics.*

———. Various years. *Direction of trade statistics.* CD-Rom.

Iriye, Akira. 1993. *The globalizing of America, 1913–1945.* New York: Cambridge University Press.

Irwin, Douglas A. 2002. *Free trade under fire.* Princeton: Princeton University Press.

Jacobs, I. Bruce, and I-hao Ben Liu. 2007. Lee Teng-hui and the idea of "Taiwan." *The China Quarterly* 190: 375–93.

Jaggers, Keith, and Ted Robert Gurr. 1995. Tracking democracy's third wave with the Polity III data. *Journal of Peace Research* 32(4): 469–82.

Jahn, Beate. 2006. Kant, Mill, and illiberal legacies in international affairs. *International Organization* 59(1): 177–207.

James, Harold. 2006. *The Roman predicament: How the rules of international order create the politics of empire.* Princeton: Princeton University Press.

James, Henry. 1923. *Richard Olney and his public service.* Boston: Houghton Mifflin.

Jarausch, Konrad. 1988. Revising German history: Bethmann Hollweg revisited. *Central European History* 21(3): 224–43.

Jervis, Robert. 1978. Cooperation under the security dilemma. *World Politics* 30(2): 168–214.

______. 2002. Theories of war in an era of leading-power peace. Presidential Address, American Political Science Association, 2001. *American Political Science Review* 96(1): 1–14.

Johnston, Alastair Iain. 2003. Is China a status-quo power? *International Security* 27(4): 5–56.

Joll, James. 1992[1984]. *The origins of the First World War.* 2nd edition. The Silver Library. New York: Longman.

Jones, Daniel M., Stuart A. Bremer, and J. David Singer. 1996. Militarized interstate disputes, 1816–1992: Rationale, coding rules, and empirical patterns. *Conflict Management and Peace Science* 15(2): 163–213.

Jones, Ronald. 1971. A three-factor model in theory, trade, and history. In *Trade, balance of payments, and growth*, eds J. Bhagwati, Ronald Jones, Robert A. Mundell, and Jaroslav Vanek, 3–21. Amsterdam: North-Holland.

Kadera, Kelly M., Mark J. C. Crescenzi, and Megan L. Shannon. 2003. Democratic survival, peace, and war in the international system. *American Journal of Political Science* 47(2): 234–47.

Kagan, Robert. 1997. What China knows that we don't: The case for a new strategy of containment. *The Weekly Standard* January 20, 1997.

Kaiser, David E. 1983. Germany and the origins of the First World War. *The Journal of Modern History* 55(3): 442–74.

Kant, Immanuel. 1971. *Kant: Political writings*, ed. Hans Reiss. Trans. H. B. Nisbet. Cambridge: Cambridge University Press.

Kastner, Scott L. 2006. Does economic integration across the Taiwan Strait make military conflict less likely? *Journal of East Asian Studies* 6(3): 319–46.

Keech, William R. 1995. *Economic politics: The costs of democracy.* Cambridge: Cambridge University Press.

Keiger, John F. V. 1983. *France and the origins of the First World War.* New York: St. Martin's Press.

Keng, Shu, Lu-huei Chen, and Kuan-po Huang. 2006. Sense, sensitivity, and sophistication in shaping the future of cross-Strait relations. *Issues and Studies* 42(4): 23–66.

Kennedy, Paul. 1980. *The rise of the Anglo-German antagonism, 1860–1914.* London: The Ashfield Press.

Kent, Bruce. 1989. *The spoils of war: The politics, economics, and diplomacy of reparations, 1919–1932.* Oxford: Clarendon Press.

Kindleberger, Charles P. 1981. Dominance and leadership in the international economy: Exploitation, public goods, and free riders. *International Studies Quarterly* 25(2): 242–54.

Kirshner, Jonathan. 2007. *Appeasing bankers: Financial caution on the road to war.* Princeton: Princeton University Press.

Kiser, Edgar. 1986/87. The formation of state policy in Western European absolutisms: A comparison of England and France. *Politics and Society* 15(3): 259–96.

Kiser Edgar, K. A. Drass, and W. Brustein. 1995. Ruler autonomy and war in early modern Western Europe. *International Studies Quarterly* 39(1): 109–38.

Kissinger, Henry. 1994. *Diplomacy.* New York: Simon & Schuster.

Kokovtsov, Vladimir. 1935. *Out of my past: The memoirs of Count Kokovtsov,* ed. H. Fisher. Trans. Laura Matveev. Stanford, CA: Stanford University Press.

Kornai, Janos. 1992. *The socialist system: The political economy of communism.* Princeton: Princeton University Press.

———. 2000. What the change of system from socialism to capitalism does and does not mean. *Journal of Economic Perspectives* 14(1): 27–42.

Krasner, Stephen D. 1976. State power and the structure of international trade. *World Politics* 28(3): 317–47.

Krumeich, Gerd. 1984. *Armaments and politics in France on the eve of the First World War: The introduction of three-year conscription 1913–1914.* Trans. Stephen Conn. Leamington Spa: Berg Publishers.

LaFeber, Walter. 1960. The American business community and Cleveland's Venezuelan message. *Business History Review* 34(4): 393–402.

———. 1961. The background of Cleveland's Venezuelan policy: A reinterpretation. *The American Historical Review* 66(4): 947–67.

———. 1998[1963]. *The new empire: An interpretation of American expansion 1860–1898.* Ithaca: Cornell University Press.

Lake, Anthony. September 1993. From containment to enlargement. *Dispatch. U.S. Department of State, Bureau of Public Affairs* 4(39).

Lake, David A. 1992. Powerful pacifists: Democratic states and war. *American Political Science Review* 86(1): 24–37.

———. 1993. Leadership, hegemony, and the international economy: Naked emperor or tattered monarch with potential? *International Studies Quarterly* 37(4): 459–89.

———. 1996. Anarchy, hierarchy, and the variety of international relations. *International Organization* 50(1): 1–33.

———. 2007. Escape from the state-of-nature: Authority and hierarchy in world politics. *International Security* 32(1): 47–79.

Lake, David A., and Scott C. James. 1989. The second face of hegemony: Britain's repeal of the Corn Laws and the American Walker Tariff of 1846. *International Organization* 43(1): 1–29.

Lampton, David M. 2005. China's rise in Asia need not be at America's expense. In *Power shift: China and Asia's new dynamics,* ed. David Shambaugh, 306–26. Berkeley: University of California Press.

Langdon, John W. 1991. *July 1914: The long debate, 1918–1990.* New York: Berg.

Lardy, Nicholas R. 1992. *Foreign trade and economic reform in China, 1978–1990.* Cambridge, U.K.: Cambridge University Press.

———. 2002. *Integrating China into the global economy.* Washington, D.C.: The Brookings Institution.

Laslett, Peter. 1988. Introduction to *Two treatises of government* by John Locke. New York: Cambridge University Press.

Laves, Walter Herman Carl. 1977. *German governmental influence on foreign investments, 1871–1914*. New York: Arno Press.

Layne, Christopher. 1994. Kant or can't: The myth of the democratic peace. *International Security* 19(2): 5–49.

______. 2006. *The peace of illusions: American grand strategy from 1940 to the present*. Ithaca: Cornell University Press.

Leamer, Edward D. 1988. Measures of openness. In *Trade policy issues and empirical analysis*, ed. Robert E. Baldwin, 147–200. Chicago: The University of Chicago Press.

______. 1993. Factor-supply differences as a source of comparative advantage. *The American Economic Review* 83(2): 436–9.

Leffler, Melvyn P. 2007. *For the soul of mankind: The United States, the Soviet Union, and the Cold War*. New York: Hill and Wang.

Lenin, V. I. 1993[1916]. *Imperialism: The highest stage of capitalism*. New York: International Publishers.

Levi, Margaret. 1988. *Of rule and revenue*. Berkeley: University of California Press.

Levinsohn, James. 1993. Testing the imports-as-market-discipline hypothesis. *Journal of International Economics* 35(1–2): 1–22.

Levy, Jack S. 1987. Declining power and the preventive motivation for war. *World Politics* 40(1): 82–107.

______. 1989. The diversionary theory of war: A critique. In *Handbook of war studies*, ed. Manus I. Midlarsky. London: Unwin Hyman.

Levy, Jack S., and William F. Mabe. 2004. Politically motivated opposition to war. *International Studies Review* 6(4): 65–83.

Lieber, Kier. 1998. Grasping the technological Peace: The offense–defense balance and international security. *International Security* 25(1): 71–104.

______. 2007. The new history of World War I and what it means for international relations theory. *International Security* 32(2): 155–91.

Lieven, D. C. B. 1983. *Russia and the origins of the First World War*. New York: St. Martin's Press.

Lin, Tse-min and Yun-han Chu. 2008. The Structure of Taiwan's political cleavages toward the 2004 presidential election: A spatial analysis. *Taiwan Journal of Democracy* 4(2).

Lindblom, Charles. 1977. *Politics and markets: The world's political-economic systems*. New York: Basic Books.

Lipset, Seymor Martin. 1994. The social requisites of democracy revisited: 1993 presidential address. *American Sociological Review* 59(1): 1–22.

Lipson, Charles. 2003. *Reliable partners: How democracies have made a separate peace*. Princeton: Princeton University Press.

Lobell, Steven E. 2003. The challenge of hegemony: Grand strategy, trade, and domestic politics. Ann Arbor: University of Michigan Press.

Locke, John. 1988. *Two treatises of government*. Student Edition. Ed. Peter Laslett. Cambridge, U.K.: Cambridge University Press.

Lodge, Henry Cabot. 1891. Protection or free trade–which? *Arena* 4: 652–67.

______. 1893. Outlook and duty of the Republican Party. *The Forum* 15: 250–8.

______. 1895a. Our Blundering Foreign Policy. *The Forum* 19: 8–17.

______. 1895b. England, Venezuela, and the Monroe Doctrine. *North American Review* 160: 651–8.

Long, James William. 1968. The economics of the Franco-Russian alliance, 1904–1906. Ph. D. dissertation. University of Wisconsin, Madison.

Long, J. Scott. 1997. *Regression models for categorical and limited dependent variables.* Thousand Oaks, CA: Sage.

Looney, Robert. 2002. Problems in using trade to counter terrorism: The case of Pakistan. *Strategic Insight* 1(8). Available online at http://www.cc.nps.nav.mil/si/oct02/southAsia.asp.

Macdonald, James. 2006. *A free nation deep in debt: The financial roots of democracy.* Princeton: Princeton University Press.

Macmillan, John. 2003. Beyond the separate democratic peace. *Journal of Peace Research* 40(2): 233–43.

MacPherson, C. B. 1962. *The political theory of possessive individualism.* London: Oxford University Press.

Maddison, Angus. 1991. *Dynamic forces in capitalist development: A long-run comparative view.* Oxford: Oxford University Press.

Mainland Affairs Council. 2007. *The cross-Strait economic statistics monthly*, No. 178. Available at http://www.mac.gov.tw/english/index1-e.htm.

Mansfield, Edward D. 1994. *Power, trade, and war.* Princeton: Princeton University Press.

Mansfield, Edward D., and Jon C. Pevehouse. 2000. Trade blocs, trade flows, and international conflict. *International Organization* 54(4):775–808.

Mansfield, Edward D., Jon C. Pevehouse, and David H. Bearce. 1999/2000. Preferential trading arrangements and military disputes. *Security Studies* 9(1):92–118.

Mansfield, Edward D., and Brian M. Pollins. 2001. The study of interdependence and conflict: Recent advances, open questions, and directions for future research. *Journal of Conflict Resolution* 45(6): 834–59.

———. eds. 2003. *Economic interdependence and international conflict: New perspectives on an enduring debate.* Ann Arbor: University of Michigan Press.

Mansfield, Edward D., and Jack L. Snyder. 1995. Democratization and the danger of war. *International Security* 20(1): 5–38.

———. 2002a. Democratic transitions, institutional strength, and war. *International Organization* 56(2): 297–337.

———. 2002b. Incomplete democratization and the outbreak of military disputes. *International Studies Quarterly* 6(4): 529–49.

———. 2005. *Electing to fight: Why emerging democracies go to war.* Cambridge, MA: MIT Press.

Maoz, Zeev, and Bruce Russett. 1993. Normative and structural causes of the democratic peace. *American Political Science Review* 87(3): 624–38.

Marshall, M. G., and K. Jaggers. 2003. *Polity IV Project: Political regime characteristics and transitions, 1800–1999.* Available online at http://www.systemicpeace.org/polity/polity4.htm.

May, Ernest R. 1961. *Imperial democracy: The emergence of America as a Great Power.* New York: Harper.

McCormick, Thomas J. 1995[1989]. *America's half-century: United States foreign policy in the Cold War and after.* 2nd edition. Baltimore: Johns Hopkins University Press.

McDonald, David McLaren. 1992. *United government and foreign policy in Russia 1900–1914.* Cambridge, MA: Harvard University Press.

McDonald, Patrick J. 2004. Peace through trade or free trade? *Journal of Conflict Resolution* 48(4): 547–72.

______. 2007a. The purse strings of peace. *American Journal of Political Science* 51(3): 569–82.

______. 2007b. Revitalizing grand strategy: America's untapped market power. *The Washington Quarterly* 30(3): 21–35.

McDonald, Patrick J., and Kevin Sweeney. 2007. The Achilles' heel of liberal IR theory? Globalization and conflict in the pre-World War I era. *World Politics* 59(3): 370–403.

Mearsheimer, John J. 2001. *The tragedy of great power politics.* New York: Norton.

Medeiros, Evan S., and M. Taylor Fravel. 2003. China's new diplomacy. *Foreign Affairs* 82(6): 22–35.

Mehlinger, Howard D., and John M. Thompson. 1972. *Count Witte and the tsarist government in the 1905 revolution.* Bloomington: Indiana University Press.

Merk, Frederick. 1967. *The Oregon question: Essays in Anglo-American diplomacy and politics.* Cambridge: Belknap Press of Harvard University Press.

Miller, Kenneth E. 1961. John Stuart Mill's theory of international relations. *Journal of the History of Ideas* 22(4): 493–514.

Milner, Helen V. 1998. The emerging synthesis of international, American and comparative politics. *International Organization* 52(4): 759–86.

______. 1999. The political economy of international trade. *Annual Review of Political Science* 2: 91–114.

Mitchell, B. R. Various years. *International historical statistics: Africa, Asia, and Oceania, 1750–1993.* London: Macmillan Reference.

______. Various years. *International historical statistics: The Americas, 1750–1993.* London: Macmillan Reference.

______. Various years. *International historical statistics: Europe, 1750–1993.* London: Macmillan Reference.

Mitchell, B. R., Sara McLaughlin, Scott Gates, and Havard Hegre. 1999. Evolution in democracy-war dynamics. *Journal of Conflict Research* 43(6): 771–92.

Mombauer, Annika. 2001. *Helmuth von Moltke and the origins of the First World War.* Cambridge, U.K.: Cambridge University Press.

______. 2002. *The origins of the First World War: Controversies and consensus.* London: Longman.

Mommsen, Wolfgang J. 1973. Domestic factors in German foreign policy before 1914. *Central European History* 6(1): 3–43.

Montesquieu, Baron de. 1966[1748]. *The spirit of the laws.* Ed. Franz Neumann. Trans. Thomas Nugent. New York: Hafner Publishing Company.

Moore, Barrington, Jr. 1966. *Social origins of dictatorship and democracy.* Boston: Beacon Press.

Moore, Thomas G., and Dixia Yang. 2001. Empowered and restrained: Chinese foreign policy in the age of economic interdependence. In *The making of Chinese foreign and security policy in an era of reform*, ed. David Lampton, 191–229. Stanford: Stanford University Press.

Moravcsik, Andrew. 1997. Taking preferences seriously: A liberal theory of international politics. *International Organization* 51(4): 513–53.

Morrow, James D. 1999. How could trade affect conflict? *Journal of Peace Research* 36(4):481–89.

Mousseau, Michael. 2000. Market prosperity, democratic consolidation, and democratic peace. *Journal of Conflict Resolution* 44(4): 472–507.

———. 2005. Comparing new theory with prior beliefs: Market civilization and the democratic peace. *Conflict Management and Peace Science* 22(1): 63–77.

Mousseau, Michael, Havard Hegre, and John R. O'Neal. 2003. How the wealth of nations conditions the liberal peace. *European Journal of International Relations* 9(2): 277–314.

Mueller, John E. 1999. *Capitalism, democracy, and Ralph's pretty good grocery*. Princeton, N.J.: Princeton University Press.

Naughton, Barry. 1995. Deng Xiaoping: The economist. In *Deng Xiaoping: Portrait of a Chinese statesman*, ed. David Shambaugh, 83–106. New York: Oxford University Press.

———. 2007. *The Chinese economy: Transitions and growth*. Cambridge, MA: MIT Press.

Neilson, Keith. 1985. Watching the 'steamroller': British observers and the Russian army before 1914. *The Journal of Strategic Studies* 8(2): 199–217.

———. 1995. Russia. In *Decisions for war 1914*, ed. Keith Wilson, 97–120. London: UCL Press.

Nevins, Allan. 1930. *Henry White: Thirty years of American diplomacy*. New York: Harpers and Brothers Publishers.

Nicholls, David. 1991. Richard Cobden and the international peace congress movement, 1848–1853. *Journal of British Studies* 30(4): 351–76.

North, Douglass C. 1981. *Structure and change in economic history*. New York: Norton.

North, Douglass C., and Barry R Weingast. 1989. Constitutions and commitment: The evolution of institutions governing public choice in 17th-century England. *The Journal of Economic History* 49(4): 803–832.

Ohashi, Hideo. 2005. China's regional trade and investment profile. In *Power shift: China and Asia's new dynamics*, ed. David Shambaugh, 71–95. Berkeley: University of California Press.

Oneal, John R., and Bruce M. Russett. 1997. The classical liberals were right: Democracy, interdependence, and conflict, 1950–1985. *International Studies Quarterly* 41(2): 267–93.

———. 1999. The Kantian peace: The pacific benefits of democracy, interdependence, and international organizations, 1885–1992. *World Politics* 52(1): 1–37.

Oneal, John R., Bruce Russett, and Michael L. Berbaum. 2003. Causes of peace: Democracy, interdependence, and international organizations, 1885–1992. *International Studies Quarterly* 47(3): 371–93.

Oneal, John R., Bruce Russett, and David R. Davis. 1998. The third leg of the Kantian tripod for peace: International organizations and militarized disputes, 1950–1985. *International Organization* 52(3): 441–67.

Oren, Ido. 1995. The subjectivity of the democratic peace: Changing U.S. perceptions of imperial Germany. *International Security* 20(2): 147–184.

O'Rourke, Kevin H., and Jeffrey G. Williamson. 1999. *Globalization and history: The evolution of a nineteenth-century Atlantic economy*. Cambridge, MA: MIT Press.

Owen, John M. 1994. How liberalism produces democratic peace. *International Security* 19(2): 87–125.

———. 1997a. *Liberal peace, liberal war: American politics and international security*. Ithaca: Cornell University Press.

———. 1997b. Perceptions and the limits of liberal peace: The Mexican-American and Spanish-American Wars. In *Paths to peace: Is democracy the answer?* Ed. Mirian Fendius Elman, 153–189. Cambridge: MIT Press.

———. 2005. Iraq and the democratic peace. *Foreign Affairs.* 84(6): 122–7.

Paine, Thomas. 1995[1791]. *Rights of man, common sense, and other political writings.* Ed. Mark Philp. Oxford: Oxford University Press.

Paléologue, Maurice. 1924. *An ambassador's memoirs.* New York: George H. Doran.

Papayoanou, Paul. 1999. *Power ties: Economic interdependence and war.* Ann Arbor: University of Michigan Press.

Paul, James C. N. 1951. *Rift in the democracy.* Philadelphia: University of Pennsylvania Press.

Pearson, Jonathan. 2003. *Sir Anthony Eden and the Suez crisis: Reluctant gamble.* New York: Palgrave Macmillan.

Perkins, Dexter. 1937. *The Monroe doctrine, 1867–1907.* Baltimore: The Johns Hopkins Press.

Pevehouse, Jon C., and Bruce Russett. 2006. Democratic international governmental organizations promote peace. *International Organization* 60(4): 969–1000.

Phillips, Steven. 2005. Building a Taiwanese republic: The independence movements, 1945–present. In *Dangerous Strait: The U.S.–Taiwan–China crisis,* ed. Nancy Bernkopf, 44–69. New York: Columbia University Press.

Pipes, Richard. 1999. *Property and freedom.* New York: Knopf.

Pletcher, David M. 1973. *The diplomacy of annexation; Texas, Oregon, and the Mexican War.* Columbia: University of Missouri Press.

Pogge von Strandmann, Hartmut. 1988. Germany and the coming of war. In *The coming of the First World War,* eds R. J. W. Evans and Hartmut Pogge von Strandmann, 87–123. New York: Oxford University Press.

Polachek, Solomon W. 1980. Conflict and trade. *Journal of Conflict Resolution* 24: 55–78.

Polanyi, Karl. 2001[1944]. *The great transformation: The political and economic origins of our time.* Boston: Beacon Press.

Pollard, Robert A. 1985. *Economic security and the origins of the Cold War, 1945–1950.* New York: Columbia University Press.

Powell, Robert. 1999. *In the Shadow of Power: States and Strategies in International Politics.* Princeton: Princeton University Press.

Powell, Robert. 2002. Bargaining theory and international conflict. *Annual Review of Political Science* 5(1): 1–30.

———. 2003. Nuclear deterrence theory, nuclear proliferation, and national missile defense. *International Security* 27(4): 86–118.

———. 2006. War as a commitment problem. *International Organization* 60(1): 169–203.

Przeworski, Adam, and Michael Wallerstein. 1988. Structural dependence of the state on capital. *American Political Science Review* 82(1): 11–29.

Przeworski, A., M. Alvarez, J. A. Cheibub, and F. Limongi. 2000. *Democracy and development: Political institutions and well-being in the world, 1950–1990.* New York: Cambridge University Press.

Ray, James Lee. 1995. *Democracy and international conflict: An evaluation of the democratic peace proposition.* Columbia: University of South Carolina Press.

———. 1998. Does democracy cause peace? *Annual Review of Political Science* 1(1): 27–46.

Reed, William. 2003. Information and economic interdependence. *Journal of Conflict Resolution* 47(1): 54–71.

Reiter, Dan. 2003. Exploring the bargaining model of war. *Perspectives on Politics* 1(1): 27–43.

Reiter, Dan, and Allan C. Stam. 2002. *Democracies at war.* Princeton: Princeton University Press.

Reiter, Dan, and Erik R. Tillman. 2002. Public, legislative, and executive constraints on the democratic initiation of conflict. *The Journal of Politics* 64(3): 810–26.

Ricardo, David. 1951[1820]. Funding system. In *The works and correspondence of David Ricardo*, Volume 4, ed. Piero Sraffa. Cambridge: Cambridge University Press.

Rigger, Shelley. 1999. *Politics in Taiwan: Voting for democracy.* New York: Routledge.

———. 2005. The unfinished business of Taiwan's democratization. In *Dangerous Strait: The U.S.–Taiwan–China crisis*, ed. Nancy Bernkopf, 16–43. New York: Columbia University Press.

Ripsman, Norrin M., and Jean-Marc F. Blanchard. 1996/97. Commercial liberalism under fire: Evidence from 1914 and 1936. *Security Studies* 6(2): 4–50.

———. 2003. Qualitative research on economic interdependence and conflict: Overcoming methodological hurdles. In *Economic interdependence and international conflict: New perspectives on an enduring debate*, eds Edward Mansfield and Brian Pollins. Ann Arbor: University of Michigan Press.

Risse-Kappen, Thomas. 1996. Collective identity in a democratic community: The case of NATO. In *The culture of national security: Norms and identity in world politics*, ed. Peter J. Katzenstein. New York: Columbia University Press.

Rock, Stephen R. 1989. *Why peace breaks out great power rapprochement in historical perspective.* Chapel Hill: University of North Carolina Press.

———. 1997. Anglo-U.S. relations, 1845–1930: Did shared liberal values and democratic institutions keep the peace? In *Paths to peace: Is democracy the answer?* Ed. Miriam Fendius Elman. Cambridge: MIT Press.

Rodrik, Dani. 1995. Trade policy and industrial reform. In *Handbook of development economics*, volume 3B, eds Jere Behrman and T. N. Srinivasan. Amsterdam: Elsevier.

Rogowski, Ronald. 1989. *Commerce and coalitions: How trade affects domestic political alignments.* Princeton: Princeton University Press.

———. 1999. Institutions as constraints on strategic actors. In, *Strategic choice and international relations*, eds David A. Lake and Robert Powell. Princeton: Princeton University Press.

Rohl, John C. G. 1973. *1914: Delusion or design? The testimony of two German diplomats.* London: Elek.

———. 1995. *Germany.* In *Decisions for war, 1914*, ed. Keith Wilson, 27–54. London: UCL Press.

Romberg, Alan D. 2003. *Rein in at the brink of the precipice: American policy toward Taiwan and U.S.–PRC relations.* Washington: Henry L. Stimson Center.

Rosato, Sebastian. 2003. The flawed logic of democratic peace theory. *American Political Science Review* 97(4): 585–602.

Rosecrance, Richard. 1986. *The rise of the trading state: Commerce and conquest in the modern world.* New York: Basic Books.

Ross, Michael J. 2001. Does oil hinder democracy? *World Politics* 53(3): 325–61.

Rousseau, David L. 2005. *Democracy and war: Institutions, norms, and the evolution of international conflict.* Stanford: Stanford University Press.

Rousseau, David L., Christopher Gelpi, Dan Reiter, and Paul K. Huth. 1996. Assessing the dyadic nature of the democratic peace, 1918–1988. *American Political Science Review* 90(3): 512–33.

Rowe, David M. 1999. World economic expansion and national security in pre-World War I Europe. *International Organization* 53(2): 195–231.

______. 2005. The tragedy of liberalism: How globalization caused the First World War. *Security Studies* 14(3): 407–47.

Rowe, David M., David H. Bearce, and Patrick J. McDonald. 2002. Binding Prometheus: How the 19th-century expansion of trade impeded Britain's ability to raise an army. *International Studies Quarterly* 46(4): 551–78.

Rummel, R. J. 1983. Libertarianism and international violence. *The Journal of Conflict Resolution* 27(1): 27–71.

Russett, Bruce, and John R. Oneal. 2001. *Triangulating peace: Democracy, interdependence, and international organizations.* New York: W. W. Norton and Company.

Scherer, Paul. 1999. *Lord John Russell: A biography.* London: Associated University Press.

Schneider, Gerald, and Gunther G. Schulze. 2003. The domestic roots of commercial liberalism: A sector-specific approach. In *Globalization and armed conflict* eds Gerald Schneider, Katherine Barbieri, and Nils Petter Gleditsch, 103–22. Lanham, MD: Roman and Littlefield Publishers.

Schultz, Kenneth. 1999. Do democratic institutions constrain or inform? Contrasting two institutional perspectives on democracy and war. *International Organization* 53(2): 233–66.

______. 2001. *Democracy and coercive diplomacy.* Cambridge, U.K.: Cambridge University Press.

Schumpeter, Joseph A. 1951[1919]. The sociology of imperialisms. In *Imperialism and social classes*, ed. Paul M. Sweezy, trans. Heinz Norden, 1–130. New York: Augustus M. Kelley, Inc.

______. 1942. *Capitalism, socialism, and democracy.* New York: Harper and Row.

Sellers, Charles Grier. 1966. *James K. Polk, continentalist.* Princeton, N.J.: Princeton University Press.

Shenton, James Patrick. 1961. *Robert John Walker: A politician from Jackson to Lincoln.* New York: Columbia University Press.

Shifter, Michael. 2006. In search of Hugo Chavez. *Foreign Affairs* 85(3): 45–55.

Shirk, Susan. 1994. *How China opened its door: The political success of the PRC's foreign trade and investment reforms.* Washington, D.C.: The Brookings Institution.

______. 2007. *China: Fragile superpower.* New York: Oxford University Press.

Signorino, Curtis S., and Jeffery Ritter. 1999. Tau-b or not Tau-b: Measuring the similarity of foreign policy positions. *International Studies Quarterly* 43(1):115–44.

Silberner, Edmund. 1946. *The problem of war in nineteenth-century economic thought.* Trans. Alexander H. Krappe. Princeton: Princeton University Press.

Simmons, Beth. 1994. *Who adjusts? Domestic sources of foreign economic policy during the interwar years.* Princeton: Princeton University Press.

Singer, J. David, Stuart Bremer, and John Stuckey. 1972. Capability distribution, uncertainty, and major power war, 1820–1965. In *Peace, war, and numbers*, ed. Bruce Russett, 19–48. Beverly Hills: Sage.

Smith, Adam. 1937[1776]. *An inquiry into the nature and causes of the wealth of nations.* New York: Random House.

Smith, Alastair. 1996. Diversionary policy in democratic systems. *International Studies Quarterly* 40(1): 133–53.

———. 1998. International crises and domestic politics. *American Political Science Review* 92(3): 623–38.

Snidal, Duncan. 1985. The limits of hegemonic stability theory. *International Organization* 39(4): 579–614.

Snyder, Jack. 1984. Civil-military relations and the cult of the offensive, 1914 and 1984. *International Security* 9(1): 108–46.

———. 1991. *Myths of empire: Domestic politics and international ambition.* Ithaca, N.Y.: Cornell University Press.

———. 2000. *From voting to violence democratization and nationalist conflict.* New York: Norton.

Solingen, Etel. 1998. *Regional orders at century's dawn: Global and domestic influences on grand strategy.* Princeton, N.J.: Princeton University Press.

Sontag, John P. 1968. Tsarist debts and tsarist foreign policy. *Slavic Review* 27(4): 529–41.

Souva, Mark. 2004. Institutional similarity and interstate conflict. *International Interactions* 30(3): 263–281.

Souva, Mark, and Brandon Prins. 2006. The liberal peace revisited: The role of democracy, dependence, and development in militarized interstate dispute initiation, 1950–1999. *International Interactions* 32(2): 183–200.

Spiro, David. 1994. Given democratic peace a chance? The insignificance of the democratic peace. *International Security* 19(2): 50–86.

Spring, D. W. 1988a. Russia and the Franco-Russian alliance, 1905–1914: Dependence or interdependence? *Slavonic and East European Review* 66(4): 564–92.

———. 1988b. Russia and the coming of war. In *The coming of the First World War,* eds R. J. W. Evans and Hartmut Pogge von Strandmann, 57–86. Oxford: Clarendon Press.

Staley, Eugene. 1935. *War and the private investor: A study in the relations of international politics and international private investment.* Garden City, N.Y.: Doubleday, Doran and Company, Inc.

Stein, Arthur A. 1993. Governments, economic interdependence, and international cooperation. In *Behavior, society, and nuclear war,* vol. 3., eds Philip E. Tetlock, Jo L. Husbands, Robert Jervis, Paul C. Stern, and Charles Tilly. New York: Oxford University Press.

Steiner, Zara S. 1977. *Britain and the origins of the First World War.* New York: St. Martin's Press.

Stevenson, David. 1996. *Armaments and the coming of war: Europe, 1904–1914.* Oxford: Clarendon Press.

Stigler, George J. 1971. The theory of economic regulation. *The Bell Journal of Economics and Management Science* 2(1): 3–21.

Stiglitz, Joseph. 2002. *Globalization and its discontents.* New York: Norton.

Stinnett, Douglas M., Jaroslav Tir, Philip Schafer, Paul F. Diehl, and Charles Gochman. 2002. The Correlates of War Project direct contiguity data, version 3. *Conflict Management and Peace Science* 19(2): 58–66.

Stolper, Wolfgang F., and Paul A. Samuelson. 1941. Protection and real wages. *The Review of Economic Studies* 9(1): 58–73.

Taylor, A. J. P. 1954. *The struggle for mastery in Europe, 1848–1918*. Oxford: Oxford University Press.

Thompson, W. R. 1996. Democracy and peace: Putting the cart before the horse? *International Organization* 50(1): 141–74.

Tian, John Q. 2006. *Government, business, and the politics of interdependence and conflict across the Taiwan Strait*. New York: Palgrave Macmillan.

Trubowitz, Peter. 1998. *Defining the national interest: Conflict and change in American foreign policy*. Chicago: Chicago University Press.

Tucker, Nancy Bernkopf. 2005. Strategic ambiguity or strategic clarity? In *Dangerous Strait: The U.S.–Taiwan–China crisis*, ed. Nancy Bernkopf, 186–211. New York: Columbia University Press.

Tully, James. 1980. *A discourse on property: John Locke and his adversaries*. Cambridge: Cambridge University Press.

Turner, L. C. F. 1968. The Russian mobilization in 1914. *Journal of Contemporary History* 3(1): 65–88.

U.S. Census Department. 2005 foreign trade statistics. Available at http://www.census.gov/foreign-trade/statistics/country/sreport/textile.html.

Van Evera, Stephen. 1984. The cult of the offensive and the origins of the First World War. *International Security* 9(1): 58–107.

Varian, Hal R. 1996. *Intermediate microeconomics: A modern approach*. 4th ed. New York: W. W. Norton and Co.

Verdier, Daniel, and Mette Eilstrup-Sangiovanni. 2005. European integration as a solution to war. *European Journal of International Relations* 11(1): 99–135.

Viner, Jacob. 1951. *International economics*. Glencoe, Ill.: Free Press.

Wachman, Alan M. 2007. *Why Taiwan? Geostrategic rationales for China's territorial integrity*. Stanford: Stanford University Press.

Wagner, R. Harrison. 1988. Economic interdependence, bargaining power, and political influence. *International Organization* 42(3): 461–83.

______. 2000. Bargaining and war. *American Journal of Political Science* 44(3): 469–84.

______. 2007. *War and the state: The theory of international politics*. Ann Arbor: University of Michigan Press.

Walker, Thomas C. 2000. The forgotten prophet: Tom Paine's cosmopolitanism and international relations. *International Studies Quarterly* 44(1): 51–72.

Wallerstein, Immanuel. 1974. The rise and future demise of the world capitalist system: Concepts for comparative analysis. *Comparative Studies in Society and History* 16(4): 387–415.

Walter, Andrew. 1996. Adam Smith and the liberal tradition in international relations. *Review of International Studies* 22(1): 5–28.

Waltz, Kenneth N. 1959. *Man, the state, and war: A theoretical analysis*. New York: Columbia University Press.

______. 1979. *Theory of international politics*. New York: McGraw-Hill.

Waterbury, John. 1983. *The Egypt of Nasser and Sadat: The political economy of two regimes*. Princeton: Princeton University Press.

______. 1992. The heart of the matter? Public enterprise and the adjustment process. In *The politics of economic adjustment: International constraints, distributive conflicts, and the state*, eds S. Haggard and R. R. Kaufman. Princeton, N.J.: Princeton University Press.

Way, Christopher Robert. 1998. Manchester revisited: A theoretical and empirical evaluation of commercial liberalism. Ph.D. dissertation, Stanford University.

Weede, Erich. 1995. Economic policy and international security: Rent-seeking, free trade, and democratic peace. *European Journal of International Relations* 1(4): 519–37.

Weingast, Barry R. 1995. The economic role of political institutions: Market-preserving federalism and economic growth. *The Journal of Law, Economics, and Organization* 11(1): 1–31.

Weinthal, Erika, and Pauline Jones Luong. 2006. Combating the resource curse: An alternative solution to managing mineral wealth. *Perspectives on Politics* 4(1): 35–53.

Welch, Jr., Richard E. 1988. *The presidencies of Grover Cleveland*. Lawrence, KS: The University Press of Kansas.

Wendt, Alexander. 1999. *Social theory of international politics. Cambridge studies in international relations*, vol. 67. Cambridge: Cambridge University Press.

Widenor, William C. 1980. *Henry Cabot Lodge and the search for an American foreign policy*. Berkeley: University of California Press.

Williams, William Appleman. 1959. *The tragedy of American diplomacy*. New York: Dell Publishing Company.

Williamson, Samuel J. 1988. The origins of World War I. *Journal of Interdisciplinary History* 18(4): 795–818.

———. 1991. *Austria–Hungary and the origins of the First World War*. London: Macmillan.

Williamson, Jeffrey G. 1998. Globalization, labor markets, and policy backlash in the past. *Journal of Economic Perspectives* 12(4): 51–72.

Williamson, Oliver E. 1985. *The economic institutions of capitalism: Firms, markets, relational contracting*. New York: The Free Press.

Wilson, Keith M. 1984. Imperial interests in the British decision for war, 1914: The defence of India in Central Asia. *Review of International Studies* 10: 189–203.

———. 1995. Britain. In *Decisions for war 1914*, ed. Keith Wilson. London: UCL Press.

Winch, Donald. 1978. *Adam Smith's politics: An essay in historiographic revision*. Cambridge, U.K.: Cambridge University Press.

Wolford, Scott. 2007a. The turnover trap: New leaders, reputation, and international conflict. *American Journal of Political Science* 51(4): 772–88.

———. 2007b. In the shadow of the successor: Leadership turnover as a commitment problem. *Typescript*.

World Bank. Various years. *World development indicators CD-ROM*. Washington: World Bank.

Wu, Yu-shan. 2005. Taiwan's domestic politics and cross-Strait relations. *The China Journal* 53: 35–60.

Yahuda, Michael. 1993. Deng Xiaoping: The statesman. *The China Quarterly* 135: 551–72.

Yergin, Daniel. 1991. *The prize: The epic quest for oil, money, and power*. New York: Touchstone.

Zakaria, Fareed. 1997. The rise of illiberal democracy. *Foreign Affairs* 76(6): 22–43.

———. 2003. *The Future of freedom: Illiberal democracy at home and abroad*. New York: W. W. Norton and Co.

Zheng, Bijian. 2005. *China's peaceful rise: Speeches of Zheng Bijian, 1997–2005.* Washington, D.C.: The Brookings Institution.

Zoellick, Robert. 2004. When trade leads to tolerance. *New York Times*, A13, June 12, 2004.

Zorn, Christopher J. W. 2001. Generalized estimating equation models for correlated data: A review with applications. *American Journal of Political Science* 45(2): 470–90.

Index

Made in the USA
Lexington, KY
17 January 2015